MAGIC and RELIGION

MAGIC and RELIGION

THEIR PSYCHOLOGICAL NATURE, ORIGIN, and FUNCTION

by

GEORGE B. VETTER

PHILOSOPHICAL LIBRARY

New York

Printed in the United States of America

CONTENTS

PLATES

PREFACE

Man's religious behavior has long been treated as though it were a mystery or an enigma. It is more than likely that it has been thus treated because we much prefer to leave it as something mysterious and awesome.

It is as human behavior that the subject is approached in this volume, for the good and sufficient reason that there is nothing else about it that can be approached by the methods of science. In view of the almost endless and incredible varieties of behavior to which the adjective "religious" is attached, it is assumed that what we must be dealing with are some of the many and varied aspects of the learning process, or habituation, if for no better reason than the improbability that there could be as many diverse instinctive behavior patterns inherent in a stock otherwise so homogeneous. There are, however, far better reasons than that for a recourse to the psychology of habit.

Let us face matters frankly. Some 95% of us continue to believe throughout our entire lifetimes the religious ideas taught us when young, regardless of what that faith may have been. So it should be apparent to all but the willfully blind that factors other than a scientific logic determined the acceptance of those beliefs, or held sway when they were acquired. Most of the literature pretending to inquire into the nature of religion proves upon examination to be but more or less subtly disguised attempts to justify varying portions of these early indoctrinations.

There has been no previous attempt to examine the major premises of supernaturalism in the light of the modern objective approach to the more complex symbolic processes so long thought of variously as "spiritual" or "mental." Nor has religious behavior been subjected to analysis in the light of the newer knowledge of the objective nature of the learning process, which has, at long last, entirely freed itself from dualistic and teleological assumptions. Much of profound significance for all religion has developed in this area during the last three decades. Yet that work and those findings have been all but completely ignored by the religious and philosophical fraternities. With due humility, the author hereby submits his interpretations of the significance of recent psychological findings for that section of our social customs broadly designated as the magico-religious.

G. B. V.

ACKNOWLEDGMENTS

The following publishers have graciously given permission for quotations from their published works:

George Allen & Unwin Ltd., from V. Ferm: "Religion in Transition"; the American Psychological Association, from its various journals; Appleton-Century-Crofts, Inc., from Smith & Guthrie; "General Psychology in Terms of Behavior", and from M. K. Thomson: "The Springs of Human Action"; the Atlantic Monthly Press from William James' Letters; The Canadian Journal of Psychology, from article by E. H. Page; the University of Chicago Press, from Wach: Sociology of Religion; Columbia University Press, from Thorndike: "History of Magic and Experimental Science" and from Kardiner: "Psychological Frontiers of Society"; the Free Press of Glencoe, Illinois, from Goode: "Religion Among the Primitives", Malinowski: Magic, Science, & Religion, and Parsons: "Structure of Social Action"; Froben Press, Fort Pierce Beach, Florida, 1943, from Victor Robinson, M.D., "The Story of Medicine"; Grune & Stratton, Inc., from Moore's "Driving Forces of Human Nature"; Harcourt, Brace & Company, Inc. from Stern's "The Third Revolution" and from Leuba's "Psychology of Religious Mysticism"; Harper & Brothers, from Guthrie: "The Psychology of Learning", Guthrie & Edwards: "Psychology", and Wright: "The Religious Response". Also from Harper's Magazine, from the article "Religious Beliefs of American Scientists" by James Leuba; the Harvard University Press, from Kluckhohn & Leighton: "The Navaho" and from C. W. Heath: "What People Are"; Henry Holt & Company, Inc. from C. M. Child: "Physiological Foundations of Behavior" and from Bergson: "Two Sources of Morality and Religion"; the International Universities Press, from Ostow & Scharfstein: "The Need to Believe"; the Journal Press, from Article by Anne Roe; the Journal of Pastoral Care, from article by A. T. Boisen; Alfred A. Knopf, from Mencken's "Treatise on the Gods"; Life Magazine and Mrs. Paul Hutchinson, quotations from an article by Paul Hutchinson; The Month, magazine, London, from article by F. A. Voigt; J. B. Lippincott Co., the extensive quotations from "Religion and the Modern Mind" by W. T. Stace, Copyright 1952 by W. T. Stace; Longmans, Green & Co. from William James' "Essays in Radical Empiricism" and "Varieties of Religious Experience"; Look Magazine and Dr. Warren Weaver for a quotation from the article "Can a Scientist Believe in God?"; Macdonald & Evans Ltd., from W .G. de Burgh, "From Morality to Religion"; the Macmillan Company, from Allport, "The Individual and his Religion", and from Hedley: "The Superstitions of the Irreligious", and from Whitehead: "Religion in the Making"; Methuen & Company, from MacDougall; "Body & Mind", and R. R. Marett: "The Threshold of Religion"; Thomas Nelson & Sons, from Raymond Cattell: "Psychology and the Religious Quest"; the Oxford University Press, from R. Otto's "The Idea of the Holy"; the Partisan Review, for quotations from John Dewey; the Princeton University Press, from W. T. Stace: "Time and Eternity"; the Ronald Press, from C. J. Ducasse; "A Philosophical Scrutiny of Religion"; Routledge & Kegan Paul Ltd., from J. C. Flower: "Psychology of Religion"; the Smithsonian Institution for a quotation from the publications of the Bureau of American Ethnology; the Williams & Wilkins Company and Dr. L. W. Max for the lengthy quotations from Professor Max's articles in the Journal of Comparative Psychology; the Yale University Press, from E. W. Hopkins' "Origin and Evolution of Religion", and from Truman Arnold: "Folklore of Capitalism"; The New York Times has granted permission for the various quotations from its pages, as has the New York World Telegram & Sun for the quotations from Earl Sparling's articles "Sight: The Great Adventure"; and so also has the New York Herald Tribune for the quotations from their despatches. Professor N. R. F. Maier has given permission to quote from his volume "Frustration". Rupert Brooke's poem, "Heaven" is reprinted by permission of Dodd, Mead & Company, from the Collected Poems of Rupert Brooke, Copyright 1915 by Dodd, Mead & Company. Copyright renewal 1943 by Edward Marsh.

The lines of verse on page 43 are from: "A Treasury of Humorous Verse" by Samuel Hoffenstein, Copyright: R 1955 by David Hoffenstein, Permission of Liveright Publishers, New York.

My former student, Mr. Osborn Andreas, a rare combination of scholar, businessman, and experimenter in the art of living, has provided important material and aid for the volume.

George B. Vetter
New York University.

MAGIC and RELIGION

1. INTRODUCTORY

Signs are not wanting that there is an increasing interest in at least certain academic circles in the entire subject of the magico-religious. It has long been observed, at times with regret, and again with satisfaction, that the American institutions of higher learning, originally founded to prepare young men for the ministry, and perhaps a few for the law in addition, have practically ceased to pay any attention whatsoever to the entire subject of theology. Now for this historical process, as well as for all other events that occur, there are perfectly adequate causal factors, frequently prejudged and oversimplified as an "increasing Godlessness" by various members of the professional clergy. For one thing, it was always some particular sectarian treatment that religion had at the hands of a particular institution; and our country was blessed, or cursed, depending upon the point of view, with an increasing diversity of religious faiths. And, drawing students from wide areas with diverse local sectarian individualities, it became increasingly advantageous to separate sharply the sectarian theological education from rapidly growing fields of secular knowledge in the sciences and medicine. Thus, the American standard today in this matter is the isolation of the education for theology into a completely separate school. Many a now seemingly completely "secular" college is by historical tradition actually a sectarian college in origin; but one might well be associated with such a school for a quarter century without ever being reminded of it, or even without ever discovering the fact in the first place. But by all odds, the chief reason for this historical divorce of religion from secular learning has been the simple fact that much of what theologians had traditionally believed and taught was increasingly in conflict with current scientific findings. While many individuals, both clerical and lay, developed a fairly effective system of logic-tight compartments in which to keep their various conflicting systems of belief, nonetheless both theologians and scientists found it expedient to adopt a 'let sleeping dogs lie' attitude. And such an attitude is well nigh impossible to maintain if the same students are in alternate classes taught a special creation hypothesis, and natural selection. Trouble enough of that sort in these days where a student might be taught the traditional metaphysics of mind and matter in one class, only to encounter a modern objective psychology being taught in the next.

But whatever the exact balance of forces operating in each particular institution, the fact remains that for a time the abandonment of religion as a subject for study in the secular college was well nigh complete. But it should be emphasized that what thus disappeared from the liberal arts college was the teaching of any one religion as the true faith. But such is the diversity and uneven development in the educational world that even while this divorcing process was not yet begun in some schools, in others, courses dealing with at least some aspects of religion, but in secular and objective fashion, were being introduced. Frequently spearheaded by philosophy departments were courses under titles such as "The Philosophy of Religion" which usually made it possible for the instructor to acquaint his students with much that lay beyond the narrow limits of local sectarianism, even if, for the most part, the men entrusted with the teaching of such courses could be depended upon not to give any too great offense to the local campus chaplain; all, no doubt, in the interests of the peace and dignity necessary to the academic life. Great variability, of necessity, obtained in the content and point of view taken in these courses, varying all the way from a mild form of Christian apologetics to a thinly disguised atheism or agnosticism. But objectivity in the treatment of religion as a course subject matter probably began in the safe form of courses in departments of Anthropology under the title of "Primitive Religion," where it is relatively easy to be objective. It is well to note that it was the prior accumulation of new and factual data on primitive society that provided the bases for a new approach to the subject. In much the same way it was recent factual accumulations that made possible a comparative Sociology, and academic courses in the Sociology of Religion. And where courses in Comparative Religion returned to the Liberal Arts curriculum one is safe in assuming that the pro-Christian bias typical of such courses in theological seminaries was considerably minimized. On occasion, such courses might even be taught by an instructor with a decided weakness for the mystical who left at least a few of his students at the courses' end fancying themselves Buddhists or devotees of the Bhagavad Gita.

But it has long been apparent that most aspects of anything that could possibly be called religion must at bottom be psychological phenomena. That indeed was the assumption implicit in the long and futile attempt to reconcile religion and reason in Western Europe. Even the dramatic attempts on the part of some to make the very unreasonableness of religious faith the basis for its acceptance still left religion in the psychological sphere. The secularization of the soul into the "mind" and the consequent emergence of "experience" as the fundamental psychological reality apparently brought religious phenomena even more firmly into the psychological fold. Identifying the religious as something in the private experience of the individual made it at least a possible subject for empirical study; and the work done around the turn of the present century by Coe, Ames, & Starbuck, and brilliantly presented with its proper linkage to religious history by William James, set the pattern for American and British religious psychology well down into the 1930's. The last two decades have seen a decided decline in the number of texts in psychology and religion that continue to build upon this phase of American psychology. The vein seems to have been "mined out."[1] But during that same period a veritable flood of books and articles capitalizing upon the dramatics of the Freudian psychology have appeared, dealing with religion in a most irreverent but at least stimulating manner.

However, the lack of scientific knowledge of the nature of the mind or of human behavior has not prevented the formulation of a great variety of theories as to the nature and origin of religion. Of necessity, any theory of any aspect of human behavior, whether individual or social, must consciously or unconsciously make more or less systematic assumptions in regard to the nature of the human equation, the more sophisticated theoreticians being quite aware of such assumptions as are made and reasonably consistent in them; the naive remaining happily content with the convenient inconsistencies of common sense psychology, and usually, blissfully quite unaware of them. Nor should it be assumed that a certain psychological naiveté has of necessity vitiated or invalidated all observation and theorization in the field. Much important spade work has indeed been done. There is something about even an obviously bad theory that frequently drives its proponent into meticulous and exhaustive research and scholarship that at worst calls attention to obscure source material, or sets some egregious error into sharp relief, or calls attention to some otherwise overlooked aspects of a problem. Like the wildest trials in a trial-and-error problem, even the most preposterous theories have at least the virtue of not repeating familiar errors. Much of our learning is obviously the making of new errors, out of which emerges an occasional hit!

These theories of the nature and origin of religion are numerous and varied. This writer is unaware that any serious attempt has ever been made to classify, organize or compare the various theories that have been put forth, other than a very casual designation of three different classes of theories by Hopkins.[2] These he designated as (1) animism, or the English theory; (2) naturalism, the fear and awe theories with which the name of Max Mueller is commonly identified and which he calls the "German" theory; and (3) collectivism (illusionism) with which Durkheim's name is closely identified, and which he calls the "French" theory. Even a casual pursuit of the literature will turn up many more, each usually sponsored by a passionate advocate so that the enthusiastic novice in the field is rather likely to be successively swept off his feet, figuratively speaking, by each ardent champion. H. L. Mencken once wrote somewhere that in America, anyone who had read three good books automatically belonged to the Intelligentsia, but the net effect of reading about that number of books in the field of the nature and origin of religion is usually a firmly convinced advocate of one of the very many theories already put forth, while yet blissfully unaware even of the existence of the others. Thus it will perhaps be not amiss to present here a somewhat systematic listing and at the same time a rough classification of the theories that happen to have fallen under observation during a period of some thirty-five years. No pretense is made of all-inclusiveness for this listing, nor of any special or esoteric merit in the system of classification used. No system of taxonomy can be more than an effective mnemonic device at best. Some of these theories will have more thorough consideration in later chapters; others might only be given simple mention. In the case of others it may well be assumed that their merits, limitations, and shortcomings will be apparent from the general discussion. Definitions of religion very frequently imply theories as to its origin and some of these might well be found in the classification. Proper names in parentheses indicate names commonly identified with such theories. Some names are identified with more than one.

I. The Traditional-Philosophical Theories
   1. Revelation, Divine Origin, usually implying true vs. false revelations and religions; supplied to all true believers.
   2. Teleological theories, implying that the purposes served by the religion explain or account for that religion. (Conservation of values, Harald Höffding.)
II. Physiological-Psychological or Instinct Theories
   3. The "religious instinct" theory.
   4. The special religious "sense" which may or may not be well developed in any given individual. (W. T. Stace)
   5. The "fear" theory. (Rabbi Lewis Browne, Wm. Howells, etc.—most widely held)
   6. The "awe" or "sympathetic love" theory. (Max Mueller, Tiele) (Specifically awe of the phenomena of nature) (Robert R. Marett)
   7. The emotions generally in the social situation. (Robert H. Lowie, Emile Durkheim)
   8. Sex. (Freudians and neo-Freudians, Schroeder)

III. The Psychological Experience and "Rationality" Theories

9. The religious metaphysics is based upon the subjective experience in sleep and dreams.

10. The abnormal experience of drugs and hallucinations provided the bases. (Gruppe)

11. There is a specific and unique religious experience. (a) an individual product, (Wm. James); (b) a social product, (Durkheim)

12. The mystical state is fundamental; it may or may not be exactly identical with the ordinary religious experience, but all religions are but theories about the mystical experience. (W. T. Stace)

13. Religion the product of an attempt at redemption from sin and suffering, whether physical or "spiritual."

14. Religion a product of man's inability to face an Unknown; he "has to believe something"; the phenomena of psychological "closure."

15. Religion a rational deduction from the facts of the cosmos: the existence of a god deduced from ontological, cosmological, and teleological "evidences."

IV. The Psychological-Developmental and Frustration Theories, involving various aspects of the learning process.

16. The product of habits, "complexes," acquired in the family situation. (C. G. Jung, E. D. Martin, Sigmund Freud)

17. Disappointments and shortcomings of the world create the belief in a more perfect order which rewards one for virtues and tribulations of this world which would otherwise be meaningless. (A popular lay theory.)

18. Religion a product of the felt inadequacies of the human equipment, the "inferiority complex" theory. (R. H. Thouless, J. C. Flower)

19. Religion produced by the desire to escape from reality, to retreat into a fantasy-world nearer to the heart's desire.

20. Religion is the embracing of a collective neurosis to save oneself from an individual neurosis. (Sigmund Freud)

V. The Historical-Developmental Theories

21. Religion evolved out of animism. (E. B. Tylor)
22. Religion evolved out of animatism, which is a personalizing of the impersonal, treating impersonal phenomena as if they had or were personalities. (R. R. Marett)
23. Religion evolved out of the "mana" concept. (A. A. Lovejoy)
24. Religion grew out of the failure of magic. (J. G. Frazer, et al)
25. It evolved out of totemism. (F. B. Jevons, E. Durkheim)
26. It evolved out of private fetishes which are simpler and probably antedate totems.
27. Religion evolved out of ancestor worship. (H. Spencer)
28. It begins as Euhemerism, the deification of kings or heroes. (P. H. Buck)

VI. The "Ill Will" or Conspiracy Theories.

29. Religion is a creation of the medicine-man or priests who discovered that the average man could easily be exploited for the priests' own ends and purposes. (H. L. Mencken, Upton Sinclair)
30. Religion is an opiate, deliberately applied to, if indeed not devised for, the purpose of keeping subject classes distracted from their mundane miseries, by concerns over things post-mortem. The priests may be the exploiting class, or they may be merely the lackeys or servants of such exploiters. (K. Marx, F. Engels, V. Lenin)

VII. Miscellaneous, otherwise unclassified theories concerning nature and origin

31. Religion originates in any excessive, or fanatical, zeal for causes or beliefs. (G. LeBon)
32. Religion arises from any socially shared frame of reference and object of devotion. (E. Fromm)

This rather extensive list of theories certainly testifies to the importance of religion in man's life, as well as to our curiosity about it. In 1940 an analysis of the figures describing journal circulation in the United States showed that where the combined circulation of all that could be classed as "general" stood at about 60 million, religious journals totaled 45 million, as compared to a total circulation of all scientific journals of but three and one half million. A recent study of the religious press[3] indicates that while there is of course a steady decline since 1840 when it is estimated that three-fourths of all the reading done by the American people was religious, still the religious press is far and away the largest serving a special interest in the community. Church and state may well be separate in the United States and there may be no state subsidy of religion other than tax exemption, but that still leaves religion an important influence upon the body politic. It must be taken into account in the launching of any important social program; no candidate for high office must even be considered without a primary check on the religious implications of his candidacy. The basic magico-religious attitudes of the populace provide an important part of the apperceptive mass that greets whatever transpires.

Hence, of the basic importance of the entire range of magico-religious behavior there can be no doubt whatever. Even in the United States, a land perhaps unjustly much maligned for its materialism and godlessness, the total amount of human energy absorbed in religious activities of all sorts, is still, in spite of its overall general relative decline during the past century, an important item in the total budget, as a glance at such documents as those released by the Treasury Department on consumer expenditures will reveal. It runs currently to almost exactly one half of the amount spent for private secular education and research of all sorts, a not inconsiderable sum, even if relatively picayune in comparison to the amount spent for its philologically kindred "spirits". But even more interesting is the role of religion in providing a generalized background of guilt-feelings for many piecemeal or wholly backsliding individuals which must be added to the debit side in any over-all evaluation of the very real services rendered by institutionalized religions. It would indeed be a challenging bit of research to try to discover the long run consequences upon personalities, vacillating on the brink of sin, of the almost continuous reminders of their ritual sinfulness. It is highly probable that the dire consequences presumed to spring from this source are seriously overestimated in anti-religious circles. A recent bit of research revealed only a small percentage of Americans who felt that the inhibitions induced by their religious convictions were any great bar to their overall enjoyment of life. Some psychiatrists, however, are impressed by the high incidence of religiously induced guilt feelings in their patients. This may well mean that with our relatively fluid sectarian allegiance in the predominantly Protestant United States we simply tend to move over into a church where our Sunday golf or other relatively innocuous vices are not too frequently and publicly castigated as cardinal sins. There is, in short, great need for data on the precise effects of religious influences on the contemporary basic personality pattern.

But be that as it may, there is room for much sound research that might dig up a few factual grains that could well provide an effective antidote to the strident claims of rivalling vested interest groups. Let me reiterate, it is the effect of such persistent institutional forces upon the individual personality that must be considered to be of more far-reaching importance than the mere economic cost so frequently stressed by those critical of traditional institutions. Should the vulgar economics of modern social life so impress anyone that he would begin by weighing religion in dollar scales he should have his attention called to far greater apparent costs and wastes in current economic life; for example, the hundred-odd percent we somehow manage to add to the cost of goods at the point of production, in the process of placing them into the hands of the "consumer," that much lamented fellow who seems of such vital concern in the current struggle betwen entrepreneurs and tradeunionists. No, the simple truth is that most Americans, some 90-odd percent, think of themselves as religious, feel a bit guilty that they do not engage more regularly in devout observances, think of religion as playing a rather vital role in their affairs, and frequently join new cults in millions, all of which constitutes eloquent enough testimony of the importance of the subject in contemporary social processes, if for no other reason than for the light it throws on the basic habits of thought of the citizenry. Small wonder, then,

that scientific objectivity was slow in reaching the general field
of the magico-religious. One needs but remember that there still
are five sovereign states in the Union upon whose books are
laws making the teaching in public schools of man's descent
from other animal forms a punishable offense. It is no doubt on
the whole a good omen that we have achieved sufficient emotional distance from our provincial sectarianism that we can
begin to discuss religion as an objective social phenomenon.
Certainly the individual teacher in the field has difficulty enough
with his own private emotional conflicts over the subject matter
without having to deal with social and institutional pressures,
tending to distort his objectivity, in addition. It might be remarked parenthetically that where as recently as 1928 the
author of a textbook in the Psychology of Religion could make
the specific assertion that no one not having had a personal,
religious experience could possibly consider himself qualified to
deal with the subject, today's widespread recognition of the
traumatic and biasing effects of early indoctrination would
prompt one to look for objectivity elsewhere, namely in individuals with less dramatic emotional involvement with the subject.

It is the unhappy duty of a psychologist invading any aspect
of social phenomena to puncture a few fondly held illusions. The
first of these is the idea, assiduously cultivated on occasion by
various vested interests, that all things social are of so profound
a degree of complexity as to baffle all but a few, perhaps divinely
chosen, individuals in perpetuity, and that it is this complexity
that provides the primary difficulty in their comprehension.
Let us concede that there is enough complexity here to satisfy
anyone with a taste for something other than the simple. But
the error lies in attempting to ascribe to this complexity the chief
practical difficulty in dealing with social phenomena. For it is
the emotional nature of the subject matter that causes far more
difficulty than the sheer complexity of any social question, unless,
of course, these emotional attitudes are specifically designated
as constituting the complexity. This fiction of complexity is commonly invoked to discourage the sort of objective inquiry into
some aspect of social relations that would perhaps appear dangerous to stable and well-ordered social relations. It was, and

still is, one of the chief weapons in the arsenal of laissez faire social theory, which provided such an excellent ideological basis for leaving a variety of strategically placed people and classes in peaceful possession of their privileges; a condition no doubt essential to a peaceful and stable society.

Perhaps much of what seems to be on the face of it the "complexity" of social phenomena is in reality a relative inaccessibility of many critically significant facts. All too frequently critically important and vital social "facts" are information that is the private possession of individuals or small groups who in the nature of the situation must be strongly motivated to keep such essential facts as private as possible in the protection of what they readily perceive to be their private well being which is frequently disguised, even to themselves, as "the best interests of the institution," or "business," or "the country," and which frequently is genuine enough. But it must be remarked that such motives are not too difficult to surmise or even to ascertain with reasonable accuracy, once we cease to be hypnotized into inactivity by the presumed imponderability of the social whole confronting us.

A second, and even more insidious illusion, is the fiction of impartiality. Beware of anyone claiming impartiality in anything. To make any such claim at this stage of our knowledge of human behavior brands anyone as either very naive psychologically, or an out and out knave. Let me repeat: it is absolutely impossible for anyone to be impartial about anything! I might, for example, be emotionally relatively *indifferent* about many things, but that is not *impartiality*.[4] To assert my impartiality about any question would mean that I should have to assert that nothing in my entire make-up or history were stacking the cards one way or the other in my appraisal or evaluation of the situation! I would have to believe that nothing in my past experience, directly or indirectly, consciously or unconsciously, had been such, up to the present, to make my appraisal or evaluation of a situation favor one side of a dispute, or question of fact, or moral judgment, more than the other. Such impartiality would demand a Free Will of unheard of potency, one that could, in the first place, identify all possible past influences on emotion and judgment, and then in the second place effectively neutralize each and every one of these past influences to precisely the same degree of ineffectiveness! It is ridiculous even to suggest such a possibility! Such a process would have to wipe out all past learning in all fields, for who could tell what indirect influences might be at work loading the dice for the judgment in question! No! Impartiality is impossible of attainment. But we can strive for *objectivity*. We can learn to ask the sort of questions and to find the kind of answers that others too can ask and answer with similar results. We can begin the task of unravelling the chain of significant factors in the attitudes and beliefs and actions of ourselves as well as others. We can learn to recognize the historical factors that have made our judgments and values what they are, and at least no longer delude ourselves that we are, or even can be expected to be, impartial. We can reconcile ourselves to a determinism even in the field of the subtleties of personality variables. This is not meant to imply that there are no more unknowns in that field; it is merely to assert its general inclusion in the domain of the relatively knowable where predictions with some degree of improvement above chance can be made. Perhaps, most important of all, it can remind us that where morals and values clash an appeal to "impartiality" must of necessity remain meaningless, and that objectivity provides an assignment that is difficult enough.

That there is a very special emotional attitude quite generally reserved for the entire area of religion and theology cannot be denied. It is a topic that must be treated gingerly if at all. It is frankly assumed that discussions and arguments in regard to it are in the worst of bad taste. Like all beliefs not based upon empirical evidence, they are adhered to with great tenacity and even greater heat. It is commonly taken for granted that ordinary rules of fact and evidence have no jurisdiction in this area. And, while the matters religions typically deal with are presumed to be of an almost unbelievable complexity, and in authoritarian sects the individual has nothing to do but believe the official interpretations, in the more individualized cults and faiths, each individual is somehow presumed to be in a privately authoritative position in regard to the cosmic mysteries; at least current religious etiquette demands that he be socially treated as if he were. Above all, the entire subject is blanketed with an awesome taboo against its being approached or handled by the same techniques and attitudes found acceptable and effective in other dimensions of human experience and behavior. There is, as H. L. Mencken so aptly put it[5] "—the general feeling that religion itself is a highly complicated and enigmatical thing, with functions so diverse and sinister that plain men had better avoid thinking of them, as they avoid thinking about the Queen's legs or the King's death." Such attitudes must be gotten rid of, if there is to be any hope of insight or understanding. In this scientific age, anything thus hedged in by taboos can at once be suspected of having plenty to conceal from the prying eyes of critical inquiry. But most of all, the emotional sensitivity in regard to religion is a product of the elaborate pattern of logic-tight idea systems which current beliefs and practices demand if they are to be maintained. The degree of sensitivity provides an excellent measure of the amount of conflict to which the "believer" is subjected, in the process of hanging on to his various and more or less contradictory idea-systems. In any objective inquiry, such emotionality merits no especial respect; it is merely one of the difficulties and complexities of the subject matter.

Our language habits tend to disguise the fact that all social phenomena are but human behavior. With such institutional fictions as "The State," "The Church," "The Law," not to mention "economics," "politics," or "religion," we can abandon the embarrassing realities of individual motives and the vested interests of groups in favor of convenient abstractions whose pure attributes are practically immune to the facts of the particular. We succeed too well in our institutional substitution of the "role" for the individual personality to the point of denying or at least forgetting the personal bases of social phenomena. We forget that our economic laws are but the behavior norms of a particular culture. We come to assume that what we call "religion" must somehow be a universal and pure essence; or, which is worse, when a common term has been applied to a diversity of behaviors, we insist that there must be an essence common to all. (Such are the tricks played upon us by our own verbal behavior!) Or worse, in the case of "religion," we insist that whatever fails obviously to fit our formula is not "true" religion; a but slightly less naive version of the definition of religion given us by Parson Thwackum in Fielding's "Tom Jones"[6] "—When I mention religion, I mean the Christian religion; and not only the Christian religion, but the Protestant religion; and not only the Protestant religion, but the Church of England."

The anti-religious societies have overlooked a bet in failing to collect and give wide publicity to the various definitions of religion! Nothing could quite so effectively destroy the idea that some single Platonic universal underlies all the individual and particular religions; that there is a universal, bona fide, essence that is "the religious," even were all the definitions submitted by anthropologists, skeptics, and unbelievers ruthlessly eliminated! Let us examine a representative few. For Bishop Butler, religion was "The belief in one God or Creator, and moral governor of the world, and in future retribution." This would simplify matters enormously. After a little preliminary witch-hunt to determine the status of Trinities and Madonna worship, we could just limit ourselves to the simon pure monotheisms. All else would presumably fall under the rubric of superstition. For Kant, religion was "The recognition of our duties as commands from God." Such a definition would rest uncomfortably alongside of Schleiermacher's assertion that ideas are all foreign to religion, which is, rather, just an innate consciousness of the Deity. William James[7] says it is "The feelings, acts, and experiences of men in their solitude." For Professor Floyd Allport, religion is something so individual and private that it resists all attempts at communication to others.[8] Professor Haydon calls it "the co-operative quest for a completely satisfying life," and Robertson Smith is convinced that primitive religion was essentially an affair of the community rather than of individuals.

Sometimes it requires rather extensive and flowery verbalization to convey the subtle shades of meaning that for some particular individual spell out religion. Alfred N. Whitehead[9] provides us with as good an illustration as any:

"The religious insight is the grasp of this truth: That the order of the world, the depth of reality of the world, the value of the world in its whole and in its parts, the beauty of the world, the zest of life, the peace of life, and the mastery of evil, are all bound together—not accidentally, but by reason of this truth: that the universe exhibits a creativity with infinite freedom, and a realm of forms with infinite possibilities; but that this creativity and these forms are together impotent to achieve actuality apart from the completed ideal harmony, which is God."

Such a definition obviously must be supplemented with a definition of God, which he provides as follows:[10]

"God is that function in the world by reason of which our purposes are directed to ends which in our own consciousness are impartial as to our own interests. He is that element in life in virtue of which judgment stretches beyond facts of existence to values of existence. He is that element in virtue of which our purposes extend beyond values for ourselves to values for others. He is that element in virtue of which the attainment of such a value for others transforms itself into value for ourselves."

Previously, in a somewhat different mood, he says:[11]

"Religion is the last refuge of human savagery."

It is apparent that anyone essaying to write on the subject of religion should first of all thoroughly digest a modern treatise on semantics. Poetical rhapsody must not be confused with objective fact, particularly not when man is trying hard to free himself from the tyranny of the past. Insofar as these quoted paragraphs have content, they are somewhat flowery elaborations of the Kantian conception of religion: an identification of religion with ethics.

Elsewhere Whitehead says religion is "what the individual does with his own solitariness."[12] To G. B. Shaw religion is that which binds men to one another. Then too there is that old mediaeval aphorism which holds that "one Christian is no Christian!" For Höffding religion is faith in the conservation of values, but Reinach tells us that religion is a body of scruples which impede the free exercise of our faculties! Professor John Dewey once wrote that "whatever induces genuine perspective is religious," but Professor Shotwell defines religion as man's reaction to experiences apprehended but not comprehended.

Professor E. G. Ames sees it as the pursuit of the highest social values, but the sociologist J. Wach writes,[13] "We have tried to show that social integration is not the aim or purpose of religion. Religion is sound and true to its nature only so long as it has no aim or purpose except the worship of God." The anthropologist, R. H. Lowie, finds the essence of religion in the sense of something transcending the expected or natural, a sense of the Extraordinary, Mysterious, or Supernatural. For Santayana, religion is the poetry we believe in, and God is a conceived victory of mind over nature. For the geologist, Lyell, religion is simply a case of "I give so that you may give," and Sir J. G. Frazer finds "entreaty" to be the hallmark of religion. In the Euthyphron, Plato has a character describe the then current rituals to the Gods as "the science of begging and getting." Talcott Parsons[14] quotes Professor A. D. Nock from a lecture at Harvard as having defined religion as: "The active attitudes of men to those parts of their life and environment which do not to them appear to be wholly controlled, conditioned or understood by human agency, and all that they do, say or think in virtue of such attitudes." Such a definition has the virtue of sharply separating the practical, the mechanical or the deterministic from all ceremonial, ritualistic or piacular activities. But the difficulty with that from the standpoint of understanding either of these is just that man himself frequently neither knows nor observes the distinction. Such a dichotomy can only be made by man insofar as he has a scientific mastery over a given range of phenomena, where he has identified all the causal elements in a given situation. Widely viewed, of course, no such distinction is recognized or observed. The old Scottish herb doctor from whom the medical world got digitalis as a heart stimulant knew neither what was causing the symptoms of the "dropsy" he was treating, nor did he know which of the ingredients of his concoction, including the phases of the moon in which some were gathered and the prayers the patient was taught to say, had any physiological effect. He knew only a total "formula" and that it "worked." The religious and the pharmacological were all one to him.

Similarly, the old rural American formula for removing warts,

PLATE 1. A "spook" cemetery near New Delhi, India. The Goblin like effect is produced by the presence of hundreds of white clay pots which the native Mohammedans place on sticks "to remind the dead that they have not been forgotten by their relatives."

PLATE 2. "Tongue Tied." Yoga Dixon, Indian Fakir, shows that his tongue is firmly attached to the wooden plank with a silver plated nail, without loss of blood.

—*courtesy World Wide Photo*

PLATE 3. Prayers for Hidden Sun God. During an eclipse of the sun, Indian Hindus prayed by the thousands that the Sun God be released from the grip of Rahu, the demon snake. Hindus feared that the unusual duration of the phenomen created a danger that the Sun God might be swallowed before prayers could save him. Here, a sadhu, or holy man, lies on a bed of thorns.

—courtesy World Wide Photo

PLATE 4. Interior Hogan, chanting before the sand painting to be used to heal a sick child.

—*courtesy The American Museum of Natural History*

usually from a cow's udder, which ran: "Tie a hair from a horse's tail tightly around the base of the wart every evening at sundown," we dismiss today simply with a comment that it utilizes the principle of stricture, a shutting off of the blood supply. To the peasant it was far more than that: it was something that worked! And, psychologically, there is far more to it than just the stricture principle: it is functionally workable and contains the elements necessary to assure the working of that principle. First of all, it specifies a good material that is always readily available at the time specified in the formula, namely at sundown when both horse and cow are in the barn. Is the item "at sundown" nothing but a mnemonic device where the setting sun gives the time cue and reminder? Probably not: there is a magical linkage of the setting sun with the wasting away of the wart: 'as the light fades, so does the wart.' The formula provides material, proper timing, mnemonic device, and confidence-giving formula. And it works! But the ingredients of this formula are not subjected to an analysis into their true natures. The non-mechanical elements in this routine are at a minimum, but they are yet there. We can sharply define and distinguish them; but the distinctions are ours, and of recent origin.

The Oxford dictionary defines religion as "recognition on the part of man of some higher, unseen power as having control of his destiny, and as being entitled to obedience, reverence, and worship." This is an excellent statement of the completely authoritarian conception of religion, a point of view which is currently in almost complete disfavor in democratic societies. No better illustration exists of the extent to which religious concepts are subject to modification by intellectual innovations and developments in the other aspects of the culture. The general acceptance of the concept of biological evolution had a similar effect upon the anthropomorphic character of popularly accepted supernatural agencies.

E. B. Tylor, the anthropologist, suggested as a common denominator the belief in spiritual beings, which would rule out the teachings of Gautama the Buddha. Upon reading Charles Guyau's volume entitled "The Irreligion of the Future," Professor Royce remarked that its title should have been "The Religion of the Future." Where Professor Mehran K. Thompson, in his "Springs of Human Action," writes, "Whenever the satisfaction of a human need is sought by communion with a source other than human (supernatural) there is present, at least in germ, the religious attitude," Professor Gordon Allport writes in his recent and very challenging volume, "The Individual and his Religion,"[15] "—the explanations involved in religion have very little to do with the clamorous wishes of ordinary life. What is demanded by the great religions is self-abnegation, discipline, surrender,"—far from providing us with devices for the satisfaction of ordinary wants or needs! No wonder that Professor Marett[16] complained long ago that definitions of words are always troublesome; and religion is the most troublesome of all words to define. Now a word troublesome to define is simply one that the lexicographer finds used in many different and often contradictory ways. That is very obviously the situation in regard to the word "religion." The culturally naive apply the term to a segment of the socially acquired practices to which they conform without even questioning the content. A variation in form or content, a concern with problems not normally considered as coming in that class, might well be greeted or perceived as "superstition," or at best met with a "do you call that Religion? —oh no!" as the old Negro spiritual has it. Even minor ritual or ideational deviations from the familiar are likely to be so met. Apparently no matter what the word or symbol to which one owes emotional allegiance, a specific content comes to be assigned to it; and deviations therefrom are emphatically rejected. The symbol or term "religion" certainly has no monopoly on this process. Note the instance of the earnest Nazi who, in the latter days of the Hitler regime wrote—"Don't ever think that the perversions of anti-semitism, concentration camps and aggressive warfare represent the *true spirit* of National Socialism!" But there is no denying the intensity or tenacity of such beliefs. Small wonder that an irreverent student came up with a definition of religion as "the beliefs that cannot be destroyed by the presentation of contrary evidence, and the practices whose continuance is independent of their efficacy"! And then there is that definition of faith, reportedly obtained from a naive, but literally

minded student as: "—the power which enables us to believe
what we know to be untrue"! Certainly there is no lack of evidence of the tenacity with which even irrational beliefs are
adhered to, in the name of religion, by people far removed from
any suspicion of psychotic taint.

In the usage of the term "religion" there are thus to be observed not only wide and contradictory deviations in content,
but also a tendency to hair-splitting niceties of distinction between the acceptable and the rejected. A slight difference in
goal, purpose, ritual, or emotional attitude is often the basis for
a total rejection of a belief or practice as not "truly religious"
or not constituting "true religion." Certainly this is no recent
phenomenon, for already Omar Khayyam could speak of the
"two and seventy jarring sects." And the centifugal process certainly did not cease in his time, as the two hundred-fifty odd
Protestant sects in the United States today can testify. But let
the question of the universality of "religion" arise and at once
a quite different mood and spirit seems to dominate. Here the
thinnest evidence, the most diverse beliefs and practices, are at
once accepted as evidence for the universality of religion. The
traditional explanation of this dilemma is of course that there
are 'true' and 'false' religions, but that in no way answers the
questions as to the basic element or elements that underlie both
the true and the false. Recently Professor Gordon Allport has
introduced a more sophisticated note into this perennial chestnut by referring to the type of belief and practice acceptable
to him as "mature" religion.[17] But of course that still leaves
unanswered the question of the common denominators underlying both 'immature' and 'mature' religions! Let it be emphasized here that it is precisely at this common denominator underlying both 'true' and 'false' religions, both 'mature' and 'immature,' 'primitive' and whatever is the opposite of that, that this
inquiry is aimed. It can hardly be doubted that there are in all
this diversity common denominators of some sort, no doubt in
the domain of the human behavior involved, whether emotional, ideational or overt. There are real reasons, even if only
'psychological,' for the existence of this category in current
usage. The antecedent factors are probably neither conscious

nor rational in the ordinary sense, but certainly adequate, causally.

But there's the rub! How *did* we "get that way," how did or do we happen to have "religion," be "religious," to "have faith," to "believe"? It is perhaps far more significant than we realize that for so long it has been felt that some special explanation, reason, or theory should be necessary to explain this part of our reasonably well-ordered lives! And obviously the basis for this need is just that we now see a difference between our secular, mechanical, industrial, or material lives, and this aspect on which we agree so badly in definition and content: the magical, ceremonial, ritualistic, or religious. It was not always thus, nor is it everywhere now! Where contact with the western world has not brought our categories of thought we simply do not find a concept or category corresponding to that which we, however badly, agree in calling "religion."

The Greeks did *not* have a word for it! Certainly not the early peninsular cultures; and even later, the Greek *polis* was a social entity that included official ceremonial—what we would call religious functions, perhaps,—as well as political, military, and judicial institutions and customs. But no Greek thought of himself as having a "religion," any more than he thought of himself as a "scientist," even if on the one hand he joined in public ceremonies to the gods, and on the other made the perhaps accurate observation that certain cloud formations presaged rain. Nor were these Greeks any great exception in this matter. You will look in vain in the Old Testament for a distinction between the religious as opposed to the secular. Those lusty and confident old tales limit themselves to no such modest sphere as we, today, conceive the field of religion. On the same page, and with equal confidence, it will invade what to us are the fields of jurisprudence, medicine, social ethics, and religion. And why not? For in those days such specialization of human knowledge, social functions, and institutions was unknown. One workable, social behavior pattern under which they could hope to survive was problem enough for them. Before ever they knew that they had any science, jurisprudence, or religion, the various cultures had worked out, by trial and error habit fixation, innovation, and improvisation, a more or less workable set of behavior habits that we commonly call a pattern of culture. Equipped with these habits, a culture might prove to be dynamically expanding, perhaps conquering, by force or by example. Or it might well prove unequal to a changing and unstable environment and meet with a slow or rapid decline, or even complete extinction. Many the culture groups that disappeared without leaving a trace! The natural selection process operates effectively in the social world as well as in the biological. But the individual, in his short life-span, is usually being kept more than busy with his day to day problems. Trouble enough to discern what is effective and important in the immediate present! Whether the "culture" as a whole is flowering or declining, current situations must be met, decisions be made. And, as situations recur, the habits and experience of the past are drawn upon. And in spite of the changing world, there is also much recurrence and repetition. For a predictable world we can, and do, develop habitual adjustments, standards, and codes of conduct. We learn these as specific habits, as approved conduct, as correct techniques. Much of such particular wisdom, learning, or tradition must accumulate before we begin to group it, classify it, or, even later, organize it into logic-tight systems or topics: into technology, epidemiology, law, agronomy, or religion, each with its special skills, personnel, and of course its vested interests. Our early Greek, like primitive man generally, had acquired a way of surviving. He knew it just as his way of doing things. For the most part he knew too, that just across the river, on the other side of the mountains, or on that next island there were other people with quite a different way of doing things. He may well have generally, but did not always think of his way of doing things as necessarily superior.[18] We all well know the advantages the familiar has in our own eyes! But rarely is there to be found a distinct category corresponding even roughly to our current conception of the "religious."

Let us take, for example the Navaho.[19]

"In another sense, speaking of 'Navaho religion' does violence to the viewpoint of The People. There is no word or phrase in their language which could possibly be translated as 'religion.' " What they do have is a set of cosmological beliefs and an organized and predictable way of meeting those segments of experience which are not subject to rational or objective means of control. Furthermore, they do not have a separate category for the phenomena that western religions classify as the supernatural. Their eschatology has a non-positive character; the good, as opposed to the evil, which may or may not be synonymous with breath and/or life. The good may or may not go to the afterworld. It is here at once obvious that such ceremonial practices as they have do not follow from specific beliefs, simply because they have no positive or specific beliefs in such matters. They have no equivalent of the Christian belief in a soul or immortality. But they do have regular, habitual, predictable ways of meeting situations in which man is otherwise functionally impotent.

Similarly, the ancient Canaanite "religion," if indeed one is warranted in applying such a term to their way of doing things, showed no separation of sacred from secular:

"From this it follows that Canaanite religion was more of a public institution than of an individual experience. In its outward manifestations it was, in fact, barely distinguishable from the ordered regimen of society. Its headquarters were just as much a city hall as an abode of deity. Its officers, the so-called priests were just as much judges and physicians as sacristans and hierophants. Its rites were public exercises, and its 'sacrifices' included taxes and levies, fines and imposts, no less than purely piacular or propitiatory offerings. In short, while it doubtless inspired feelings of individual piety and devotion, it was, in essence, an expression of communal economy. Sacred and Secular were met together; church and state kissed each other."[20]

It is apparent that it would be far better to put it that sacred and secular did not exist as separate categories, nor had church or state emerged as separate entities. They obviously made no great distinction between the things they did in solving a mechanical problem and what they found effective in keeping organized life moving in the face of frustration or failure. The practical, the essential, in a mechanical sense, were not marked off sharply from the activities that had no function other than to maintain organized activity or cohesion in the crises for which they had no practical remedy or solution.

Many years ago as a young and very unsophisticated lad I recall discussing "religion" with a Haida Indian on the west coast of Vancouver Island. I brought up the subject with a question as to his religious beliefs. His answer was a puzzle to me for quite some time; it ran about as follows: "Well you see, we don't have one of those religions like you have that you don't use much." I thought at the time that he was referring to the discrepancies between the expressed pieties and the sharp business practices of traders and merchants. I recall being quite surprised to discover that he was on the contrary, quite well satisfied with the pale-faces on that score. The difficulty was simply that I could not even imagine the "religious" not sharply separated from the "secular."

A Pueblo Indian similarly, once tried to enlighten me. Driving over the bad roads of New Mexico of twenty-five years ago I came upon an even worse one pointing in a direction indicated upon my map as leading to some ancient cliff-dwellings. Having long heard of these relics but never having seen one, I was shortly within sight of a cliff, and, what little road there was having completely disappeared I proceeded on foot. A short climb, and there they were! Not only the cliff-dwellings, but a leathery-faced Indian, all alone, sitting where he could overlook the site. It seems that some excavations had been recently made at the site and it was his task to keep away any unauthorized diggers.

Many of the rooms and chambers had been completely cleared of debris; others only partially. Conspicuous among the structures were a few cylindrical, shaftlike chambers, sunk perpendicularly into the relatively soft rock of which the cliffs were composed. One of these structures was located at the top of the mesa, and another already excavated, was on a shelf of rock along the cliff-face. Strolling over to the Indian, I asked him about these unusual structures, pointing to the completely excavated one.

"That is a kiva," he said, in a very matter-of-fact tone of voice. To my inquiry as to the nature and function of the room he replied in a tone of veiled contempt:

"The archaeologists say it was a ceremonial room."

Having gathered from the tone of his voice that he did not think too highly of the opinion of these professionals, I asked him what their use and function "really were." His ready reply was simply: "For weaving."

"That's *very* interesting," I ventured, "what makes you think so?"

"Those holes in the floor," he said pointing, "they are spaced just like the poles in the weaving frames my people use today."

"Well, well," said I, "the kiva had a practical rather than a ceremonial function!" To which he replied in the manner and voice one uses when the too obvious has to be specifically stated:

"Well, weaving is ceremonial too!"

Now it is immaterial if this Indian's guess as to the significance and use of the kiva is right or wrong. What is important, however, in his answer is its portrayal of the point of view of cultures other than our own; namely that our distinction of the practical from the ceremonial is meaningless to them. Incidentally the Indian was probably correct in his interpretation, as he is now generally conceded to have been on his assertion that the cliff-dwellings were built and lived in by the forefathers of his tribe, the Pueblo Indians. I mention this only by way of adding weight to, or emphasizing the objectivity of the observation of the Indian on his culture where he fails to find a distinction between the practical and the ceremonial-religious.

It is more than likely that the term 'religion' in anything like its contemporary meaning (if indeed we can get any agreement on that!) does not antedate the Christian era! The Latin word, *religio*, has several derivations, and champions can be found today for all. Cicero, and many since his time, have derived *religio* from re—'back' and legere—'to pick.' The meaning, 'to read,' is a developed meaning of more recent vintage. Another traces it to *lego*—'meticulous observance,' from which the verb *religio* was derived. Hence meticulous exactness, conscientiousness, and 'religious' aversion—taboo! The other derivation agrees that the *re* has the meaning 'back,' but derives the latter part of the word from *ligare*—'to bind.' Where learned philologists disagree most of us might well concede the apparent plausibility of both! The sense of the word in Latin is "awe" and it is often used in a sense closely resembling our "taboo." The Romans used *res divinae* and *sacra* more nearly in our sense of "religion." And when the Christian sect, then a Jewish splinter-group, appeared in Rome it was of course classified as "superstitio," namely, foreign practices.

When the Jews are referred to as 'the most religious people in the world,' as they very frequently are, what is the basis for that judgment? Perhaps that their codes prescribe in greater detail than any other the entire lives of their people. But nowhere in the Old Testament can one find even a reasonable equivalent for our word 'religion'! If there is a competitor for the title of 'the most religious people' it must be the Hindus. But oriental scholars tell me they know no such equivalent word! Their term 'dharma' comes a bit closer to our word than any other, but it derives from *dhr*, to hold, and dharma implies that to which one holds or cleaves to, that which gives form and direction, and many other things foreign to our concept of the religious, things we classify as purely secular, and which, with us, are freed from the emotional loading characteristic of the religious. At the other extreme, the unreligious, stand perhaps the Chinese. Their 'chiao' is probably best rendered as simply 'doctrine,' or 'that which is taught' (German 'Lehre') and covers a quite different range from our familiar term 're-ligion.' The Japanese converted this to *tsung-chiao*—"direction-giving doctrine" in which form it has been replanted in modern China! The Tibetan Buddhists have an equivalent in their language for the Hindu dharma, but the Mongolian Buddhists and the Manchurian use for this purpose a word derived, of all things, from the Greek word *nomos,* that must have made the journey across Asia by way of Syria, Persia, and then eastward.[21] All these are terms not too different from the *hodos tu Xristu* as it appears in the Acts of the Apostles. But this "way of Christ" is a bit embarrassing to Christians because it of course assumed and included the entire Jewish law and tradition, hardly acceptable to many Westerners as a basic definition of Religion!

But whether these people in primitive, naive, cultures know it or not, at least we know, or confidently feel that we know that they too have a "religion." And while most of us would do a rather poor job of identifying just what the common essence is in all these "religions," we nonetheless feel that such essence must exist. And of course, such an essence must have an origin, a "cause," a history! It is safe to presume that an answer of some sort is provided in every culture, if one remembers the significant fact that the "answer" will cover not only what we call the "religious" but also the secular aspects of the culture in question. We can confidently expect to be met with "explanations" such as the following: "we have always done things this way," or "Whozzis, our culture-hero taught us to do things this way." Such explanations we recognize as but naive forms of the revelation theory, twin brother to the special creation dogma, now beginning to acquire a quaint, nostalgic touch for some of us, like furniture out of the gay nineties. For we are now far beyond such naive true-false beliefs and look to the "scientific," or at least the "philosophical" for answers to our questions. And in those circles, theories of divine origin or of a revealed religion are now, even if perhaps reluctantly in some philosophical circles, laid aside. Satisfactory explanations must now be of a very different fibre.

CHAPTER II

SOME POPULAR "EXPLANATIONS" OF BEHAVIOR AND RELIGION—TELEOLOGY AND INSTINCT

Amusingly enough, we seem to feel that religious behavior calls for a very special type of explanation. The ordinary, run-of-the-mill sort of theory that might do very well for some other part of a culture, seems, almost by definition, to be inadequate when it comes to religion. That always seems to demand something very special! Let us review briefly, some of the more outstanding brain-children of this varied crop of explanations. The business of all true religion, writes Professor Harold Höffding,* is the conservation of the highest spiritual values. Here we have illustrated as well as anywhere, one type of explanation, not only of religion but of a great variety of phenomena, particularly human or animal behavior. Note that it is the function or the purpose served by religion that is presumed to account for it or explain it. Similar is the familiar explanation offered for the existence of religion in terms of the need of it in providing effective moral sanctions in behavior. Such explanations may well be "good" or "adequate" from the standpoint of the objectives of some people, but they are not to be confused with scientific or instrumental explanations. Scientific knowledge must be instrumental, it must be useful for prediction or control of the materials or phenomena in question. Common sense makes no such rigid demands of explanations in the religious or philosophical sphere. Here, explanations in terms of purpose served, "teleological" explanations are perfectly acceptable. Let me illustrate: Ask almost anyone but a modern physiologist or psychologist, why a bird sits on its nest of eggs. The answer "In order to hatch them" will no doubt be forthcoming. That is a teleological explanation, an explanation in terms of the purposes served by the act. But that is not an instrumental explanation, one that might be of any conceivable use to you in case you were an amateur poultry raiser and had just bought a big incubator to do your hatching for you, and what you wanted was hens back at their proper business of laying eggs instead of fussing around with a mere dozen when your incubator handles thousands at a clip! The kind of knowledge, of explanation of chicken behavior, you then want is definitely of an *instrumental* character. You want information you can use to control the behavior of your material, knowledge of a very *materialistic* sort! And in our workaday world, that is precisely the sort of knowledge we demand. If you, as a poultryman at odds with the behavior of your hens, consulted an "expert" on animal behavior in the matter and he sagely informed you that the hens had "egg-hatching instincts" or "philoprogenitive instincts," or "race-preservation instincts"; or if he offered you any other such tautological or teleological substitutes for practical, useful advice in the control of such phenomena you would consider him a mountebank, and rightly so. In our practical, workaday world we demand just this kind of knowledge and explanations. Why are we not equally hard-headed in all other fields?

Well for one thing, we are dualists in our common-sense metaphysics, our habits of speech in regard to what we hold to be "real" or existent. We simply assume that there are two quite different realms of reality, the "mental" and the "physical," and we define these largely in terms of negations of each other. A favorite joke in Wm. James' day went something like this: to the question, "What is mind?", the answer was, "No matter." Then to the question, "What is matter?" the reply was, "Never mind"! However, after having assigned these two entities to entirely different realms we promptly set them to interacting causally with one another! That is, we blithely assume that *of course* physical events can cause mental events and *naturally* mental events or processes can cause physical or material things to happen. It all seems very simple, but the bitterest quarrels in the entire history of philosophy have grown out of the varied attempts to bring a bit of consistency into this casual "common sense." But that is another story. For the moment it is enough to note that in our common-sense concepts of causality and reasoning, we fall into bad habits with this convenient dualism of mind and matter. If we run out of "explanations" in the one sphere we quite casually switch over into the other! And so if we know nothing of the whole complicated physiological and endocrine cycle of egg-laying and hatching in birds we simply "explain" what goes on in terms of non-material instincts or purposes which somehow "cause" the material events to happen. In much the same way, the "values" religions presumably conserve are felt to be the explanation of the religion itself. Thus do the words we use play tricks on our logic!

Then there is that belief, fondly held by many, that man is religious, forsooth, because he has a religious instinct! This is a particularly amusing development of theory in view of the fact that in theological circles there was for long considerable resistance to the acceptance of the notion of human instincts. Such acceptance was tantamount to a general acceptance of the doctrine of the descent of man from lower animal forms, and one might well wonder how quickly time put a different face upon the matter. One is reminded of the old American political maxim, "If you can't lick 'em, jine 'em," as it is expressed in the rural vernacular. Yet it would be all too easy to oversimplify the question or dismiss it too cavalierly. Such a question must always be examined in the light of the current popular usage of a term if one is to get at the question actually at issue. Here a rather detailed examination of the current popular usage of the term "instinct" is in order.

Popular usage attaches varied and contradictory meanings to the term "instinct." To begin with, there is the meaning that the instinctive is inborn, that it does not have to be learned; in fact, it definitely appears without opportunity for learning. But in addition, popular belief has it that any behavior found universally in man must of course be instinctive too. And the lay mind is easily convinced with a small sample that any given item of behavior is truly universal, what with the whimsical reversal of meaning that current usage has given the perfectly sound old adage 'the exception *proves* the rule,' i.e., puts it to the proof! In addition, the "instinctive" is also felt to be purposive, somehow to cause the individual to do just the right thing at the right time; that it is the end-result, goal or purpose served by an act that determines or "causes" it. Thus the term instinct becomes a by-word for the irresistible, the inescapable. No wonder then that it is also applied to very well practiced habits that have reached a stage of being spontaneous, unpremeditated, automatic, or unconscious. Somewhere within this generous range of meanings the layman is more than warranted in his use of the instinct concept as applied to religion. The facts in regard to the inborn or native character of religion are however quite otherwise. In fact, recent experimental findings make increasingly dubious the whole instinct concept as applied not only to man but to the higher mammalian groups. This, of course, does not mean to imply that such primitive motor patterns as walking must be learned. The best evidence still seems to indicate that these basic motor performances wait only upon certain maturational processes, and that even complete immobilization prior to the normal age for walking has no marked effect upon the appearance of the locomotor behavior. That even elementary performances such as the catching of rats and mice by cats are enormously subject to modification by environmental influences has long been known. And recent, highly ingenious experiments on rats have shown clearly that if the female rat is raised in an environment where it is effectively prevented from getting any practice whatever in the manipulation of solid objects it is then completely lacking in even the most elementary manipulative activities essential to the care of the young when they arrive. In short, while there can be no denying that some basic reflex patterns are ready to function at birth and that others wait merely upon some maturational processes before the activities appear, it is becoming increasingly apparent that at the more complex levels of behavior the instinct concept is of dubious validity, even in much sub-human behavior.

However, it is the criterion of universal occurrence that

most deserves inquiry in regard to religion. It takes but a cursory glance at the available data in this field to make a very interesting discovery, namely that the criteria of what constitutes religion are one thing when evidence is being sought for the universality of religion, and quite another when invidious comparisons are being made between one religion and another! In fact, it had better be remembered right at the start that if one sets out with the determination to find religion everywhere, among all people, one had better put very wide limits to his criteria of the religious; they will be needed. Rivers, commenting upon the small island groups in the South Pacific, concluded that one must be prepared to count as "religious" any habitual or traditional treatment of the sick or the dead if one expects to find religion in all cultures! We would, on our part, be outraged at any system of classification that counted the functions of doctor and undertaker as religious, but one can be sure that such judgments as that of Rivers are not made lightly. It might well be that the same group in which one observer would find nothing more "religious" than their therapy, would at other times or seasons reveal some rituals or ceremonials that would seem quite devout to the same or a different observer. But there is no denying that in some cultures there is little enough that seems to warrant the term religion. And very frequently it is obvious that the supernatural per se, is of little interest to people; such interest as they show in that dimension is likely to be in direct relation to the satisfaction of some obvious need, as Nansen observed in regard to the Eskimo.

The argument for the innate character of religion encounters another serious obstacle in the form of enormous variations in beliefs and practice from individual to individual in the same culture. Particularly where there is no specialized priestcraft, no written scripture, one can expect to find enormous variation from individual to individual within the same tribe in just what is believed, practiced, or recited. Paul Radin, who has gone thoroughly into this question is his "Primitive Man as Philosopher," assures us that there now is, and there always has been, enormous variation from individual to individual in the extent to which the sacred myths, fictions, or traditions are believed. This range of variation always has run from an extreme literalist fundamentalism on the one hand to the complete skepticism of the village atheist on the other. There never has been uniformity of belief in such matters any more than we find it now among ourselves. Far from the sort of uniformity one comes to expect in the instinctive or inborn, we find in that which must be classified as religious in order to make it a cultural universal, great variability, first of all in the socially acceptable norms of such behavior, and then even greater variability of belief and practice from individual to individual within each culture. All of which adds up very badly for any sort of an instinct theory of religion.

The Emotions

The shortcomings of the instinct theory have long been apparent to all but the more naive levels of literacy. Yet the conviction could not down that religion was somehow a psychological phenomenon, if but the correct psychological mechanism that would account for it could be identified. The emotions, particularly that of fear appealed to a large number of writers, probably more than any other theory. And, not wholly without cause, what with some theologians making such pronouncements as "the fear of God is the beginning of wisdom." Certainly the early Old Testament Jehovah is no fellow to trifle with; you obeyed his rules without question; you violated them in fear and trembling. The wrath of an angry god was something to be avoided. The simple facts are that much of trial and error learning is a matter of emotionally reenforced, conditioned avoidance of a variety of situations and responses. Most any aspect of every culture is bound to contain some considerable amount of emotionally reenforced rules of avoidance of a variety of behavior alternatives; the religious could hardly be expected to furnish an exception to the general principle. Certainly most all religions will be found to contain accounts of things to be avoided as well as positive prescriptions of what should be done. It is safe to assume that religious leaders in the past as well as political leaders in the present find it easy and tempting to use fears of all sorts as effective organizing principles. Small wonder that it has been easy for writers to find convincing evidence of the role played by fear in the motivation of religious belief, practice, or ceremonial. These theorists are fond of drawing a picture of Primitive Man (with a capital P!) cowering in terror of animals, streams, storms, sicknesses, and just about everything else. His religion then, was a device hit upon to counteract or neutralize these terrors, real or imagined. But I rather suspect that such speculation deals with what is at bottom rather bad psychology, a bad account of the basic animal behavior in man. The simple facts are that every animal, man included, if he is to survive in a given environment, must and does arrive at a relative emotional equilibrium, no matter what the environment. A living organism is, after all, a regulatory, or homeostatic (the now fashionable term) mechanism. A change of environment might bring its terrors, but no one can live in a perpetual state of fear or serious emotional disturbance. You either adjust, move out, or die! And by and large the changes man has made in his environment have been gradual; he has remained adjusted, after a fashion, even under his most drastic changes. So it would take a lot of gratuitous stretching of points to make fear the basis of all religions. Agricultural rites and deities would have to be rephrased as somehow the product of the fear of hunger, the obviously phallic in some practices would have to be a fear of impotence or a fear of racial extinction, etc. And even the obviously joyous in many a religion would then presumably call for an interpretation as some sort of Freudian reaction formation that would make it out to have at bottom some deeply disguised fear-motivation. That fear mechanisms are being played upon in many a religion there can be no doubt. But it is quite another matter to claim that so extensive a social complexity is to be charged to a single, narrow emotional motivation. Besides, one might ask, where is the evidence that man anywhere slinks through life, hounded by perpetual terrors? The appearance of new and strange phenomena is indeed likely to produce a temporary period of wariness. But if it persists, man adjusts to it, even the soldier to the terrors of battle. And the habits he acquires there are rather likely to be specific to the situation. Nor is there any good evidence that things were significantly different during the period we refer to as pre-human. Certainly our nearest anthropoid relatives now living give no more evidence of a dominance of their behavior by fear.

Howells,[1] in ascribing religion to "fear," stretches this concept to include all forms of anxiety, insecurity, frustration, maladjustment, apprehensiveness, inadequacy, dissatisfaction, disappointment, vulnerability, and so on. Such definition certainly takes in a lot of territory and there is no denying that a variety of ritualistic practices are engaged in under situations and circumstances where such motivation is present. But certainly not all that is done under such circumstances could by any stretch of the imagination be called "religious." Much purely secular activity is similarly motivated. Furthermore, there is much of ritual and ceremonial, commonly classed as religious, that is engaged in when no such "fears" are involved, when in fact there is joy, elation, triumph, lust, and practically the entire gamut of human emotions and motives other than the fearful or the depressing. Yet there is no intention to deny here that religious activities are prompted by very real motives; all behavior has its "motivational" factors. In its historical origins there is no evidence of religion for religion's sake. What is emphatically denied, however, is that there is any limitation of the religious to any specific or particular drives or motives.

The objections to a general fear theory have been apparent to many. Furthermore the whole notion never did appeal too well in a culture area where the religious traditions were increasingly emphasizing the characteristics of the chief deity as kind, omniscient, and loving. Such a religion could hardly be a function of fear, even if, perhaps in the past it had played a larger role. The emotion, awe, commonly defined as fear generously diluted with love and perhaps other acceptable ingredients seemed to many to be nearer the essential core of religion and its predominant attitudes. Certainly the predominant attitude toward deities in the western world is moving farther and farther from any pure fear state, and, if religion were to be explained by "emotion," then certainly an emotion more compatible with the indigenous religious attitudes must be found. But since the deities seem increasingly reluctant to put in personal appearances these days the specific cues or stimuli actually eliciting this awe had to be identified. The Anthropologist, Marett, found this original arouser in the phenomena of nature, the mountains, the clouds, the sky, the storms, the sun, the rain. And make no mistake about it, pull apart almost any religion and the role obviously played by these factors becomes apparent at once, if the origin of the gods themselves is at all synonymous with the origin of religion. There is more than a suspicion that Jehovah is the product of the fusion of a rain and a sun god, with a possibility that a volcanic deity entered into the picture somewhere along the line. Many of the Greek gods were thus identified with the various aspects of nature, and they all dwelt up on the highest mountain in the region, a fairly common place of abode to be assigned to gods. In Tibet it is on the high mountain tops that gods are presumed to dwell. Similarly here in America wherever geysers, hot springs or high mountains occur they are almost certain to color the local demonology or whatever supernaturals are presumed to exist. Then again, the major portion of the myriad Vedic gods certainly are nothing if not personalizations of one aspect or another of the major geological, solar, or cosmological phenomena. Probably the commonest gods everywhere are the solar and meteorological. And one might well be tempted to speculate on the fortuitous factors that have been decisive in the assigning of sex or gender to these deities; certainly the periodicity of the moon's phases did not escape observation; with but one or possibly two exceptions the moon is a feminine deity everywhere! This deification frequently reflects the vital role in the economy of a particular natural phenomenon. Thus the Murngin think of some of their totemic spirits as residing in their vitally important water-holes. That agriculturalists in an area of marginal rainfall should view the rain with a somewhat loaded emotionality is quite understandable, and that rites concerned with the "production" of rainfall should play a central role in such ceremonial life as there exists is equally to be expected. Nor is such solar religion necessarily limited to the sun, moon, or planets. The Mandaeans of southern Babylonia have a religion organized around the assumption that all the heavenly bodies revolve around the pole star, Polaris; they face it while praying, place the dying so that face and feet point in its direction, and orient their architecture with reference to it.

The ancient Canaanite culture, the precursor of Judaism, made a most ingenious use of human emotion in the determination of its supernaturals, which were of two classes: El, and Baal. The first, (plural elim or elohim) were personifications of the power believed to dwell in any object or phenomenon which excited awe in man, gave him "goose pimples" or sent shivers up and down his spine. Thus majestic mountains were "mountains of el," tall trees were trees of el, mighty winds were the "breath of elohim." In the Arabic language a similar word denotes the sensation of numinous awe and wonder. But the elim are also minor ghosts, demons, spirits, etc., and were held to cause plagues and disasters. Such primarily impersonal power seems of a piece with the impersonal energy concepts common in most societies, but there is no denying that this Canaanite usage is a transitional stage to a more complete personalization that the concept acquired at the hands of the Hebrews. Yet even in the Old Testament we find, for example, that a man who was liable to ecstatic trauma and supersensuous experiences was called "a man of elohim," as in Deut. 33:1; Sam. 2:27; 9:9-10. The second (plural, Baalim or Bealim) were what can only be described as personifications of the dynamic, indwelling forces which activate or give energy to objects or phenomena, or determine their effectual and organic existence. Thus, in Semitic idiom, an eloquent man is a Baal of the tongue; a husband who brings his wife to sexual fulfillment and energizes her womanhood is her Baal! A wide range of objects or phenomena might well be thus energized by a Baal: the earth, the sky, the thunder or the rain. But it could also be the living community of men and beasts, or collectively the total of all actually or supposedly animate objects in a given place. It is because they were thus so often regarded as personifications of the collective self of such places that the Canaanite Baalim usually bore names signifying their attachment to particular localities or places. Hence the conception of the Baalim as village gods, which in truth it would be difficult to deny of some. The facts seem to be that there frequently was a blending of the characteristics of Elohim and Baalim. Yet in general the relation of man to the Baalim was a more horizontal one, a participating, or cooperating relationship rather than one of worship or adoration. A great range of variation seems to have existed at various times and places in regard to these basic attitudes toward the supernaturals.

Yet one could make no greater mistake than to think that no other emotional attitude toward supernaturals, gods, if you please, could be the social norm anywhere. Man does not everywhere nor always stand in awe before his gods or supernaturals. The proper attitude toward supernaturals among the Kwakiutl of the Northwest American coast is to abuse, shame, or even kill them! For those to whom such an attitude toward the supernaturals seems unthinkable it might be well to note that the social scene teaches the individual what kind of behavior is effective in social relations. If a person's social world rewards a particular behavior approach, be it one of entreaty on the one hand or an aggressive demanding at the other extreme, that is the behavior pattern that can "come natural to" the individual in any similar problem situation. As in any trial-and-error learning situation, the likeliest response to be elicited is the one last practiced in that or a similar situation. So we are forced to conclude that the "awe" theorists are a bit weak in both their anthropology and their psychology. Their position drives them into holding, either that the Kwakiutl do not possess any religion at all, or that religion does not necessarily involve awe of anything, least of all of the supernatural.

Aware of the difficulties involved in trying to find a single, specific emotion present in all religions, some theorists have contended that religion is a matter of the emotions generally. One might be a bit more impressed with such an observation if emotions were somewhat more specific and particular entities whose presence or absence could be positively ascertained. As things now stand in matters of human behavior there seems no basis for any claim that emotions are an all-or-none entity of

some sort, or that it could be reasonably claimed of any behavior
that it did not involve emotional activity of some sort. And as
for identifying the visceral, glandular, or skeletal components
peculiar to a religious pattern of emotions one need but give a
glance at the difficulties encountered in attempting to find reliable differentiae of such elemental patterns as those commonly designated "fear" and "anger" to abandon the quest before it is well begun. Then too, just whose "religious" reactions
should be used as a criterion? The visceral and skeletal activity
in a member of some ecstatic or orgiastic cult feeling the inrush
of "the Power," or the physiological norms obtained from a
staid and somber citizen who feels that he has renewed his
covenant with the higher powers by putting in his appearance
at the ten o'clock services where he perhaps reluctantly found
that his plans for a minor coup in real estate seriously interfered with his best intentions to give his undivided attention to
the sermon? A little acquaintance with current research on emotions makes it at once apparent that it is nothing distinctive
whatever to say of any manner of behaving that it involves "the
emotions generally." What behavior, might one ask, does not?
This is not to deny, of course, that in terms of the old dichotomy
of the intellect vs. the emotions, all the phenomena of religion
are far more a question of emotional rather than intellectual behavior. But so for that matter are plenty of other questions of
socio-economic creeds, morality, and even sports and recreations.
Hardly a unique or distinctive criterion. Some writers find that
this general emotionality must be supplemented by a fairly particular and distinctive social situation in order to produce religion. But that would certainly call forth a loud protest from
the fraternity that holds that religion is in its essence a highly
private matter!

Frustration and Religion

It has often been observed that we cease trying to get by
religious devices the things we have learned to achieve by more
direct means. Veblen long ago pointed out that the animistic
habits of thought tended more strongly to survive among indi-

viduals whose occupations involved a considerable amount of uncontrollable hazard.[2] A couple of millennia earlier, Lucretius pointed out that under trouble there was to be expected an increase in the attention paid the gods, as at deaths, during famines or other individual crises. The religious zeal of convicted criminals is considerably in excess of that in those of us still at large. In some cultures there is a great increase in interest in the subject at puberty. No survey has ever failed to reveal a higher level of religiosity in women than in men. In America the overall correlation between the amounts of education and religious belief and observance is negative: the more education, the less piety. The defeated and the frustrated likewise frequently find solace in religion. It has often been suggested that the firm adherence of the Jews to their faith is a result of the persecution they suffered for it. There is not the slightest doubt that the recent persecutions initiated by the Hitler regime in Germany increased the degree of overall attachment of the Jews to their traditional ways of life. Rabbis have frequently observed it with regret, not unmixed with at least a small amount of satisfaction. Then there is a not infrequent return to religion that comes with senescence, an interest in the non-corporeal life or the possibilities thereof. As the anthropologist, Paul Radin recently put it:[3]

"It has always been the welcome and happy hunting ground for mystics of all ages and all races. It has not infrequently enabled tired intellectuals to spend the evening of their life in tragic solace and in romantic expiation for the sin of having attempted to think logically and realistically in their more robust years."

The common denominator of all these instances or situations seems to be that of more or less frustration, disappointment, or defeat. That is the thesis developed by Flower in his Psychology of Religion.[4] As he put it, religion grows out of the— "—discrimination of a situation in relation to which existing equipment, in the form of original or acquired tendencies is inadequate, and may be said to break down." When, in other words, the shortcomings of mundane existence become a bit too apparent a certain percentage of us turn to speculations on a post-mortem order, particularly where such traditions are already firmly established in the culture pattern. The poet, Rupert Brooke, captured the core and essence of this behavior tendency in his poem, "Heaven."

> "Fish say, they have their stream and pond;
> But is there anything Beyond?
> This life cannot be All, they swear
> For how unpleasant, if it were!
> One may not doubt that, somehow, Good
> Shall come of Water and of Mud;
> And, sure, the reverent eye must see
> A Purpose in Liquidity.
> We darkly know, by Faith we cry
> The future is not Wholly Dry.
> Mud unto mud!—Death eddies near—
> Not here the appointed End, not here!
> But somewhere, beyond Space and Time
> Is wetter water, slimier slime!"[5]

Here the poet has expressed the sentiments that many feel but could not by any means verbalize as effectively in deadly earnest as the genius of the poet manages to do in satirical jest. The attitudes toward life here satirized are more or less products of the robust western culture. They would sound strange in Buddhist or Hindu ears. This sentiment asks for more of that which the Buddhist tries his best to get away from!

There are many minor variations in this frustration, disappointment, or inferiority-feeling theory of religion. No one could pretend to deny that life for the average mortal in many cultures was hedged in and more or less baffled by unresolved worries, anxieties, sex drives, loves not specifically sexual, egocentric desires for social recognition or approval, and baffled aims of possession or achievement. If not before that time, then surely all but a small minority, see death coming too soon, with so many things left undone, so many wines still untasted, and without having perhaps ever owned a brand new automobile! What boots it to have the good pastor reassure us on Sunday that "you can't take it with you" when a ravishing wench we can't have greets us out of every advertisement, and a succession of brand-new cars parade by so rapidly one cannot even learn their identities before still newer ones appear. Renunciation here, comes easier with promises of unutterable bliss beyond the grave. It has been shown again and again that the fuller, the more satisfying the life the less concern for things post-mortem. Such individuals, even if regular church-goers, demand intellectual stimulation from their pastors rather than threats of hell-fire for ritual violations. There may well be no better measure of the worth of a civilization than the percentage count on its "frustrated" citizens, of those for whom life is so bad that the uncertainties of death seem roseate by comparison. Evidence of an increasing mastery over the environment has generally produced optimistic outlooks in people. The United States at mid-century fits well this general picture. A recent survey conducted for a women's magazine and, as published, lacking all statistical information except percentages, reported but five percent of the populace as volunteering the information that they felt in the need of a redemption from sin. The picture as presented was on the whole that of a people seriously guilty of the sin of self-sufficiency, which is hardly to be wondered at in an age when scientific knowledge and method have removed so much uncertainty from life, and with it the bases for so many frustrations as well as fears. There are undoubtedly indi-viduals at all times and in all cultures for whom the religious beliefs and practices act as balm for their emotional bruises and disappointments, and certainly more at some times than at others. Some beliefs can very readily be put to such use. But probably as much of ritual and belief has provided stimulus to action as has been used to lick emotional wounds. The one is probably no more universal nor characteristic of what man has been up to than the other.

CHAPTER III

SEX AND RELIGION

Physiology and the hormones, being what they are, sex is a topic not likely to be ignored in any culture. And while it is no doubt an exaggeration to say, as some writers have, that religions revolve madly about sex, it is nonetheless true that regularity and predictability in regard to sexual behavior is highly essential to any stable form of social organization. Hence of necessity, religions, always an integral part of their cultures, are rather likely to reveal, openly or in disguised form, considerable concern with sex in some fashion. This concern may indeed vary from the lusty and enthusiastic phallicism of some Hindu variants to the generally unsuccessful attempts on the part of other cults to exterminate, repress, or at least bemoan it, the latter attitude so well caricatured by Samuel Hoffenstein:[1]

"The sexes aren't very nice:
They are but instruments of vice.

If the obscure amoeba can
Get on without them, so should Man."

Indeed the entire possible gamut of attitudes can be found to have been illustrated at some time or place in past or present cultures. One might easily be biologically minded enough to suspect that any culture that is really successful in combating sex would have but a relatively short life expectation. That is indeed true, but it is amazing how close determined social

effort and organization can come to flouting the best of biology!
Some of the Shaker groups did succeed in ending reproduction
in their own ranks, but they kept the organization going with
converts for several generations and by the systematic adoption
of foundlings and orphans. The Russian sect of Skopts made
a close approach to the same dim view of sex as did the Shakers.
But they prescribed castration for their males after they had
sired a son, which, if strictly adhered to, would only slow down
a bit the rate of biological extinction of the culture.

One might here observe that such inadequacy of sexual
mores illustrates but one of many possible ways in which a culture pattern might prove to be handicapped in many dimensions
other than the social-sexual. An "extinct" culture is nothing
other than one that failed to leave behind it an organized group
of people living under the pattern of life once extant. Such a
condition might well be brought about by an almost limitless
number of failures of habit adjustment in a great variety of
spheres of social or biological functions. Such failures may or
may not have had any direct relation to the religious aspects
of the cultures. But these extreme forms of repressive social
measures but illustrate asceticism in general which in some form
is likely to appear in every culture. As before remarked, sex
with its emotion arousing potentialities demands channeling
and regulation of some sort in the interest of peace and quiet
and social efficiency in general. No single function of life dares
make too excessive demands upon human time and energy lest
that additional energy cost prove the proverbial straw that breaks
the back, if not of the proverbial beast of burden, then of that
delicate balance or margin of efficiency which may well just
permit that particular culture to survive. Any excessive energy
expenditure in any other dimension might prove equally fatal;
it is merely being asserted here that the sexual sphere is no exception to the general principle. This must of course in no way
be construed as holding that no society can tolerate any gross
inefficiency in any of its social dimensions. But where any great
wastage of energy exists in some one dimension, if that society
is to survive the odds increase that such wastage must be made
up for with exceptional efficiency in some other dimension or

with good general competence in the balance of the pattern. Our western capitalism, for example, suffers a cruel inefficiency in the form of distribution costs considerably in excess now of over-all production costs. But this is more than compensated for in comparison with other cultures by the fantastic efficiency of our productive machinery and productive skills. But when an approximate equality of technological competence exists, as it long did between many primitive cultures, the odds increased that efficiency of energy expenditure in the sexual sphere became critical for survival.

It cannot be too strongly emphasized at this point that it is not so much the sheer efficiency of the one set of customs as against the other that is immediately and critically important; it is the contrast between the unpredictability that the full gamut of possible sexual behaviors and variability that any group could provide, and any pattern of regularity and predictability. Man can, and does, adjust to anything, from having a hundred wives to celibacy, once the habit pattern is set. That many a culture should take a rather dim view of sex is quite understandable. In a sense, control of the reproductive process marks a significant beginning in man's battle to become the master of his fate. Paradoxically, the more man won the battle for survival against the natural hazards of the non-human environment the more quickly he found a battle on his hands against his own Malthusian dilemmas. Hence the more likely it is that under such conditions man hedges in his reproduction with restrictions, many of which will be found to be closely related to economic motives and considerations. The almost fanatical identification of sex with sin in the western European cultures is probably not so much chargeable to Christianity per se as it is to the total cultural complex in which the survival rate had rather rapidly caught up with the improved technology and lowered death rate, making each new arrival something of an economic commitment, and the whole also probably complicated and given emotional loading by venereal diseases taking on an almost epidemic character in the sixteenth century. This puritanical Christianity was itself a deterministic product before it in turn became a prime mover in promoting the currently much maligned

puritanism. What better morality, one might ask, could any
sober judgment provide in a world where the population
pressed heavily on the food supply, where venereal diseases
had no known specifics, and contraception was unheard of? On
top of that it must be remembered that this puritanism had
to be superimposed upon a lingering pagan tradition that harked
back to the time when it took about all the reproducing that
could normally be done if the population was to be held even
against the various hazards that keep the life-span in primitive
societies down to a twenty-five or so year average, and in which
a goddess of fertility was generously honored and her rites maintained even well into the period of the Christian dispensation;
with of course a slight reinterpretation of motives for the traditional eating of fish on Freya's day (Friday). The tradition that
the eating of fish is stimulating to the philoprogenitive procliyi-
ties is far older than the quaint notion that it is a brain food.
In fact the now current attitudes in regard to sex and reproduction that seem to us the natural order of the universe are but
a more or less fortuitous product of historical and human determinants that have elsewhere in the world taken quite another
turn. Where the struggle for the survival of a group is a dubious
battle and the death rate high, births are prized in and of themselves. Sometimes even, a young woman has a much higher
marriage market value if she can come into the bargain already
equipped with a few offspring as eloquent testimony to her
fertility. Yet it must be quite understandable that wherever
any group assumes social leadership, whether religious or secular,
the responsibilities loom almost as large as the privileges, and
the failure to provide effective leadership is rather likely to have
swift repercussions. If then, a religious leadership comes to
emphasize a particular motivational dimension one may be quite
certain that there were sound factors in the situation making
them capitalize it, whether for short or long term considerations
or a mixture of both. Within limits, it was a formula that
"worked," that struck a responsive chord or perhaps even had
salubrious consequences for the longer run. And the young
Christian church that attempted early to assume responsibility
for the suffering, the poor, and the orphaned, might well be

pardoned for its moral zeal in a program whose practical consequences in the here and now were all too obvious to its mundane leadership, and hence presumably also to its gods.

It is not here intended to deny or minimize the role played by personal or emotional factors in clerical as well as in secular leadership. One might indeed profitably speculate on the anti-contraceptive animus currently shown by a celibate clerical leadership. Just how much of this zeal stems from a shrewd calculus of the consequences of, or possibilities in the differential reproduction rates in a population? Just how much is a historical hang-over from the aforementioned battle in the Christianizing of the European pagans? And just how much of it is to be sought in what in these post-Freudian days might be referred to as the darker levels of the Unconscious of these celibate policy-makers? For the development of reasonably effective contraceptive measures has certainly shifted the bases for any possible hedonic calculus from what it was in the past when the only morally approved alternative to a career as a celibate was the almost mortal certainty of being confronted with an organ-pipe series of offspring, together with the inescapably concomitant economic responsibilities such a herd entailed. It is then no great surprise that, as recently quoted in the New York Times, a dignitary of some considerable importance in this celibate hierarchy complained of both the quantity as well as the quality of the crop of candidates offering themselves for admission to the priesthood. What else might one expect against the almost brutally seductive competition offered these days by the secular life?

No inquiry into the phenomena broadly referable to as religious could make any claim whatever to inclusiveness unless it came effectively to grips with this question or phenomenon of clerical celibacy. Certainly it was not new to the world when it appeared in the Christian church circa three or four hundred A.D. The Buddhist world had long known the celibate monk, and such profound scholars in the history of religion as F. Max Müller think it not at all unlikely that it was wandering Buddhist monks that introduced the idea to the western world, along with rosaries, tonsures and other paraphernalia in which

Buddhism anticipated Christianity. Certainly such example might have been effective here and there, but that would still leave unanswered the problem of original beginnings as well as the question of what there was in the current scene compatible with it so that it could take root. The forest sages at whose feet Gautama imbibed Vedic wisdom were probably celibates. I say "probably" because the then current tradition did not permit a man to become a "forest dweller" until after he had become a grandfather, and by Hindu tradition and on the basis of the accounts of them written by those observant Greeks of Alexander's time who marveled at them, these forest retreats were filled with old men who spent their time in philosophical speculations in which they were rather expected to come to conclusions quite the opposite of what they had spent their entire previous lives in believing! Tradition has it that the wives of these old men might go to the forest with them, but the best opinion now has it that they seldom did. In such an age class, the practice of celibacy probably preceded it as a theory. One of the heresies of which Gautama was considered guilty was that of seeking to advance the normal season of things, specifically to advocate celibacy as part of the program of negating desire, the root of evil. But Buddhism probably always lacked an effective machinery for the enforcement of uniform rules over any great geographical areas. It is more likely that Christian celibacy had rather independent origins. The historical evidence seems to indicate that the control of the early church machinery had gravitated into the hands of celibates, probably rather elderly ones at that. The factors tending in that direction are varied. At the stage in which a rising social movement is a fighting organization, leadership tends to pass into the hands of those whose emotional allegiance and energies are not claimed by family responsibilities. There is no doubt but that the responsibilities of wife and children tend to divide loyalties as well as motivate individual economic accumulations. Properly qualified church zealots should not be thus handicapped. The same is no doubt true for any fighting social movement. That was the sad conclusion reached, apparently, by the Greenwich Village girl whom I heard to complain that "Communists make lousy hus-

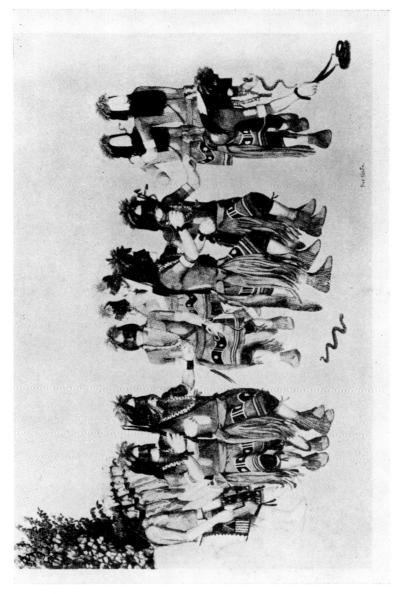

PLATE 5. Hopi Snake Ceremony. (Painted by Fred Kabotie, Hopi artist)
    —*courtesy The American Museum of Natural History*

PLATE 6. Corn altar of the American Indian. The six-direction altar.

—courtesy The American Museum of Natural History

PLATE 7. Sun-worship. The royal family (Ikhnaton's) making offerings to the sun.

—*courtesy New York Public Library Picture Collection*

PLATE 8. Milk Bath for a God. Every twelve years the statue of the Rain God Gomateswara, in Southern India, is anointed with milk, curds, sacred water and sandal paste by pilgrims. The statue is 57 feet high, and a thousand years old.
—*courtesy New York Public Library Picture Collection*

bands." Either organizational interest or family concerns come
to dominate. The church as a fighting organization saw the
advantages of ruling out this divided allegiance, no doubt after
finding that leadership selection had already for the most part
established it de facto before it was made official.

But an effective organizational technique for the short run
is not necessarily a desirable long run policy. Every culture
constitutes its own bases for biological selection; it becomes,
willy-nilly an eugenic force. One might well question the long
run merit of any social policy that prizes highly certain abilities,
selects them by a careful winnowing process, and then sentences these selectees to biological extinction. Naturally enough,
such a policy lasting only during a half-dozen generations
and involving only a small sample of the population would
be absolutely nothing about which to waste a breath of
concern. The current apprehension felt in some circles as to the
dire eugenic consequences of the differential birth rate in the
United States of the various social strata, during the period in
which the planned family is moving from the upper strata toward
the dismal bottom might bear examination from this point of
view. That process has been under way at most two generations since significant fractions of the population have been involved, and already the practice has worked down through two-
thirds of the population. It is probably now true that the bottom one-third of the socio-economic scale is producing two-
thirds of the people that are to constitute the coming generation
of Americans. The long run consequences of such differential
fertility would no doubt be eugenically catastrophic. And the
ardent environmentalist, completely unconcerned with the loss
of desirable genes, might well shudder at the consequences of
producing so large a proportion of the population in sub-stand-
ard environments. But the few generations thus raised and already water over the dam, so to speak, should at most prompt
us to keep a weather eye on the current process and do what
we can to speed up the process of motivating the lower strata
to put their biology under control. Paradoxically enough, in the
strata so far penetrated the process has been a concomitant
of an increased standard of consumption which seems to have

thumbed its nose at the Malthusian dogma of the relation between food supply and reproduction. And there is no reason for
fearing that the same process might not continue further on
down the scale if economic betterment with its concomitant
social motivation of not only keeping up with the Jones' but
going them one better if possible, can be continued. Effective
eugenic techniques can no doubt be devised to take up where
this form of motivation fails to penetrate. But one might well
wonder if the millennium and a half during which such questionable eugenics have obtained in some cultures might not have
left a mark of statistically identifiable proportions by this time.
The significant facts seem to be about as follows: first it is
apparent that the selection of candidates for the priestly caste
was on the basis of recognizable aptitude for the symbol manipu-
lating, "academic" abilities now apprehended in what are popularly called intelligence tests. This selection represents no mean
fraction of the total populace, particularly when the state or the
whole culture approaches a theocracy. Accurate ratios of clergy
to the balance of the population are difficult to obtain for the
past, but where one finds today the arrested mediaevalism of a
theocratic society such as in Buddhist Tibet some rough idea
of the size of the clerical fraction of the populace can be had.
Professor Joseph Rock[2] reported some years past on a little
Buddhist principality, largely Tibetan in population in the
province of Kansu. A largely nomadic people, its capital city
consisted of some 400 families, yet the monastary then housed
700 monks and during a previous period had housed 3800.

Until quite recently, Outer Mongolia provided an illustration
of just such a society. New York Times correspondent, Mr. Jack
Raymond reported the following item from that country:

"When the Communist revolution came in 1921, with the
successful Russian-aided revolt against the Manchus, there were
100,000 Lama monks among a population of less than 700,000.
Today there are about 300 Lamas in a population of about
1,000,000."[3]

In his Encyclopedia of Religion, Pike estimates that one in
every four Tibetan males belongs to the celibate orders.

This state of affairs is probably not too different from the norms of the mediaeval Christian culture, naturally with great variability from place to place and from century to century. The exact ratios of clerics to the balance of the population is of no moment. It suffices to recognize that this celibate fraction represented a sizable and not insignificant fraction of the populace to be selected out for special functions involving their prized abilities, and then promptly eliminated from the biological strain. Any such breeding practice in animal husbandry circles would fail to pass muster in even the slowest-witted rustic circles, and had such been the rule for an equivalent number of generations in the barnyards of the Western civilizations then milk, eggs, and beefsteaks would be luxuries indeed. The evidence that any damage has been done to the human strains involved must in the nature of things be purely inferential. But several lines are well worth noting. A recent inquiry into the parentage of the people listed in "Who's Who in America" revealed many times the chance expectancy of offspring of members of the clergy. Let it be granted without further argument that a similar deviation might have been discovered for the offspring of any equivalent professional group. But the significant fact to be noted is simply this: had the current culture demanded a celibate clergy then those particular individuals would simply have been missing from the roster, their places filled by some second-raters not now included.

Perhaps more significant is a series of comparisons that can be drawn with a culture that has never included a celibate clergy in its traditions, to wit, the Jewish. Far from requiring a celibate priestcraft, the rabbi that in orthodox circles, pauses in his reproduction short of four sons is by general agreement what would correspond to a "piker" in the American vernacular. Frequent samplings by the author among Jewish college students have revealed a surprisingly large fraction with rabbinical ancestry in the direct line. And in the not too distant past in that culture they even ran to a generous polygamy for its outstanding citizens, if, of course, one may believe their surviving written traditions on such points as this. The eugenic consequences of this type of polygamy might well bear scientific investigation. In this field a scientific gold mine is being neglected here in America where the descendants of the Latter Day Saints who had a brief period of polygamous enthusiasm are still available for study. Educators with first-hand acquaintance with this stock are unanimous in assuring me that the scions of these old polygamous families are at least a cut or two above the run of the mill Saint of monogamous lineage. But the errors possible in such unstatistical impressions are notorious; the facts are interesting enough and important enough to warrant serious study while yet the material is at hand. But to return to the subject of the Jewish-Christian comparison. Here it is increasingly evident that a real difference exists, even if it is not of the order of the vulgar libel, popular in underprivileged Christian circles, that "all Jews are clever." Yet there is just no possibility of dismissing lightly as insignificant, the weight of evidence of differences of a significant order that has been accumulating for some time. First of all, every measuring process that has winnowed out children of abnormally high intelligence quotients in the U. S. has turned up at least twice the chance quota of Jews. One of the largest of these, Professor Terman's study of the one thousand brightest children in California found twice the chance quota of Jewish children among these children with very high intelligence quotients. In Who's Who listings the ratio is even higher, particularly so over Catholics.

An examination of the 1956 list of state scholarship winners in the New York City schools, giving the names of 1460 winners, reveals even greater differences. A count of the typically Jewish names came to 874. Not counted as Jewish names were such as Green, Schwartz, Davidson, Cook, Stone, Cooper, Brown, Fisher, etc. unless accompanied by given names practically never given to non-Jewish children such as Hyman, Moses, or other highly typical Jewish names, or unless the winner was identified as coming from a Rabbinical school. The accuracy of this method of identification was checked in one large school having forty-odd winners, where it was found to have missed in six cases, failing to identify Jews in every case. It is safe to assume that the rough method of identification here used underestimated the percentage of Jews by ten to fifteen percent. Estimates of the percentage of Jews in the city vary from one fourth to one third of the population. The World Almanac of 1948 gives the former estimate. In 1939 and 1940 when most of these winning children were born, the percentage of Jews in the population of the city was almost certainly not higher than that. These winners must then represent somewhere between two and three times their chance quota.

The superiority of this Jewish sample is now so apparent that even the Ivy League Colleges, large and small, with their stringent scholastic requirements now have admitted Jews to the extent of some 23 to 25% of their student bodies. This well over chance representation is certainly not the product of any secret, pro-Semitic bias on the part of their admissions machinery. The monstrosities of the Hitler machine, and the needs of "cold war" policy, have produced a climate in which the crassest discrimination can no longer be permitted.

Selection of immigrants to the U. S. is at once offered as an explanation but it will probably not hold water. Similar or even more impressive facts seem to be apparent in Europe. In Germany, for example, with a Jewish population in pre-Hitler days of approximately three-fourths of one percent, this small fraction yet managed to include twenty percent of all Germany's Nobel Prize winners! Are we then to conclude that the Jew has some twenty-five times the incidence of genius calibre than the ordinary German apotheosized in the Hitlerian mythology? Hardly. Such a difference is probably primarily, but not entirely, a cultural one, with its roots far back in the mediaeval scene where the Jew was denied the right to become a land owner. In his process of adjustment to such a scene the Jew turned to such occupations of dubious, borderline respectability as merchandising, money-lending, or secular medicine then largely under an interdict as 'alchemy' and under suspicion by all right-thinking people, and of course only resorted to under dire need. But such is the irony of history that land holders became loutish peasants, and these pariah occupations became in effect "the tail that wags the dog" in the homely American idiom. Where merchandising was once an occupation for a vagabond peddler it spawned the merchant prince; the money-lending usurer, whose soul was already hopelessly damned be-

yond redemption but whose accessible financial resources
bought him a grudging tolerance, became in time the respectable
institutions of finance.[4] As for the alchemist, his successors provided not only an effective secular medicine but also the scientific inquiry and sound scholarship that was unhampered by
considerations of concern for the interest of institutionalized
theology. And in the days before the existence of schools of
medicine, not to even mention colleges of business and finance,
such skills tended to remain family vocations and interests in
much the way that today a disproportionate fraction of say,
Iowa farmers, will be found to be the sons of Iowa farmers.
Where the mediaeval Christian was brought up in an attitude
toward secular inquiry and scholarship that could at best be
described as a suspicious and grudging tolerance, the Jew suffered no such traumatizing retardation. A head-count of those
engaged in the activities in which outstanding successes on
occasion receive Nobel or similar prizes would tend to show
almost the same disproportion of Jews to Christians. In one
of the few areas in which accurate data are available, the medical and dental professions, for example, the percentage of
members of Jewish extraction runs to some 22%, where their
total representation in the population at large is currently estimated at 3.5%. It is thus obvious that this disproportion of representation in certain areas of achievement is in good part a
cultural-traditional product and not an index of the incidence
of the higher levels of intelligence of the respective groups.
Much the same historical-cultural process accounts obviously
for the almost dramatic underrepresentation of Catholics in any
roster of scientific achievement, so obvious that it has been
commented upon publicly by church dignitaries. Such cultural
compulsives are not lightly redirected. Let one child stand out
obviously above the rest in nimbleness of wit and general edu-
cability and it is even today a rare Catholic family in which
there does not at once develop a conspiracy, aided and abetted
of course by the family priest, to educate him for clerical orders.

Yet it would certainly be rash to conclude that all discernible
differences in measure or status must of necessity be purely

cultural. Some fifty to sixty generations of dubious eugenics cannot help but leave their biological mark on a populace. The central tendencies of the respective groups have probably not been seriously separated by the process, but were the incidence of cases at the extreme upper ends of the distributions still to remain the same after so long a period of bad eugenic practice, I for one would be compelled to take a very dim view of the entire Darwinian natural selection theory. An alternative possibility remains in the interpretation of the evidence that the Jews seem now to have the edge on Christians in the higher echelons of the intelligence scale. If for any reason it seems unacceptable to hold that the many generations of clerical celibacy of one group can account for the differences now discerned, one can simply concede that the "chosen people" have had an edge all along, a theory certainly not wholly incompatible with the point of view of the compilers of what has long been referred to as "Holy Writ."

Nowhere will this thesis encounter greater resistance and emphatic denial than among Jews; at least in their public pronouncements. Certainly no other group has fought more valiantly or effectively to abolish discriminations because of race, creed, or color. It is amusing how even their social scientists can close their eyes to the mounting evidence that their own fraction consistently turns up with far more than its chance quota of writers, artists, scientists, inventors, jurists, musicians, millionaires, composers; religious, political and social leaders and innovators, as well as child prodigies. It is as if they feared desperately that the facts might be discovered and trouble result. Let me reassure them: the rest of the world perceives the *consequences* of that fact consciously, but in part represses the full realization of the reasons for those consequences. The result is that the non-Jewish world repeats the sterotype that "all Jews are clever," the "cleverness" here conceded being a quality assumed largely to be composed of chicanery, trickery, and unscrupulousness. That is to say, not being compelled to identify the specific traits and abilities that constitute intelligence they tend instead to ascribe the achievements of the Jews to undesirable personality traits. Here again, as in most all questions, the long run advantages are all with presenting an unvarnished truth.

There is a tendency for many social scientists and psychologists to deny the fact of genuine differences between various samples or "races" of man, even when differences are clearly apparent. They do this no doubt with the best of motives and intentions. But the chief consequence of such denial among laymen is just to discredit the scientists, along with their opinions and scientific results. Facts persistently loaded in a particular direction cannot be prevented from registering with the populace. But these perceptions will be distorted by hates, frustrations, and ancient animosities over differences in creed and ritual, into something upon which they can vent these spleens, hates, inferiorities, and frustrations, if they are not forced into admitting the simple fact of individual and group differences. One could well appreciate the considerations of modesty which would motivate a. Jew publicly to play down such differences where they are in his favor. All the more reason why the rest of us should insist upon the cold, unvarnished, facts, because for the long run, fictions, however well-meant, are always dangerous. One wonders, had the numerous Germans who readily became such vicious exponents of anti-Semitism, been frankly taught all along that the Jewish sample among them contained proportionally a much larger fraction of genius, would they have so readily consented to its destruction? As it was, it was the *undesirable* qualities of the Jew which Hitler supplied or they invented to *explain away* his achievements that permitted mass anti-Semitism.

When specific abilities are pointed up, and we are forced to face them frankly, their constructive role in the community becomes focal, and it is easy to demonstrate how all share in such contributions, be they a magic bullet to hit spirochetes or a polio vaccine. Attention should be focused upon the fact that whenever the best man for a particular task is assigned to it *we all gain;* that whenever anyone is being made to function in a capacity, other than the one in which he is most efficient, *we all lose.* If there must be hostilities, let them be directed against anyone who would substitute *any other criteria* for this simple one in the problem of role determination, or who would wish to make any abilities, regardless of how rare or important, or any disabilities, regardless of how handicapping, an excuse for the exploitation of *anyone by anyone.*

In the interests of a proper evaluation today of the eugenic merits or demerits of an institution such as clerical celibacy it should be added that the damage done today by its continuation has obviously shrunk to a relative insignificance compared to its probable role in the past. Where up until practically the current generations the priesthood represented almost the entire intelligentsia of our western culture, they now have lively competition from dozens of equally respected and far better rewarded professions and skills, none of which demand any such preposterous violations of nature as celibacy. So the clergy can claim but at best a small fraction of the high I.Q.s where once they claimed, practically without competition, the whole. In fact, there is even a sporting chance that from here on out a celibate clergy might have eugenic rather than dysgenic consequences for the foreseeable future. When it is recalled that even so sympathetic a student of religion as a phenomenon of individual behavior as William James was driven to the conclusion that the religious virtuoso would be found to have as a highly probable concomitant a variety of undisputed symptoms of pathologies in the mental sphere one can readily see that it would be all too easy to oversimplify the entire problem.

So there probably are some live alternatives to the theory advanced by the Reverend Wesley Shrader[5] to account for the impressively high incidence of "nervous breakdowns" he has observed in the ranks of the clergy, both in his own and in other faiths. He ascribes it to simple overwork. One should first of all question the adequacy of the sample upon which he based his conclusion that there is such a rising rate of behavior pathology among the clergy. But even if we take his observations at face value it should be pointed out that "overwork" as a cause of mental disorders is mostly a polite fiction. There just is no evidence that hard work, up to the point where neither rest, sleep, nor adequate food is possible, as in the case of what is now known as "battle fatigue," can be properly charged with producing mental pathology. But both sound laboratory experiments and clinical observations have left no doubt that the stresses produced by long-continued conflict situations can be a very real culprit. Anyone confronted with the problem of reconciling the ancient theologies with the fruits of modern scientific empiricism is certainly in an unenviable position. If an environmentalistic theory must be found for an increase in breakdowns among the priesthood, certainly such a source of conflict cannot be left out of consideration. Surely the minister who had abandoned his profession over such conflicts is a familiar enough figure. As one put it to the author: "It was the only way I knew to save my sanity."

Should a celibate institution then draw in more than a chance quota of the mentally unstable, that would be no cause for alarm from the standpoint of eugenics. And certainly such individuals would be far less menacing in such a role than anywhere in the secular power heirarchy. The world has recently had all too vivid experiences with abnormal men in high political leadership. Even America has not been spared. But we could view their roles in a religious machinery with relative equanimity. For who is to say that society does not need its quota of men bitten with a little divine madness, as ferments, as innovators, as thundering Isaiahs to rouse it out of the ruts of complacency? There is no doubt that there have been periods of history when the premium was, and rightly, on conformity and stability. It is equally beyond doubt that at other times mankind can profit from the ardent, disgruntled innovator.

But sex and religion have met in relations other than clerical celibacy. In fact the concern of so many religions with so many aspects of sex has given a certain amount of warrant to those who have taken great delight in making all of religion but a sexual derivative. Certainly considerable emotionality was aroused around the turn of the century when Professor Starbuck reported his findings in regard to the age of occurrence of the then typical religious conversion. That the central tendencies thus found coincided so neatly with the puberty norms, about a year earlier on the average for girls than for boys, seemed in that statistically naive age to practically imply that the one was the cause of the other! Furthermore, linking religion even thus remotely with sex seemed a serious affront to all right-minded piety. Little did even the serious students of religion at that time suspect that the conversion experience itself was almost entirely a cultural rather than a hormonal phenomenon! Most important for an insight into the mentality of the day, which has changed but little enough in the years since, is this quite unconscious assumption that implies in effect that sex is an evil thing, and that nothing good could come out of it. Yet that is hardly to be wondered at after almost two millennia of preaching a doctrine of the essential sinfulness of sex, of talk about being "conceived in sin," of an almost transcendent virtue in an "immaculate conception,"[6] and of sex standards set by a celibate clergy. Small wonder that in the language sex had become almost a synonym for sin! Yet let it not be forgotten that few indeed are the cultures that ignore sex. This preoccupation with sex and sin is but one of the possible ways in which sex can and does color human behavior. There are others.

Cultures do not necessarily meet a problem of population pressure by hedging sex around with the taboos and restrictions of celibacy. They might, as some do, meet the problem with contraception, abortions, infanticide, or even cannibalism. Population has certainly pressed upon the food supply for a long time in India, yet here the culture seems to have attached no conception whatever of sin to sex. They have adopted customs of broad family economic responsibility for all in the family group and have continued to marry their offspring off as early as possible. Unwanted girl babies were disposed of in some areas. But it might well be noted that the life-span and survival rate have always been low in this area and until of recent date it took about all the reproducing each family could do to hold its own, what with epidemics, chronic food shortages and outright famine. Serious population pressure followed upon the heels of the control of epidemics which enormously reduced death rates but left the family mores unchanged. But this is the area in which the frankest of phallic worship abounded and where sexual intercourse, far from being a sin, was rated a religious duty, insofar as one is justified in speaking of a highly ritualized life as "religious." In places, service by all women as temple "priestesses" for longer or shorter terms was obligatory, such priestesses are, to western eyes indistinguishable from prostitutes, except that the temple "god," i.e., a group of priests, collected the fees. In some areas the "surplus" girl babies became such priestesses at the age of five or six years to serve in the holy rites of sex.

In every culture there is always the problem for some individuals of infertility. Lacking anything even approaching a scientific technology in this area it is obvious that their only recourse was to the ritualistic or the "religious." Almost invariably the wholly unwarranted assumption is made that the difficulty lies with the woman, so she is frequently subjected to a variety of indignities or penances involving fastings, eating of or refraining from particular foods, visiting shrines, sacred trees, stones, or temples. Since the infertility of any given pair is in at least a sizable fraction of the time the result of shortcomings on the part of the male it is not at all surprising that in a variety of cultures the remedy for sterility includes sexual intercourse with a temple priest; a remedy which anticipates by some millennia the latest scientific techniques of the "artificial insemination" to which a good fraction of the contemporary priesthood objects so strenuously and gives every possible ritual denunciation, but between the abandonment of the temple priest's services and the use of "artificial insemination" the women of the west have at various times and at places run to some strange techniques to achieve pregnancy, as witness the following account:[7]

"Down to the revolution there stood at Brest a chapel of St. Guignolet containing a priapean statue of a holy man. Women who were, or feared to be sterile used to go and scrape a little of the prominent member, which they put into a glass of water from the well and drank. The same practice was followed at the chapel of St. Pierre-a-Croquettes in Brabant until 1837, when the archaeologist Schayes called attention to it, and thereupon the ecclesiastical authorities removed the cause of the scandal.— At Antwerp stood at the gateway to the church of Saint Walburga in the Rue des Pecheurs a statue, the sexual organ of which had been entirely scraped away by women for the same purpose."

There was considerable phallicism in pre-Christian western Europe, and, with the church's happy capacity for compromise with local paganism, much of it long remained. The decree of Mans in 1247 forbade it, as did the Synod of Tours in 1396. In 1781, Sir William Hamilton visited Naples and found in Isernia phallic images being sold on the streets and placed in the church like candles today.

Orgiastic sects in Christianity survived in Russia down to relatively recent years.[8] They are referred to as the Khlysti, but there were others. Some of these really "put on a show!" In one account the communicants danced around a naked fifteen year-old virgin sitting in a tub of warm water while some old women cut off one of her breasts. This breast was then cut up into small pieces of which everyone ate one, after which the worshippers paired off in a sexual orgy. One might well gasp in amazement and wonder how such a performance could originate. It is a safe bet that the surgical innovation was the contribution of some demented person, but the capacity of the "normal" population to follow such perversions once initiated is, alas, familiar enough. Social theory has probably underestimated the importance of the roles played by individual innovators and initiators generally, the sane as well as the paranoid, in determining the social norms of particular groups.

It is nothing unusual whatever for the priestly caste to lead abnormal lives in the area of sex. Probably every possible variant and perversion has appeared at some time or another. Chastity for the priesthood was no Christian invention. As far back as three to four hundred B.C. the old Roman priesthood practiced varying taboos on sexual intercourse, sometimes lasting for long periods of years. Then again, the period of chastity may have been confined to a given period before the performance of certain rites, much as the dairyman-priest among the Todas of India must remain chaste for a particular period before and during his tour of duty at taking care of the dairy products or milking the buffalo in the temple-barn that is the only sacred edifice in their cultural pattern. The Roman vestal virgins simi-

larly were committed to a long period of chastity, usually thirty
years. At one time the penalty for being caught breaking such a
vow was burial alive!

Creator gods frequently indicate the sex drives as the creative power, and their rituals are often frankly phallic. It may
have been this aspect of some rituals that prompted Aristotle to
say that to love a god is indecent. But creator gods did not get
too much attention from Greeks, Romans, or Teutons.

Mohammedanism and Christianity from the start inherited
the generally low opinion in which the Jews held women. It was
not until the Council of Macon in 585 A.D. that women were
officially conceded to have souls. The Mohammedans still deny
women immortality, but this discrimination does not prevent
them from being faithful believers. St. Paul's famous dictum
that 'it was better to marry than burn' gave but grudging sanction to that institution. Somewhere in the gospels I seem to recall
something about eunuchs which have made themselves such
for the Kingdom of Heaven's sake, without any additional comment or moral judgment on the practice. This probably provided the scriptural authority for such sects as the Skopts. About
the middle of the 16th century the Council of Trent made marriage one of the sacraments, the delay being very revealing of
the generally dim view of sex taken by the early church leadership.

Sometimes the attention paid to sex takes the form of mutila-
tions. Even a cursory examination of the various practices of
bodily mutilation found about the world will show that the
primary sex characters come in for more ceremonial trimming
than the entire balance of the human body. Usually these are
disguised or explained as "improvements" and almost universally
accompanied with an enormous amount of ritual and ceremonial.
One might almost come to think that nature had done a very
bad job in the evolution of the sex apparatus were it not for
the fact that there is but poor agreement indeed as to the direction these "improvements" should take. This is of course not to
imply that the evolutionary process has done anywhere nearly
a perfect job in its random variations and survivals. It has been
said, and no doubt with considerable justice, that any apprentice

plumber that did as bad a job in any building as "nature" has
done on the human urinary system not only would, but should
be fired as an utterly hopeless bungler, incapable of ever being
a credit to his craft. But few indeed of these "improvements"
have any sound bases in physiology or anatomy. They are probably just monuments to the fact that sex is a rather intriguing
business, and as such will come in for an enormous amount of
attention. And since much of such attention is likely to have a
ritualistic, ceremonial character it is almost certain to be perceived as "religious"; with which perception there certainly is
no sound basis for quarreling.

There is much argument as to the role played by sex in the
ecstatic subjective religious experience.[9] It is certainly true that
a considerable number of religious mystics used sexual language
in their attempts to describe the intense joys of the religious experience. But it is probably a mistake to take this too literally or
to make too much of it. St. Augustine made use of musical terms.
St. Theresa used the language of courts and etiquette. There are
after all, but a limited number of dimensions of intense feeling
known to the human organism, and no matter how unique the
experience, it must be communicated in terms of familiar sense
modalities. And the senses involved in sex and nutrition make
powerful appeals. How else account for the lugubrious title
bestowed upon an early colonial catechism:—"Spiritual milk for
Christian babes, drawn from the breasts of both testaments."
And there is no denying that many a cult leader made the discovery that sex could be used in various ways to make a rising
religious movement more attractive or to increase the zeal of
his following. Let it not be lightly assumed that this process always took the form of a moral laxity or a breaking down of
normal inhibitions as was indeed frequently the case in many
a springtime fertility rite of which Easter with its emphasis
upon eggs, and the lower mammals of renowned philoprogenitive prowess, is a much chastened survival. Far from it. In some
segments of the Christian culture where sex had become a synonym for sin, and where technological efficiency had practically
reduced the effective sphere of the magico-religious to the task
of first of all convincing the communicants that they were

steeped in a type of sin that urgently needed a serious ritual cleansing, and then of course providing the ablutions, sex proved a mainstay. Since sex was by definition practically identical with sin, and, biology being what it is, it was easy to use this as a leverage to start the sinner on the path to reform, once he had admitted his sinfulness. But there was the rub! Lest an individual was indeed impressed with his own sinfulness it was difficult to convince him that he needed "salvation." And right there you have the bases for that tempting, recurrent, perennial, the doctrine of the necessity of sin for salvation which played a considerable role in the hold Rasputin had over his followers, and, before his time, many another had hit upon the same device, whether or not it was enunciated as an avowed doctrine. A variant on this device seems to have been hit upon by a contemporary group known variously as Buchmanites, the Oxford Movement, or Moral Rearmament Movement. Here again, sex is the great Sin, but the cathartic effect of its public confession is effectively used not only in aborting any possible repressive mechanisms that might be incubating within the individual, but also at the same time creating an effective fellowship in the combating of sin by mutual aid, much after the manner found effective by the much publicized "Alcoholics Anonymous." One cannot help but suspect that these periods of public confession, where in the refined atmosphere of an unimpeachable suburban home the Buchmanite hostess might perhaps confess an adultery in the presence of the cuckold husband, are no small aid in the recruitment of new communicants. Often enough have sinners come to scoff or snicker and remained to pray!

The old fashioned camp-meeting type of religious revival is now looked upon in general as a rather dubious bit of past in American Protestantism. On the thinly settled frontier it was no doubt true that the objective conditions existed for the formation of quite new and different standards of morals in a people who yet carried with them quite effective memories of a stricter moral clime. The exhorting revivalist was expert in the business of awakening strong guilt feeling in his auditors and it was not long before he discovered the general correlation between the fact of having sinned and the acute need for salvation. However it was but rarely and in small circles that deviant, splinter-group leaders made use of the principle as an articulate doctrine. I can find no record of any of the major revivalists having even flirted with it coyly or indirectly. But the emotional excitement, incident to meeting large numbers of strangers and being assembled in a compact throng which was encouraged to give vent to its feelings by overt expressions of all sorts, was more than enough to make the institution a success. The more suggestible, and no doubt too, the more recently sinful, would be likely first to feel the need of a saving grace as promised from the rostrum, and their overt expression in word and act would provide the balance-destroying stimuli just still needed by others slightly more resistant to suggestion or less recently sinful. This has gone on until entire audiences have "accepted grace," and on the frontier many a stable organized congregation remained behind as a monument to a successful revival meeting.

Social movements are sometimes more often remembered for some of their more exceptional and perhaps more dramatic concomitants than for their more routine, prosaic accomplishments. This is probably the case with regard to the revival. What with the relative ease of transition from one type of excitement to another it is small wonder that these early camp-meetings, so named because those that attended frequently came from many miles and camped in the woods nearby, served also as a more or less extemporaneous mating ground. The parson being handy, many of these matings were then given official sanction, but there remained enough unsanctified onces, with their biological dividends, to make the parents of nubile daughters a bit apprehensive, particularly in the later frontier years when a settled, orderly life followed close behind with its reduced economic opportunities which made it rather more difficult for the adolescents to achieve an effective economic base. In his youth the author recalls an episode that highlights this phase of the question. The conversation around the rural smithy concerned itself with a certain young lady who was "in trouble" as the local vernacular had it. Directly this was revealed there was a quite understandable zeal to discover which of the local swains was involved. But it developed that all that was known at the moment was that it had occurred at the last nearby camp meeting. At this the unregenerate blacksmith spat a huge mouthful of tobacco juice preparatory to unburdening himself of the following:—"I allus did think there was more souls made than saved at these here campmeetin's!" It takes but a few of these more dramatic episodes to provide the bases for the literary use made of them in current fiction dealing with certain marginal rural areas in the United States. And, of course, it is always possible that in some limited area a more or less orgiastic tradition can get under way, and become a local norm. Witness the spread in recent years from Virginia to Alabama of this preposterous cult perennially matching "faith" against rattlesnake venom. The resulting fatalities are about the percentage long known to medical science, but here in a sizable percentage of the population the more archaic, animistic interpretation of such phenomena survives. And if such can get a foothold in a populace, what, might one well ask, could not?

So there should be no attempt to deny that some religions seem to be concerned primarily with sex, either to deify it or to repress it, nor even that most of them give it a reasonable amount of attention and concern. But over against that is the undeniable fact that some other cultures pay a minimum amount of attention to sex in their ceremonial or ritual behavior, far from making it the chief item of concern. On an average, sex gets about the attention, ritual, ceremonial, emotional, and practical that its role in the physiology of human motivation might be expected to predict for it. That it then comes in for an average amount of attention in such organized schemes of values, of formalized or ritualized sets of rules, directions, or generalized codes of conduct is only to be expected. But this is no warrant for expecting any too close correlation between physiological norms and the specific patterns of social or institutional norms. Social habits can almost directly fly into the face of physiological reality. One need but mention that much quoted and whimsical custom, the couvade that has appeared in several widely separated spots on the earth. On sheer physiological grounds one might expect to be safe in predicting for the mother the role of invalid in childbirth, rather than for the father. And, in truth, so it usually is. But not always. For in these few cultures it is the father that assumes the role of invalid while it is the duty of the freshly parturient mother carefully to minister to both father and child. Similarly, in the western world with its tradition of a "weaker sex" it seems almost preposterous to us that any culture should assign, excepting in a purely figurative sense, greater hardness to women's heads than men's. But such is the case with the much quoted Arapesh of Dr. Mead. In justification of their assumption these mountain people of New Guinea point to the heavy burdens women are expected to, and do, carry, balanced upon their heads. In their zeal to justify the existing order of things the males conveniently overlook the long course of training, beginning in very early childhood, with the small girl children being given larger and larger loads to balance upon their heads. In short, given sufficient motivation the norms of human physiology can come in for considerable competition in the determination of human behavior.

Illustrative of the general principle of human physiology bowing to social motivation of one sort or another are the whole array of bodily modifications in the interest of local esthetic whims with the foot-binding, teeth filing or extracting, ear and nose piercing, circumcising, infibulating, wasp-waisting, head binding, lip stretching, etc. Here behavior norms can be established clearly in direct violation of basic, specific, and innate structural or reflexological norms and processes. Lest this seem to anyone a proof of the irredeemable perversity and stupidity of man, let it be remembered that as a basic behavior process these preposterous violations of physiology make use of the same habits and functions as those involved in surgery or dentistry. The latter merely had to wait until the trial and error process hit upon an effective pattern. What we are dealing with, at bottom, is the inhibitory power of the cortex over lower-center reflex action. It is that capacity that is distinctive and characteristic of human behavior, not any sterotyped, one-to-one correspondence between any innate physiological or neurological pattern and an established social norm or custom. And this is the basic error made by any theory depending upon some single motivating agent to account for any particular aspect of society.

The advent of Freudianism enormously increased the already generous latitude the proponents of a sexual theory of religion were allowing themselves in the interpretation of phenomena as evidence for their thesis. The magic key was "symbolism." Thus where snakes appeared in any form of ritualism the Freudian needed to look no further; for was not the snake a most brazen phallic symbol and any to-do being made over serpents ipso facto sexual, even if the culture in question was obviously free from the socially repressive mores in regard to sex that obtained in the culture where psychoanalytic theories were first formulated. A far safer bet would be that it was the killing power of the snake's venom that drew ceremonial attention to it in the first place, particularly in view of the fact that it is the venomous snake that is typically given credit in primitive cultures for having whatever their term or concept is for spirit, soul, ghost or similar animistic agent. It is not the garter snake but the rattlesnake that in stone images surrounds some Mexican pyramids. It is again the rattlesnake that is used in the Hopi snake dance, and in general it is a safe bet that a venomous snake will be used in ceremonial if there is one indigenous to the culture area. It is the extraordinary potency in any animal or thing that increased the chances that it will get ritual or ceremonial attention. In the languages of at least some primitive tribes the nearest thing they have to a concept of the supernatural is that of the extraordinary, the highly dangerous, or the unusual.

One could make out an excellent case for the very important role played by food and nutrition in religion. The variety of the rituals that can be collected bearing on one phase or another of food gathering, hunting, trapping, assuring a plenteous supply of such natural food sources, planting, watering, fertilizing, cultivating, guarding against enemies, and harvesting, will no doubt match anything that can be collected in the entire domain of sex and reproduction. Did a snake goddess survive in ritual practices in a Cretan cave for three to five thousand years? Yes,

but she survived by incorporating so many other homely functions that the line between her worship and a monotheism must
be drawn finely indeed, and these nature-cults were always
heavily loaded with concern for the nutritive side of life
wherever there was any pressure of population upon available
food supply or where irregularities of seasons made adequate
nutrition a touch and go business. For a stretch of over 2000
years Demeter was worshipped at Eleusis. Rain and Sun gods
are almost standard equipment for agricultural societies. And a
glance at the Old Testament, or better yet, at modern Judaism
would make almost anyone wonder as to just where a line between dietetics and religion is to be drawn. It is not for nothing
that the first request in the Lord's Prayer is for the daily bread!
Whatever may be of serious concern to man is likely to be found
dealt with in his religions. A seventeenth century prayer book
has long been in the writer's family, and the exhaustive index
of topics and situations provided for with a specific prayer was
long a marvel to him. He won numerous wagers against his
fellow adolescents who were confident enough in their imaginative powers to specify a situation, not anachronistic for the date
of the prayer-book, for which a prayer could not be found.

Finally, it must be remembered that even where sexual
taboos are at a minimum there may still be found a rich ceremonial or "religious" life.

Chapter IV

MIND AND RELIGION—ANIMISM

Our religious ideas, and of course the ideas we have had about religion, have been intimately linked and related to our conceptions of ourselves, our souls, our minds, spirits, ghosts, our doubles, and in short, whatever we believe it was that accounted for what we did. And typically we have at least talked as if we believed that there was some single entity within the material body that accounted for its actions, that differentiated the living from the dead, that was perhaps even our "real" essence. Yes, typically we have subscribed or given lip allegiance to such a simple dualism, but along with that we have carried a generous vocabulary of other or supplementary entities or agencies presumably responsible for some particular or peculiar aspects of our behavior, such as our will, our conscience, our intelligence, our "heart," our "self," our "ego," and not to forget the "right minds" we were *not* in when we did some stupid or villainous thing at which we were later caught. The multiple souls of the Eskimo, the old Egyptian, and so many other cultures are at bottom not too different from our practical language of description of our behavior, which indeed, seems quite different from our avowed theory! The term *animism* has come to be applied to all such concepts of activating principles of whatever sort, presumed to account for or explain the activity of some object or body. These animistic principles or entities and of course the names for them have had a very interesting developmental history. To us, the term *mind* seems very prosaic and secular, free from any dubious theories of immortality, hell-fire, or metempsychosis. In its present form and usage it is something of a newcomer. Many languages do not yet have such a secular term and continue to use instead, a term identical with our word soul. And whatever term a language has for this soul or animistic principle it almost invariably has a suspicious philological kinship with words for breath, shadow, image, or reflection. Likewise, the terms for death very frequently say in effect "breath gone," or "breath departed."

Doubtless our metaphysics of mind and matter had its origins in this humble, naive, animism. This dualism, this apparent separateness of mind and matter, was no doubt given substance by the familiar phenomena of sleep and dreams, hallucinations, and drugs, probably by way of the prior development of language habits, verbal designations for these vivid, consciously experienced, subjective kinds of "reality," as opposed to socially verifiable events. For purposes of social communication in regard to such subjective and baffling experiences as dreams and hallucinations specific verbal distinctions had to be made. Once made, words are all too easily reified into a kind of reality that is very much lacking in the original experience. Once a name is assigned to anything, the name itself becomes a substantial entity. Note the highly emotional attitudes widely held toward personal names, which may go the length it reputedly has in China where one's "real" name remains a closely held secret, while another, usually of a derogatory sort, must serve for practical purposes. In old Egypt the *Ren* was the name of anything, and had a separate existence and was thought to be the underlying and permanent substances of things. It may well be that Pythagoras learned similar notions from the Egyptians, along with the geometry he admittedly got there, namely the conception of the "reality" of the properties of numbers and geometrical forms. There can hardly be a doubt but that Plato's ideas of an immaterial reality derived from these Pythagorean doctrines and from the Socratic theory of the reality of ethical universals. Such doctrine of course presumes the non-material character of human thought processes, an assumption increasingly difficult to maintain in the light of modern psychological research.

This evolution of primitive animism into the sharp duality of soul and body, mind and matter, or flesh vs. spirit is in itself a most interesting phenomenon. In the Philosophy I class it might well be made to seem that mind and matter had always been the obviously different things they are now credited by common sense with being. But the historical facts are quite otherwise, and so are the facts of modern anthropology. To what we call primitive peoples, the idea of a completely incorporeal reality is preposterous. A soul, a ghost, or a demon of whatever persuasion must be capable of furnishing sense impressions of some sort at some time or other. There are perhaps some special exceptions; one of the American plains tribes credits one type of being with the whimsical capacity of making itself invisible whenever humans look at it. This instance but emphasizes the general principle that such ghostly entities are by definition capable of furnishing valid sense impressions to mortals. Rarefied, attenuated, even "gaseous" might the material be of which they are composed, but the notions of reality that were acceptable to Pythagoras and Plato will not pass muster with what we used to call "the untutored savage." Their souls, spirits, or shades by whatever name, if indeed they assume them to exist, are rather likely to have the ordinary human ills and needs of the flesh, but not without plenty of exceptions. They may even be highly dependent upon surviving mortals for ritual attention of various sorts if they are to continue their existence. Many a sophisticated, modern religious communicant still carries on some of these ritual attentions to the dead. The overt behavior remains much the same, the motivation for doing it is probably identical, but the verbal account offered, the rationalizations now given, will probably differ a bit. It is of these verbalized "reasons" for the activity one must learn to be suspicious. They are not an account of how the behavior or ritual practice came to be.

But there can be no denying that in the western world an increasing sophistication in regard to the material world served for a time to "dematerialize" the ghost or spirit concept. In Homer the spirits of the slain in battle are to be "seen" as wraiths of mist hovering over the field, probably in the morning when there actually is a bit of mist about to aid the perceptive process! But even as early as this there are but a few scattered hints in Homer of any remaining fear of the dead. As in so many primitive cultures, there seeemed definitely to be lacking any formal, authoritative, or official doctrine in these matters. To us, in this day, the attitude and behavior of the Greeks in such matters seems more secular than sacred. This Homeric view of the soul, concurred in by the Orphics and other theologi in spite of other differences, held the psyche to be a unique creature of combined spiritual and material nature, which, regardless of the manner of its origin, now actually dwells within man. But at this time this "psyche" seems to have been considered a sort of second self that carries on a more or less separate existence, but making itself felt when the normal, visible self loses consciousness in dreams, swoons, "ecstasy," "mania" or other deviant mental states. Note that this "psyche" was not the agency that carried on the normal functions we now think of as "mental," the sensing, perceiving, even thinking and reasoning. It seems to have been limited to the relatively abnormal states of consciousness, which were always more or less detached from the normal personality or self. It seems reasonable to suppose that when some Greek philosophers began to play with the idea of an immortal soul the point of departure in their thinking very probably was this more or less abnormal "psyche." Certainly this seems to be the case with the philosophy of Empedocles who thought of the soul as confined within the body but having a separate existence there, not at all concerned with sensation, perception, or even thinking, which latter function he ascribed to the heart's blood. Its activity was confined to what Empedocles thought of as "higher" modes of knowledge such as in ecstatic inspiration, in profound philosophic insights that transcend sensory perception and ordinary experience and in effect can grasp the universe as a totality and in its true nature. To it belonged the requirements of ethical and religious systems and duties. In fact, it had many of the characteristics we now commonly ascribe to the "conscience." But note: its highest duty was to free itself from its unhallowed union with the body. Thus far this certainly has many of the characteristics

of later "soul" doctrines, but amusingly enough, Empedocles
thought of these souls as relatively long-lived but certainly not
immortal!

In Democritus we have an early and specific denial of the
possibility of immortality since the soul would of necessity be
made up of the same kind of basic atoms which in dispersal
would destroy any pattern of which they may once have been
a part. Six centuries before Christ a scoffing Hindu is credited
with saying that the soul is only a sort of bodily effervescence
like the foam on beer; which makes both beer and materialism
considerably older than many of us had thought.[1] Anaxagoras
was certainly an early, if not the first, emphatic and conscious
dualist among Greek philosophers. For him the mind concept
was something distinct from everything material; it is absolutely
immaterial and incorporeal. But these "minds" or "souls" could
not survive the dissolution of the material "concretions" in which
the moving and animating soul-force once lived!

So much for the philosophers; what about the lay attitudes
of about that period? Such funeral orations as survive of the
5th and 4th centuries B.C. make no assumptions of survival for
the soul, beyond that credited to the activities of the "cult of the
dead." Such survival as was assumed was in terms of what we
today would call the germ plasm, or in terms of the memories
held by the living. Incidentally, there was at this time also no
assuming of a desirable state of affairs, post-mortem, nor even
do high hopes for such appear in these orations. In Pindar's
victory odes, heroes only are presumed to have an exalted post-
mortem state of being; a theory, amusingly enough, not too infrequently encountered in primitive cultures! Far more common than the assumption of an exhalted state post-mortem, is
a general skepticism as to any survival that might by any
stretch of the imagination be construed as an assumption of
immortality. Much more common is the belief that the dead
survive for a time; the length of time being a highly variable
factor not only from culture to culture but also within the culture itself where a great variability obtains from person to person. An interesting variant is the belief that the dead survive as
long as anyone remembers them; this is probably the proviso

that assures a relative immortality to culture heroes; they have it by virtue of the fact that they are remembered! This process is no doubt closely akin to all sorts of ritual duties and observances in regard to the dead. To us there is something profoundly disturbing about an immortality that is created for the dead by the memories and rituals and observances of the living. But there is no denying that whatever else the dead may be up to, as memories in the living they remain here as active and effective agents of a sort. And that sort of effective reality apparently is given official recognition by the literal realism of the naive mind. The other sort of immortality seems to be a much later product in cultures where symbols have graduated to a somewhat different role.

The intimate relation long felt to exist between intoxicants and drugs, and animistic ideas of all sorts is not entirely without foundation. No doubt it was the capacity of ethyl alcohol to induce rather interesting changes in the subjective state of consciousness that earned beverages containing a sufficient quantity of it the title of "spirits." The languages of some cultures fail to distinguish between getting drunk and getting into contact or communion with such spirits as they may presume to exist; in short, they have not yet made separate categories of getting drunk and "getting religion." Let us not get too uppish about that shortcoming; the language of the Good Book is not any too clear on the difference either! And the William James who wrote:[2] "The plain truth is that to interpret religion one must in the end look at the immediate content of the religious consciousness," was in deadly earnest when he tried each new drug or intoxicant that he heard about as having the capacity to influence the conscious experience or conscious state. He may indeed have been convinced by that time that the conscious state as altered by alcohol did not put him in tune with the infinite but he certainly had not given up the hope that some other drug might well have that happy effect or at least be able to add to the all too meagre reality as experienced in the normal conscious states. Almost without exception the drugs and intoxicants found in nature or discovered by primitive technology were used more or less as the nucleus of rituals and ceremonials of a profoundly religious character, not to forget or overlook the role played by wine in "Communion," a peculiarly revealing term for the ideas and beliefs of yesteryear. Time was not too remote when that "communion" was more than the figure of speech it is now pretended to be in some circles. Small wonder that howls of indignation went up from some of the very churches that had been instrumental in passing the prohibition amendment when it was to be carried to the point of prohibiting wine for the sacraments.

Just what the nature of the soma plant was, even its botanical character, is apparently not known today.[3] But the people who wrote the Vedas knew it, and used it, and organized some of their most solemn rituals about it, and, in effect, raised it to the level of a deity; not too great an honor in a culture that could deify practically anything, including cows and monkeys. Tobacco has gone far afield from its initial use as a ritual agent that gave solemnity and permanence to the memory of agreements, contracts, or negotiations. It seems on its way to becoming a general nuisance attached to everything, to the tune of a total money expenditure almost exactly the size of the budget of private education and scientific research combined! But it still lags half-way behind the current expenditure for "spirits," even if we now are a bit less animistic as to the character of their potency!

There can hardly be any doubt that it is the nature of our subjective experience that provides the background for the development of an animistic terminology or habits of speech. Not only that convincing anomaly, the dream experience, where the dreamer apparently spends at least part of the night under conditions that demand a violation of the ordinary ordinates of space and time, but also the more prosaic, everyday capacity for thought and imagery that seems so convincingly to many people to take place without regard for material processes, equally bring to birth a set of terms to designate this type of activity, event, or process. Once separated in language habits, the separation becomes a part of our thought processes. This is not to imply that it is a universal "must." Emphatically no! It is merely made possible, and indeed, a variety of widely separated cultures have achieved what are in effect highly similar language and thought habits. Once standardized as the official manner of speech in a culture, children acquire it quite as a matter of course. But far from universally; Dr. Mead reports that she finds no animistic ideas among the Manus children in New Guinea. And in the European scene it will be remembered too that Professor Piaget was most surprised when he found that his studies showed clearly that children do not spontaneously separate "thought" from "thing," that they do *not* speak of thought as a disembodied, animistic process but instead stubbornly insist that they think with their mouths, tongues, voices, or even with their stomachs, if the questioner persists in confronting the child with the facts that no mouths were seen to move and no voices heard. Somewhere along the age scale, of course, the cultural fiction that thinking is done with the "mind" is learned. At the age of three years and ten months one of the author's children was heard to use the expression "think." Upon being asked exactly what he did when he thought, the following answer was forthcoming:—"Well, I have to get real quiet, and then my throat tells me." This seems all the more amusing to a psychologist in view of the fact that this child reports a variety of imagery of exceptional clarity, and hence might well be much less dependent upon kinesthesis. Seven years later the same child has a quick and ready answer to the same question, namely, the thinking is located "in the head," but he has no more specific localization for the process than the head in general, and even that localization is no doubt the product of the conventional identification of "head" with "brains," which are credited with involvement in the higher thought processes.

An interesting reversal has developed in the modern world in its attitudes toward visions and hallucinations. It is apparent that in what is loosely referred to as "Biblical Times" the hallucination was in excellent repute as an authoritative source of dependable guidance. However, already at the turn of the last century William James was moved to direct his most eloquent verbal darts at what he called "medical materialism," the dismissal out of hand as beneath contempt any beliefs or opinions based upon, or involving any abnormal mental state whatever.

He saw no reason why an abnormal temperature or physiological state might not be better for incubating some profound truth. James was, after all, interested in the validity of the so-called religious experience, its significance, and its effect on the moral life. But all that is beside the point of the present inquiry. Here the question of moment is merely this: what role did such states play in providing a background in thought and language of an animistic sort to influence in any marked degree the development of that entire segment of culture commonly designated "the religious?" Far from seeking to "discredit" anything, we are interested only in answering the question that might be crudely put: "how did we get that way?" Seen from this point of view, the significant facts are simply that these dreams, visions, hallucinations if you will, do occur universally in all cultures, some to all persons, some to only a few. But a terminology for these events does everywhere develop, and these events and processes cannot help but be incorporated into the overall scheme of things. The subjective experiences are there, the language designations for them develop, they enter into the reality of the social, conversational world, they are assigned causal efficacy and reality whenever the time sequence of their occurrence interposes them into an event sequence. Thus are created in speech habits what the metaphysician later utilizes as hard and fast dichotomies or metaphysical categories that were never implied in the original verbal usage. These categories of soul versus body, spirit versus flesh, or mind as opposed to matter, in which the qualities of the one are denied to the other, are of recent vintage. Insofar as religions represent then any form whatever of an elaboration upon or development from any kind of notion of two (or more) kinds of reality with an emphasis upon this non-material "reality," then surely it is the character of the human organism, with its dreams, visions, imagery, symbolization or abstract thought, as well as its capacity for occasional hallucinations that has provided the background for the systematic development of such ideas. How could it well be otherwise?

An examination of specific religions confirms the role played by these phenomena with a monotonous regularity. Almost invariably there lurks in the background the leader, the founder, the "savior," or the "enlightened one," whose authority stemmed largely from such vivid subjective reality, induced either in himself or in others with sufficient vividness to convince at least some plausible fraction of his fellow citizens of its significance. It is these subjective "mental" phenomena that have provided the pattern for the spiritual, the animistic, the personalized aspects of the supernatural, for primitive savage as well as for today's sophisticated metaphysician. If there is any reality in mind, soul, or spirit, it must stem from something convincing in human experience. At one cultural level the literal reality of the dream, vision, or hallucination may be unquestioned along with simple memory or direct sense impressions. The sophisticated philosopher puts it thus: "Das Dasein der Seele besteht in ihrem Leben, in der Einheit aufeinander bezogener psychischer Vorgaenge; nehmen wir diese weg, so bleibt kein Rueckstand."[4] Or again, "Seele ist die auf nicht weiter sagbare Weise zur Einheit verbundene Vielheit innere Erlebnisse." In both cases there is this unquestioned reliance upon the reality and significance of the subjective.

But what is the nature of this subjectively experienced reality? As we have seen, the older traditions did not even question its basic similarity to the material, the objective world. The older Greek philosophers had this in common with primitive thinking almost everywhere. The relatively elusive pneuma of the Stoics was but a slightly modified version of the air or the breath which was obviously highly essential to the living individual and more or less inseparable from it, but also definitely palpable to the senses. In later speculations this concept persisted as a much disputed "spirit," whose relation to the concept of a soul has almost continually been in dispute and upon which there is no agreement among theologians to this day. It is of course true that in some of the Platonic dialogues the concept of a completely non-material soul is defended. But it found little favor in the eyes of his contemporaries. The Neo-Platonists who combined eastern mysticism with Hebrew theology and Greek philosophy found the idea acceptable, and it is apparent that this brand of metaphysics became a part of official Christian theology only slowly, and against great opposition. For as late as four hundred years after Christ the conception of both God and the soul as it emerges from the writings of the church fathers is indistinguishable from that of the gaseous, vaporous, but still material substance of the ghost or soul of primitive animism.[5] Both soul and body were still *material* to early church fathers. And immortality was not one of the attributes of this quasi-material soul. It was much more closely akin to the Aristotelian concept of the vital principle that could, of course, have no existence apart from a material body. But this vital principle accounted for the activities of the organism. Now the Platonic conception of the soul presumed that it could have nothing in common with the body. But at the same time it was the soul that caused the movements of the body, a not unimportant part of its total functions! This is certainly one of the earliest instances of the assumption that the wholly other, the wholly different can none the less causally interact. The other principal functions of the soul were what we would today generally call the cognitive. The soul could contemplate the Platonic Ideas and thereby attain to true knowledge. Such activity was designated as Reason. Plato had a relatively lower opinion of the mental processes resulting from direct, sense-stimulation by the objective world; that was mere opinion! One might well wonder what a keen intellect such as his would have emerged with in the way of conclusions had he known of the role played by the kinesthetic senses in the processes he thought of as Reason!

Whether or not the idea of a completely non-material soul was Plato's "true" belief, it is obvious that the theory acquired no great following in the centuries immediately following. By what processes of change in the intellectual climate did the idea become acceptable? What happened after or during some seven hundred years of relative neglect of this Platonic metaphysics that it finally found favor? Probably as likely a summing up of the process as any is given by Professor McDougall.[6] "The spiritualization of the soul seems to have been achieved by way of the refinement of the conception of God. This refining process consisted in successively denying Him all the distinctive attributes of matter, until the conception of an immaterial spirit was reached. And then the conception of the human soul was assimilated to this more refined conception of God. Thus man, having created God in his own likeness in the course of his first speculative efforts, reversed the order of procedure at a later stage and shaped his idea of himself on the model of his more refined idea of God."

It is certain that to the early church fathers God and all animistic agents were presumed to be corporeal, and they could cite Scripture to prove it. In short, their animistic ideas were precisely those of practically all primitive peoples. It may well be that the general mysticism of the east reached the west by way of Alexandria and the Neoplatonists and their forerunners. Certainly where Plato seemed to assign immateriality and reality to both Ideas and Souls he excluded the latter from what he conceived to be the realm of true Being. In at least some of his writings this intermediate position of the soul with respect to true Being and Becoming is clear. Sometimes it seems not too remote from the vital principle of Aristotle. Interestingly enough, in those parts of the New Testament credited to St. Paul there appears, in contrast to the balance of the text, a doctrine, not too different from that of Plato, in which a similar tripartite division of body, soul, and spirit is presumed. Here the soul is much like the Aristotelian vital principle, inseparable from the flesh, and mortal. It is the spirit (pneuma-breath), coming directly from God that is immortal. This is very closely akin to the metaphysics found in some of the later writings of the Old Testament. But there remains a conspicuous difference: this spirit that came to man from God retains, at death, its individuality and provides the basis for personal immortality. In the later Judaism of the Old Testament it is held that this individual spirit is somehow reabsorbed into the Godhead, and so of course loses its former individuality.

Should one seek to establish more accurately of what Professor McDougall's "refinement of the conception of God" consisted it is rather likely that a problem of considerable complexity would confront one. What process could make the conception of a material god increasingly inacceptable? Probably an increasing sophistication in regard to the material world, for one thing. Then again, any gods left within the material realm would be an invitation to endless jurisdictional disputes that could not but result in a weakened authority for all parties to the controversy. Material things and events have a stubborn and sometimes embarrassing conviction about them that will not down. In fact even the most preposterous dogma or metaphysics has its foundation in some aspect of objective reality, in some possible interpretation of some palpable process. The material world tends to develop a logic and a dynamics all its own. It is not for nothing that it has been many times pointed out that it is the not otherwise predictable or controllable that becomes the domain of the gods. Yet it must be remembered that the Orphic priestcraft taught a doctrine of personal immortality long before Plato at a time when such belief was entertained only in aberrant Greek cults, and where it was linked with doctrines of metempsychosis and a primitive materialistic animism. In short, souls were held to be immortal before they lost their material character. At the hands of Plato the soul already lost its material character before the gods were thus conceived. And yet it is probably true that the dematerialization of the soul in the Middle Ages had the sequence as outlined by McDougall in the above quotation. And certainly the official theology of Christendom since that time, and many philosophers, have accepted it without question. There remains only the question of the extent of its acceptance at the present time. By the time the institutionalized cultural leaders have accepted and taught an official doctrine for some fifteen hundred years it can be expected that the deviants rejecting the official views will be few indeed. But apparently there always have been, at all times and in all cultures, a minority that has rejected the local, official doctrines. And on occasion the deviants have transformed themselves into the majority. This process is sometimes referred to as progress, and at times it might well be.

But there is no denying that the rise of the scientific method in the world has brought on dark days for animism of all sorts. And it is obvious that animism of some sort constitutes the foundation of every system of religious belief and practice with the possible exception of certain rigid pantheisms. And it is a matter of serious moment to all organized religious institutions that they have to "do business," as the vernacular has it, in a world in which animism in any form is no longer in good repute. As Professor McDougall[7] so eloquently puts it: "I believe that the future of religion is intimately bound up with the fate of Animism; and especially I believe that, if science should continue to maintain the mechanistic dogma, and consequently to repudiate Animism, the belief in any form of life after the death of the body will continue rapidly to decline among all civilized peoples, and will, before many generations have passed away, become a negligible quantity.—And it seems to me highly probable that the passing away of this belief would be calamitous for our civilization." This is an alarm widely felt and frequently expressed with great eloquence and even greater apprehension in Christendom where it seems to be conveniently forgotten that the parent religion, Judaism, of which Christianity is an offshoot, rose, flowered, and persisted without any such belief! And that in Hinduism the survival of the individual beyond death is conceded—but emphatically bemoaned! It would seem rather likely that such apprehension of the dire consequences of a change in a belief structure are the familiar reactions of the well habituated to any innovation that does violence to old habits.

It is of course undeniably true that no one institution in a culture can indefinitely remain at loggerheads with the entire cultural pattern. And if an increasing segment of the lives of a people comes under the influence of a materialistic determinism the odds increase that a generalization of thought habits is to be anticipated. There is, after all, a dramatic, convincing vividness to the day-to-day miracles worked by organized scientific research in therapeutic agents, for example, that can be quite confidently expected to displace amulets, fetishes, or other nonmaterial therapeutic proceses. And it is by this wise that scientific empiricism has tended to become the norm of the culture with a consequent loss of prestige for animistic habits of thought in general. Yet it would be all too easy to exaggerate the speed with which such generalization takes place. Habits are, after all, in large part specific to the situation. And unless a new technique is a dramatic improvement over the old in the specific situation and produces its results in such a short time span that the average person can at once perceive it as causally effective, it might indeed have a hard row to hoe. The net result in contemporary culture has been almost as profound a change in religious practices and beliefs as in the overall secular aspects of the culture. Some conspicuous lags admittedly exist, notably in the highly authoritarian religions that seem to be devoted to the thesis that poor mortal man was doomed to bungle along twixt salvation and perdition on a few meagre Revelations of Truth vouchsafed him some millennia ago. And even here the fiction of timeless truths has taxed the ingenuity of the ablest of rationalizers who seek by means of subtle taxonomic devices to fit embarrassing new discoveries into the framework of the old beliefs. Admittedly their efforts have prevented wholesale defections of the Faithful, excepting for such periods of cataclysmic social change as sweep away political and economic as well as religious institutions.

Mind in the Twentieth Century

On the record then, it seems that the soul-mind idea began its existence as a concept of a diffuse, material, causal agent of some sort at a time when man knew even less about the nature of matter than he does now. Only by devious and varied steps did it come to be thought of as a *causal agent lacking both extension and substance*. Where, one might well ask, did the concept of a causality wholly divorced from all materiality, yet effective in and on the material world arise? There probably is but one answer to this query, and a simple one at that: in the subjective, the symbolic, imaginal, or thinking processes which go on privately, or at least relatively privately, within each individual. Even a cursory glance at the record of man's past ideas and beliefs on this matter show clearly that the dualistic-interactionistic metaphysics that is standard adult equipment today is but a cultural product and a relatively late one at that, and in but a limited number of cultures. And even here we find that our children do not automatically begin thinking in these terms. Since the adults are in large part unconscious of their

beliefs in such matters they are not moved to indoctrinate the
children deliberately; yet in due time the children acquire the
language and thought of the adults anyhow. But even cursory
research will reveal that, to children, thinking is very much a
materialistic process with its locus, in the normal child, in the
region of the mouth, tongue, or larynx. But it must be remembered that this "common sense" is the end-result of some sixty
generations of people subjected to official, institutional controls
in educational and theological machinery, during which time
language habits as well as beliefs have attained considerable
stability. And what, might one ask, is precisely the gist of these
common-sense assumptions? Well, first of all this assumption
of a non-material, soul-mind process which directs the activity
of the individual himself. Next comes the quite plausible assumption that other humans, like ourselves, are similarly
equipped and function similarly, although there has frequently
arisen considerable skepticism as to whether people of different
skin-color, different language, or of different culture were not
lacking in some vital aspect or other. Then, wherever an obvious
material agency seemed lacking in any effective ongoing process,
a similar, directing force, much after the nature of the individual human, non-material, soul-mind would be credited with
the initiation and direction of the activity. In fact, it is obvious
that any concept of a personal god must be a projective product
of this sort. It is the thought habits engendered by a presumed,
but apparently effective private "will" that set the pattern for
the acceptance of animistic agencies in general, gods with a definite plan or purpose encompassing their acts, or the humbler,
lesser agencies assumed when, as the poet has it: "Every clod
feels a stir of might, An instinct within it that reaches and
towers—." And indeed, such gods were assumed, long before
they were handicapped by the dubious metaphysics of non-
materiality! It must also be remembered that gods or other effective agencies were constructed or assumed long before the private, subjective thought processes themselves were held to be
of a non-material character! In short, whatever man's conception
of himself and his capacities, it was these that set the pattern for
his perceptions of the external world. Did he see purposeful

action in himself? Then what could be more "logical" than to assume that other events were willed by some similar agent!

Already during the 19th century the grounds under animistic agents of all sorts were becoming increasingly shaky, particularly in the domain of physiology. The increasing popularity of various sorts of psychophysical parallelism is eloquent testimony to increasingly complete cycles of material causality disclosed by researches in physiology and neurology. There was a zealous pursuit of physical correlates of the phenomena of "mind," an apparently well motivated attempt to establish or describe "mental" processes in such a way as to avoid assigning causal efficacy to "mind" at any point. As always, the evaluations of the degree of success in these efforts vary with the point of view. Some reduced the "mental" to the role of an innocuous epiphenomenon. A die-hard core of animists remains. For them non-material mind plays a truly causal role in memory, will, reason, and purpose. It may even be frankly assigned all the functions and characteristics of an orthodox soul, complete with its unity, immortality, and kinship with a diety. What are the phenomena that make these ghostly demands? The prize exhibit seems to be a phenomenon that goes by the name of consciousness.

Semanticists of recent vintage have what will probably prove to be a lifetime job ahead of them in reforming our language habits. The mischief of centuries just is not undone overnight. Their chief theme song indeed bears frequent and emphatic repetition: words, particularly nouns, should have objective references of some sort. Otherwise we are rather likely to deceive ourselves with our own noises! And just that is what our philosophers and metaphysicians seem to have been doing with their favorite noun, "consciousness." Now the word "conscious" is an excellent adjective; it tells us something very specific about a particular act or behavior. To be "conscious" is to be very actively responding to at least certain classes of stimuli, to be responsive to other individuals if there are any about, and, after a given series of events have transpired, be able to give a reasonably accurate account of at least some of the more significant occurrences of the period in question. Nor is there any point in attempting to force an all-or-none option at any point or in any particular instance. There is no such thing as a blanket "consciousness"; rather one can say without fear of contradiction that a particular act was apparently "conscious," namely, that the distinctive or individual aspects of the particular situation were being reacted to, that the responses made by the person or individual were not of the character of a spinal reflex, nor even of that of the simple conditioned reflex such as the "automatic" adjustments made to visual cues on the steering mechanism of an automobile, and involving latency periods of the order of something under a tenth of a second. No, your "conscious" act, almost of necessity suggests the presence and the functioning of inhibitory mechanisms, of compromise responses, of an action that is the product of an entire constellation of stimuli or influences, a Gestalt if you will. But there is no blanket "consciousness," conscious of everything, or apart from the specific reactions made by the individual, and which might be aptly describable as "conscious." The term "aware" might indeed serve as well, and a noun constructed from that adjective would be equally dubious. That the human organism happens to be one whose activities are progressively modified more or less by each of its successive responses, conscious or unconscious, yet withal retaining some considerable degree of stability or permanence, has frequently been given such designation or interpretation as the "unity of consciousness." Should one wonder what the animus behind such reification is, it will not be difficult to find. Lotze, for example, found it sufficient ground for assuming an *indivisible* soul, in the face of a long popular tradition of "possession" by evil spirits and devils, not to mention a variety of specific directions for exorcising them. This simple 'unity of consciousness' has ever higher hurdles today in the form of split, dual, or multiple personalities, not to mention the interesting inroads made into the normal 'unity' by hypnotic techniques. As for the convincing logic of the unitary ego, self, or soul, that has seemed so fundamental to many a thinker both before and after Descartes, it should be apparent that the individual organism is in a particularly strategic position to speak authoritatively on a considerable variety of events whose locus happens to be inside the skin of that animal or individual. And yet in this day of increasingly accurate instrumental techniques we have in a sense more than taken the measure of just what this advantage consists in, and are becoming increasingly aware of the limitations on the reliability and dependability of this "subjective" reality. Consider, for example, the findings of Professor L. W. Max[8] in a monumental piece of research, this particular aspect of which he sums up as follows:

"We found that below a certain microvoltage, which varies with different individuals, the subjects did not kinaesthetically perceive feeble muscle contractions, though they were definitely present. This fact may help to explain, for the kinaesthetic sense, the imageless and non-sensory experiences of the imageless thought school; muscular activity might actually be present throughout a given experience, without being introspectively detectable. In the present study, we have repeatedly come upon instances of thinking without the subject being able introspectively to detect concomitant motor activity of an order easily recorded by our amplifiers."

The subjective "experience," the private "consciousness," provides no magic key to spiritual certainty, nor even to mundane wisdom. It is neither more nor less dependable, fool-proof, or real than any other general class of evidence. For some problems and questions it has decided advantages; for others it is notoriously fallible. The precise content of immediate thought processes and imagery is of course best reported by the person himself. But the accuracy of the location of organic distress in the body is notoriously bad, even apart from the whimsies of 'referred pains'. The subjective report on the motivation or causality of attitudes, emotions, and overt acts has such notoriously low relevance and reliability that even the mythology of the Unconscious with its teleology, hedonism, and complex metaphysics represents in some areas a considerable improvement over the traditional rational mind concept. It must be admitted at the outset that the last forty years have seen a greater increase in the scientific understanding of what has long gone under the name of soul or mind than had the two preceding millennia. And philosophers, metaphysicians, and even to a much

greater degree, theologians, have been understandably reluctant
to acquaint themselves with these findings, not to speak of
bringing their traditional doctrines into line with these more
experimentally and empirically based points of view. The situation is met by all too many such specialists with a variety of
evasions. A favorite dodge consists of conveniently dichotomizing phenomena into sharply distinct categories: The Scientific
and The Religious. Anything classified as 'religious' is then
automatically freed from any compulsion to conform to scientific principles, and old beliefs and ideas can then remain sacrosanct.

A similar semantic solution is frequently attempted in
which the concept "philosophical" is contrasted with "scientific."
But such is the prestige of the rubric "scientific" that the professional fraternity of philosophers prefers rather to sail under
the same emblem. Where, then, the current findings of psychologists fit badly with the traditional metaphysical concepts it is
standard practice to dismiss the more realistic interpretations as
the product of but an aberrant cult of psychologists. A straw
man named "The Behaviorist" served in the role of whipping
boy for the profession for almost two decades. A similar maneu-
ver consists in finding within the scientific fraternity, men,
usually of advanced age and of some considerable eminence in
some non-psychological field, whose views of the nature of
mind are completely uncontaminated by any recent psychological findings, and publicizing the opinions of these gentlemen on
matters philosophical, psychological, or religious as proof of the
upstart or heretical character of any contrary opinions. By further semantic ingenuity this is expanded into the dogma that
"Religion" and "Science" are not, and could not possibly be, in
conflict. These myths will no doubt continue to be repeated in
spite of the fact that well over fifteen years ago Professor Leuba
showed by a careful statistical and attitudinal study of scientists
that amount of training, degree of eminence, and youth of the
individuals all correlated negatively with degree of religiosity.
In addition, the closer the field of a man's expertness approached
the study of man himself the lower was the average degree of
addiction to animistic thinking. One is reminded of the seven-

lived persistence of the belief in phrenology and its founding saints, Gall and Spurzheim. For over a century this naive whimsy has persisted in spite of the fact that shortly after the first publication of these bad guesses by the eminent anatomists, they were found to be completely wanting in value. But the nonsense persists providing an interesting topic for the study of the psychology of belief.

It will be well to review here precisely wherein modern psychology differs from that varying mixture of animism, theology, and philosophy that constitutes the traditional account of mind, human nature, or the soul that has obtained with minor variations since Aristotle's day. Let us begin with the assumption of the teleological character of the behavior of living things: the assumption that in some way the purposes to be served by an act actually determine the act. Now of course, in a certain historical-evolutionary sense it is true that the activities of organisms do have to be such that the needs of the organism are met in that particular environment. By the elimination of species and individuals whose behavior fails to "serve their needs" the environment thus forces a spurious purposefulness. But that is not what is ordinarily thought of as the purposefulness of an act. No; when the overwhelming majority of people are asked for an explanation of what makes the leaves of a plant grow upward or the roots downward, or why a squirrel stores nuts in October, or what makes a bird sit on its eggs, they reply that it is the nature of living things that in some unspecified way they "know" what to do, and hence do it. The indwelling agent responsible for this is conceived as in the nature of a mind or soul, lacking of course many refinements and powers presumably possessed by the human mind or soul. Frequently the agent is designated as an "instinct," which is held to be a purposive force or "power," in some way kin to the power or powers presumed to run the universe as a whole, and commonly offered as evidence that the universe is run by an over-all intelligence.

This well illustrates the lag that always occurs between the discovery of knowledge by specialists and its incorporation into the common sense of the layman. To botanists it has long been known that the upward growth of plants is a reaction to very real stresses in the cell sap produced by sunlight, gravity, and similar known forces. The nut gathering and storing of the squirrel is part of an elaborate metabolic cycle in the rodent, involving a dietary cycle in which the nut storing can appear only after a period of normal diets, including the eating of both immature and mature nuts to a point where the animal's metabolism has stored up minimal amounts of certain particular body fats, among other definite physical changes, which will not take place on, for example, a fruit diet. Note that squirrels kept on a fruit diet long after they would normally be eating nuts will then be busy eating them, if they can find them, even while snow clouds threaten to cover up such nuts as may remain to the laggard. As for the hatching of eggs by birds, that too is the product of a similar cycle, closely related to both solar radiation and seasonal dietary cycles during which the immediately critical factor seems to be that the production of fully matured eggs exhausts the stored elements composing eggs, leaving the bird with a profoundly changed metabolism, much as parturition in mammals produces changes, including the onset of lactation. In the case of the birds the effects of the exhausting egg-laying are an increased body temperature, drowsiness, loss of appetite, and an acute irritation in the breast region which apparently is minimized by the application of a counterirritant such as a mustard plaster, or more normally, by prevention of heat loss and the pressing of hard objects firmly against the breast; conditions normally realized in the usual position of the bird on its nest. The earlier phases of the reproductive cycle are similarly the product of material processes, including in many species the activation of the gonads by the pituitary gland which in turn has been aroused by the diurnally increasing doses of ultraviolet radiation incident to the spring phase of the solar cycle. The migratory behavior of birds, the mechanics of which is far from completely untangled at this stage of the operation of human curiosity, is similarly sparked in its northward phase by this same mechanism in spring, and it is the decreasing solar radiation of late summer and fall that must reach a given point before the southward flight will get under way. At any event, it has been established that migratory birds in the north, subjected at the end of summer to artificial and regular *increases* of ultraviolet radiation will, when released, spend some considerable time in northward flight, instead of southward as would be dictated by any conceivable grade of mind or intelligence.[8a]

A word might well be in order here on the nature of an "explanation." Just what constitutes a "satisfactory" explanation? Time was when the moon was satisfactorily explained as a device to provide light for man at night. Or that opium put one to sleep by virtue of its dormitive potency. Many an explanation merely reconciled or classified an unknown with the familiar, thus ending curiosity. People with practical problems to solve in regard to these unknowns are understandably impatient with such "explanations." They want explanations that have an instrumental, a practical character. They want answers they can put to some sort of use. If, for example, the birds whose nest-sitting behavior is in question, happen to be poultry on which you hope to make a profit, and your motivation is the quite understandable one of minimizing the time spent in a brooding coma and a maximizing of the egg-laying part of the cycle, it is some specific directions you will want for intervening somewhere in the "normal" cycle and giving events a more favorable turn. Happily for the consumer of eggs, precisely that has long been done by the poultry experts. They assiduously pursued this type of instrumental knowledge. They have of course begun with genetic selection of individuals showing an emphasis upon the desired traits. The result over the years has been the production of what amounts to a biological monstrosity that could not possibly survive in the "normal" or "natural" environment, where its behavior would not be at all appropriate for survival. Scientific diets to maintain this abnormal metabolism have also been worked out. By this means we have more than tripled the "normal" egg production of even the most enthusiastic wild fowl, with a corresponding reduction in the cost of that dietary staple.

So it would seem that what will pass muster as an explanation is a variable that depends upon the kind of information we happen to want at the moment. So long as we wish merely to have and hold our traditional beliefs undisturbed, then the criterion of a "good" explanation is simply that it shall be emotionally satisfactory. When we are confronted with a practical problem, we want instrumental explanations, useful knowledge. And there is but little of a useful character in any teleological explanation. Scientists have long provided us with concepts that are a great improvement over this naive teleology or purposivism of common sense. Here is one: the behavior of all living things is, *in general,* regulatory. This means only that by and large, or in the average, it works, it keeps the organism alive, it keeps the members of the species replaced—after a fashion. But it is a dubious battle; in the end, every multicellular organism is doomed to death. Individual immortality was left behind with the unicellular organisms, apparently discarded by the evolutionary process as a handicap, or at best something unimportant. But when an organism's behavior is described as "regulatory" we know and expect that often indeed what the living thing does is not the "correct" thing. Instead its behavior is such that, given certain physical or material conditions, it reacts in fairly predictable ways. Now *in general* the conditions which arouse an organism to action are disturbances of that delicate equilibrium that is a living organism; and *in general,* the activity thus aroused in the animal is such as to reestablish or maintain the required states. But, it must be emphasized, only with some slight margin of long run successes over long run failures. One might indeed question even this pessimistic account of its successes by pointing out that from the standpoint of the organisms considered as a species, the end for all seems to be extinction! The individuals that survive are those that are just a bit different from their predecessors, and in the long run, constitute new "species." But we do not take this too seriously because we now know that a "species" is but an artifact of a short period of observation during which we cannot observe the slow but cumulative changes by which organisms are transformed. But then, if a living thing is not a little spark of mind or soul or guiding intelligence or vital principle, how can we describe it, characterize it, without invoking animistic concepts of some sort? Let us see how a great physiologist, C. M. Child,[9] tries his hand at it: "Each living thing represents an order and unity of some sort, maintaining itself ·with more or less success in a changing environment." Yes, the living thing has "order and unity," it is more or less predictable, and, in spite of the fact that the world in which it exists varies somewhat from moment to moment, it yet manages somehow to "maintain itself." But how? Is that "maintaining itself" not evidence of "reason," guidance, or a vital spark? Let us rather put it this way: a living organism consists of a multitude of *homeostatic mechanisms* or physiological norms, and *never* remains exactly the same from moment to moment. Heraclitus was exactly 100% correct when he shocked his listeners by telling them that they could not ever talk to the same person twice! It is the nature of the living organism that it is a continually changing thing. And what is it that changes? Why each of these many homeostatic mechanisms, or *norms*, if you please. Living protoplasm has a variable rather than a fixed chemical composition. But there are decided limits within which the makeup of any living matter may vary—and still remain "alive." And as the make-up of protoplasm changes, so does its activity, within limits. And, in general, the changes in the way the living thing behaves are such as to reestablish the "norm" whose disturbance it was that initiated the new behavior! But remember, only *in general*.

There are decided limits to the range of disturbances of norms that an organism can compensate or correct for. Body temperature can be allowed to vary some few degrees either way from the norm; but there are critical points beyond which the organism's unaided efforts will fail to reestablish normal life functions. The fluid concentration of the body can vary but little before death ensues. The delicate recovery processes that take place during sleep and whose actual character is almost wholly unknown, are equally vital. The precise amount of the secretions of a great variety of endocrine glands can, and does, vary. But for some of the secretions there comes a point beyond which the resulting changes are irreversible, and death ensues. Similarly with variations in the kinds and quantities of a large variety of minerals, vitamins, fats, and amino-acids. Now in an organism's normal environment, the normal functioning of the organism loses only slowly the battle for norm-maintenance. Invading organisms may hasten the process, indeed they might even, and frequently do, give it a coup de grâce before the corrective processes of the organism can get under way. In any case there are decided limits to this "wisdom of the body" as it has been called. And such "wisdom" consists of its inherited organic constitution with the reflexive, adjustive, and "regulatory" mechanisms of the animal world, plus the specific immunities, sensitizations, and changes in the gamma globulin acquired by each individual in addition to the more readily observed habit sophistications which are the specific instruments of norm maintenance. These individual instruments, not some blanket purposive force or agency determine the moment to moment fate of the individual.

The confusion in the controversy over the possession of "animal instincts" by man stemmed largely from the question of the purposive character of such behavior. The common-sense assumption of the fundamentally purposive character of inborn behavior was seen to be unwarranted the minute behavior was subjected to careful scientific scrutiny. When it was denied by some students of human behavior that man had any "instincts" what was actually being denied was the purposive character of his inborn reactions, not the existence, *prior to learning*, of predictable, reflexive, or even primitively patterned behavior. It was of course obvious that man, in common with all vertebrates and more particularly in common with mammals and primates, arrived here at birth with a more or less predictable repertoire of responses which were obviously independent of any possible learning process. What they were heatedly denying was just that the goals, functions, or the purposes served by these acts, in any way caused or determined them. Such behavior, they were insisting, was a function of the organic structure of the organism. A given structure would respond in a given way to particular energy changes, or stimuli, arising in the environment of the organism or within the body of the animal itself. Some such predictable patterns of behavior can be observed at the birth of the animal. If the young are observed prior to the time of normal birth, such differences in behavior as appear can be presumed to be a function of the differences in structure between a full-term animal and one prematurely made available for observation. Then too, behavior appearing later, yet not related to any learning process, can be presumed to be a function of further change and development in the organism itself. In the case of animals not protected by law or convention against detailed dissection and study, specific correspondences between particular organic changes and the appearance of particular reactions have been established. It is to be presumed that the same process obtains in man.

That such behavior as is "native" to an animal should be, on the whole, useful in its life economy should cause no surprise. The animals now living here are the end-product of a billion or so years of a natural selective process during which time there has been a ruthless elimination of all organisms whose reactions left too wide a margin of failure. No wonder then that a short period of observation of the animals' activities should show the almost infallible workings of the marvels of instinct. But it must be remembered that the price of just one wrong response is usually *finis* for the animal that makes it. A split second too late in a response can mean that the animal provides the meal in the regulatory processes of another organism. There is no room for "purposive" forces here: those of the rabbit would of necessity run counter to those of the fox, or whatever preys on rabbits. And the rabbit's purposive forces would certainly run counter to those in the grasses and cabbages it eats. It is far simpler to assume a materialistic determinism for what happens to both rabbit and fox. Time was when it was assumed that the entire universe was purposefully attuned to human needs and desires: when the sun was put there to give us light, the earth to feed us, etc. We now laugh at that sort of bumptious egotism. Such "explanations" are not exactly applicable in the practical problems of making a reluctant earth yield up its nutrients, or in adapting our tasks and labors to the horse's or elephant's reflexes or inborn action patterns.

If a careful analysis of the behavior of living things finds no use for, or need of, purposive forces in animal behavior, one might well ask if the concept of instinct has any relevance whatever for human behavior. In any attempt to formulate an answer to such a question a sharp distinction must be made between the concept of instinct as a teleological, a purposive force or agent, and the term "instinct" used simply as a term to designate behavior that is a function of the original structure or maturational development of the organism, which is in no way determined by any aspect of the learning process. Apart from their use as instruments of emotional "shock therapy" in psychiatric or psychoanalytic "couch-time" stories, modern psychology finds no use for teleological accounts of human behavior. "Purposes" are at best inferences from a record of past performances and can contribute no new details of the causal processes involved. They have no instrumental value. But the term "instinct," used to denote an inventory of actions patterns available for the conditioning or learning process to operate upon, often has both theoretical and practical value. The careful studies of infant behavior have provided us with statistically reliable data on just what is to be expected from the human infant in the way of behavior that has been modified little, if any at all, by the learning process. These inborn or native behaviors of man reflect in good part the basic vertebrate and mammalian activity patterns, as indeed they should. Man generally arrives here on this earthly scene with a full complement of the basic vegetative functions of respiration, circulation, temperature maintenance, digestion and the metabolic processes generally. Given time, and survival, maturational processes will complete the development of the reproductive functions. Motor and locomotor processes await maturational development. Were the head of the human infant not so large and heavy, nor the point of air-intake so unfavorably located the human infant could probably swim at birth or thereabouts. A helpless creature, the human young, completely incapable of extracting its organic needs from its environment except by making a noisy nuisance of itself when any sort of need exists, thereby inducing the adults in its environment to make the necessary adjustments for it. Beyond these capacities, the human equipment comprises but little in the way of effectively functional, cut-and-dried, specifically functional or adjustive behavior. Man has survived in his environment not by means of his specific, inborn behavior equipment, but rather by virtue of his capacity for adjustive habit formation.

Not even the fastest pace of natural selection could possibly evolve an organism equipped with the specific reflex or instinctive behavior necessary for survival in a complex and highly variable environment. By a natural selection process, however, what has survived has been a creature with a habit capacity so flexible that each individual could evolve or develop a behavior pattern custom-made to even the subtlest environmental variations, and frequently do it rapidly enough to save its own skin and then live out a long life with the new behavior pattern as a more or less permanent behavior acquisition.

While the adult human behavior normally encountered is of course primarily learned rather than inborn, yet it must not be forgotten that the limits to any learning are strictly set by the inborn, physiological structures whose functions and activities can at best be restructured and repatterned by the learning process. It is these limitations to the learning process laid down in the original inherited structures that are the bases of the individual differences that loom so large in the educational and social world generally. Much is still to be learned in regard to the effective timing of teaching efforts to coincide with the precise period of structural maturity at which particular skills, attitudes, and abilities can be acquired most efficiently. Yet it is not in the area of the inborn or instinctive that man is most marked off from the lower animals; it is in the capacity for behavior modification that the difference is most marked. Does this mean that "mind" should be identified with the phenomena of behavior variability or learning, rather than with the mysteries of life and instinct?

Just where mind, purpose, or intelligence is to be found has long been a moot question. The orthodox Hindu seems to see it in the entire animal kingdom though on occasion he might concede spirit to a tree in the vegetable world. Normally he worries only about the insects he might swallow or inhale, not about the rice he eats. Limiting it to man certainly simplifies life and morals if not logic. Champions can be found setting the limits of mind at all possible levels; conceding it to animals with a nervous system is a favorite. But the evidences for behavior modifications very suggestive of learning in protozoa and other micro-organisms argues strongly for a wider dispersal. The changes and mutations in viruses provide more grounds for speculation. If one were to insist that man had a corner on mind he would then be confronted with idiot humans, and "genius" apes like Koehler's "Sultan."[10] The common denominator of the claims to "mind" is simply that the performances attributed to it are asserted to be impossible of explanation under any system of scientific determinism. There are still plenty of unknowns in the domain of living things. Just exactly what sort of an explanation of precisely what aspect of human or animal performance will impress as convincingly "adequate" will depend upon the individual in question. One will be convinced of the determinism in living things by a mechanical heart that keeps an animal alive; another will hold out till he sees a full-panoplied bishop emerge out of a test tube, right under his own eyes; anything short of that and he will remain an animist and a supernaturalist. The progress in the hundred-odd years since the synthesis of the first organic compound has been dramatic. But at best the barest outlines of the problems to be solved in the chemistry of living protoplasm are now in sight. Meantime the dramatic synthesis of more and more complex organic compounds goes on apace. So does the empirical discovery of the control by chemical means of human abnormalities formerly credited to animistic agencies, as is the case of the control of grand mal seizures by sodium dilantin. Each new discovery convinces the materialist that deterministic answers will ultimately be found to all the questions now in sight. But the same discoveries seem equally to convince the animist that there is an ultimate Mystery behind all the little mysteries of life and mind; that it is not in the chemistry of life that the mystery resides, but in the activities of life.

Here again, there is some considerable disagreement as to precisely which activities demand or embody this mysterious Something that is more than the material activities which can be apprehended and measured. A position commonly taken by those not familiar with lowly organisms is that inasmuch as no living organism has been synthesized out of the non-living, it is precisely the activities of living things that are a function of an

agency such as mind, soul, or spirit, This would of necessity
include tropismatic, reflex, and all primitive regulatory reactions
such as those of growth, reproduction, nutrition, and norm maintenance generally. Experimenters with first-hand knowledge of
the behavior of lower organisms tend generally to see these
activities in terms of the known forces or processes of the
familiar cycle of energy and matter. Descartes, and many since
his time, held that familiar material forces and matter could
account for all the activities of all organisms other than man.
What he would have said had it not been for the omnipresent
Inquisition of his day is any man's guess. It is significant that
he burned one manuscript out of fear of the consequences of its
release or publication. Such an arbitrary line between man and
the lower animals is not frequently drawn these days, outside
the circles of orthodox theology. Far more frequently will one
find that it is learning, wherever found that is the dependable
ear-mark of "mind"; that it is the learning process that transcends the limits of the purely material, the deterministic. And, if
it is not ordinary, or rote learning that demands a mind or spirit,
then it is any creative discovery or invention that requires it.
As more and more determinants of animal activities are identified, the more does animism retreat into the remaining unknowns, just as it has during the past centuries in areas other
than the psychological.

An examination of the nature of the learning process would
seem to be in order at this point, to discover, if possible, just
what there is about learning, and the higher mental processes
generally, that has so long made them a refuge of animism in
all of its varied forms.

Much of a practical nature as to the conditions of learning
has accumulated in the folklore of practically every culture. In
general, devices had been hit upon for inculcating such behavior
patterns as were essential to the maintenance of a well-ordered
society. For the most part these devices consisted of associative
techniques of one form or another. Particular responses were
called out, by fair means or foul, in particular situations; shortly
the situation alone elicited the proper response without the aid
of the fair or foul. At first little Oswald must be reminded to

"Tip your hat to the lady." Shortly the situation alone suffices. The tale, the genealogy, the list of taboos must be recited with prompting till it can be recited letter perfect without the prompting. But was there any general principle at work and underlying all these varities of learning? Or was each case a law unto itself? By the 19th century there were at least some thinkers who were ready to concede that learning was a matter of sense-data and "associations in the mind," the entire process being assumed to be, with perhaps rare exceptions, conscious, and of course "mental."

When Professor Pavlov found that his nice quantitative experiments in digestion were being ruined by similar associative processes effective on glandular secretions he drew the quite reasonable conclusion that these processes were identical with psychic or mental processes of association. He proceeded to test the hypothesis that any stimuli, acting just prior to, or during the time that already effective stimuli were causing the dog to salivate, would themselves become capable of making the saliva flow. An annoyance in one research program thus became the basis of what is probably the most significant and fruitful work ever done on the phenomena long referred to as the domain of the mind. Left at issue is only the question of how much of the total problem of mind is encompassed by the basic mechanisms of the conditioned "reflex," as Pavlov called it while yet asserting that the processes were identical with what is popularly called the "psychic." Some contemporary psychologists are ready to concede that even the highest of mental processes are but elaborations and complications of the same basic conditioning process. Others hold that conditioning can account for but a small fraction of the phenomena of mind. Some hold that all learning is but conditioning; others that there are several distinct kinds of learning processes, of which conditioning is but a crude and simple form. The importance of the question in the psychology of today is suggested by the growing list of titles in any bibliography of conditioning. From a few dozen articles by other than Russian authors in about 1925, the list has grown into the many thousands today, and bids fair to continue mounting at a dizzy pace.[11]

An intelligent judgment of the merits of the controversy is impossible without at least a glimpse at some of the more critical experiments in the area of conditioning, which have gone far beyond the simple pairing and association of bell with food till the bell alone elicits a flow of saliva without the presence of the food. What should be emphasized here is that the Russians did go to the trouble to demonstrate that any sense modality could be made use of in establishing such associations with any response. These will be referred to as "simple conditioning."

By introducing a delay in time between the application of a new stimulus and the use of the original cue to call out the response, *delayed* conditioned reactions can be formed. Let us suppose that a bell is sounded before food is presented to the animal. With the increase in the time interval between bell and food the response of salivation is now delayed for an interval corresponding to the interval used in the training period. Such delays have been built up to many minutes in dogs, and even longer in children. In these experiments the bell or other cue to be conditioned is kept operating until the food is presented. When the new cue is permitted to stimulate only momentarily, after which nothing further is done till the food is presented to the subject the result now is a response which occurs, apparently "out of the blue," perhaps a half-hour after the bell or other stimulus was administered, but very accurately timed to correspond to the period of delay used in the training series. Needless to say, such results can be obtained only under carefully controlled experimental conditions in light-proof, sound-proof, vibration-proof experimental chambers. The theoretical importance of these *trace* reflexes, as the Russians call them, has been largely overlooked by contemporary students of conditioning. What, might one well ask, is the dog or child responding to when, perhaps a half hour after a bell stopped ringing the saliva flows? There is no known mechanism permitting an auditory stimulus to remain "stored up," like current in a condenser, and then discharged on a definite time schedule. It is apparent that *the organism itself must be providing* the cues which produce this salivation after a nicely timed interval. A careful observation of such experimental animals during the delay period, as the author was once privileged to make in Pavlov's laboratory, will reveal that during this period the animal is actually very *active*. but the activity is one of maintaining an almost perfect immobility, much like a pointer having spotted a pheasant. Maintaining so rigid a behavior set means a definite cycle of vigorous activity during which it is the cues provided by the animal's own responses that keep the continuity in this postural activity. When some muscle fibres have contracted they must in turn relax and recover from their refractory phases. Meantime, other muscle fibres must take over, and any such shifts in the tension of a group of muscle cells produces specific and distinctive changes in the pattern of kinesthetic cues coming from the various innervated structures. Such cycles of activity have a "logic," a predictability all their own; given constant conditions a predictable cycle of activities is set up in the experimental animal. The food, when it comes repeatedly at a definite time interval after the bell signal that initiated the postural rigidity, now coincides in successive practice periods *with a definite point in the activity pattern with its concomitant specific cues,* and it is these self-provided cues which shortly become capable of eliciting salivation without the original food being present. It is probable that the cues principally involved are the kinesthetic cues from the skeletal musculature but there is no reason why cues from the hollow organ systems might not also contribute.

But it is for the light it throws on simple conditioning that an understanding of the "trace" phenomena is important. While Pavlov was probably one of the really great experimental scientists that the past century produced, he had very naive ideas or theories of the nature of the conditioning process. He presumed that the simultaneous activation of two sensory projection areas in the cortex somehow opened up rather direct paths in the cortical neurones between these areas, over which nervous impulses would then flow, even in the absence of the innervation or activation of one of them. There is much experimental evidence against this simple thesis. Lang and Olmstead[12] established a conditioned flexion of a dog's leg to an auditory stimulus. Then the *sensory* fibres leading *from the leg* to the central nervous system were cut. This destroyed the conditioned reactions of this leg as effectively as if the dog's auditory nerves or the motor fibres to that leg had been severed. A similar operation will destroy all "voluntary" control of a limb in humans, even if all the structures presumed to be essential for conditioning under Pavlov's theory are left intact, as well as those essential under any naive "will" theory of behavior. Other experiments have shown the significance of the role played by the normal flow of sensory impulses from the structures to be conditioned or under "voluntary" control. Conditioning, then, is no simple system of reflex pathways; it is an activity in which an important part is played by the residual cycles of reflex activity going on in the organism, as well as by the variable cues in the animal's environment. A glance at the latency periods of various kinds of reactions will bear this out; a simple spinal reflex will require in the neighborhood of .035 to .040 seconds, the simplest of conditioned reactions at least twice that time. "Voluntary" responses, such as pressing a key upon signal will require approximately .2 second. These "higher" mental processes seem tied to pedestrian steps of some kind in the organism for their operation; no evidence here for an instantaneous flash, freed from material processes or activities! Even the simple conditioned reaction is dependent upon the animal's self-provided cues in much the same way that the trace conditioning process demands it.

Many other experiments have clearly demonstrated the widespread validity of the conditioning process in the more complex aspects of human behavior. There is, for example, the phenomenon of experimental extinction, or rather "inhibition" of conditioned reactions once acquired. Many successive repetitions of a conditioned stimulus will temporarily end its power to elicit a reaction; but a single pairing with the original, action-getting stimulus will reestablish its power to call out the conditioned reaction. This characteristic of conditioning will assume great importance in any analysis of the psychology of belief and faith.

Higher order conditioning but illustrates in elementary form the complexities of "mind" that we take for granted. Let us say that a conditioned reaction has been established in a dog such that he flexes his leg upon the sounding of a bell. This is easily accomplished by following the bell sound with an electric shock to the foot. Now the bell alone will cause the dog to lift his foot. Then we accompany the bell with a flash of light during a training series. Shortly the flash of light will elicit the response previously given only to the electric shock or the bell. With human subjects such transfers of stimulus efficacy apparently go on indefinitely, as when "meaning" transfers from spoken to written word and from one language to another. With dogs it requires special devices to exceed the third order.

Smooth muscles, such as the iris muscle of the eye, are subject to conditioning as well as glands and striped muscles. Here is your mechanism whereby annoyances at the breakfast table destroy appetites!

Several stimuli, neither of which alone could elicit a reaction, may be administered in a combination so as to produce a summation effect and call out a response, in conditioning experiments as well as in everyday life.

A conditioned reaction can be made specific to a particular intensity or pitch of a sound stimulus, up to the limits of the animal's capacity to discriminate. Similarly with any other sense modality, the conditioning can be made specific to one of a series of similar cues.

The Russians recently reported evidence for the conditioning of the activity of internal organs as well as the metabolic activity of the tissues.[13]

The electrical activities detectable in the brain cortex and commonly referred to as "brain waves" have been conditioned to other than their normal activity.[14]

By using stimuli previously conditioned to elicit salivation and then given experimental "extinction" by repeated administration not followed by food, the Russian experimenters produced what they called "Storage and Discharge," namely a salivary reaction conditioned specifically to a succession of cues in a definite time order, where neither of the cues alone, nor both cues in any order but the practiced one could call out salivation. However, given the familiar cues in the practiced order and separated by the practiced time intervals, the salivary response would be elicited. Not the individual stimuli themselves suffice; they must occur in a definite time relationship. Such responses to "relations" between stimuli have long been cited as evidence that the higher mental activities of man, and even of some lower animals, somehow transcend any possible mechanistic determinism. It is interesting to note that predictable conditionings can be established that involve patterns of stimuli and time intervals to precise "relations" between cues.

The processes of perception have long been held to be of a mental sort, transcending the mere sense data upon which they are admittedly dependent. The high priests of the Gestalt school have long cited perceptive processes as evidence of the inadequacy of any stimulus-response or deterministic theory of the higher mental processes. Perceptions are not by any stretch of the imagination simple reflex reactions to raw sense data, but do they actually transcend the conditioning process? Professor Wertheimer was fond of pointing out that one might hear a melody played, let us say in the key of "C" major on a piano, long or often enough so that the melody became familiar. Should one then hear the same melody, but played in the key of D flat major, the black keys, one would unfailingly recognize the tune without a single one of the previously stimulated receptors having been put in action! No simple theory of pathways "worn" through the nervous system would here suffice since there is good evidence that there is differential sensitivity of the hair cells on the basilar membrane and that different pitches involve the stimulation of different receptor cells. Such theorizing about perception is sadly lacking in even a rudimentary understanding of elementary conditioning where, as has been previously pointed out, the critically significant cues in conditioning are not only the paired cues manipulated by the experimenter, but also the return afferent nervous impulses from the structures involved in the conditioning process, as was eloquently shown by the Lang & Olmstead experiment. In the case of the identification of such a melody, the process is made clear by the addition of a little old-fashioned introspection. When we try to identify a melody that is not immediately familiar we all hit upon the same process, namely we "pick up" the few notes of the tune that are available, hum or sing them more or less overtly, and *it is the cues provided us by that performance* that call out the identifying reactions. Humming such a tune, particularly if it is a song, shortly initiates some well-practiced serial reactions in which the words of the song as we sing them frequently provide the critical words of the title. The "perceptive" response is thus rung out of us by the cues our own activity has provided. To perceive visually demands not only the visual cues from the object but the equally important cues that are provided by the, perhaps unconscious, adjustments we make to those visual cues. On April 14 and 15, 1931, the New York World Telegram reported in some detail the experiences of a 22 year old man in acquiring visual perceptions. This man had lacked pupils in the iris muscles of his eyes. But in one eye there was a small break in the iris which enabled enough light to enter to permit distinguishing daylight from night and which permitted him to "feel," not see, the difference between bright red and bright blue. At age 22 an operation was performed, opening a pupil to admit light and give him about 30% vision. Note the process of acquiring perceptions in this unfamiliar modality as described by the reporter:

"Some weeks after the operation he saw some children skipping rope. 'What are those kids doing, Earl?' he was asked.

He didn't know. He had to think back to his past.

'I figured it out,' he explains, 'by the sound of the rope against the sidewalk. I had heard that sound when I was blind. Slap, slap, slap, like that. The first time I heard it when I was blind I asked what it was. Someone told me it was little girls skipping rope.'"

Note the process of perceiving as here described. With the aid of socially provided cues he is able to react with "rope skipping" while the sound peculiar to that activity is stimulating his ears. Now, as an adult and beginning to acquire visual perceptions *he depends upon the sound to call out the response:* "rope skipping." After this one experience the visual perception functions; the activity and objects involved are, after all, fairly specific and distinctive. Not so with the problem of "learning" to perceive faces, because visually, a face is different each time the angle of vision is changed. Let us see how our reporter described the problems of the formation of visual perceptions of faces in this erstwhile blind man:

"He was shown, when he could see that well, the likeness of a human face, and illustration in an advertisement.

'What is that, Earl?'

'Now let's see,' said Earl, his eye down close to the magazine. He had to give it up. He had never seen a human face at that time, much less the dot and line symbol which the seeing world accepts conventionally as the pictured representation of a face.[15] They explained that he was looking at a human picture, and he asked, 'Is it a lady or a man?' His chief way, even these weeks later, of distinguishing the picture of a man from the picture of a woman is by looking for the tie.

'If there isn't a tie I know it's a lady.'"

There were other problems of physiognomy. That first printed face he looked at was a full face view. Later he was shown another printed face in profile. 'What was that?' He didn't know.

He was completely bewildered when told that that was a human face too. No seeing person can imagine what a shock it was to him to learn that the human face could look so different by a mere change in viewpoint. How could a face look this way if you looked at it one way and an entirely different way if you looked at it another way?

The complaint, familiar in every race, that members of all alien races look alike is magnified many times for this man as he tries to distinguish one face from another. He does not yet automatically and unconsciously make those specific reactions to a face which will later provide the differentiating, self-provided cues enabling him to "perceive" the difference between Fred and Jim. Once he can make a specific reaction to a necktie or its lack, he has a basis for at least some distinctions. It must not be forgotten that the perceiver may not be at all aware of precisely what detail or aspect of a given object or situation is providing the differentiating cues. But it is these responses called out in us by the thing perceived that provide the significant differentiating cues.

An experiment by Gellerman,[16] using apes and young chil-

dren as subjects, probably best illustrates or demonstrates the
dependence of "perception" upon self-provided cues. Food was
placed in drawers for the subjects to find. The position of the
drawers was varied. But the front sides of the drawers had geometric and other figures carved into the wood, and in a given
learning problem the reward was always to be found in the
drawer having a particular figure carved on its face. What is of
greatest theoretical interest is the fact that the "perceiving" of
the correct drawer by both apes and children did not occur
until in their random exploration the subjects got their fingers
into these carved figures and "explored" them with finger movements. At a particular stage in the learning process, there would
come a time in this tracing-out of the figures with the fingers
that the subject would suddenly abandon the drawer altogether
or else lunge at it in opening it. Those identifying patterns when
explored by a finger would provide distinctive patterns of kinesthetic cues which were conditioning avoidance or attack upon
the drawer, as the case may have been. With children, there
would come a point in the tracing of the figure where the child
would say "No" or "Yes" as part of the process of "decision."
But it was the movement-produced stimuli that elicited both
the overt and the verbal responses. In 1921, Smith & Guthrie[17]
summed up this process very succinctly as follows:

"When, by this process of conditioning, any stimulus from
the object furnishes a cue for the early occurrence of responses
that were originally given only as the result of further acquaintance, the baby is said to *perceive* the object."

False perceptions, or illusions, of course occur. For such mis-
takes in our perceptions we have no difficulty in discovering
deterministic explanations. The reluctance to accept similar factors at work in correct perceptions where perhaps higher order
or trace conditioning may be at work accounts for the proliferation of theories that involves animistic conceptions of behavior,
or that invent or postulate a variety of learning or reasoning
processes, or different levels of "mind." Such theories frequently
attempt to hold that perceiving and learning are very different
phenomena. One might well ask, is such a distinction meaningful
in an understanding of the behavior revealed in Gellerman's

experiment? It is all too apparent that whether we say the children "learned," "learned to perceive," or just "perceived," the process involved was simple conditioning in which, as in all conditioning, a vital part is played by the cues provided by the perceiver. It was probably a misfortune for the early understanding of conditioning that so much attention was focused on salivary secretion, a reaction ill-suited to a close analysis of the conditioning process.

Soul and mind theories of human action are always invoked where a knowledge of the stimulus-response process ends. All current animistic theories of human behavior antedate our knowledge of the role of kinesthesis in behavior, the receptors for which each and every response of the organism provides a distinctive pattern of stimulation. We are probably but rarely made acutely aware of such stimulation, but it no doubt contributes a major portion of the cues and sensations that constitute the general background of being alive and "aware," and what was once thought to be "experience" that "lies beyond perception." As it was once well put:[18]

"There is a precategorical state of bare experience, sheer being, that is homogeneous; that is not experienced as belonging to the subject; that lends itself inadequately to classificatory description. This mental matrix, our reports reveal, is, when put into categorical terms, like a pressury gray extension that is somehow lively. These three are not in any way differentiated one from the other; they constitute an existence, a being."

Whether the author of this statement knew it or not, this is really an excellent attempt at describing the subjective experience of kinesthesis, sensations which ordinarily are not sharply identified, since of necessity, kinesthetic cues are always present as a background to any other, and can never be completely shut out after the manner in which one can close the eyes and shut out vision. What is always present tends to be ignored in "conscious" processes, but these cues need only be somehow interrupted from a limited bodily area to impress their importance upon us. As has been pointed out above, all conditioned and voluntary activity of a limb is contingent upon their presence. This is that "sixth sense" so bitterly fought over in medieval

Europe. That this motion sense should have been denounced with vehemence by an organization that had a vested interest in an animistic view of nature can hardly have been accidental. Without this "motion sense," organized, integrated behavior would be an impossibility. It would leave psychology no other option, no other alternative, but some form of animism, where a non-material agent of some sort, "causing" the body to do things would have to be presumed. The classical, the traditional theories of metaphysics and epistemology as well as the language habits we call "common-sense" were formulated and hallowed long before kinesthesis and self-provided cues generally were even dreamed of, let alone pin-pointed and identified in histology and neurology. Given sufficient time, they cannot help but reflect the impact of such significant and relevant facts. Can anyone really believe that The Stagirite would have written his metaphysics as he did, had he known the brain function to be something other than providing tears to prevent the eyeballs from drying up, and if he had known the details of the kinesthetic sense? But what is one to say of contemporary philosophers whose speculations in regard to "mind" involve nothing more modern in the field of psychology than the sadly obsolete "Five Senses" and whose knowledge of volitional processes contains nothing more modern than the shibboleths that were hurled about during the 19th century? It is no accident that Scholastic psychology still insists that there are but five senses in the human body in the face of the clear neurological and histological identification of at least three times that proverbial number. Only by this device can the "key" sense, kinesthesis or the motion sense be ignored or denied. Its importance in any scientific account of the higher "mental" processes is all too obvious. Without it, the case for an animistic metaphysics can long be made to seem intellectually respectable. Once the critically important role of this sense is understood and conceded, a complete overhauling of the classical and traditional conceptions of metaphysics and epistemology is unavoidable. It is all too apparent that these philosophical disciplines have had but little genuine independence from religion. As Peter Damian, the twelfth century scholastic philosopher, put it rather brazenly:

"Philosophy is but the handmaiden to religion, and like her must once a month be purified."

Only recently have there been signs that the philosophical fraternity might some day be ready to begin building on scientific probabilities rather than on the "purified" ideas of two millennia ago. For the most part they seem contented with Aristotelian or Platonic theories of mind. If they have taken any cognizance of the experimental phenomena of conditioning they concede it no role in human behavior beyond its accounting for a few whimsicalities such as inappropriate mouth-waterings or irrational emotional reactions.

To have scientific respectability today any speculations on the nature of mind or the higher mental processes must not only take cognizance of the more advanced work of Pavlov and the Russian experimenters generally, but must consider in detail the monumental ventures into the conditioning of more and more complex processes so ably pursued by Professor Razran over the past twenty-five years.[19] His facility with the Russian language has enabled him to keep abreast of the not insignificant work being done by contemporary Soviet scientists in spite of their doctrinal handicaps. Their work in the establishment of visceral conditionings seems on the face of it to be nothing short of monumental and will probably be found to be of far reaching importance in the area of psychosomatic or "functional" disorders.[20] Far from overestimating the importance of the mechanisms of conditioning over the entire range of human behavior it seems to this author that Razran continually underestimates the role of conditioning in the higher mental functions. What appears to Razran as evidence for the existence of "higher levels" of learning seems to me but the effects on any particular learning or conditioning situation of previous habits or conditionings involving some or all of the same stimulus elements. That is of course the reason Razran gets his best conditioning results on human subjects when they are distracted by cues and activities other than those whose linkage it is sought to establish. Children, similarly, make excellent conditioning subjects showing a regular average decrease in the number of pairings necessary to establish a linkage up to about age five, the correspondence being closer with mental than chronological age. After age five, conditioning begins to take on the erratic and unpredictable character of the process in the *undistracted* adult. The individual stimuli used have been components of too great a variety of stimulus patterns in previous associations which in the particular experimental situation might have facilitative or inhibitory effects, depending upon the specific history of each individual. That the response of the adult human should be less and less a function of the immediate, specific environmentally provided stimuli, and increasingly a function of self-provided cues produced by what are apt to be minimal, symbolic, or other partially inhibited reactions immediately and perhaps almost reflexly made to the situation, is precisely what we expect and demand of the individual as proof of his fitness for adult status. But such behavior could hardly seem a warrant for postulating the existence here of an entirely different kind of a learning process. In such activities are to be recognized elements or characteristics of higher order conditionings, trace conditioned reactions, conditioned inhibitions and other processes that the experimenter can isolate and explore independently if only he has sufficient ingenuity. But the real life situations always deal with an organism literally "loaded" with past conditionings involving almost all possible cues and situations. No wonder that in such a case an increasingly important role is played by the behavior patterns already built up in the organism and less and less by the experimenter's newly juxtaposed stimuli. We tend to forget that the sophisticated, the skilled acts of an individual in a particular situation are the responses he is now making *instead of the naive* reactions he formerly made overtly and conspicuously and which are now reduced to that bare minimum necessary to provide the cues which now condition the sophisticated responses. The small boy, bravely whistling his way through a cemetery illustrates this process very well. With a history of a belief in ghosts and a fear of them current in his culture, the boy, upon finding himself in a dangerous proximity to their haunts is of course prompted to flee. But his training has also put a premium upon bravery in the face of danger and a disguising of apprehension. Having probably used whistling previously as a device for disguising apprehension of a minor sort he now whistles in response to an even greater tension or fear. To "whistle to keep up your courage" has become proverbial. Many cultures put a premium upon those completely reversing the reactions more nearly normal or inborn to the situation. But that does not alter the fact that these approved behaviors are now conditioned reactions called out by that particular situation in a person properly conditioned so to respond.

It is man's behavior that seems to be most closely related to the higher mental processes and which will probably provide the best clues to their nature and functioning. So much of our thinking takes a verbal form that we are more than justified in studying it in this modality. It has long been recognized that "thoughts" can produce effects in the body but precisely what kind of effects are produced by what kind of thoughts? Professor Razran hit upon a very ingenious device for making quantitative comparisons of the relative efficacy of the same word in a variety of languages on himself as subject. The word chosen was "saliva" in six languages in which he had varying degrees of fluency and one language of which he knew no other word. A nonsense syllable and a time period without any verbal cue served as controls. What was studied was the effect of "thinking" continuously the particular word in but one language, upon the amount of saliva secreted during a two minute period. This was achieved by using a roll of dental cotton, weighed before and after the two minute period in the mouth. The amount of saliva collected by this means corresponded nicely with the degree of familiarity and fluency with each of the languages. No experiment has ever more clearly demonstrated the far-reaching possibilities of the self-stimulation process, of "mental" effects on the body, or of the intimate relationship between "thoughts" and bodily processes—call it what you will. We have here a quantitative invasion of the mysteries of "the mind," and I rather suspect that the result is that the mind seems a bit less mysterious, and much more a part of the material universe.

But we dearly love our mysteries and in general resent their being "reduced" to material determinants. A recent popular article on sleep says:

"We still cannot fathom the mechanism of that built-in biological clock which enables some peope to "set" their minds at a certain hour—and wake up on the dot without alarms or any other external signals."

There are people whose performances approach this. My grandmother could awaken us at 3:00 a.m. for an early fishing trip, without the aid of an alarm clock. She was a light sleeper and could hear the old kitchen clock strike even if it was some distance from her room. Her method of "setting her mind" was to strike the bedstead vigorously as many blows as the hour at which she wanted to awaken. With such a firm "set" or "einstellung" she would remember her assignment when the clock struck. A few controls and the elements essential to a properly timed awakening can readily be ascertained. With a little practice in getting up at varying hours the cues finally fall into a pattern of some sort. Simplest of all is the situation that develops when one has to arise at a particular time every morning. At first it might well take a loud and persistent alarm clock to interrupt sleep. But shortly the constant cues provided by the physiological condition of the sleeper, the normal and predictable environmental sounds and the cues provided by approaching daylight suffice. We prefer to tell about it as if it were a deep mystery. Even a rough check on the actual events involved quickly dispel any mystery. When enough different cues have accompanied any activity of an organism, those cues become adequate to elicit such behavior, even if none of these stimuli alone are capable of doing it.

But it is probably in verbal activity that we will fare best in apprehending the nature of "mental" processes. Riess[21] conditioned children of various ages to give electrodermal reactions to words by pairing them with the sound of a buzzer that was found capable of calling out the galvanic reaction. When the conditionings were well established he tested the subjects with homophones, antonyms, and synonyms of the words used in the conditioning process. Transfers of the electrodermal reaction were noted to these semantically related words. The youngest group of subjects, (mean age seven years nine months) gave most transfer to homophones, then to antonyms, with synonyms last. An older group (mean age ten years eight months) showed this declining order: antonyms, homophones, synonyms. The group averaging fourteen years of age gave the strongest transfer to synonyms, then antonyms, and homophones lowest. One might well ask, if a "mind" handles meanings, how is it that a lowly "body" should show such a progressive evolution in its involvement with reactions to words? Or, could it be that "mind" is but a name, like "soul," long applied to events and processes not otherwise apprehended or understood?

It is commonly asserted, in opposition to any deterministic theories of mind or behavior, that "experience" or the conscious sensation is something unique and not to be equated with any of its antecedents of "causes"; that "experience" cannot be equated with "response." Professor Clarence Leuba[22] has shown clearly that, given the proper conditions, the entire range of sensory "experience" can be conditioned, in much the same way that responses are. Such conditioned sensations strongly suggest the processes underlying imagery of all sorts. To quote from the former of Leuba's articles:[23]

"From the protocols it is apparent that the conditioned sensations (images) were frequently accompanied by objective responses, such as a movement toward, and a scratching of, the itching hand; or a wrinkling up of the nose and sniffling movement as the creosote was imaginatively experienced. These movements were quick, spontaneous responses following immediately upon the conditioned stimulus and substantiated the subject's introspective reports. *Usually, the overt movements started before the subject reported the presence of imagery.*" (Italics mine.)

Apparently these images, like other voluntary or conditioned responses, are critically dependent upon the same kind of return afferent cues as is the conditioned leg flexion of the humble dog. Leuba used subjects under deep hypnosis to get his results. He comments on this as follows:

"The hypnotic state served the same purpose as the hunger drive, the sound-proofing, and the exclusion of extraneous stimuli in general in Pavlov's conditioned response experiments. It limited the subject's attention to the pertinent stimuli, and thereby enabled the experimenters to demonstrate *a fundamental psychological principle whose functioning in everyday life is frequently obscured by the simultaneous presence of many stimuli and many responses.*" (Italics mine.)

In other words, when enough of the elements of a given situation are controlled or held constant, the behavior of the individual becomes highly predictable. When the situation is sufficiently simplified so that we can predict responses with a high degree of accuracy we speak of a "conditioned reaction" and we assume that this is a deterministic product. It would seem to be no great stretching of inferences to assume a similar determinism even if the situation is complicated by the presence of unknown and uncontrolled cues, and by relatively unpredictable outcomes. Each individual represents a quite unique loading and weighting of probabilities for a variety of possible responses. But it is surely an error to equate such uniqueness with an indeterminism in human behavior. It is interesting to note that in areas where each individual may well be quite unpredictable on the basis of our present knowledge of him, yet massed predictions might well have great accuracy. We will not know in advance who will be a highway casualty on the forthcoming three-day week-end. But how many, how they will come to grief, their probable ages and temperamental characteristics can be predicted in advance at a far better than chance rate, including even the hours of the day and their probable seating position in the vehicle involved, and the age of the driver. It is probably illusory to assume even the narrowest area, not covered by deterministic processes, where a hypothetical "mind," an agency that somehow operates outside of the familiar ordinates of causality, has dominion.

Where the crass, contranaturalistic term "soul" with its implications of immortality or post-mortem survival is no longer in good repute, and where the activities of the normal waking individual, properly describable as "conscious" are reified into a non-material entity "consciousness," this is commonly assumed to be such an agency, and it is credited with performing the higher mental functions in complete, or almost complete, independence of motor activity. It is conceded, of course, that this non-material agency needs a living body as a sort of habitat, but the truly "mental" operations are assumed somehow to be independent of that body. In experimental psychological circles such dualistic assumptions have of course long been challenged. Recurrently it would seem to some psychologist that perhaps there *always* was activity of some sort when any form of "mental" activity was afoot. The importance of the nervous system to the higher animals made it easy for some to hold that consciousness involved cortical processes only, that no other structures were or need be involved. The production of conscious experiences by direct stimulation of the cortex seemed to lend credence to this view. But there were also those who early held that motor components of some sort were essential to conscious states. Such views comprise the peripheral or *motor theory of consciousness,* in contrast to the "central" theory that held that processes in the brain cortex alone sufficed. But both of these theories assume that of necessity "mental" activities demand some sort of material activities, either as causal or parallel events, an opinion encountered well back into the fourth century A.D. when it was held by St. Augustine.

In the controversy as to whether or not the devil could read men's thoughts there were those, including St. Augustine, who held that he could. The grounds given by these apprehensive fellows was that the devil, being master in the domain of matter, could accurately deduce what was in man's mind by virtue of the fact that every thought would involve some distinctive movement of matter, however minimal it might be. This was probably no unique hunch since it is not too unusual for primitive languages, or it should better be said, for the language of primitive cultures to refer to thinking as talking quietly to oneself, or as "speaking in the stomach." Piaget found the identical opinion in the children of Geneva, and a little careful quizzing of three to six year olds will turn up the same thing anywhere, a process of reasoning not too different from that of Zeno when he held that reason cannot be in the brain, because speech derives from reason, while at the same time speech issues with the voice from the throat. Hence the road to the soul must lead through the throat!

But the distinguishing characteristic of the contemporary scientific era is just that objective verification must be found for the most brilliant new hunches as well as for the most ancient and respectable beliefs. Until some quite convincing activity can be identified as present with all thought processes, particularly those that are conscious, there will still remain grounds for an animistic view of the higher mental processes; and even finding activities concomitant with all thinking and imagery would but make a strong case for a psycho-physical parallelism, or, as with Occam, an "occasionalism."

When St. Augustine concluded that there were movement correlates with every item of the thought process it is safe to assume that he reached that conviction only after some considerable introspective observation. Max Mueller was convinced that thinking without words was impossible, and William James certainly realized that Mueller's ideas were not wholly without warrant. He pointed out that it was practically impossible to think "bubble" without distinctive sensations arising in the larynx.[24] The history of the development of the ideas in regard to the role of motor activity in conscious processes has been well summed up by Professor Max.[25] An increasing awareness of the role played by kinesthesis and movement produced stimuli, coupled with observations that human imagery tended to be linked with motor movements seems to have provided the solid substance upon which speculations were based, particularly in Dunlap,[26] and Washburn.[27] Thorson[28] summed up such experimental work as had been done up to that time, and attempted to find motor correlates of the thought process, or "internal speech." As Max has clearly pointed out,[29] the limitations of the apparatus used in these earlier experiments were such as to give dubious validity to the failure of these experiments to find clear-cut motor correlates to thought processes although in some subjects there seemed to be clear evidence of correlated movements. The relative insensitivity of the apparatus left plenty of room for regular motor activity beyond the level of sensitivity of the early systems of levers that were relied upon to reveal movements.

The development of very sensitive devices capable of measuring extremely small changes in electrical potential opened up entirely new possibilities in this search for motor correlates to mental action. Jacobson[30] used such a delicate galvanometer to study motor concomitants of imagery and thinking. His findings indicate clearly that processes of imagination and thought do consistently involve implicit motor activity, and that this motor activity is an essential condition for such processes and not just an incidental concomitant. Such implicit activity tends to be confined to the muscle groups involved in the imagined act. When an act is imagined verbally, activity is recorded in the lips and tongue; when it is imagined visually, action currents can be detected in the eye muscles. Jacobson's research was motivated by the practical problem of finding means of helping tense, "nervous," or neurotic people, and those suffering from insomnia, whose troubles seem to involve self-stimulated and self-perpetuated activities to the point where they became disabling. His method of treatment, which is often very effective, is to practice his patients in what he calls "progressive relaxation," a relaxation of tension progressively over the entire body, thereby cutting off at their source the disturbing stimuli that perpetuate the neurotic behavior.

The outstanding research in this area is without question that of Professor Louis W. Max.[31] Using a pair of highly sensitive galvanometers coupled each to an especially designed amplifying system, with the changes in current recorded on photographic film, he was equipped to overcome many of the limitations suffered by previous experimenters. Using deaf subjects who use their arms and fingers for what corresponds to oral, written, and gestural speech in normal subjects, had the advantage of simplicity in the nature of the structures involved. Action currents fortuitously aroused in adjacent structures, introduce errors in attempts to measure action currents in tongue, larynx, and lips. Respiration, swallowing, and head movements frequently are sources of galvanic disturbances, not arising in the speech processes themselves, that seriously interfere with accurate measurement of the events in lips, tongue, or larynx. Normal subjects were used as controls, where records were taken from the tongue and arm muscles. Deaf subjects had one galvanometer attached to an arm and one to a leg. For certain kinds of problems the galvanometers were attached each to an arm. Some of the more important findings are best described in the author's own words:[32]

"5. Abstract thought problems elicited manual action-currents in 84 per cent of the cases and in 18 deaf subjects as compared with 31 per cent of the cases in 16 hearing subjects. The average amplitude of response was 3.41 plus microvolts for the deaf and 0.8 microvolts for the hearing. In simultaneous electromyograms from the arm and leg of the deaf, the frequency of positive responses during thought was 73 per cent in the arm and 19 per cent in the leg. Whereas during kinaesthetic tasks involving arm muscles, the percentage of positive arm responses from hearing and deaf subjects was substantially the same, during thought problems the arms of the deaf yielded larger and more frequent responses that those of normals.

"6. Simple reading and mental repetition of verbal material gave smaller and less frequent action-current responses from the deaf than reading with intent to remember, memorization and other more complex thought problems. Similarly, problems in mental arithmetic of an automatized nature yielded less electromyographic response than non-automatized ones.

"7. Vocalized speech, nodding of the head and non-manual language substitutes were frequently accompanied in the deaf, and only occasionally in hearing subjects, by simultaneous action-currents in the hand and arm muscles.

"8. In general, the more intelligent and more educated deaf subjects tended to give less electromyographic response to problem situations; previous vocational experience, fear of the laboratory situation and other emotional states were found to influence the nature of the response."

This last item probably has important theoretical implications. What Max actually found was negative rank-difference correlations between average microvoltage recorded during problem solving and test scores as follows: with the Pintner-Patterson, —0.92; Meyers, —0.90; Dearborn, —0.63; Otis, —0.33; Army Alpha, —0.26. Rank difference correlations on 18 cases are not too conclusive, but when all correlations point in the same direction the results cannot be ignored. Note also the effect of vocational experience as reported in the same study:[33]

"3. Vocational experience. The average electromyographic responses of any given subject seemed to be partly related to his previous occupational activities. Our three proof readers, for example, gave little or no electromyographic activity on most of the purely verbal problems. Counting X's, Y's, etc., in an alphabetical series almost always gave zero responses in their case, as compared with positive responses in practically all the other subjects. Two subjects who had previously employed mathematical calculations in their vocations yielded relatively small responses to the arithmetic problems."

Of similar importance is the evidence from this same truly monumental study in regard to a shifting over of minimal activity from one structure to another during the multiplying of two place numbers by two place numbers. For these problems the experimenter, again working with deaf subjects, attached a galvanometer to each arm of the subject. In one particular case the subject had been told to multiply 39 by 14. I here quote again from Max:[34]

"There is a shifting of electromyographic activity from one arm to the other during the solution period. A clue to the significance of the shifting in this subject is found in the introspections, an excerpt from which follows:

Q. What went on in your mind during the problem?

A. When the numbers were on the card (referring to the method of presentation of the problems) . . . I multiply in my mind 39 times 4—4 times 9 makes 36, then carry 3—then multiply 4 by 3 makes 12 and 3 makes 15 . . .

Q. When you say "multiplied in mind"—how do you mean?

A. I keep the answer in my hand, then for the next addition I use the number in my hand and add the number to the number in the image and so on till I get the answer.

Q. You say "Keep answer in hand." One hand?

A. I did adding in my left hand and keep the answer in right hand.

Q. Always or just today?

A. They don't teach me to keep the numbers in my hand. It is part of my personal . . .

Such shifting of the implicit action-currents from one arm to another was repeatedly observed in other deaf subjects. What the electromyograms show is not a sustained deflection in the 2 arms that might be regarded as a generalized tension effect but rather an intermittent shifting of discrete volleys of action-currents, a picture which supports the possibility of a specific functional involvement of these arm responses in the current thinking act. Such shifting was not observed between the arm and leg in the simultaneous arm and leg records.

The pattern results would indicate that in the deaf, over and above any tension effects that may be present during thought, there is in addition a differential participation of the arm muscles in the thinking process."

When it is remembered that in all these researches no more than two muscle groups could be studied during mental activity, it should come as no surprise that there were instances of zero voltage from one or two particular muscle systems during an actual thinking process. It would indeed be something of a miracle if, in view of the evidence for what is almost a regular shifting from one muscle group to another during thinking, any one muscle group were to be found to have always been active during all thought problems. What these researches have clearly shown is that thought processes can be mediated in many effector groups; that a given train of thought or problem might involve a shift from one effector group to another, and always there is the tendency toward skipping, by-passing, or shortening such activities as testified to by the relatively lower level of myogalvanic activity during given mental operations for the relatively more intelligent as well as for those more specifically skilled or practiced in a particular type of operation. Certainly the experiments on higher-order conditioned responses, in which cues that are concomitant to what are already but conditioned cues, themselves take on the power of calling out responses originally linked with neither, demonstrate the possibilities inherent in the process. These processes have been experimentally verified. Even if some evidence were to appear indicating that such processes could not be operating in particular cases and that some form of "short-circuiting" mechanisms in some higher brain centers had to be assumed,[35] that would certainly not necessitate an abandonment of a determinism in the domain of mind. There might indeed be large gaps in the procession of events of a conscious character; such gaps do not testify to an inadequacy of determinism in mental processes. We know from the electromyogram that there is plenty of deterministic activity going on that is far beyond the reach of any subjective report from the individual in whom these events transpire. The day is long past when it could be held that the conscious "experience" was the ultimate word on events inside the body or the processes determining other mental or physical events. For at least some processes the electromyogram is far more sensitive and accurate. On the basis of any conscious precursors, some mental events might well be "uncaused," not be deterministic products, or be the effect of some divine afflatus. Today the burden of proof rests clearly upon those who still hold to an indeterminism. And much more clearly than in William James' day it also rests upon those who would make a noun out of the adjective "conscious." As he so forcefully put it:[36]

"It (consciousness) is the name of a nonenity, and has no right to a place among first principles. Those who still cling to it are clinging to a mere echo, the faint rumor left behind by the disappearing "soul" upon the air of philosophy."

A materialistic theory of mind certainly commends itself on the basis of simplicity, as well as on the factual evidence. Any alternative necessitates the assumption of an entire and additional reality dimension, of which, almost by definition we can never have any scientific knowledge. It is interesting to note that children brought up with a materialistic account of "mental processes" are but mildly amused at any sort of dualistic metaphysics. The concept of "mind" as it appears in common speech gives them no more trouble than the term "sunrise" causes in learning the more accurate account of the relative motions of the heavenly bodies.

One wonders, does it ever occur to the addicts to the ancient

animism that in the development of every child they are witnesses to the slow, piecemeal, and deterministic process that
creates the "mind" of the child. There is never more mind,
reason, or intelligence in any child than the growth, maturational, and conditioning or learning processes have produced.
If there is here a distinctive entity having an entirely different
basis in reality, how does it happen that it is unimaginatively
tied and limited, step by step, to the material events and processes that have very definite, predictable, yes, deterministic
sequences? The child's behavior waits upon the maturational
processes. The specific content of that child's "mind" is a function of the conditioning processes it is subjected to. Given the
proper environment it will acquire a "mind," a "rational" one,
mind you, for which hepatoscopy, genethlialogy, zoomorphism,
or malicious animal magmetism are the quintessence of logic.
Surely, a "mind" so constructed is a deterministic product. We
can see the sequences of environmental events that inflict such
monstrosities on the behavior patterns of helpless infants and
children. So too, in precisely the same manner might that "mind"
come to consist of similar, quite predictable habits that make
up its "logic," only this time it contains, let us say, the thirty-nine
articles of some specific creed, plus enough habits corresponding to an objective reality which provide the bases for his organic subsistence. With John Locke, one might well ask, where
is there any evidence of "mind" other than the specific products
of a variety of events in space and time? Any dualistic assumption could but insist that all these material events were but a
shadow, an echo, a fortuitous by-product of the "real" events
that took place in a realm of spirit, something after the theories
of Hegel and the absolute idealists. All of which has an odor
reminiscent of the phlogiston theories of combustion. Fire was
a unique essence that transcended such fortuitous facts as the
material details of what went into a combustion process. Mind
and spirit too, are presumed to be "something more" than just
the objectively identifiable process that scientific methods identify. To limit theories of human activity to objectively identifiable entities is to be guilty of a heinous sin indeed: reduction-
ism! But such is the fate of superfluities.

Free Will and the Reality of Religion

When the "reality of religion" is under discussion the fact of the existence of religious beliefs and institutionalized religious behavior is commonly not in question. It is the reality of some sort of force, energy, or power, not measured or identified by the common gram, centimeter, second units of science that is perhaps in dispute. It is the reality of what the layman probably calls 'spiritual power' or even 'God' that is under fire.

But what sort of phenomenon is it that calls for or demands the postulate of some such spiritual power? Where does the admittedly very impressive array of scientific knowledge fall down so badly that some other agency must be postulated? The answer to these questions will be found to vary with the level of scientific sophistication of those asked. The fact that there is a certain predictability to the phenomena of inanimate nature constitutes proof to some that an active intelligence of an anthropomorphic sort must have constructed Nature in that way. For others it is the complex chemistry of carbon as manifested in living organisms that demands a spiritual power of some sort as an adequate explanation. But these positions are the earmarks of the relatively unsophisticated, of those who are relative strangers to even the commonplaces of today's science. It is in the more complex, symbolic, or "mental" processes of man that "spiritual" powers are commonly presumed to operate by those relatively well informed in modern science. Or, it is the phenomena of human choice reactions, volition, or "free will" as it has long been called, that seem to involve processes or events beyond any imaginable "determinism." Let me quote here from a most brilliant and scholarly volume, "Origin and Evolution of Religion" by E. Washburn Hopkins, Ph.D., LL.D., Professor of Sanskrit and comparative philology at Yale University:

"The very investigator who proves by an indisputable array of facts that nature is subject to mechanical laws and then argues from this that life is mechanical, is himself a part of nature; but no one can predict what he will do; *he is not himself subject to material laws in his volition.*"[37] (Italics mine.)

And again: "Life then possesses an immaterial something actually existing as an objective reality. Whether nature is dual or one of these phases by an expression of the other, in either case an immaterial power must be accepted. If we reduce matter and force to different manifestations of the same thing, we shall still have to admit that the forceform cannot be explained, for example, as electricity, *for electricity has no will power. There must be a power implying will,* of which electricity is one expression, for will cannot be referred to matter without force, only to force or energy. Energy operative with will must then be assumed in the infinite as it is revealed in the finite. Whether it is called energized will or willing energy or some unknown power, which for want of a better term may be described as spiritual power, is unimportant. Some call it God." Again: "Life as it now is thus demands the explanation of an immaterial power, infinite energy or will, operative in the universe and controlling it."[38]

Similarly Stace: "I shall first discuss the problem of free will, for it is certain that if there is no free will there can be no morality. Morality is concerned with what men ought and ought not to do. But if a man has no freedom to choose what he will do, if whatever he does is done under compulsion, then it does not make sense to tell him that he ought not to have done what he did and that he ought to do something different. All moral percepts would in such case be meaningless. Also if he acts always under compulsion, how can he be held morally responsible for his actions? How can he, for example, be punished for what he could not help doing?

It is to be observed that those learned professors of philosophy or psychology who deny the existence of free will do so only in their professional moments and in their studies and lecture rooms. For when it comes to doing anything practical, even of the most trivial kind, they invariably behave as if they and others were free. . . ."[39]

It is thus apparent that to Professors Hopkins, Stace, and to untold others far less well-informed, our acts of *will,* free or otherwise, constitute an effective roadblock against the extension of a determinism into the domain of "the spirit." However, scientific curiosity has not been wholly idle in this field during the past generation, and many insights have accrued to the contemporary scientific tradition, even if they have not yet become part of the traditional thought pattern of even the sophisticated layman. Let us then examine this hoary old chestnut, our "free will" in the light of the more recent scientific findings and analyses.

Popularly, an act of will or of volition, whether "free"or not, is one that is initiated, or certainly preceded, by "mental" or "spiritual" activities presumed to be of a non-material nature, and to be "in the mind." In what is, superficially at least, a completely immobile and inactive "body," a very much active "mind," 'soul," or "spirit" seems to be able to engage in flights of fancy, plots, schemes, plans of action, hates, loves, rages, prayers, curses, and blessings as well as quantitatively exact calculations. These processes might well be accompanied by convincingly vivid imagery sometimes seemingly as clear as if their particular sense-modality were under actual stimulation by the realities of the external world. It is this dynamically active process, apparently independent of actual, measurable, and material activity that has no doubt provided the pattern for all the many and varied forms of animistic habits of speech, of postulated souls, spirits, gods, devils, and even of an "animate nature," whether of the cosmos generally or limited to the apparently directed but certainly regulatory activities of living things generally. Man has long interpreted the events in the universe about him in terms of this type of his own activities. This activity, in unfamiliar situations at least, is often, but far from always, preceded by such apparently non-material, private, processes. Where better explanations are lacking for any phenomena, it is not to be wondered at that he "projects" what he presumes to be his own processes and procedures into the events about him. Certainly the existence of such non-material agencies could not be established by the conventional, the objective criteria of reality. But if we assume that a non-material agency within us, somthing not dependent upon bodily energies, or something categorically different from the material flesh and its functions, is actually an effective "cause" of the events that follow in the material world, what could be more natural than to presume that similar agencies are at work, each in its own unique sphere, and responsible for the events and processes therein! There is nowhere any postulated spirit, devil, god, or animistic agency that is not all too obviously a product of such an interpretation in terms of the processes going on within ourselves. Gods, devils, or spirits generally, are presumed to make things happen in this world and beyond, by the sort of magical fiat that our own volitional processes seem to exercise in "making" the body respond "at will." Given this "sample" or illustration of causality of a non-deterministic sort where physical or material events seem to have mental or spiritual rather than material antecedents, the habits of thought or logic that apparently carry over seem to be about as follows: "My little spirit makes these important things happen; in much the same way, other and otherwise unexplained or mysterious events are the product of agencies that are in some way similar, but of course more powerful." *The prototype of all non-material forces or agencies conceived to exist is the subjective thought or volitional process that is the common experience of all mankind.* It is this subjective process that provides the terms and symbols of a communication process that have been elaborated into a category of reality in metaphysics. What begins as an adjective for the covert, the symbolic, the private, the mental, becomes Mind, Spirit, or Soul by a process of reification, the conversion of adjectives into nouns of dubious validity.

There is of course, no question whatever as to the effective role played by these private, subjective, symbolic processes in the determination of the behavior of the individual. They are indeed sometimes causally effective, if anything in the universe can be said to "cause" anything else. The error is in the assertion that these processes are not of a material, mechanical, or other measurable energy form or sort, that an "act of will" involves non-material determinants, processes just not to be subsumed under the familiar categories of the scientific world.

Animistic theorists seem to be fascinated by their "free-will" power to lift their arm on a signal from themselves, or of others, or indeed to inhibit the raising of the arm under circumstances ordinarily calculated to produce such an elevation. This ability was of course established as a deterministic process so early in life that they know nothing whatever of the steps in its formation. So they assume the action of a spiritual agency in its operation, and offer it as exhibit "A" in anti-deterministic disputes. Let us now follow the very real, materialistic, deterministic, and *conditioning* process by which such "free-will" control is established over anatomical units, to see if a gap exists in such processes that must be filled with a mind, spirit, soul, or other animistic entity or agent. Hudgins[40] made use of the pupillary reflex in human subjects in exploring this problem of volition. Normally, the iris muscle of the eye reacts in a reflex manner to bright lights by contracting, thereby decreasing the size of the pupil. Focusing upon near objects also touches off a reflex that diminishes the size of the pupil. On the other hand, any rather intense stimuli, such as a loud noise or a sharp pain will normally dilate it. Hudgins conditioned the pupil to contract at the sound of a bell by pairing the bell with a flash of light. By arranging an electrical circuit so that a contraction of the subject's hand closed the circuit on both the light and the bell when the experimenter gave the command "contract," and opened the circuit again when the command was given to "relax," several hours of training made it possible to eliminate light, sound, and hand grip; just to say the word "contract" alone called out the pupillary contraction. Some subjects said the word "contract" out loud during the training period. After training these subjects needed but say the word "contract" and a pupillary contraction would result. Other subjects but whispered the word, while still others merely thought "contract." In these subjects also, whispering or thinking "contract" sufficed to bring about such a diminution of the size of the pupil. They had acquired "free will" or volitional control of a visceral sphincter muscle, a problem of a difficulty comparable to that confronting a child in acquiring "control" of its bladder sphincter, surely a problem of "will" if ever there is one! Should the reader not have "voluntary" control of the retrahens muscle, the striped or "voluntary" muscle which enables one to wiggle his ears, a much prized ability in small-boy circles, such "control" can

easily be acquired. Direct stimulation of the skin over this muscle with a mild electrical current will cause the muscle to contract. While closing the circuit on your stimulus, "try" to move
the muscle by contracting any muscle anywhere in the general
region, or anywhere at all for that matter. Shortly, whatever it
was you did while the retrahens muscle was contracting will
provide sufficient conditioning stimuli to cause your ear to
"wiggle." If you just "think" any signal word, or whisper during
the training period, that thought or whisper will now do the
trick. You now have "free-will" control of your ear-wiggle. Perhaps you have a "mind" or a "will"; but whatever you may
have, it is impotent until the conditioning process has linked
the cues provided by some response already under "voluntary"
control with this new reaction. Then, and only then, does the
"will" seem to have any power or existence. Our every "volitional" act has precisely such a "conditioning" history in its
acquisition.

It would seem then that a concept like "will" had better join
terms and expressions like "sunrise" and "sunset" into the limbo
of common sense expressions, useful enough for a certain short-
hand of communication, but simply not to be confused with
scientific accounts of the processes involved. The acceptance of
a heliocentric astronomy did not come easily either. The language habits and perceptions of a lifetime do not easily succumb
to the remote mathematics and experimental subtleties of the
experimenter. Even the most apparently obvious "facts" of common sense must in the end be reinterpreted in the light of more
exact knowledge of the nature of the processes in question. A
recognition of the determinants in all acts of volition would seem
to be simple compared to being compelled to accept the fact
of the "up" falling of objects at the southern end of the earth!

It is at once apparent that even the subtlest of moral hair-
splittings in any free-will option must constitute a 'choice' of
some kind, a reaction of one sort rather than of another. Such
'choices' of course, vary in complexity, and in the manner of
their acquisition from subtle value judgments in aesthetics to
inborn, tropismatic attractions or avoidances. Now the question
must be raised as to just where deterministic explanations be-

come inadequate. It is safe to say that there is no general agreement to be found among the fraternity that holds determinism
to be inadequate. Some hold that the movements, behavior, or
"choices" of even the lowliest amoeba involve some subtle trace
of the spiritual factor. But the studies of surface tensions, of
reversible sol-gel reactions in the protoplasm of microorganisms
have made these survivals of animism sound like phlogiston
theories of combustion. But the tests and researches themselves
which first of all exploded whatever may have remained of the
respectability of all purposive theories of animal behavior, have
paved the way for highly significant findings in parasitology. The
reactions of these organisms to "choice" in their environments
proved to be subtle matters of chemical effects on surface tension and the relative fluidity of a living protoplasm rather than
the reflections of some purpose. An organism might well retreat
from some agents actually noxious to its life-processes; but then
again it might be fatally attracted to its doom at the hands of
another. To the agents normally present in its traditional environment the reactions of any organism can be described as at
best, regulatory, or homeostatic. So much for choices at the
lowest levels.

It will probably be argued at once that such tropismatic reactions or adjustments are not to be confused with true acts of
volition, and indeed the differences between them must not be
minimized. But precisely what are the earmarks of the act of
will or volition that distinguish them from the lowly, reflexive
or instinctive actions? Any careful, quantitative approach to this
question will at once reveal a rather significant finding: what we
commonly recognize as an act of "volition" or "choice" or "free
will" will involve a certain amount of delay in the choice reaction. Common sense long has made the distinction between
a choice or a reaction that involved a certain amount of blocking, of hesitation, of considering of alternatives, as against a reaction in a given situation in which the individual was apparently not aware of the options available. In the latter case
we do not say that an individual "chose," or exercised his volition. We give deterministic accounts of his behavior; we say he
absentmindedly made his familiar reactions to but one aspect of

the situation; we say he did not know that a choice existed, etc. But to constitute an act of volition there must be present this element of delay. And just what is it that goes on in such a period of delay? Is this process that goes on in such a period something completely outside of the realm of the material? Is this a manifestation of what Professor Hopkins calls "spiritual power"? Many years ago Professor Hunter[41] made some very significant beginnings in the study of this problem with his experiments on the delayed reaction. His problem was that of exploring the capacity of an animal to react correctly when there were no longer any objective cues present to determine the correct choice. In the first stage of the experiment the animals were confronted with three doors, any one of which might lead to food; but the door with the food was always lighted as against the other two unilluminated doors which did not lead to food. Under these conditions the animals shortly learned to go to the lighted doorway. Such learning conforms to the simple formula of the Pavlovian conditioned response, a purely deterministic process, and clearly shown not to involve volitional processes, or conscious direction on the part of the conditioned animal. At this point in the experiment complications were introduced by the experimenter in the form of a period of delay before the animal was permitted to start for the correct doorway and after the light over the doorway leading to food had been extinguished. What was being tested was, in one way of describing it, the ability of the animals to react to "stimuli no longer present," or so it seemed to be in the terminology then current. Actually, no cue can be reacted to if it is not acting on an organism, no matter what animal is involved, including man. But are we then dealing in this instance with some form of what Professor Hopkins called "spiritual power" or "immaterial power"? Let us observe the behavior of these animals a bit more closely. It was shortly observed by Professor Hunter that the rats that could still choose correctly after some five to ten seconds delay, and his dogs with a tolerance for delay running into several minutes, had to maintain a postural set or orientation toward the correct doorway during the entire period of delay if they were to choose correctly upon being released. If even momentarily the animal shifted its set to another direction its success was then purely a matter of chance, i.e., one in three. In the case of the rats it was established that the critical determiners were somehow located in the neck muscles: if these were shifted from their correct orientation toward the correct door the rat's "memory" for it was lost. Should one now say that when the rat is released it goes to the correct doorway "of its own free will"? Or shall we say that it is making a "choice"? To imply such human functions in the performances of these animals is hardly warranted, and it is fortunately not necessary; we need only point out that the rats and dogs are responding to *cues provided by their own reactions* which were initiated by the lighted doorway and maintained in circular fashion after the manner of a Pointer dog keeping "set" in the direction of the game animal. Specifically, the cues involved are provided by the animal's own reactions; the senses involved are the kinesthetic, the much disputed motion sense, the specific receptors for which are located in all muscles and tendons, and on all joint surfaces. Each movement of the animal is registered in a pattern of kinesthetic cues, which, in this case provide the stimuli giving the animal its direction when released. To put it in other words, the dog's "memory" consists of these self-provided, kinesthetic cues provided by a steadily maintained pattern of activity in the dog. Any break in this pattern of activity means a loss of "memory." The animal's "choice," or "volition" then proves to be a reaction touched off by cues provided by the activity sustained during the period of delay or blocking. It would seem that there was no need here to invoke the activities of any form of "spiritual force."

Such a performance is indeed a far cry from the subtleties of human decisions and preferences. But are we dealing here with differences in kind or only in degree? To return again to Professor Hunter's experiment, let us examine the performances turned in by some other animals, the raccoon for example. This animal's tolerance of delay is much less than that of the dog, at best somewhere under a minute. But it has a distinct advantage: it does not have to maintain a constant set, a steady pointing at the door in order to choose the correct one when released. Nor do monkeys, tried in the same situation. Nor do young children! What kind of a "mental" or "spiritual" performance are we dealing with here? Shall we say that the raccoon's *memory* lasts thirty seconds, or that he can exercise an effective free-will choice over that period of time? At this point one might well ask just what kind of a process such a choice reaction involves. It is at once obvious that whatever it is, it differs in degree but not in kind from the human performance. And just how *does* the human make a correct choice in such a situation? It is apparent that such a problem is far too easy for man to reveal the process that underlies his correct choice. For a comparable problem in man the number of doors would have to be increased to a dozen or so. *Then* how do we meet such a problem? Very simply: we count in (or out) to the end of the line of doors, thus identifying the correct door by a system of *self-provided cues,* and should we have failed so to identify a particular door we would be forced to resort to trial and error guesses such as we actually are driven to if we have failed to note the number on a door in a corridor with many similar doors! With the simple three-door situation the process is somewhat as follows: when the light flashes on, identifying the correct door, the animal makes obvious overt movements in that specific direction. It is this, *last practiced response in this situation* which is again called out when the barrier is released, permitting the animal to go to the food. For the raccoon that is a problem of comparable complexity to the seven symbol telephone number that we look up before dialing. Were we to be interrupted in the process, for example by giving someone else a few other numbers before having an opportunity to dial our own, the odds would rise that errors would result.

The psychologically naive person will probably object at this point and say that we are here dealing only with "memory" and not "will" or "volition." But every choice, every act of "free will" is similarly determined *by the cues provided by the reactions called out in us by the choice situation!* In one case it might merely be the process of counting that provides the identifying cues; in another we might be confronted with a situation that we would identify with the label "stealing," and the reactions called out in us by that word would provide the balance-destroying stimuli that enter into a moral choice. In any situation where alternative actions are possible, we react with whatever verbal or imaginal activities have in the past been associated with such situations or elements thereof. It is always these reactions called out in us by these situations that provide *the cues that in turn call out the responses that are in effect our choices,* or our "free will." The complexity and subtlety of factors involved may indeed vary enormously, but at bottom the same basic pattern of activity is always involved.

Let us examine the process in detail in what is no doubt a relatively simple situation involving "free" choice. Take for example, the situation in which a small boy is confronted with, and offered a choice from, one of these boxes of candy in which no two pieces are alike. The situation is relatively simply in that the small boy must make his choice on the basis of purely visual cues. Now of course our subject has already had considerable experience with candies of various sorts and appearances. On the basis of purely visual cues he already distinguishes large pieces from small, chocolates from gum drops, caramels from crunches, even if not by name. Certain visual appearances of these particular pieces became "associated" with distinctive gustatory reactions, and it is the reactions called out in him by these visual cues that provide the balance-destroying stimuli that make possible a choice, that prevent him from remaining permanently frozen in immobility like the donkey in the famous fable. Let us suppose that these candies differed only in size. Then, assuming our subject were too young to have acquired the social inhibitions in regard to "hogging" the large pieces where a large piece now calls out a very subtle kind of avoidance, it would be the differences in the effect of the larger visual image that would constitute the effective bases of a free "choice." His reactions to a large piece, being different from those to smaller ones provide the balance destroying cues. If the distinctive striping of the peppermint stick identified a candy to which in the past he had given an avoidance reaction, that striping now would touch off avoidance reactions, no matter how large the piece. The options offered by the box of sweets tap these and many other specific conditionings out of the past of the choosing subject, and it is these conditioned reactions that provide the cues that constitute such a "free choice." Once this is grasped we have a simple explanation of what seems to be a moral perversity of the young in such situations where, before summary disciplinary measures have been applied, they may well pick up one piece, then promptly drop it, take another only to again drop it for still another choice. The explanation for this unseemly conduct is simply this: their choices are based on conditioned reactions to *visual* cues provided by the individual pieces. But when once their fingers pick up a piece these same fingers obscure the piece chosen and thus destroy its stimulus value in competition with the other pieces remaining in the effective field of vision. In such a situation some other piece now provides more potent stimuli, so the first one is dropped in favor of the unobscured one. This can go on more or less indefinitely; six such successive "choices" have been reported by interested observers. In the small boy's performance we merely see illustrated in simpler form the processes underlying the adult "acts of free will" that tradition has long assigned to the operation of some subtle, "spiritual" factor or force. These determining factors can indeed be rightly called "covert," "private," "minimal," or "symbolic"; but the facts hardly warrant their isolation into a distinctive metaphysical category.

An approach such as this to the traditional controversy in regard to the freedom of the will calls for a reappraisal of the old arguments and the motivations behind them. One might ask, first of all, what is the psychological validity behind the vivid, convincing, subjective feeling everyone has that it is indeed he that is making his choices and decisions? The simple and obvious fact is, of course, that the critical, determining, or balance-destroying cues do indeed come from the individual himself. At the moment of choice the predominantly important role in any decision is being played by those activities actually going on within the individual. It is those processes that even naive introspection reveals as being critically important in the decisions of the moment, and it would be silly to deny the obvious fact that the drama of decision is here being played off, that the activities of the thinking, reasoning individual at that moment are critically important. It is only when the proponents of free will theories fail to recognize that each of these possible activities, or self-provided stimulus patterns, is also a deterministic product of the historical past of the individual that one must part company with them. For determined they indeed have been, by possibly any or every preceding event in the entire history of the universe, including every possible chance factor determining the biological character of the animal kingdom, his own particular animal order, family, genus, and species, and particularly the fortuitous factors determining the individual genetic constitution of his particular combination of chromosomes and genes. Beyond these are of course the myriad factors in the life history of the individual, the nutritive, pathologic, familial, and social-cultural factors, any slight variant of which might indeed be shown to weight the scales of probability in the behavior of the moment. To deny the historically determinitive character of the individual's behavior is to fly in face of all that man has learned in the past three millennia.

One might well wonder at the intensity of the emotionality with which such a determinism in human actions is rejected not only by certain individuals but also by some organized social groups. It is apparently felt by these persons to constitute a debasing of the individual human, to initiate a moral loss of some sort, or to be contrary to the scheme of things presumably laid down by the postulated anthropomorphic agencies responsible for the current cosmic order. To others it seems to make meaningless any orderly strivings, particularly those of a moral sort. This attitude results apparently from a confusion of practical, disciplinary techniques with a system of metaphysics. It would indeed be impractical to punish a child caught redhanded stealing strawberry jam, simultaneously with indoctrinating him that children have an uncontrollable jam-stealing instinct or to point out at the same time that nothing could be done to change a child's inborn penchant for sweets. Yet this is the dilemma the professional moralist visualizes when confronted with a theory of determinism in human behavior. It would apparently rob him of his moral "right" to punish for misdeeds, and that makes him uncomfortable, as indeed it should. *Questions involving any "right to punish" should of course be rephrased into questions regarding effective sequences of events designed to establish desirable patterns of behavior.* The introduction of consistencies and predictable sequences into the environment of any individual results in orderly behavior if that person is not psychotic. His behavior simply reflects, insofar as we are dealing with learned acts, the interaction of a particular organism with a particular environment. Intelligent human action must go far beyond any mere "right to punish" for particular deviations in conduct. It must recognize in full detail the nature of the deterministic process that produces desirable as well as undesirable conduct in an individual. And these facts are no state security secrets to be kept from the trainee; his complete insight into the basic principles of the process are for the most part effective aids in the acquisition of desirable habits.

The normal personality has no serious difficulty in adjusting to the complexities of his environment that do not exceed the limits of his capacity to discriminate. If any of his acts have predictable consequences the learning process usually fixates or eliminates the acts involved in the direction of workable behavior adjustment. Such problems of adjustment produce no soul-searching in the individual. If some practical situation is to be met the individual will usually mobilize his own or the resources of others to meet the situation effectively, without concern as to whether it is a "free will" that is determining his conduct. It is interesting to note that the question of the freedom of the will became a matter of serious concern when behavior standards were at issue whose validation was contingent upon post-mortem events about which the ordinary process of learning and logic were of necessity mute.

The plausibility of the free will hypothesis was no doubt improved by some aspects of personality dynamics. Once certain mechanisms are developed in a particular personality an increasingly important role is played by the personality vis à vis that played by the environment in the further acquisition of traits. No doubt this shift in the determining process toward the individual and away from environmental factors helped contribute to free-will doctrines, much as the same observed consistencies and predictabilities in the personality provided the bases for theories of predestination and infant damnation, given the theological animus that dominated human thinking at that time. In a later, less animistic period of human thinking the same facts were perceived as evidence for the operation of mechanisms of heredity, or of the inborn.

Champions of a free will doctrine commonly charge that deterministic philosophies are fathers to pessimism, despair, and a surrender of moral effort. Nothing could be further from the truth. Once the individual has grasped the fact that the world of the determinants of personality and history is one in which "almost anything is rather more than likely to happen," as a poetic novelist once put it, in which it is at least theoretically possible that even the most trifling event can have the most tremendous possibilities in consequences desired or undesired, the entire process being subject to materialistic, deterministic laws rather than to the whims of anthropomorphic agents, it would be difficult to imagine an atmosphere more conducive to intelligent empiricism and research. The whole constitutes a situation replete with endless challenging problems and a maximum of motivation for their solution. Once our acts of "free will" are seen *not* to involve or demand "the explanation of an immaterial power, infinite energy or will, operative in the universe and controlling it" (as Professor Hopkins put it) we can well introduce a significant reassignment of the very real energies now spent in praising, adoring, invoking, wheedling, contemplating, or entreating forces of whose existence there is not one shred of scientific evidence. Such efforts and energy should obviously be devoted to a study of the bona-fide determinants of human behavior, the genetic, bio-chemical, endocrinological bases of activity in the organism, the nature of the conditioning or learning process in the individual, and the role of the social pressures and influences which seem even to determine out of hand whether the evidence and arguments for "free will" or for "determinism" seem "valid" to human "reason." There is more useful knowledge to be obtained from the careful study of one experiment on the "delayed reaction" in man or beast than from a rehash of all the ink ever spread in the controversy over free will or determinism. Watch the ardent champions of "free will"; they are 100% determinists when they are confronted with the practical problem of making converts and adherents to the free will doctrine. They provide us with particular verbal response patterns and see to it that we have plenty of practice in repeating them under considerable "pressure," evidence, and argument against the thesis being defended. That is the accepted process by which "right reasoning" is produced. Our "reasons" and our "free-will" are the product of the cues provided by the responses habitually elicited in us by particular questions or situations. They are indeed deterministic products, the critical or balance-destroying stimuli being provided primarily by the activities going on within the "willing" individual. But these activities do not take place in a void, or a world of spirit or mind. They are very much a function of discernible activities presently going on in the human body. These activities can be and have been recorded. The action currents liberated when muscle cells contract or relax are much in evidence when "mental" processes are going on, even if there are no signs of overt activity.

The die-hard dualist will assert that these galvanometric deflections which reveal the presence of muscular activities are not the "mental" or "spiritual" processes themselves. These, he will assert, are not "the same as" the muscle twitches there recorded. Such an assertion seems to make some people happy. What, might one ask, can then be evidence of the existence and function of this mind stuff? The subjective "experience" of thinking or "willing" or "reasoning," the "awareness" of such processes? Objectively this must refer to the problem of whether the person in question is able to give a fluent, and usually verbal, account, play by play of the events and processes going on. This is a highly variable factor. If the "mental" were to be limited to the processes man can thus verbalize or report on while the events in question are in progress, then there would still be a great mystery hovering over a major portion of man's activities which would then still need "explaining" or accounting for. To identify "mind" with that small fraction of activity can only

make two unknowns grow where but one grew before. If it is
asserted that the muscle twitches recorded on the galvanometer
are actually caused by the mental process which is something
other than the muscle activity itself one can only ask how it
happens that such mental process are always dependent upon
intact sensory-motor, neuro-muscular structures? The mind or
spirit hypothesis seems to be a superfluity that contributes nothing whatever to understanding, predicting, or controlling behavior. It is a hold-over from the days when the functions of the
nervous system were not even guessed at, and the higher
thought processes were presumed to be a function of the viscera.

Whether or not an individual can make a concomitant
and usually verbal report of activity going on in his organism
seems to be a highly variable and even fortuitous matter. Unfamiliar situations, unusual combinations of cues, rapidly changing stimuli, all seem to set in action the activities commonly
characterized as "conscious," the distinguishing feature of which
is a high responsiveness to exteroceptive cues, a capacity to
report on some kinds of ongoing activities, and usually the
ability to recall at least some of the details of the process for
varying times afterward. To use the adjective "conscious" as the
basis for a noun, "consciousness," may be good grammar but
it is undoubtedly bad science. As previously indicated, even
William James considered it at times a dubious business.[42]

The efforts to show that it is precisely the conscious activity
of man that initiates the new, makes the inventions and discoveries as if it were the central spark of directing intelligence,
meet with dismal failure. The "new" is not foreshadowed "in
consciousness"; it usually comes as a complete surprise; our conscious processes have not anticipated it. More commonly our
overt activity of some sort has stumbled into a new way of doing
things or a new juxtaposition of familiar elements which our
conscious processes did not anticipate or foreshadow. To trans-
late such discovery into communicable symbols however, usually
requires considerable activity commonly considered "conscious."
Almost any well-practiced activity then again tends to lose its
conscious character. This may progress to a point where we are
completely unable to identify the details of our activities in

any conscious sense, although there might well be no question whatever of our competence in that particular performance. The "conscious" character or attribute of any activity is a highly fortuitous matter. Items or events may remain conscious to us far past any possible point of psychological usefulness, as when such activities perpetuate an insomnia. Then again, the ordinarily very familiar might baffle our best attempts to "bring them to consciousness" as it is popularly called. During crises we frequently fail to "become conscious" of items or elements that might well mean our salvation. What we do in a given situation is far better predicted from a record of what our past behavior was in that situation than from a record of just what we were conscious. As for the noun "consciousness," animism has retreated into this reified adjective like Hitler into his Berlin bunker.

Chapter V

MAGIC AND RELIGION

The Concept of the Magical

Any inquiry into the nature of religion is rather likely to pay its respects to the term or concept of magic. At some time in the course of its analysis or classification of its subject, a consideration of "magic" can hardly be avoided. What is this magic? How does it differ from "religion"? In popular parlance "magic" is of course characterized variously as untrue, disproved, false, or, if there are magical forces or processes they are at best evil, and to be resorted to only in the grimmest of straits or emergencies when all legitimate or respectable means of attaining an end have failed. Or, it is often believed that in some distant lands there are wonder-workers who have at their command and under control a variety of highly potent forces not available to their own specialists in religion nor even to their scientists. Particularly, it is believed that "science" cannot explain the miracles they confidently believe these potent fellows capable of performing. A recent survey by the author found almost 50% of a large sample of college students holding this belief. Our own culture has no corner on such notions; it is probably as old as the awareness of the existence of cultural differences in our neighbors. Chantepie de la Saussaye tells us in his "Religion of the Teutons"[1] that these generally tough-minded fellows nonetheless harbored this same belief over a long period. It was the Finns in particular that they believed to possess such uncanny powers and agents, and many an innocent Teuton, male

and female, was put to death on the suspicion of having had
truck with these evil Finnish masters of illicit forces. Among
American Indians there was a similar tendency to ascribe highly
potent powers to specialists in distant tribes. Lynn Thorndike[2]
finds the belief so common that he makes the generalization
that the wonder-workers of distant tribes are always presumed
to be more powerful than those at home. Certainly the commonest alibi for a failure of magical or priestly efforts is to
charge that failure to the action of a more powerful counter-
magic. Rivers finds it common in the Melanesians.

This concept "magic" has a most interesting history in western
Europe. Let us begin with the word itself; the ancient Iranian
medicine men, shamans, magicians, or priests were called magi
in the plural form; singular: magus. These fellows were
equipped with a considerable "bag of tricks," a combination of
medical and practical knowledge, with an impressive ritualism
bolstered by an imposing array of devices for deceiving the eye.
In their day they were a very effective combination of Bishop
Sheen and Duninger or Houdini. Pliny, the old Roman historian,
about as shrewd as they came in his day, knew these Iranian
magi well. It seems that around the beginning of the present era
these fellows often wandered far afield into other lands where
they fared well with their skills and no doubt picked up a few
more ideas that would be useful back home. At any rate, Pliny
credits these magi with having probed deeply into the secrets
of nature—perhaps even too curiously or too deeply! Even *he*
was a bit jittery about the powers these fellows seemed to command! Certainly there was no doubting the impressiveness of
their skills. It must be remembered that at home in Iran these
magi were the priests, the learned men, the specialists in the
sacred. In fact, the name of these specialists is philologically of
the same root and structure as the Iranian word for "the sacred,"
i.e., the correct practices vis à vis the divine, the contra-natural,
the noble. Their profession was in excellent repute at home.

Pliny credits Zoroaster with having been the originator of
the skills of these magi. He was not lacking in skepticism in
regard to this "magic" of the Iranians but thought of it as a degeneration from ancient skill or knowledge. Where the "magic"

consisted of crude thaumaturgy he objected to it. Thorndike reports that Pliny rejected many crude "magical" ideas, but accepted much else that would hardly rate credence today. Of prayers he held that if they were accepted as efficacious, then incantations had as good a claim to respectability. But he even added—'the wisest believe in neither.' Obviously aiming to be critical and empirical, yet Pliny accepts whole bodies of the lore of the magi that seem preposterous to us today. It is diffi-cult indeed to know without empirical trial what to accept and what to reject. Thorndike unwittingly illustrates this problem when he describes as preposterous the stories that fish can be killed by crushing a particular plant and throwing it into the water. The first volume of his monumental History of Magic and Experimental Science was published in 1923. Since that time the use of rotenone for killing out completely the fish in streams or lakes before restocking with game fish has become a commonplace. It is no wonder then that Pliny was frequently in error in the days before the development of the scientific tradition! We can then forgive him his credence in the impor-tance of moon-phases, in the gathering of herbs, or in the neces-sity of a state of chastity or virginity in the operator of particular processes.

Written during the second century of the present era, the Golden Ass of Apuleius depicts magic as being irresistible and occult, but also criminal and false. But it is also regularly referred to as an art and a discipline. Small wonder then that the three magi linked with the Christian story of the Messiah were pre-sumed to be fellows of substance and their link with magic graciously disguised by New Testament translators under the rubric of "wise men." These magi had a good reputation in their day. Thorndike[3] thinks that the evidence is fairly clear that the term came to be applied generally to the practices of any recently displaced or abandoned cult or "religion." Practices once standard but now forbidden or abandoned became "magic." But the rejection or abandonment was not a function of their demonstrable falsity or untruth. Until well into the Middle Ages the learned men of the time thought of magic as true but evil. All during this first millennium there was great

variability and unpredictability as to what was accepted and
what rejected as true or false, good or evil. Dreams have their
ins and their outs; so does astrology. An era of skepticism might
appear during which one or the other of such items might fall
into disrepute; but equally preposterous beliefs of a different
sort might well be retained. The church certainly did not invent
belief in astrology, dreams, numerology, amulets, and lot-casting; these beliefs were simply a part of the pre-Christian heritage. But the church did long hold to belief in the existence of
evil spirits who worked their wills effectively through their
knowledge of the forces of nature. This is not surprising in an
era in which there is widespread acceptance of the occult
powers of gems, herbs, stars, animals, and a wide variety of
spirits. The first millennium showed no sharp break, intellectually, with the generally "magical" past. The acceptance of Christianity meant no general rejection of previously accepted gods,
charms, or beliefs. Christ was merely added to the list of things
"believed." In general the same old magic and astrology were
believed in. Even St. Augustine conceded powers to magic that
Christians and saints could not duplicate. He thought it was
part of the divine plan to make Christians humble. In general,
these mediaeval authors lacked consistency in regard to the
beliefs of the past. At one time an author might denounce
astrology, numerology, or lot-casting in one context, and some
time later accept them in slightly different situations. In this
period the arts too generally continued to be a mixture of the
"magical," the "religious," and the "technological," nor were
there distinctions drawn between any of these areas that would
be meaningful or significant today.

It has been pointed out above that older or discarded or
outlawed practices are likely to be regarded as magic. It should
also be added that when a new religion or ritual is being introduced into a culture and is still the private worship of a small
minority and regarded by the majority as a foreign practice it
is rather likely to be regarded as an outlandish or preposterous
magic of some sort. The term "superstition" currently used
almost as a synonym for magic, has an interesting history. The
old Greek usage of the term was to indicate an excessive fear

or dread of the gods or demons. The normal attitude of the Greeks toward the gods in the Hellenic paganism was a cheerful and friendly familiarity. They were, as characterized by Norman Douglas in the novel "South Wind," "horizontal" gods, and, one might add, human, perhaps "all too human." My colleague, Professor Casper Kramer, assures me that the Romans used the term "superstition" as a general term to designate all foreign religions. Private opinion has pretty much retained that same usage today, with varying inhibitions on its public expression. Any excessive dread of the supernatural drew Plutarch's ire. Such fear was worse, he held, than to deny the existence of gods, for it makes men unhappy and it is at least as bad to believe ill of the gods as not to believe in them at all. He denounced the excesses of such superstitions with their magics, their "impure rites, their purifications, their filthiness and chastity."[4] No pathological preoccupation with evil here!

The Status of Magic in the Early Christian Period

To understand sympathetically this period of our past one must remember that at this time there was no separation of natural science from magic; there were no traditions of scientific method, no solid body of experimental knowledge. It is apparent that even the most sophisticated of individuals was confronted with officially believed and accepted "miracles," both of the past and in the present. How was one to distinguish genuine miracles from similar performances on the part of pagans and Jews? The evidences for the one were as good and no better than those for the other. There was no question of the genuineness of the performances. While yet functioning in a "free market," Pagans, Christians, and Jews hurled charges at each other of magic, sorcery, devil mongery, and witchcraft, even then terms of denunciation and reproach. The competing specialists no doubt were willing to appropriate methods, skills, and techniques from one another, much after the manner of rival professional magicians in the theatrical world today who try to protect their special skills and tricks by the use of assistants who must furnish bond to guarantee that they will not reveal their employer's secrets. It was no easy matter to distinguish "genuine" Christian miracles from the performances of the godless or rival sects. Whatever proves to have been beneficial is rather likely to acquire good repute. In the Apochrypha Peter distinguishes the Christian miracles from magic on the grounds that the former are beneficial while magic is not. No doubt such distinctions then gave rise to the separation of magic into "black" and "white," the latter being beneficial if a bit outside the official Christian ritual or doctrine. It is apparent that all magic was thought of as an art, a special skill, the efficacy of which was simply not even questioned. A similar embarrassing dilemma was provided by Divine Prophecy as opposed to horoscopes and divination, and Christian ritual as against magic. In the 3rd century A.D. Origen grappled with such problems and came to the conclusion that these were really very different. But he did not attempt to deny the effectiveness of these evil activities; he just assumed that their effectiveness was a function of the work of evil spirits and wicked demons, acting in the service of magicians. It is difficult for us to imagine the intellectual climate of Origen's times. He thought that stars were powerful personalities. Words too, he thought to be powerful agents, not only when used by God, but also when spoken by man. He objected to the casting of horoscopes on the ground that it meant the destruction of the free will of the individual whose future was thus being determined for him! Over 150 years later we find St. Augustine still holding that miracle-working magicians got their results with the aid of demons that they had in their service.

This lack of separation of science from magic persisted well through the 13th century.[5] Roger Bacon shows clearly in his writings that he was still a long way from the contemporary conceptions of magic, science, and religion. He wrote "—the prayers and sacrifices of Aristotle and other philosophers were licit and not idolatrous." He also speaks of "—those magnificent sciences"—which properly employ—"images, characters, charms, prayers and deprecations" as *magical sciences*"! And he apparently used the terms "astronomy" and "astrology" interchangeably. In view of the long years Bacon spent in prison

because of his questioning mind it would not be easy to overestimate the dominance of the church over science during the
Middle Ages. It must be remembered that Bacon was a very
special friend of the then current Pope, Clement IV, who
shielded him for a time. And it was at Oxford that even the
students joined with the monks and friars in denouncing Bacon
as a magician for attempting a few demonstrations or experiments in what we now think of as "science." The cry, "Down
with the magician" echoing there in the halls is eloquent testimony to the total absence of even the faintest trace of a scientific attitude in the world of learning, dominated by the church.
Since the powerful Dominican and Franciscan orders had inter-
dicted research by observation and experiment and the latter
order specifically forbade its members the study of medicine
and natural philosophy about the middle of the 13th century,
it is at least obvious that by no stretch of the imagination could
the church have been described as a patron of science. Against
such a hostile institution even an enlightened Pope was helpless.
Perhaps the kindest thing that can be said is that the church was
a creature of the times. But one would have to add in all honesty
that no other single factor contributed so much to the character
of those times as did the church.

Since the citizen of the Middle Ages classed as "magic" the
phenomena we now think of as "science" it is no wonder that
even learned men of that time thought magic to be true but
evil. What they then accepted as true was not only what we
would today call magic and science, but also the occult arts,
astrology, divination, sorcery, witchcraft, counter-magic, and
superstitions generally. Some Medieval writer might appear
skeptical about some of these beliefs but retain his faith and
confidence in the others. In general there was widespread acceptance of "occult" influences of animals, gems, stars, spirits,
planets, and herbs. Amulets, numerology, lot-casting, the casting
of horoscopes, and dream interpreting were in good repute,
holdovers from the pre-Christian period. Of course the church
with its persistent belief in the existence of evil spirits working
through their knowledge of natural forces, and with its opposition to observational and experimental knowledge was in no

position to offer any systematic attack upon the older superstitions. Official "miracles" violating normally understood causal processes provide perceptive patterns and habits of thought conducive to the acceptance of similar beliefs not officially sanctioned in situations where the personal motivational factors for believing are strong. Medical "miracles" are far more frequently expected currently in cultures whose official religions include traditions of such miraculuous cures. The intellectual climate produced in a culture where those in authority accept miracles, revelations, and incantations, and set their faces firmly against even observational evidence on controversial matters is hardly conducive to objectivity. The "true but evil" magic, or "powerful but evil" knowledge, skills, and techniques were subsumed under the common term "magic" and were officially denounced, as in Roger Bacon's case, as "suspicious novelties." Innovation and newness alone were sufficient for condemnation. As Thorndike eloquently puts it:

"Yet our material has conclusively shown that the history of magic is bound up with the history of science as well as with folk-lore, primitive culture, and the history of religion."—"It is not without reason that the magi stand out in Pliny's pages not as mere sorcerers or enchanters but as those who have gone farthest and in most detail—too curiously, in his opinion—into the study of nature. It is not without reason that we have found experimentation and magic so constantly associated throughout our period."[6] And again—"It is therefore perhaps not surprising that men like Galen, Apuleius, Apollonius, and Dunstan were accused of magic by their contemporaries; that men like Gerbert (Pope Sylvester II!), Michael Scot, and Albertus Magnus (the teacher of St. Thomas Aquinas!) were represented as magicians in later if not contemporary legend; that Lithica and Roger Bacon tell us of the danger of sages being accused of magic; that the Book of Enoch, Cyprian, Firmicus, and Picatrix confuse magic with other arts and sciences; and that no one of our authors (12th and 13th centuries)[7] try as he may, succeeds in keeping magic entirely out of science, or science entirely out of magic."[8] And the intellectual equipment of that day simply did not have separate categories for the miracles of the wonder-workers and the predictable but to them "suspicious novelties" that were emerging at the hands of Roger Bacon and others. All were equally a threat and a challenge to the practices, doctrines, and control of the official priesthood. Even popes like Clement IV and Sylvester II could not go against the main current of the whole institution, and themselves fell under serious suspicion. In the popular mind of the time any close familiarity with the works of nature was inseparable from some unholy connection with the powers of evil. One might well speculate and ponder on the question of what had produced such a state of affairs in western Europe. Just what was the intellectual dead-end that had evolved? Whose vested interests were identified with such a state of affairs?

But a secular wisdom did eventually grow in spite of the severest interdictions against it. Even the unfavorable cultural contact of wartime with the hated infidel brought important secular knowledge into Europe where the crude empiricisms of the alchemists slowly took on organization and practical usefulness. Motivated to cure diseases or produce gold out of baser substances, the kind of knowledge we now know as "scientific" slowly emerged, leaving a residue of discredited beliefs and practices to which the term "magic" clung. Local "magic" first fell into disrepute, but to this very day there persists even in otherwise intelligent circles, a popular belief in the potent powers of a variety of distant specialists in the "occult" that "science" cannot explain; the miracles of Hindu fire-walkers, or of Arabs whose ropes somehow are believed to develop sky-hooks of some sort, enabling these fellows with potent supernatural powers to throw a rope skyward after which they can climb up the otherwise unsupported hemp. Where such feats are solemnly believed to be performed they are not typically referred to as "magic"; they are accepted as good evidence of the existence of forces that transcend the matter, forces, and energies dealt with in modern science. They but reenforce faith in the fundamental rightness of religious beliefs. Such beliefs are eloquent reminders of the state of human wisdom before the emergence of organized scientific knowledge.

One need but turn to the orthodox theological literature of

the 18th and 19th centuries for numberless illustrations of the complete failure to separate "magical" from religious beliefs, practices, and functions. The Jesuit fathers, writing about the New World inhabitants[9] were frequently surprised to find that what the fathers considered ordinary events were ascribed to supernatural agents by the Indians. But sometimes on the same page one will find where the cure of some savage patient or a favorable turn in the weather will be laid to the prayers of some devout priest or to the exhibition of the sacraments. Perhaps a few pages later the author will be berating the savages for blaming some bad weather upon the operations of his pendulum clock. These same missionaries thought the savages gullible to believe their cosmological myths, and perversely wicked for failing to believe the Christian cosmology. But it is not at all unusual to find that the missionary suspects devil-mongery when a tribal medicine-man puts on a good "magical" act whose mechanics he fails to grasp. Even today it is still firmly believed by the "faithful" in many sects that prayers and rituals, that is, those of the *true faith*, will cure the diseases and bring a favorable turn to the weather; and they manage to do this in a cultural atmosphere in which new drugs and vaccines are a commonplace in the news, as is the daily weather-map showing the location of the storm and pressure areas and wind directions that clearly anticipate the weather probabilities.

Let us review then, briefly, the historical background and current meaning of the term "magic" at the end of the 19th century when the European anthropologists began their systematic study of primitive cultures. We find that primitive societies lacked completely any terms or concepts even approximating our usage of the terms: magic, religion, or science. Instead they had established patterns of behavior, habitual ways of behaving under all familiar and recurrent circumstances which they held to be the correct or proper procedure. They might even have had sufficient contacts with other cultures to know that there were also a variety of other, apparently workable, ways of doing things. But in general, foreign ways and practices tended to be suspect, not so much impotent or untrue, but rather evil. In the Roman world the term magic, derived from the name of the

Iranian "specialists in the sacred" tended to become attached to previously held but now outlawed practices as well as to current innovations of minority groups within the Roman culture. These practices were generally held to be potent but evil, along with any and all innovations or probings into nature, and have continued so to be regarded in some areas of inquiry, as for example that of human sex, well into the middle of the 20th century, as illustrated by the reactions in some circles to the famous Kinsey reports on human sexual behavior. Long before the sphere of the scientific was distinguished from the magical the obvious virtues of some processes and techniques that lay beyond the approved "religious" gave rise to the division of magic into black versus white magic, the former malign or evil, the latter benign or desirable. While the term "superstition" was at times in Rome applied to all foreign rites, beliefs, or practices, it also was used to indicate an excessive fear of gods or the supernatural of whatever form, particularly in the areas of beliefs, attitudes, and purely ritualistic observances. It was the more or less overt, specifically and functionally motivated activities aiming at the control of the elements, illnesses, the behavior of other persons, or their well-being or the reverse, that more commonly became categorized as magic, particularly if they pretended to a coercive character, or claimed or pretended to get results directly rather than through the good offices of benign supernaturals. It was, hence, the "mechanistic" character of the embryonic scientific discoveries and devices that caused them to seem to the mediaeval mind identical with the "magical." The transfer to the domain of science of all the genuinely effective processes formerly called "magical" left a residue, a discarded miscellany of false beliefs, reasonings by vague analogies or fortuitous contacts or similarities that were part of the ancient cultural heritage to which the term magic still clung. *By definition*, any beliefs or processes, that were neither part of the accepted ritual of the currently accepted religion nor in themselves demonstrably efficacious, were *magic*. It was this conception of magic that was the basis of Tylor's dichotomy of magic and religion and upon which Frazer elaborated his theory of the nature of magic, and of the evolution of religion out of magic.

Magic and Religion in the 20th Century

Subjectively, the distinction between magic and religion seems to practically everyone simple and obvious enough. Magic, being by definition false or wicked, or both, couldn't possibly be confused with "religion" which was equally by definition true and virtuous. These two categories cause the layman no trouble whatever. He knows exactly what belongs to each. With the serious students of religion and magic, however, matters stand very differently. Quite unconsciously, they practically all seem to assume that magic is a lamentable business at best, while religion is something very different. The question is, however, just exactly what is the difference? Just how are they to be separated, once and for all? What seems obvious and simple to the layman becomes bewilderingly complex the minute curiosity leads one to examine the beliefs and practices of cultures beyond our own. It is the rare treatise on the nature, origin, or evolution of religion that fails to separate the two by a gulf of at least a chapter or two.

A dilemma confronts the large majority of these authors on the subject of religion and magic, resulting from preconceptions out of their past and background. They come into the problem firmly committed to the belief that man, everywhere and always has been and is "religious." They are likewise committed to the conviction that "religion" and "magic" are very different. Hence, what will be accepted as "religious" when it is a question of establishing the universality of "religion" might be indignantly rejected as "not truly religious" when it comes to the question of a distinction between religion and magic! This writer has yet to find where these two questions are considered simultaneously, where the practices and beliefs accepted as evidence of man's universal religiosity are also recognized as "truly religious." Typically, the universality of religion is assumed, after which it is sharply separated from magic, without stopping to consider if the classification of certain practices and beliefs as "magic" might not leave some groups devoid of "religion," as would indeed frequently be the case.

What then, are the distinguishing characteristics of religion and magic that are commonly discovered, or depended upon to make good the dichotomy? Typical is the distinction made by Leuba.[10]

"It appeared to me that the only clear way of separating the religious from the rest of life was not by their end, but by the method or means they use to reach their end. That method is appeal to, and reliance upon, superhuman beings." Burris[11] separates truly religious prayer from magical incantation on the grounds that the former invokes a god or a personal agency of some sort. Also, the prayer assumes that the volitional element rests with the god, but with the operator in magic. Malinowski[12] sees a significant difference of another sort: "While in the magical act the underlying idea and aim is always clear, straightforward, and definite, in the religious ceremony there is no purpose directed toward a subsequent event." Now this really is news! In other words the rainmaking ceremonials of the Indians of the American Southwest are not really religion; any prayer for recovery from illness, or for victory, or even for peace of mind could not be "religion"! On this criterion there would indeed be but few cultures that could be said to have any religion whatever. Yet let us not forget this criterion of Malinowski's; others have expressed similar ideas. They can help us to some real insight into the psychology of religion. What shall we then say of the Kwakiutl who may well revile, curse, threaten, or even "kill" their supernaturals should they fail to "deliver the goods" on demand? Here too would be another group without religion on such a criterion. What shall we do about the Winnebago "practitioners" whose performances are claimed by them to "compel the spirits"; and similarly, gods are "compelled" or coerced to the wills of the practitioners in a wide variety of cultures. The line between such performances and the devout observances in which it is confidently felt that the gods must answer the pleas addressed to them in indeed thin. What shall we say about the many rites and rituals that are on the borderline between all definitions separating religion and magic? There is but one thing that can be said, namely, that there cannot be found any objective distinctions. Any distinctions we make will be meaningless in any culture other than our own. What, for example, are we to do about the beliefs, practices, and criteria of the Zuñi? The nearest thing they have to prayers are fixed formulae that have value only when acquired by purchase from someone who had a previously recognized right to them. Commented a Zuñi on the Christian missionaries: "They throw away their religion (prayers) as if it weren't worth anything and expect us to believe it."[13] That our dichotomies are meaningless in other cultures is apparent from any glance at languages. Except in the western world they uniformly lack words or concepts even for our idea of "religion," let alone for magic or science. Nor do they observe such distinctions practically without the verbal categories. "When the god Pambi sends a drought upon the Manganjas, the priestess of this god offers him a handful of grain, crying out, 'Enjoy this grain and then hear our prayer,' at the same time offering the god a libation of beer, and flinging water into the air, with the usual combination of religious petition and magical science which appears in the ritual of the Australian who seeks magically to control while he religiously entreats the grain power."[14] Nor is this obtuseness limited to the Australians. Chantepie de la Saussaye[15] has this to say: "Jacob Grimm begins his chapter on magic by drawing a distinction between divine Wundern (miracles) and devilish Zaubern (magic),[16] not altogether justly so, inasmuch as Teutonic paganism did not observe the distinction." We have already seen that our word "magic" was derived from a Persian term having with them a meaning equivalent to our word for the sacred. And the name for the Hindu priesthood, Brahman, stems from the terms for charm, rite, formulary, or prayer. The Brahmans were the men who had "brahman" or magic power. No separation there of magic from religion.

Probably the very best summary of the *generally held* similarities and differences between magic and religion is to be found in Goode.[17] Let us note first his excellent summary of the similarities:

"The rather close similarities to be observed in the concrete phenomena stem, naturally, from their relationship to the supernatural. They are (1) both *concerned with the nonempirical.*

They refer to a realm beyond that of the "logico-experimental," to the nonmeasurable, the intangible, where the nonbeliever "cannot see" those elements which are real enough to the faithful. Thus, (2) they both stand in somewhat the *same relationship to Western science,* which itself has imposed this distinction on the primitive. To the primitive society, of course, such a distinction is impossible: the supernatural is as real as what we call the empirical, and the world does not stop at the borderline of the Western scientists' senses.

"Further, (3) both are pervasively *symbolic.* That is, objects which may be ordinary in one situation are endowed with religious or magical significance in another: they *stand* for something else, such as a magical force, an idea, an occurrence, etc. This suggests another similarity: (4) they both deal with nonhuman forces, sometimes called the sacred.

"A systematic symbolism suggests, (5) however, a *ritual system,* and this too, is common to both, the rituals frequently functioning as external representations of the supernatural. As to the things or forces symbolized in the rituals, both systems (6) contain many "anthropopsychic" entities. That is, the entities are dealt with frequently as though they had mentalities like the members of the society; they can be threatened, cajoled, or addressed; they may be whimsical, moody, or vain; their definition of who is worthy to approach is similar, etc. Now as to practitioners, (7) there is usually a specialized (a) *set of skills,* and (b) *select group* holding those skills, for dealing with such forces."

To this excellent summary one might be tempted to add but one more items of similarity: both are held to as beliefs with the tenacity peculiar to all behavior habits acquired under conditions of frustration and conflict,[18] providing thereby some psychological evidence for what is sometimes suspected, namely that there is a qualitative difference in the beliefs held in the area of the magico-religious as opposed to the beliefs held in regard to the workaday world.[19]

If there are seven similarities between magic and religion, there are, according to Goode, no less than eleven differences. These differences, however, are not absolute, yet the distinctions are popularly made in anthropological writing, and seem to be based upon concrete criteria upon which there is considerable agreement. Yet he emphasizes that no sharp, concrete line can be drawn between the two. However, he applies to the problem the concept of polar ideal types in which it is assumed that any given magical or religious system is not concretely found at either extreme, theoretical pole, but somewhere between the two; that any given system of supernaturalism can be expected to exhibit varying characteristics of both religion and magic. To quote Goode:[20]

"The characteristics most prominently emerging in anthropological writings as theoretical aids in distinguishing these two complexes seem to be the following:

1. *Concrete specificity of goal* relates most closely to the magical complex. This overlaps toward the religious pole more than most characteristics, since religious rewards are usually to be found in this world. However, religious goals do lean more heavily in the direction of "general welfare," "health," "good weather," and eschatological occurrences.

2. The *manipulative attitude* is to be found most strongly at the magical pole, as against the supplicative, propitiatory, or cajoling, at the religious pole.

3. The *professional-client relationship* is ideally-theoretically to be found in the magical complex. The shepherd-flock or prophet-follower, is more likely in the religious.

4. *Individual ends* are more frequently to be found toward the magical end of this continuum, as against groupal ends toward the other.

5. The magical practitioner or his "customer" *goes through his activities as a private individual,* or individuals, functioning much less as groups. At the religious extreme pole, groups carry them out, or representatives of groups.

6. With regard to the process of achieving the goal, in case of magical failure, there is more likely to be a *substitution or introduction of other techniques.* Stronger magic will be used, or magic to offset the countermagic of enemies, or even a different magician. Since much of religious activity is less specifically instrumental, is concerned more with the intrinsic meaning of

the ritual, and is expected to achieve concrete goals indirectly, by maintaining the proper continuing relationship with the gods, such a substitution is far rarer in the area of the religious pole.

7. Although the practitioner may feel cautious in handling such powerful forces, a lesser degree of emotion is expected at the magical end of this continuum. This may be described as *impersonality*. At the religious end, one expects a greater degree of emotion, possibly awe or worship.

8. The *practitioner decides whether* the process is to start at all, toward the magical pole. Toward the religious, the ritual *must* be carried out. That it must be done is part of the structure of the universe.

9. Similarly, the *practitioner decides when* the process is to start, in the case of magic, more often than in the case of religion. Toward the latter end of the continuum, the time relationships of rituals are fairly fixed, within rough limits, even when not calendrical.

10. Defined as instrumental by the society, magic is thought of as at least *potentially directed against the society*, or a major accepted group within it, or a respected individual in good repute with the gods. Religious rituals are not thought of as even potentially directed against the society or such respected people.

11. As a final, ideally distinguishing characteristic, magic is *used only instrumentally*, i.e., for goals. The religious complex may be used for goals, but at its ideal pole, the practices are ends in themselves. (All italics as in Goode.)

Now this is really a very excellent summary of characteristics that are *presumed* to distinguish magic from religion in the Western literature of the past seventy years. But it must never be forgotten by the seeker after insight into the psychology of religious behavior that all this dichotomizing is nothing other than a more or less accurate pin-pointing of what the western, predominantly Christian-Jewish culture has rejected as not being properly or truly "religious" out of the varied behaviors we find in other cultures that do not have an obviously instrumental or directly practical character. The evidence is unimpeachable that our separation of the magical from the religious is completely meaningless to the people of other cultures. Slight changes in attitudes or beliefs on the part of the practitioners of these magico-religious performances and we would change our classifications of them. These distinctions between magic and religion but mark the changes in our own culture that have been varying the techniques with which we meet particular problems. Whatever smacks a bit too strongly of methods or practices we no longer apply is now rejected and hence classified as "magic." There is even a tendency, as is the case with outmoded styles, to be most resentful about, and to be offended most by, the very rituals (or styles of dress) that we have but recently, and probably tardily, discarded. I have a friend who becomes ecstatic over an Indian snake dance but cannot bear a hymn-singing Methodist congregation, of the kind he was brought up in. What happens here when behavior, beliefs, or ideas, once psychologically acceptable as "religion" cease so to be? For the most part, the ideas or practices have become technologically obsolete. It is a safe bet that few "Christian Scientists" survive a professional training in bacteriology, or that trained bacteriologists join that church. The Catholic church last pitted prayer against vaccination for small-pox in Quebec about the year 1885 with disastrous consequences for a lot of the faithful. A natural selective process is at work with a vengeance at such times, sharply emphasizing the boundaries of the magico-religious and the scientific-technological. Usually a bit less dramatic but none-the-less effective factors are at work in shaping the boundaries of religion and "common sense" and forming jurisdictional lines that are perhaps never formally established but are yet given practical recognition. To classify the customs of people as "magic" or "religion" on the basis of such polar-ideal type concepts can then at best but anticipate, with considerably better than chance accuracy, what a sampling of observers *out of our culture also,* will do by way of classification of those same customs. That there should be a discernible trend in matters called "magical" or "religious" should not be surprising inasmuch as the separation is increasingly a function of the secularizing consequences of scientific and technological innovations.

One need but examine the concrete history of each of the

eleven differences between magic and religion in our culture
to reveal the changing character of the processes in question.
Take the "concrete specificity of goal" that characterizes the
magical, for example, Every prayer for victory, for recovery
from illnesses, then belongs in the category of "magic." In the
author's library is a Christian prayer-book dated 1689, containing upward of fifteen hundred prayers. These prayers are
specifically tailored to the particular need and request. Practically the entire content would have to be rejected as magic
on this criterion. Or take this matter of the "manipulative attitude"; what are we to do with incense, baptisms, bead-telling,
genuflexion, or candle lighting? As for the "professional-client"
relationship characteristic of magic, how is this to be distinguished from the psycho-therapy the pastor is expected to provide even in the faiths officially lacking the confessional? The
theological seminaries are increasing the time devoted to these
specialities in their ministerial training. "Individual ends" may
be more characteristic of magical attitudes, but there is a large
school of thought that holds that religion is fundamentally an
individual matter, that the social aspects are but the trimmings,
(Wm. James et al). "Variations and innovations in techniques"
certainly have long been under suspicion as magic and opposed
to religion. It is this flexibility of magic, its readiness to try something new and different that gave it credit for being the parent
of science. No doubt there were behavior tendencies making for
stereotypy and repetitiveness as well as for innovation in the
history of various cultures. The psychological and social factors
involved are indeed worthy of extended consideration. It is
rather probable that any behavior that has become a matter of
public performance and hence involves the critical expectational
norms of an entire population would find innovations encountering serious public resistance. Innovation would tend to appear
more often in areas where no such broad social role was
involved, where but a few individuals were immediately disturbed by each variation. It is factors such as this, rather than
anything distinctively "religious" or "magical" that would be
found to be correlated with innovations, or their absence.

If we tend toward a taxonomy of the magico-religious in

which the term "religious" is increasingly reserved for acts lacking specific, individual motivation, then of course such behavior would have to be attached to social situations, seasons, etc. and not to individual, personal, needs or motives. Lacking any immediate bases in native or acquired motives in the individual these "religious" acts would have to become conditioned to particular social cues or situations in which collective patterns of behavior are the initiators, rather than the motivation of particular individuals. Unless, of course, we count the institutional personages in organized religion who collect fees or taxes for their services, or whose prestige is enhanced when they find sufficient grounds for a public performance. Again, this criterion is but a product of a culture in which the practical problems of life are solved on the technological level, leaving little indeed as function for the magico-religious techniques. To say of religious practices that they are ends in themselves, and to literally mean it, is to reveal what is for this day and age a psychological naiveté of a high order. That we no longer cure diseases with religious techniques, nor even attempt to, may well be true of a considerable fraction of the sophisticated contemporary world. But to say of rituals or ceremonials that they are ends in themselves is in effect to leave a mystery as to how they were acquired in the first place. Obviously the communicants who share a given ritual or practice must have at some time or other learned this behavior as "the proper thing to do" in particular circumstances or situations. Are we to hold then that such acts have no behavior history, no antecedents? Or did we come already equipped with these rituals from the hands of the creator-gods as many people have it in their myths? Obviously, all social behavior has a history of some sort. But has there been any rhyme, reason, or direction to that history? Has there been an evolution of some sort in man's magico-religious behavior?

Tylor made his separation of magic from religion at a time when the thinking of the western world had been strongly stimulated by the dramatic, convincing power of Darwin's contribution to the theories of biological evolution. No area of human thought or controversy was immune to its effects. Having been generally identified with the losing side of the evolutionary controversy, organized religion found itself fighting a defensive battle against militant materialists who were all too ready to put theology and theologians into the same category with vestigial organs. It was undeniably true that organized religion in Europe had been locked in a "no holds barred" battle with inductive science almost from the beginning of Christianity.[21] The obvious conclusion from the general evolutionary hunch that the contemporary religions were but the slightly evolved descendents of the crudities of belief and practice of the rudest of cultures was highly unpalatable to all people who respected their religious faith. To separate from "religion" at one stroke all the embarrassing crudities, errors, and stupidities of the past was a taxonomic and philological triumph. The things we no longer believe or practice never were "religion" in the first place! They are mere magic! That too, had its historical precedent: when there was a change in the official religion in ancient Rome, the older practices, now obsolete and forbidden, were designated as magic!

Not only did Tylor separate magic from religion, but he removed magic from religion's family tree by making it a "pseudo-science" which was based upon erroneous association of ideas. Magic then, becomes the progenitor of science instead of religion. Religion remained a pure and undefiled Platonic essence. Frazer[22] agreed as to the basic relationship of magic and science. Thinking in terms of the then current associationistic psychology, Frazer saw magic simply as the product of invalid associations, while science was the product of valid and empirically tested associations. The invalid associations of magic were understandable enough as errors, since they usually involved errors of association by similarity or by contiguity, "homeopathic" and "contagious" magics, respectively. How else could an apparently normal and sane human come to "believe" that damage to a doll gotten up to resemble in some detail a hated person or enemy, would provoke similar damage in the enemy? Just an erroneous association of ideas, thought Frazer. Here we have the effects of the rationalism of common-sense psychology at their worst! Frazer asked of himself, in effect, "what would I have to actually believe to make me construct such a figure or image, then damage it and say that the process will inflict a similar damage on my enemy?" Such logic is the exact equivalent to asserting that the devout Christian, taking the host, is saying to himself, "Now I am a frustrated—or reformed cannibal!" Were one to ask instead "what effects does this sticking of pins into the image have on the feelings and emotions of the practitioner of magic" there would still be left something of a problem in the psychology of learning, but at least we would be on the trail of a deterministic explanation of his actions. But such was the world of magic as Frazer saw it.

In contrast to this magical world of coercive, "deterministic" devices, Frazer saw "entreaty" as the basic rationale behind "religion," but the coercive practices of magic were held to be older, and of course, more primitive. The "age of religion" had everywhere been preceded by an "age of magic," and he held magic to be far more widespread than religion. I quite agree that your typical Christian observer, confronted with the diverse magicoreligious practices in the world would cry "magic" far oftener than he would be moved to say, "there is true religion." The point will not be argued further here. But to return to Frazer's evolutionary interpretation, it has been noted that he assumed that in general, magic preceded religion. In fact, it is Frazer's contention that magic failed, and this failure was first perceived by the brighter intellects of the leaders, while the weaker minds tended to continue clinging to their magic. This is the "failure of magic" theory of the origin of religion. It has a very wide currency; it fit nicely into the frame of thought provided by the theory of evolution, and permitted us to think of religion as a surviving, and hence "fit" entity, and of course disposed of the embarrassing and discredited aspects of religion as "magic." Certainly the gods cannot be coerced, particularly not OUR god; but "entreaty," that is another matter; that is the proper and presumably successful technique that displaced the ineffective magic. The very idea of a god that can be coerced!! But how about bribery? How about a fair exchange, a quid pro quo? How about some ear-warming flattery? Are there gods who might be moved by that? Or by a heap of still beating human hearts? By the sacrifice of a first-born? Or whatever it is that

gods like. A mortal cigarette addict might well walk the proverbial mile for one of his favorite brand, (I saw far more than
that given for one in the aftermath of war in Europe,) but consider the dilemma of the Winnebago gods: for a tobacco offering they are *compelled* to grant the desired favors![23] Just where
is the line between magic and true religion in this matter of
the proper approach to the gods?

Then there is the far more touchy question of the "superiority" of any one method or approach over any other. If magic
"failed" there should be some statistically respectable data to
give the comparison. It seems to me that I recall reading that in
Old Testament days some prophets had sufficient confidence in
their powers or influence with the gods that they entered into
contests of setting their altars afire with prayers: a commendable
precedent! If there is a significant superiority of any sort, other
than of the statistically verifiable kind, then how is it that in so
many cultures both techniques survive, as well as the hopelessly
mixed "type" in which coercive magic is presumed effective
when applied to gods? Where indeed is the evidence that practices we now denounce as "magic" are any less effective than
any gods appealed to by whatever subtlety of approach? If
magic "failed" and was displaced by something that "succeeded," what is the measure of that success? No such evidence
exists of course; nor can any be educed. There is something almost perverse about the data on the favorable intervention in
human affairs by the gods. Recall your Old Testament: it records
periods during which their god seemed to be at the beck and call
of the chosen people, only to be followed by long periods during
which he seemed to turn a deaf ear to their entreaties. It
reminds one of the long runs of "successes" by subjects in "extrasensory perception" tests. They are followed and preceded by
equally impressive runs of worse than chance results. The question of the relative effectiveness of magic and religion is a
sleeping dog that had best be left to lie.

But to complicate matters, there is far from a complete agreement that religion evolved out of magic. There is the precisely
opposite theory that it was religion that gave rise to magic!
Certainly plenty of primitive people credit their gods with hav-

ing originated and given to them the practices and beliefs that
we have no hesitation whatever in calling "magic." And what
are we to say when it is pointed out to us that much of what
we now call magic is but a reversal of religious practices, as in
"black" magic? Surely the "religious" came first here! Durkheim
disagreed completely with Frazer as to just what was magic and
what religion in the life of the Australian primitives, and held
that it was their religion that gave rise to their magic. That
very learned and critical scholar in the field of religion, Hopkins,[24] comments on Frazer's theory that religion is the child
of magic by pointing out that such an origin would be no explanation of the principles of religion since magic itself is
largely religious, adding: "In fact, there is a good deal to be
said for the objection urged by Durkheim, to the effect that
magic is the child of religion rather than that religion is the
child of magic." And Malinowski[25] in speaking of totemic abund-
ance rituals, has this to say:

"This ritual leads to acts of a magical nature by which plenty
is brought about."

Having just told us[26] that ritual, ceremonial, and religion differ markedly from magic we are compelled to add Malinowski to
the list of those who hold that magic grew and grows out of
religon!

Viewed objectively, there can be but one answer to this
controversy over religion and magic: objectively there is no
difference. As Goode put it,[27] "Magic and religion are not dichotomies, but represent a continuum, and are distinguished only
ideal-typically." In other words we, here in this culture, are
making distinctions that certainly are not made elsewhere. And
how does it happen that we are now making a distinction? Very
simply: because the scientific method and habits of thought we
have developed stand at sharp opposites to both magic and
religion in the fundamental concepts of causality implied by
both magic and religion, and where we *recognize* this incompatibility with science in any activities, we call them *magic;* where
we as yet refuse to admit such incompatability but insist that
factors or forces are involved that do transcend our scientific

framework we call it "religion." The issue is very sharply drawn: either one accepts a complete determinism in the universe or he holds out on *some* areas, insisting that here are phenomena that somehow transcend all determinism, causality of a material sort, or the scientifically measurable energies in the universe. Such an area is commonly referred to as "the realm of the spirit." Needless to say, there is no agreement anywhere in the world as to just what constitutes this "realm of the spirit." The area assigned to "the spirit" is without question a rapidly shrinking one in all cultural areas in which the scientific methodology and point of view have taken hold. For good or ill, the really distinctive thing about western civilization is its progressive secularization. That secularization is at bottom a transfer of more and more of the problems of living to an area in which we deal with them by depending upon empirical and experimental findings rather than by appeal to animistic agents of whatever sort: plural, single, benign, or malign.

And just how far has this process of secularization gone in the world of today? To this question there is, of course, no one answer. The answer will, in each case, be a function of the area presumed by each individual to be occupied by, or under the influence of, animistic agents or forces. One can probably assume, and correctly, that animistic beliefs of all sorts are to be found more plentifully at the lower levels of general culture and education. Professional theologians too, are almost of necessity committed to a basically animistic framework of ideas. Yet the theologian must function in the intellectual atmosphere of his congregation, an atmosphere tending increasingly to be dominated by the secularization produced by the impact of scientific method; more, naturally, in some congregations than in others. For some, the gods can be expected to intervene in practically any process; for others there seems to be some considerable doubt that any area whatever remains for "spiritual" intervention. Thus, for example, the editor of the Christian Century, Paul Hutchinson quotes with approval one E. C. Blake whom he describes as "Stated Clerk of the Presbyterian Church in the U.S.A." as follows:[28]

"Church leaders are concerned that people with a new religious interest may attempt to turn that new religion into magic —that is, to try to use God for their own purposes rather than to serve God and find His purposes. To try to use God for any purpose, however noble, is always wrong."

Such a statement must give pause to the serious student of religious behavior. To begin with, this is something rather distinctive in the old attempts to separate religion from magic. Here, apparently, any attempt to achieve anything, presumably by methods other than those employing a materialistic determinism, is ipso facto magic and certainly not religion! Where, might one well ask, would one find agreement with such ideas? In liberal theological seminaries, perhaps, but certainly not in the marketplace where our traditional religions are in competition with Christian Science, the "New Thought" in its many and varied forms, or any of the other modern cults and minority religious movements so sympathetically described by Professor Braden.[29] To remain meaningful and significant to anyone every religion must have content, meaning, application; yes, even practical application. It must have significance and function. If the old problems a religion grappled with no longer exist, the religion must incorporate new areas of significance and meaning or that religion will disappear. Where irrigation is introduced, rainmaking beliefs or rituals, magics or religions must survive, if at all, on substitute meanings or functions still having relevance to the individuals of that group. A concern for the possible purposes of a god, or a zeal to serve such purposes, in a world replete with obvious hedonic, ethical and aesthetic values that can be served, suggests but two possible bases: either a schizoid divorce from reality or a snug, comfortable existence in which the current and practical problems are met with the convincingly adequate equipment of a culture dominated by modern scientific technology, and providing adequately for such an individual. But for the world at large, in that great cultural cradle where magic and religion arose, these phenomena emerged as the specific, the concrete ways in which particular situations were met. And these were practical, personal, or socially shared needs, crises, or even bordedoms that were met with predictable behavior, be it magical, religious, "practical," or, more commonly, a mixture of all three.

Where we meet economic crises with social organization and credit, where we meet disease with organized scientific attack, where we fill the hours saved us by technology with emotional and aesthetic thrills, there indeed we might well be driven, if we retain our gods, to pondering on their purposes or ways of serving them. Not so where famine threatens when no rain falls or game departs or an epidemic strikes; nor even where all is well, nothing to worry about, but time might hang heavily on some, or, as it was once said, the devil was putting mischief into idle hands. There the ceremonial pageantry was movies, motoring, radio and television all in one. It had a practical, here-and-now function. So, gentlemen of the foreign missions, if you hope to sell, yes, even give away, the idea of a god whose purposes are yet to be discovered, be prepared to provide for your potential customers a full, good life, replete with the latest wisdom that will leave them no mundane need to be concerned about. Anything short of that and you had better leave them a god they "can use for their own purposes." It is my considered judgment that had the Russian Communists ordered their priests to preach a religion from their pulpits whose god was not be used for any purpose they would have emptied their churches far more rapidly than they have thus far succeeded in doing by turning their naive, if enthusiastic, atheists loose on them. If any attempt with prayer or ritual to serve some human purpose is magic, then there is indeed but little religion in the world, and its origins will definitely not lead us back into a dim antiquity. We will have but a relatively modern phenomenon to deal with; and Christ, healing those who had faith in Him must of necessity be classed as a magician.

Seven Stages of Magico-religious Belief.

Briefly to condense then some three thousand or more years of the cultural history of western civilization in its relation to the magico-religious would seem to give a picture something as follows:

1. A long period when, as in primitive societies generally, no distinctions even remotely resembling the current distinctions between the magical, the religious, the scientific, or the ceremonial are known or made.

2. A period when foreign techniques or practices come under a general suspicion and give rise to equivocal attitudes. Some of these foreign skills are believed to be highly potent, particularly for evil. The term "magic" became increasingly a term used to designate foreign or outlawed practices. But some foreign beliefs or practices also came to be held impotent or false. To these, increasingly the term "superstition" came to be applied.

3. Magic then came to be generally held to be potent but evil, or sinful. Religion considered effective or potent, but good.

4. Magic is further dichotomized into black versus white magic; the former being potent but evil; the latter also efficacious but good, and distinguished with difficulty from religion.

5. Stage 4 tends to give way to a belief that only some magical powers of some, usually very distant, peoples are potent. But such powers are now held to be more or less neutral, ethically; nor are they particularly feared. Typical are such beliefs as those in the genuineness of the long fabled "rope trick," of which it is widely believed that the Arab or Hindu practitioner can throw a coil of rope skyward only to have it remain fixed there while he climbs, monkeylike up it.

6. At this stage, no magic is thought efficacious; it is, by definition false. But true religion is definitely held to be efficacious in large but generally unspecified areas of human needs and desires.

7. At this last stage it is emphatically denied that even religion has any instrumental uses for man's purposes. But it is generally held by highly advanced theologians that it can effectively be used in serving "God's purposes," the god in question being the trinitarian mystery god of the Protestant branch of western Christianity. This is apparently the position taken by the Presbyterian, quoted just a few pages past.

The first four "stages" of this evolving series of evolutionary steps could be said to have been the effects of a rather long period of contact between a great variety of cultures, and their being slowly brought under the dominant influence of organized Christianity. The last three steps reflect the impact of the slowly developing dynamics of the scientific method.

It is not presumed that exactly all seven of these stages were realized everywhere in the western world. The evolutionary process has been at best spotty and irregular, with both over-lapping and skipping of individual steps or stages. Yet the general, over-all directional trend can hardly be questioned. In every culture area, and at all times, one must expect a very uneven development in different individuals as well as in the membership of different cults and sects. The devotees of both black and white magic are still quite numerous in many cultural back-waters, even in many that have nominally been under Christian domination for centuries.

Were the parsons to begin a widespread preaching of the austere doctrines of our seventh stage they would no doubt empty their churches at a rapid rate and swell the recruits of Jehovah's Witnesses, the Spiritualists, Theosophy, Christian Science, Unity, Psychiana, Father Divine's Heaven and all the other cults preaching a far more instrumental gospel than the staid and respectable churches will allow themselves to indulge in. In fact, this stage calls for an almost unique and specific background in the individual. He must, on the one hand, have been carefully brought up in one of the Protestant branches of Christian faith that has already reconciled itself to the scientific methodology in all but matters relating to the "Spirit." Naive notions of personal salvation, by means of ritually acquired grace or gesture, from the eternal torments of brim-stone fires fed by revengeful, egotistical, and sadistic gods, must have long since become offensive to his ethical sense. He must not even question any longer the operation of a materialistic determinism in areas such as meteorology, path-ology, astronomy, and geology. In fact, he must be reconciled to the idea that such "purposes" as his favorite god has are best deduced from the "laws" under which the universe seems to operate. These laws were, of course, not revealed by this god in any of the sacred writings long ascribed to him; they had to be dug out by the methods of science, to all of which our seventh-stage person is perfectly reconciled. Furthermore, since he realizes that whatever man may wish to accomplish must be limited to a judicious manipulation of energies within the framework of the deterministic principles under which this universe operates, he has accepted all these scientific findings as "manifestations of God's laws," and is, in turn, quite suspicious of any and all claims of miraculous events in which some of these better attested of "God's laws" were presumably set aside. Large sections of today's "believers" assume that of course there are frequent instances where their favorite deity intervenes piecemeal in mundane affairs. But not our seventh-stager.

In the eyes of the exponents of the crasser forms of super-naturalism, our seventh-stager is frequently seen as an apos-tate of far worse fibre than the out-and-out atheist, who rates a certain respect for his brazen fearlessness in flaunting his whole-hearted denial of the supernatural. Yet, from the scientific standpoint, the typical seventh-stager is holding out on a completely secular-scientific slant on things in one or both of two very significant areas: those of the phenomena of the human "mind," and of social ethics. Here most of them develop a scientific blind-spot; they prefer an animistic ac-count of human and perhaps animal behavior. Their grounds for still holding the Bible sacred and divinely inspired are the presumed infallibility of ethics derived therefrom. This con-stitutes the other or alternate wing of the anti-scientific resi-due found at this general level. At bottom they are but two aspects of the same fundamental phenomenon: human behav-ior. Once reconciled to a deterministic view of human behavior one shortly outgrows the need for supernatural sanctions as a basis for ethics.

Words and Word Magic. The psychology of prayer and profanity.

Words are really quite wonderful things. We toss them off in apparently endless variety, a quarter to a half-million per language, each with its distinctive use and function. Try as we will to pin-point the superiority of man over the rest of the animals and in the end we can do no better than to point to the use we make of words. Here we can probably come closer to demonstrating a qualitative difference between an average human and even the brightest among our lowly cousins than in any area. The comparison becomes a bit more complicated when we compare the stupidest human with even an average chimpanzee; but we will still fare best in defending the theory of man's uniqueness by resting our case upon speech. Just what is speech, and what are these words?

Tradition long had it that speech was but a convenient vehicle for the expression of thought; and it was taken for granted that thought of necessity preceded speech, which was assumed to be a product of thought. A rather happy inspiration this speech was conceded to have been at some dim, distant time in the past. Its discovery was long credited with having been a happy accident which came about by some lucky, or fortuitous combination of events which "gave man the idea" of speech, which he then set about to generalize and universalize. This conception was that of man, literally bursting with thoughts and ideas to communicate to his fellow man, but frustrated in these desires till one happy accident provided the model and the insight for social communication. These happy accidents were variously assumed to have been gestural, oral-gestural, interjectional, or onomatopoeic in nature; but in any event each was presumed to have set the pattern or provided the basic hunch or idea upon which man then built systematic languages. The odds are very strongly against any such event sequence having taken place. It is a much safer bet to assume that man has been doing a little talking for a long time, actually about as much talking as he had the structural and neurological bases for; and that the facility of his speech has paralleled the evolution of the structures necessary for that speech. In fact no safer assumption can be made than that in the natural selective process of man's survival no factor other than the effectiveness of his speech mechanisms was at all important. We are, evolutionarily, merely what happened to go with effective speech machinery: tender hairless skins, preposterous kidneys, helpless and prolonged infancy, practically weaponless mouths, and monstrous heads! These things were no advantage in themselves. Far from it. We survived in spite of the handicaps they provided, given the speech mechanisms and the brains necessary for them to function.

Speech begins with the making of laryngeal noises. Noises have great advantages over any other possible cues in communication. They function equally in daylight or in dark; they do not demand a particular orientation as does any form of visual communication. They function very well at a quite considerable distance. And they consume a minimum of energy in their production. It is these characteristics that made communication auditory rather than visual or tactual. We, along with many other animals, have the capacity to make noises efficiently. These noises are in all cases but by-products of other reactions, emotional or organic. Along with other animals, children make then "instinctively"; they are products of their original structures, functioning in an active organism. Such spontaneously and unconsciously made noises disappear in deaf children; that is, most of them do. Those that remain are likely to be highly unacceptable socially and of course the deaf child has no notion of their existence. But in normal animals and children the noises take on great significance; the degree of importance being a function of the capacity the animal has for "doing thing" with the noises!

Basically, what is it we learn to do with our noises? To begin with, it is at this point that animals begin to differ remarkably in what they are fundamentally capable of doing with the noises they can make. The first hurdle on the way to what we think of as true speech, namely the kind we humans have, is that the animal must be capable of learning to imitate its own noises! To put it another way, the animal must be capable of forming ear-vocal reflexes, in which the sound the animal makes, when stimulating its own ears becomes the conditioned stimulus calling out the response of making that same sound! Such reactions are called "circular" reflexes because the response provides the cues that again call out the same reaction. This performance requires a very particular group of structure, or a very special organization of structures, which some animals have, but many more do not. Man, of course, has it. So do birds in some groups, notably parrots and some ravens. Possession of this mechanism is no guarantee of intelligence. Some idiots have the mechanism remarkably well developed; they can repeat almost anything said to them but their behavior can not otherwise be modified or controlled with verbal directions or cues. They are called echolalic idiots and frequently are far from being as bright, generally, as an average chimpanzee. Yet they can repeat words with great facility. All the apes and monkeys are conspicuously lacking in this key capacity.

If to ape intelligence there had been added a parrot's capacity for the formation of ear-vocal reflexes the theory of man's descent from the lower animals would have found far more ready acceptability. To teach an ape to say even a few words is a truly epic task, yet he has a larynx much like the human and certainly is inherently capable of making practically the entire gamut of sounds necessary for human speech. Next time you see a vaudeville performance of an "almost human" ape who is even billed to "speak," watch the performance very carefully. It is a safe bet that among the accomplishments of this lowly cousin of ours will be listed those of beer-drinking, smoking,—they become perfect morphine addicts too—, perhaps match lighting also, but certainly the ape will *blow out* a match whether lit by himself or the trainer. Note the unusual zeal the ape has to blow out that match! And for a very good reason. The lighted match was probably the first step in the painful process of teaching him to say pa-pa— or a sound we will charitably allow to pass for that! The process of education is commonly begun by tieing the animal up firmly, holding a lighted match to his nose and allowing the generalized emotional "explosion" that follows, including the sudden expulsion of air from the lungs, to put out the offending flame. A repetition of the process shortly eliminates from the ape's behavior all but the puffing of the air from the mouth—and of course the zeal to blow out the match. But he is now on the road to speech! The explosive consonantal sound this made becomes the basis for his first verbal accomplishment, which is completed when he is taught to follow that first expulsion of air with the response you make when the doctor tells you to "say ah"! A slow and laborious business at best. No wonder that the vocabulary this sub-human displays is decidedly limited!

How different things are with the normal human child! He not only makes a fine variety of sounds spontaneously but very shortly he reveals the echolalia he is capable of when he repeats the same sound or pair of sounds perhaps a dozen times as he lies on his back, well fed, and unencumbered with excessive bundling. It is when the child has already learned to "imitate itself," to repeat sounds that it has just made, that the environment begins to make itself felt. Any sound from the environment is now likely to touch off the nearest thing to that in the repertoire of sounds already practiced in the child. This is the process by which every child, if it has normal hearing and a reasonably normal intelligence, acquires the language of its land. At the start he could do as well in reproducing the sounds of one language as of another. With years of practicing only one set of sounds the others become increasingly difficult, as he learns to his regret when he begins the study of another tongue.

Speech at this stage is not the expression of pre-formed thought. Rather it is activity in its own right, an effective part of the processes of getting along in the world. Only later does he learn that certain kinds of such verbal activity are by convention kept private. Meantime, he is acquiring a word for everything. Of necessity the child lives a life of social dependency, and increasingly the premium is on effective communication of the details of his own life and social proc-

esses to others. Words become the key that unlocks everything. Instead of adjusting to objective situations he comes
more and more to adjust to distinctive patterns of words.
Verbal statements anticipate objective events; threats and in-
junctions precede and anticipate punishments; verbal requests,
put in just the right form, seem to be practically "money
in the bank," particularly in the event of genuine needs on
the part of the child, such as hungers, thirsts, and distresses
generally. Most important, we all learn to repeat certain
verbal formulae, socially appropriate to particular social situations, which act as stop-gaps, as devices to still apprehension,
to quiet doubts and permit life to go on relatively undisturbed
during dangers, crises, or any serious interruptions of the
familiar routine. A great variety of activities might well
serve as such stop-gaps, but there is such a thing as efficiency
in the human economy and there are undoubted advantages in
an activity that involves a low rate of energy expenditure
and whose pursuit interferes but little with and might even
facilitate other practical or significant operations. Verbal activities are ideally suited to such tasks. They involve a very low
rate of energy expenditure and offer minimum interference
with the activities' demanded by the workaday world.

Words have another decided advantage in the processes
of thought or of control by preestablished patterns of symbols.
Their social usage tends to give them a certain exactness, a
certain social definition impossible of attainment in the world
of private images of whatever sort. That is probably the reason
why young children begin life with a rich imagery only to
find that with the years such processes disappear, perhaps even
to the point in some people that they deny ever having had
any, and doubt very much that others have them. The socially
"standardized" words prove by and large to be so much
more useful and dependable.

Such social standardization of verbal symbols does not
necessarily produce a symbol system corresponding exactly
with reality. It can result in fictions, illusions, or social myths.
But fact or fiction, actions based upon them tend to fit
the individual smoothly into his social world. This tends to

create a social reality that is workable. Belief and credence go with such workability. Such is the psychological basis of the social fictions of the various cultures, so diverse and so obviously not based on objective fact that members of each cultural fraction are amazed that such fictions are acceptable to the people in cultures other than their own. "How can they possibly believe such things?" is the private verdict of every believer when confronted with beliefs other than those currently acceptable to him.

But the familiar beliefs are distinctive patterns of emotionally reenforced action tendencies attached to particular words, phrases, objects, symbols, or institutional persons. These actions themselves are largely familiar verbal patterns, statements of creeds believed, reiterations of principles, or denunciations of specific evils or errors. Since many beliefs consist of nothing other than a stereotyped creed or articles of faith about which little is ever done other than to repeat them when the question arises, there develops for many people an isolated realm of absolutes and certainties existing in a verbal framework, in fact having little reality outside this realm of subjective emotionality, controlled largely by social and self-provided cues. How such intense emotional reactions can become attached to particular verbal stimuli is beautifully illustrated in an experiment by Diven.[30] With a delicate galvanometer attached to his subjects to record the changes in potential that mark emotional disturbances, the subjects were instructed to give their verbal associations to lists of words. After 12 seconds of such associations they would be given another word to start a new series of associations. The list however contained the word "red" which was always followed after 12 seconds by "barn." But 12 seconds after this word was given, the subject was also given a rather painful electrical shock on the leg, before being given another word on which to associate. This sequence of "red," "barn" and then shock was repeated six times in the long list of words used. The subjects were then tested for residual evidences of emotional conditioning by running through the word-list again, but without any shock following the word "barn." Some subjects were tested five minutes after the first trials, others at 24 and 48 hour intervals. Far from a general weakening of the galvanic reaction with time, the 24 and 48 hour intervals revealed stronger residual galvanic reactions than were found only five minutes after the original conditioning. Before retesting for galvanic conditioning the subjects were asked to recall as many of the original words as they could. Recalled or not, the words would then be repeated and the conditioned galvanic reactions recorded. As was to have been expected, the word "barn," and to a less extent the word "red" which preceded it now called out strong galvanic disturbances. All words having a rural connotation such as plow, pasture, sheep, hay, and cow also now gave increased galvanic deflections in all subjects but one, and that subject knew nothing of the English language! Almost half of Diven's subjects could not recall what word or words had preceded the shock, but these subjects appear to have retained stronger conditioned disturbance to these words than did those who recalled them.

From Speech to Prayer

This then, seems to be the process by which emotions of all sorts can become conditioned to names, pictures, places, or symbols; above all, to words. Once the conditionings to words are established the words can be spoken by persons other than those whose power or prestige initially aroused the emotions in question. The same words might well come from a tape or wire recorder and still produce the familiar effect. On June 21, 1955 the New York Herald Tribune reported the following from Scarsdale, N. Y., a town situated in the county having the highest per capita income in the United States;

"Recorded one-minute inspirational prayers, available to telephone callers since the service was established early this spring by the Hitchcock Memorial Presbyterian Church here, have proved so popular that today the New York Telephone Co. added a second outlet to take care of the incoming calls."

It is interesting to note that where hypnotic techniques are used to aid an individual in overcoming insomnia, tobacco or other drug habits, the busy hypnotic practitioner often found that after some practice in hypnotizing the patient by the more usual devices requiring the presence of the operator, he can often get the patient into the proper state by means of a time-saving telephone call. It forms a happy transition stage to the desired one in which the patient in effect is able to "hypnotize" himself, to get the same effective results on his own behavior with the proper verbal formulae, much after the manner in which the hypnotist gets the results by telephone. Insofar as any therapy is possible in disorders that seem on the face of them to be disturbances of habit functions, such reform of habits must of necessity be a process of establishing a certain priority or dominance of self-provided, usually verbal, cues over the action systems of the individual. For the most part this involves rather far-reaching control over visceral activities by a proper manipulation of self-provided cues.

Unless one is to assume a crass and piecemeal contranaturalism in which the events of the world are subject to a moment to moment intervention in their normal courses by agencies at the beck and call of individuals equipped with the proper ritual devices, the actual effects of prayers and rituals of all sorts must be seen in terms of the behavior consequences such devices have upon the participants and witnesses of such acts. And make no mistake about it, these effects are very real. But it must not be forgotten that the devices used, the nature of the objectives sought by these means must be subtly attuned to the general cultural sophistication of the communicant if they are to be effective. Sensibilities are all too easily offended in this area. This is beautifully illustrated by an earnest seeker after truth in this problem who wrote as follows:[31] "Polytheism encourages unscientific prayer. Indeed, the average modern conception of prayer, as a means of bringing about a change in the purpose of God, is a remnant of Polytheism."[32] It is clear that to this gentleman any prayer or ritual aimed at any intervention in the clearly determined course of events in this universe is an anachronism, in spite of the fact that he obviously concedes that "the average modern conception of prayer" is that of a process that can achieve precisely such results. Few indeed are the devout individuals who are completely reconciled to admitting that their ritualistic procedures can at best be expected to effect certain minor changes or revisions in their own desires, frustrations, or disappointments. Even where the general level of sophistication is one at which the individual might be expected to come to such a conclusion it would not necessarily be fatal to the continuance of ritualism. There are two derivative Hindu sects in whose beliefs no assumption is made that any supernatural processes are affected by worship or supplication. In the Jaina sect temples and ceremonies with prayer and sacrifice are maintained without such beliefs, and Buddhism assumes that Gautama is unconscious and inaccessible, and the moral universe beyond man's power to alter, yet they too have devotions. Psychologically this is of course perfectly possible since religious rituals do not follow upon related or relevant beliefs; they are a function of psychological laws and processes wholly of another sort as has been fully set forth in another chapter. What must be kept in mind is simply that words and formulae become powerful emotional triggers, strong enough to neutralize the effects of previously acquired uneasiness; as for example, when an individual, made apprehensive of the dire consequences of certain almost unavoidable ritual violations, is then put at ease by another formula that guarantees, or at least promises, forgiveness or absolution. Hence too, the very real power charms, spells, and cantrips of varied sorts have to protect against ghosts, devils, jinns, or haunts. At bottom such human tribulations are contests between conditioned emotion arousing stimuli in us poor bedeviled mortals.

The advantages that prayers have over practically all other forms of ritualistic behavior are many. To begin with, words are

potent conditioners of activity of all sorts in man, due to
the vital role they play in his workaday world. A large
part of all human behavior is conditioned to verbal cues.
Words have the great advantage of requiring but infinitesimal
expenditures of energy. Then too, verbalizing can go on while
causing but a minimal trifling interference with other ongoing
activities. Everywhere, man can continue to persist in his
fairly autonomous verbalizations. Given sufficient such and
"Stone walls do not a prison make, Nor iron bars a cage." With
the aid of words, a convincing phantasy-life can come practically
to ignore grim or unpleasant realities in the world of the
flesh. Most important for our purposes, namely that of understanding the nature of religious behavior, is the unquestioned
fact that persistence of attitudes of belief toward any ritual
or prayer is almost completely unrelated to effectiveness of
such behavior in controlling the events of the world of the
believer. The psychological processes involved are discussed
in another chapter.

Profanity

All cultures apparently have some taboos in regard to the use
of certain words or expressions or the mention of particular
subjects. There are profanities and obscenities in all languages,
their origins in dim antiquity long lost. The specific commandment in the Mosaic decalogue which is invoked as the
basis for the taboo against any inappropriate use of sacred
names is apparently an evolutionary product according to some
students of such matters.[33] There is good evidence that the
commandment against taking the name of the lord in vain
started out as "Thou shalt not call on the lord when thou
art empty handed," or perhaps, "Thou shalt not see my face
empty handed." In Judaism this eventually became a complete
taboo against the pronouncing of the name of their god at all,
while with the Quakers it became the basis of a general en-
joinder against the taking of all oaths. In popular belief it
is commonly thought to forbid the use of the word "god" as

the subject of the verb "damn," or similar invocations of sacred characters.

Very interesting are the almost universal sequelae that follow upon the tabooing of the utterance of any word. Each such taboo gives rise to a whole host of nonsensical but alliterative expressions such a dog-gone, darn, dickens; oh sugar! shucks! shavings! etc. where it is easy to see what the tabooed expression is that is being capitalized upon and where the right-thinking and morally correct users of such substitutes are even a bit surprised at the shock effect produced in themselves by the use of what are on the surface perfectly innocent and "pure" words.

Where any belief exists that potent agents can be invoked by the use of words there is bound to appear apprehension as to the legitimacy of their use. There is also almost certain to be a concern that the benign agencies be not offended by any improper attitude shown toward them. Such apprehension tends to be stilled by a meticulous attention to the correctness of detail of the proper rituals, procedures, and formulae. Since the intervening agents cannot be directly observed and all that mortal man can perceive is (a) the invocation, and (b) the consequences, both praise and blame tend to attach to the invocation. In short, prayers, oaths, or curses, are perceived as more or less free-floating agents in themselves, and, like the persistent Northwest Mounted are thought, in the end, to "get their man," to have their consequences. Untoward events are likely to be laid to some preceding irregularity in the ritual attitudes and procedures. The words invoking action come to be reacted to as the powers sparking the action.

Similar processes are at work in some cultures where there is a great apprehension in regard to the use of names. The name is not too well separated, psychologically, from the thing or process itself. Piaget noted a similar tendency on the part of children unconsciously to identify the name with the thing. In a variety of cultures, notably the Chinese, there is a genuine secretiveness about one's "real" name; meantime some designation, usually of a derogatory sort, must serve for the practical purposes of social communication and control. The secret and unmentionable name of the Hebrew god is another case in point, illustrating just how far such an attitude can be carried, once initiated. The potency of the thing designated tends to adhere to this symbol which conventionally designated it. This is the essence of word magic. The invoking of the word itself is filled with dangerous potentialities. Conventions then develop in each culture as to precisely the circumstances and situations under which any such potent forces are to be invoked, and when any such words are to be spoken. The violation of such conventions tends to be taken seriously and to be conspicuous in direct proportion to the awe in which the invoked agencies are held. Nor is there necessarily any formal punishment prescribed for their violation. Far from it. As is frequently the case with taboo violations, the retribution for the offense is not one that needs a social penalty to insure its enforcement. The taboo is violated at the peril of the offender; he takes upon himself the risk in so doing. His fellow citizens may well be shocked by the violation or stand in awe of the reckless fellow; but frequently there is no social punishment prescribed.

In such a case the stage is set for an interesting development, socially. The taboo violator perceives the effects of his daring on his fellows and notes their awed reactions. The taboo violations, the utterance of dangerous words become effective attention-getting devices requiring neither great skill nor effort, once sufficient skepticism in regard to the presumed ritual dangers is acquired. Such profanity then becomes not only an attention-getting device but also a method of becoming the object of an awed respect, much after the manner of the juvenile delinquent who has become a "big shot" by a killing, and for whom the consequent prison term consists merely of a validation of his title and honors. A similar process is at work, psychologically, in the procedures by which a man becomes an hippopotamus hunter among some Nilotic tribes. He is expected to violate even the strongest taboos in demonstrations of his invincibility, the final or graduating step being to commit incest with his own daughter or nearest female relative.

The precise nature of the taboo violation is wholly unimportant. The psychologically significant factor is simply the social reactions to the behavior deviation. Of course there is a certain amount of agreement as to the nature of the verbalizations that become taboo, and hence in the areas or topics that can provide a basis for profanity of speech. In addition to the already discussed "sacred" topics and entities that are frequently objects of such speech taboos and "obscenities," references to excretory functions are commonplace. The physiological and psychological factors giving them far more than a chance quota of such attention should be apparent. Any topic or function likely to involve strong emotions, such as sex, reproduction, ancestry and heredity is likely to appear in any catalog of obscenities everywhere. The fluidity of the conditioning process is however such that almost any word or term can take on practically any emotionally coloring. In a land full of dog lovers implications of identity with that animal might well be a fighting insult, as is the charge that canine ancestry is to be found on one's distaff side. In another culture an identification with an animal might well be a form of flattery. To be verbally degraded to a pig is probably quite disconcerting in many languages; in French the pig must be blue to assign one to the nadir of the existence scale. To really insult a German he has to become a pig-dog, a hybrid in which presumably the worst traits of both animals are dominant. In England, any character or condition is terrible if qualified as "bloody." This last is a particularly interesting illustration of the fortuitous factors that can give a word emotional potency. It is probably a case of the sight of blood as a concomitant to a painful injury, or menstrual taboo that provides the basic emotional possibilities. But any word or expression can get its potency from the attitude, manner, and circumstances under which it is used. But every profanity and every obscenity derives its emotional value in the user from the attention and reaction getting capacity of the expressions in his social world. Expressions that are ignored in a culture are again dropped by the individual should he fortuitously initiate or imitate them. Before it can provide the bases for obscenities a topic must involve emotions of considerable intensity. It is its attention getting and shocking power that makes it a likely device for profanity.

The understanding of its psychological character also provides the correct key to its control in the young. If a great to-do follows on the heels of a child's chance repetition of some expressions it has heard, the odds increase that the expression will recur in any subsequent situation where the child might be motivated to draw attention to himself or where the situation is similar to the one in which the expression was first elicited. If the child is punished for such expressions in an atmosphere of hostility, then a situation involving hostility toward parents, or for that matter anyone else, is likely to elicit a repetition of the forbidden usage. An attitude of indifference is probably the best for meeting the child's first venture in obscenity. If it recurs, assume the best imitation of disinterestedness you can muster and warn the child that there are situations where such words are considered very improper and that using them might let him in for considerable unpleasantness. Worst of all is to act as if a great crime had been perpetrated. That would but serve to convince the child that it had hit upon a really potent device, something that can make adults squirm and writhe. And that is a dangerous discovery for a child to make! The avoidance of emotional tensions in regard to such items is of prime importance. If a child has already acquired such habits of expression from others it is probably quite effective to discuss the fortuitous character of the adult reactions to these words. To reveal the process in its humorous aspects is an effective tension reducing device. It is as cathartic and as effective as to point out the adolescent wanting to start smoking, the origin of his motivation in the zeal to be big, grown-up and daring, especially the latter.

Chapter VI

THE THEORY OF RELIGION IN EVOLUTION

That there has been in western civilization a general shift or change in the whole nature and scope of magico-religious practices is all too obvious. Not only within the lifetime of the ordinary individual of recent generations, but, viewed in the entire historical perspective the changes are even more marked. This has given rise to much speculation as to the general trends revealed. The most popular theory, following on the heels of biological evolution, was a similar postulate for religion, placing monotheism at the apex of the evolutionary pyramid.

Andrew Lang and other anthropologists have given this postulate sharp criticisms. It is apparent that the notion of a "high" god is not such a late or rare product as it was once thought to be and a more critical examination of our so-called "higher" religions shows them to be quite far removed from the ideal of all supernatural forces boiled down to one. Christianity is at best trinitarian, with Madonna worship thrown in for good measure. Allah has a whole host of dubious and more or less autonomous jinns sailing about. Judaism has a devil and Jehovah is content with a demand that his followers "—Have no other gods before me"—a long way from a hardy denial of the existence of others, and at best, but asserts priority over them. On top of this, it appears obvious that the "high" god notion and that of a creating spirit are fairly common among some of the most primitive of cultures,[1] even if but little ritualistic attention may be paid to them.

Father Schmidt and Catholic anthropologists and philosophers generally, have also taken sharp exception to the evolutionary view. The church, having taken a rather dim view of evolution theory from the start, and by tradition committed to the creation myth of Genesis, finds it easier to hold that primitive beliefs and practices are but a degeneration from an original, a pure monotheism. That there are quite primitive groups who accept the idea of a high god there can be no doubt. Creator gods too, are widely distributed and encountered. But a high god would rarely also be credited with the original creative activities, and, although it might be conceded in a given society that a particular god existed and was indeed a "high" or most powerful god, much more ritual observance might well be offered some deity having much more circumscribed functions or powers.[2] So too, a particular god might well be credited with the creating function but given no ritual attention whatever. Their attitude then seems to be: "yes, he created things (or the world) but now that it is here we are much more concerned with such-and-such which happens to be the province of god so-and-so!" That the high god is necessarily also the creator of the universe is far from being a universal belief. The proponents of the theory of an original, pure monotheism have been a bit too ready to interpret as a belief in a high or only god the various manifestations of the mana concept, the idea of an impersonal, unmoral energy, highly potent for both good or evil, depending upon just how it is handled or manipulated. But the weight of evidence is against them.

If then, there is no clear-cut case for the evolution of religion itself in a particular direction or toward a particular goal or culmination, and if there is a certain amount of ambiguity as to whether magic evolved out of religion or vice-versa, is there not some simple, common-denominator idea or concept or assumption, perhaps unconscious, that is nonetheless the core content of all religion and perhaps even of magic? Tylor assumed that core idea or common denominator was what he called animism: the belief in spiritual beings. Everywhere, he held, are such beings believed to exist. Now the term "spiritual" in the western world was defined as the negation of the "material"; and spiritual beings, then, could not possibly have any material attributes. A long line of philosophers beginning with Plato had been talking in such terms for some two thousand years, and western religions had adopted the idea, finding it compatible with the theory of an immortal soul. In due time it became part of the "common sense" equipment of the western layman. Matter is matter, spirit is spirit, and never shall the twain be confused or held identical. To find such a concept the unquestioned equipment of man, everywhere, gave it the respectability of universality, and seemed to provide for popular faith an instinctive or innate base. The only difficulty with this animistic hypothesis is simply that no primitive society has as yet been caught believing it! Any existence apart from materiality of some sort, however diffuse or attenuated, is rejected by these naive children of nature. With a certain percentage among us, and with some Asiatics the belief will pass muster, nowhere else. A belief so universally rejected by "primitive" people will give even an enthusiastic theorist pause in his zeal to use animism as a root idea upon which to pin the origin of religion. It shortly dawned upon at least some speculators that the western idea of a "spiritual being" was not at all a simple concept, that it was in fact a highly developed and complex idea, not to be found among nor expected of primitives.

Was there then to be found a simpler concept that might furnish a basis for religion? Marett[3] believed that the tendency of all peoples to ascribe the characteristics or attributes of the living to the non-living was such a concept: simpler, universal, and capable of serving as a vehicle for religious beliefs and practices. Viewed from a slightly different point of view this was a tendency to treat the impersonal as if it had personality. Certainly all people at some time react to impersonal objects or events with behavior patterns previously practiced toward personalities; to animals, if not to stones. And who is to say that a particular animal has, or has not, a personality? Certainly the process is universal and natural enough. Such a tendency he called *animatism,* which he held was not in and of itself religious, but was potentially, religious. Treating the impersonal universe as if it were a personal god is such an animatism.

When more careful anthropological research began to do a better job of reporting what primitive people actually did and believed it became apparent that where earlier observers had reported a local belief in a Great Spirit, or a Supreme Spirit, or powerful god, there frequently proved to be beliefs far removed from that western obsession. Instead many indeed of these primitive tribes were found to ascribe a large variety of phenomena to what was not otherwise describable but as an *impersonal* energy, force, or potency. Such forces or energies seemed to have none of the attributes commonly identified with the "religious"; but it is obvious that there is nothing to prevent such forces from acquiring the attributes or characteristics of religious agencies, or of playing characteristically religious roles. But is must be remembered that our categories of the religious as opposed to the secular have no clearcut equivalent among primitive societies. Certainly they distinguished the unusual from the commonplace; the relatively safe from the hazardous, the practically certain from the wholly uncertain outcome. Such distinctions might be illustrated by the consequences involved in the bite from a non-venomous as against a venomous snake; where venomous snakes abound the inhabitants have distinctive categories for the two situations. But such a distinction is a far cry from our distinctions between natural and supernatural. Yet it is rather likely to be the nearest approximation to such a difference to be found in primitive culture.

Where or when can a concept of the supernatural then arise? Only, of course, where there already is developed a clear concept of the "natural." The western concept of the "supernatural" has no exact equivalent in primitive society. It not only implies the immediate impression of the unusual, the uncanny, and unnatural, but it implies much more than that: it implies in addition that even if we were to become much better acquainted with the phenomenon in question it would prove in the last analysis to be outside the realm of ordinary, mundane, or deterministic causality. This implies a sophistication to which there is every evidence that primitives are strangers. The realm of immutable, mechanical, or deterministic processes is for them a much reduced area, as it is indeed for the lower levels of sophistication in our own culture. The culture pattern provides them with specific habits with which to meet particular situations. The "logic" of these patterns is seldom questioned. They might appear to us as magical, religious, or devil-mongering. They might astound us with their mechanical ingenuity, or move us to pity by their utter futility. They might seem to imply a variety of beliefs that to us are completely incompatible. We might well imply to them some amazing beliefs which seem to us to be assumed by them, but to which they are complete strangers. There are, no doubt, perfectly adequate psychological and historical bases for their behavior, but these are highly unlikely to correspond to the historical steps that produced our familiar habits of action and our thought processes.

Nor is there any evidence that any one of these concepts or habits of thought is older, or associated with the more primitive, than the other. In fact, a careful examination of both language and action in a wide variety of cultures shows clearly that everywhere the unusual, the uncanny, is contrasted with the familiar, the commonplace. Everywhere causal relations seem to be presumed to exist on the basis of dubious evidence, which we designate as a belief in magic. Everywhere relatively diffuse or invisible agencies are presumed to have causal efficacy of varying sorts, which we designate as "animism." Everywhere we find people under some circumstances or in some situations treating the impersonal with behavior "logically" appropriate to personalities. And everywhere we find the recognition of some forces, some processes, as having impersonal characteristics, and most commonly a name for such impersonal force or agency, be it mana wakan, orenda, manitou, or pokunt. Nor need such a term be always used as if it implied an impersonal agency; it might well be given the characteristics of a personality in some particular context.

Motivated by this quest for some simpler, more elementary

idea or concept that could mark the beginnings of what ultimately became full-fledged religion every angle and aspect of
primitive behavior has been examined. Durkheim sees the beginnings of the sacred in the totem which symbolizes the
social group. It is from the individual's subservience to the
group, from his dependence upon it, that he acquires his basic
concept of the "sacred," the unquestioned authority. The group
identifies itself with the totemic symbol, and the individual
comes to attach to the totem the emotions originally induced
by his relations to and dependence upon the group. An ingenious theory, and not without some plausible bases in fact.
It is probably a mistake to make the assumption that there
is one fundamental "RELIGION," everywhere the same and
having the same origin. It would seem highly probable that in
some cultures the individual might well acquire such attitudes
as he has of sacredness from or by such a process as this; a
process that is, psychologically, quite familiar in the area of
the acquisition of patriotic allegiance and devotion to the flag or
symbol of the national group. But one might well ask then,
how do non-totemic cultures acquire their religions in the absence of a venerated group-symbol? There is plenty of good
evidence in many patterns of religious behavior that the familiar
figures of the family provide the basic emotional attitudes that
are organized into the formal structure of the religious system.
The parent-child relationship has certainly colored strongly the
character of the postulated supernaturals of the Judaic-Chris-
tian religions whose god can hardly be conceived apart from
the father symbol, and more particularly in Christianity where
the balance of the family comes in for a considerable share of
ritual devotion in addition, as if to provide a clincher for the
argument. And why not? If the individual's earliest emotional
experiences are not to color his later perceptions and thought
patterns, what, might one well ask, should determine them? If
a child is brought up in a social group in which the role of his
biological parents looms relatively less conspicuously than that
of a clearly symbolized group entity, that too can be expected
to leave recognizable marks upon his value systems and thought
patterns.

If then, there is a certain plausibility to the theory of religions deriving their emotional content-value from the human social group itself, be it the family or the clan or tribe, one need but remind himself that it is probably expecting too much to find a single origin for such widely diverse behavior manifestations as those provided by the magico-religious customs of a thousand or two different culture patterns.

The custom of the fetish, the kes-kam-zit, or whatever name it goes by in its diverse manifestations also warrants consideration in this quest for religious origins. Totems and fetishes are of course nicely separable by definition; a totem is always a class of objects: all bears, crows, or ginseng plants, etc., while the fetish is always a particular object, and usually too, an object of devotion, awe, or respect of but few persons, usually only one. In actual life, it is much harder to maintain nice, clear-cut distinctions. The term fetish is derived from the Portugese name for the beads, medals, or images the Christian sailors wore "to ward off evils." The early sailors, exploring the African coast found the natives similarly wearing a variety of objects and gave them the name they applied to the things they themselves wore. The essence of the fetish belief is simply that a particular object has unusual potency for good for its possessor. It might acquire this potency by receiving special treatment at the hands of a priest. Or it might be spontaneously ascribed to it by its maker, or finder, if the object is of a ready-made sort. By whatever course of events, the object is now believed to have uncommon or unusual powers. The same kind of an object might be generally accepted in a group as effective; or, each individual could identify or select his own. Such a fetish is then often addressed, appealed to, in short, personified. At what point would such an appeal, addressed to a fetish, become indistinguishable from a prayer? It is apparent that behavior that would seem to be genuinely "religious" might have had such humble beginnings. By what sort of psychological process is the primary attachment acquired? In some plains Indians the custom of the Kes-kam-zit makes this quite clear. Here the initial attachment to the object might well have a history something as follows: A brave starts on a hunt, let say an antelope hunt. Pausing to rest, a pebble catches his eye; he picks it up for closer examination and surely enough, the pebble has an unmistakable resemblance to an antelope. Suspecting it to be an omen of good luck, he adds the pebble to his medicine bag. Should the hunt have a successful termination, credit for the success can attach to the pebble that seems in some way attuned to the hunter and his desires. It could long remain a prized possession. On the other hand, if failure followed upon failure the ill-omened pebble might be roundly cursed, spat upon, and thrown away. Later another charm might be given a chance to demonstrate its prowess. Now it is obvious that in these cultures there is built up the expectation that such valuable and potent objects are to be found, and no doubt that sets the pattern and increases the frequency of such attachments. The effects of *Einstellungen* or postural sets being what they are, predominant interests and motives are almost certain to determine perceptions. Here are the essential psychological elements that can stack the cards in favor of the formation of irrational attachments. The author recalls strolling along a pebbly beach as a small boy with several companions. One of the boys picked up a flat pebble upon which the quartz veins traced out unmistakably his initials. It is difficult to describe the reaction of the group to that evidence of the cosmic importance of one of their fellows! A great hunt followed for similar evidences of greatness, but without success. The irrationalities of the fetish have none-the-less a certain psychological logic. A variety of events can give exaggerated values to particular objects. Once an object is treated as a personality it is but a short step to addressing requests to that object, or adding anointments or libations or even sacrifices. Such activities can become a group norm. As Malinowski[4] has it: "The existence of totemic clans and their correlation with cult and belief is but an instance of departmental magic and of the tendency to inheritance of magical ritual by one family." This would seem to imply that individual innovations can become family norms, and family norms can become clan or larger group norms. How else, one might well ask, could any group behavior norms arise? This would seem to imply the possibility of religion evolving out of such individual behavior mechanisms as here suggested. Yet Malinowski[5] apparently prefers it otherwise for he says: "Totemism appears thus as a blessing bestowed by religion on primitive man's efforts in dealing with his useful surroundings, upon his struggle for existence." This obviously implies that religion precedes and is older than totemism! One is probably on safer grounds in suspecting that some activities now popularly identified as "religious" may well have had a history such as that sketched above. We can leave to the philosophers the problem of *THE* Origin of Religion or any similar question implying but a single origin for so great a diversity of activities, beliefs, and rituals as now comprise the magico-religious.

Specific practices or behaviors probably each have their individual origin. That all these diversities should have a single, a common, or a root idea or hunch behind them is hardly to be expected. Human behavior typically is not preceded by either a general or specific "theory" or "hunch" or "logic." We do not act, typically, because we have a reasoned basis for the act in question. Typically, our behavior is a function of past habits conditioned to the cues provided by each particular situation. In bona-fide trial and error situations even the "correct" reactions we finally come to make are usually something of a surprise to ourselves. We have no idea how we came to make them; no verbal logic or idea preceded their appearance. To look for a single item of logic, a common theory or belief behind all the diversities of habits mankind has acquired for situations in which he has no simple, effective, and direct solution is to look for something human behavior shows no evidence of having, even for the situations it has under effective control. The relatively diffuse, invisible, but nonetheless effective forces and agencies that man encounters produce everywhere the ideas or verbal habits we can correctly call a materialistic animism, the naive animism of primitive peoples everywhere. No child can survive without acquiring habits of behavior appropriate to personalities. Similarly, forces with which the element of personal involvement is at a minimum or even completely absent, are everywhere to be encountered, and verbal habits ap-

propriate to them inescapably follow. That man, lacking more
specific and appropriate behavior in the face of some crisis
or problem should meet the situation with such habit equipment as he has, should cause no surprise. What, then, could he
be expected to come up with? Surely nothing other than whatever it is that his past learning has provided. The world of
human experience being what it is, no individual can avoid acquiring the habit equipment that psychologically constitute
animism, animatism, and the mana concept. There is, however, no
basis whatever for holding that either of these concepts is more
primitive, or psychologically simpler than the rest. All three are
spontaneous reactions of man to some aspects of the normal
environment. It is the animism that sharply denies any materiality whatever to "spiritual" entities that is a relatively recent
and not too widely held concept.

Nor can one go along with any "failure of magic" theory
as an account of the changes that have taken place in the magico-
religious, or any evolution they may have been subject to. The
term "failure" suggests that one failed where the other succeeded. But where any sort of specific results are expected or
used as a criterion of success it is doubtful that any superiority
can be shown. The physiologist, Professor A.J. Carlson is reported
to have narrowly missed dismissal from a theological seminary
for suggesting a statistical check on the efficacy of prayers for
rain.[6] The "superiority" of religion over magic is not to be found
in such statistical criteria. Since it is frequently to discarded
practices that the label "magic" comes to be attached, one is
confronted with the problem of discovering how some practices
came to be discarded. They were not abandoned because they
were magical. They were discarded first and labeled afterward.

Probably the only thing that can be said in regard to the
direction of the changes in these practices is that they have
slowly altered so as to remain not too inconsistent and incompatible with the rest of the cultural pattern; that is with
the mechanical arts, the general trial and error knowledge, or
that derived from culture contacts. This compatability with
the balance of the culture pattern must not be interpreted
too strictly or narrowly. For, not only has man a marvelous

capacity for "segmental behavior" or "logic tight compartments," but his ability to rationalize even glaring inconsistencies in his conduct or beliefs is familiar to even the novice in the study of social behavior. Not only that, but in most cultures the human economy operates on a large, safe margin which enables many a culture to carry a surprising load of practices that are a downright handicap, not to mention many more that are at best innocuous. Then too, many a culture has disappeared under an inflexible load of obsolete customs, magico-religious as well as "practical" if we insist upon classifying them.

The best evidence of the general trend in these practices is to be found in an examination of such as survive in the present accentuated conflict with the scientific methodology. By and large they tend increasingly to remove themselves from the fields where they can be directly put to the proof. Take the evolution of that quintessentially religious practice known as prayer. While it is still socially acceptable to pray for the immediate alleviation of a crisis of a purely material nature, if it involves general or public distress,[7] it is considered in very bad form (by those whose perceptions in religious matters are attuned to the nicest discriminations) for the individual to ask in prayer for blessings of too obvious an individual or material nature. So while among the devout residuum of the uncultured it is still not a matter of religious bad taste to ask the intercession of celestial anthropomorphic personalities, in reawakening the libido in an increasingly disinterested lover, or in helping to reestablish a balance in a progressively recalcitrant economic budget, such direct and specific consolations are denied the refined religious consciousness. In such an emergency the more sophisticated and disciplined devotee is permitted such complementary and somewhat reversed requests for intercession as "shrive my heart of this unholy passion" or—"give me strength to forgo the vanities of the flesh and turn my thoughts to higher things," as substitute for the explicit naiveté of the unsophisticated. So intense do the more refined religious tastes feel on these matters that it is not at all uncommon to hear them deny the status of "true" religion to the naive graces sought by the shop-girl. And one's sympathy automatically goes out to them in their disgust at such profanations, for these are in direct violation of their conception of the nature and whims of the forces appealed to.

Here the real nature of the validity of the magico-religious practice reveals itself. Its efficacy always derives from its auto-suggestive or confidence-giving or conflict resolving or merely distracting effect. And whatever is practiced during conditions of stress, remains as a habit that will reappear and persist whenever the stress reappears, whether or not these activities in any way contributed to a previous relief. This is as true of the crassest magical rite as of the most refined prayer. The difference in their acceptability lies merely in their relation to the intellectual or emotional equipment of the practitioner or communicant. Thus, to the communicant in whatever ritual, there are very real psychological if not rational reasons for the retention of the observances in question. Not only that, but we have numerous instances in which the devotional practices are retained and observed even after the individual has obtained complete insight into the mechanisms of their operation.[8] No wonder then, that they are tenaciously adhered to by the larger masses of societies living on a far less reflective and critical level.

There have been periods during which the frank use of prayer or ritual as a confidence-giving device for purely mundane exigencies has fallen into relative disfavor. Nor is it wholly incomprehensible why this should be so, for if this phase of the religious practices becomes too obvious it becomes unpalatable to the finer sensibilities, and the whole creed degenerates to the level of Christian Science, Unity, or any other manifestation of the "New Thought." On the whole, the Protestant movements in the Christian faith have in recent years tended to frown upon the use of religion for such purposes.[9] The price the Protestant church paid for its failure to provide officially such autosuggestive techniques is a whole host of dubious offshoots waxing fat at the expense of the parent body. It is only recently, since the whole process has received something of a scientific whitewash at the hands of psychiatry, and under the threat of losing congregations en masse to the deviant cults that we begin to see symptoms of a more official recognition of this phase of religious activity. Where individual pastors have begun to deal with the problems of personal conflict they have frequently struck pay dirt and filled their churches with a cult of reassurance.

By and large the older technique had been one of resolving personal conflicts and difficulties by a general disparagement of mundane affairs in their entirety, and by deferring all satisfaction of desires to new forms of bliss in another world. That such a program should prove a favorite with the entire machinery of devout observances is hardly surprising, for it disposes at one stroke of all embarrassing contradictions, uncertainties, and failures of ritual and prayer such as of need occur occasionally when efficacy in immediate affairs is presumed. From the standpoint of a stable ritual and a constant, unchanging faith there is every advantage in giving up entirely all pretense at intervention in mundane events by ritual devices, particularly in a culture whose technological innovations are proliferating at a phenomenal rate, such as they have been in Protestant Christendom. It is seriously damaging to the prestige of a priesthood to be compelled to surrender jurisdiction to secular devices in an area long profitably exploited, or serviced if you will, by spiritual methods.

Even the general area of the ethics of human conduct which many religions claim as their own, as certainly Christianity does, is not entirely free from this problem of historical embarrassments to current claims of infallibility. When, for example, we turn to Deuteronomy xxv: 11 & 12 and read:

"When men strive together one with another, and the wife of one draweth near to deliver her husband out of the hand of him that smiteth him, and putteth forth her hand, and taketh him by the secrets:

Then thou shalt cut off her hand, thine eye shall not pity her," even the most devout Believer must give pause and contemplate the changes wrought by time. There is, of course, no more reason to ascribe infallibility to the ethical doctrines of some ancient culture than there is to claim it for its astronomy or medicine. But it is easily apparent that it is high time that we recognize that an area such as that of human conduct is definitely a problem for scientific method. The old insistence that the scientific and the value-judgmental existed in completely different realms of reality is nothing but an attempt on the part of the priestcraft to retain their prerogatives in the area of ethics by a semantic trick. Time has eroded many a function out of the hands of the ritualists, and there are today but few left.

Insofar then, as "evolution" implies simply "change," no quarrel can be had with evolutionary concepts of religion. But to imply that evolution has meant change in the general direction of some particular doctrine or article of faith such as monotheism is to be guilty of serious oversimplification if not of outright falsehood. At best, such changes as we have seen in the practices commonly called religious have been nothing other than a general trend toward a compatability with the changes in the balance of the culture patterns. Religious and ceremonial behavior cannot remain long as a thing completely apart. Any extensive changes in the basic pattern of life are practically certain to produce repercussions in even the most isolated and compartmentalized of rituals and ceremonials. In the western cultures, literally exploding under the impact of a developing science and technology the impact upon religious practices has been dramatic, to put it mildly.

If one were to make the assumption that practices follow on the heels of beliefs, or that rituals or practices were observed "because of certain prior beliefs" our western religions would indeed be a puzzle. Actually the western scientific findings have destroyed the bases of belief after belief, only to have them survive in slightly modified form or supported with a new crop of rationalizations. Overt ritual procedures appear far more readily modifiable than purely verbal beliefs. The priesthood has by and large done a very effective job of retaining its functions and role in the face of an almost complete destruction of the cultural frame that created their historical roles and functions. Or perhaps it is more correct to say that by jealously guarding and defending its vested interests, and failing in that endeavor, finding other functions, or even being content with such as were left to them, they are still with us; in most areas in the west no doubt much reduced in function, power, and prestige.

In a world in which cultural changes are taking place there is also to be expected more or less change in the area of human magico-religious behavior. Change indeed there is. But probably more to be marveled at is the lack of change in this area, the capacity of organized ritualism to survive almost intact where the pace of cultural change is admittedly slow. Consider, for example, the worship of the goddess Eileithyia,[10] a snake goddess, in the Cretan cave of Amnisos. She seems to have been venerated there for a minimum of three to five thousand years, from Neolithic to early Christian times. This deity had so many functions that a suspicion of monotheism might well arise, and provide fuel for the theorists who hold that from the very start man knew that there was but ONE god. In this same cave a pair of stalagmites were the center of an aniconic cult of some kind long before the days of the snake goddess. Numerous vases were found buried around the bases of these up-thrusting geological accretions. Lacking further details of what went on here in that dim, distant past we will gladly allow the specialists in Freudian symbolism to play around with stalagmites and snakes and draw such conclusions as they will on what went on in the lower levels of the Unconscious of these primitive fellows! But this Eileithyian cult had a subordinate male deity. It is credited with having been very humane in general temper, a nature creed, and it is thought to have contributed its general temper and spirit to later Greek practices. There was change here, but even more continuity.

The Eleusinian rites of Demeter at Eleusis were performed for over two thousand years. There was much secrecy and mystery about these cults and little enough is known of the details. They anticipated the contemporary fraternal orders and college fraternities with an elaborate three-part initiation: the things that were enacted, the things that were shown, and the things that were explained or spoken. With the introduction of Christianity to Greece, Demeter was retained as Saint Demetra, and as such she remained there until the beginning of the 19th. century![11]

In the Nile valley, change in ritual and religion seems to have consisted of adding to current practices whatever new gods were introduced by war or commerce, meantime retaining the old. The burdens of the ritual machinery must have reached monumental proportions. No wonder that Amen-hotep was driven to attempt a simplification of the accumulating menagerie of gods into a single deity, the sun-god. The astonishing thing about this is not that he failed in the end so to reduce their complex worship, but rather how closely he apparently did come to making the change stick. But there is no denying the persistent continuity of the Egyptian scheme of supernaturalism over a time span that must be reckoned in millennia ,during which persistence and survival were more conspicuous than change.

Just how old Hinduism actually is seems to be a matter of some considerable doubt. But certain it is that by the 7th. century B.C., it had been long frozen in a rigid pattern hardly compatible with the balance of the culture, and gave rise to a lively Reformation in the form of Buddhism which is now some two thousand five hundred years old! In India itself, Hinduism seems again to have displaced its reformation or at least absorbed it. But the variety of beliefs and practices discoverable in that fantastic land is such that the addition of several new systems of beliefs could hardly add significant complexity or variety to the myriad already present. There are no signs here of any evolutionary trend toward monotheism.

Judaism too has a respectable age of some four thousand years. Of the numerous splinter groups that have broken off the parent body the chief are Christianity, now approaching the end of its second millennium, and Mohammedanism some six-hundred years younger. All quite impressive spans of times over which to maintain any convincing continuity.

These relatively long-lived religions prove nothing except that some such social behavior patterns have indeed survived a long time. What would be even more impressive, statistically, would be a listing of the religions that did not survive. In some cases, the balance of the culture seems to have survived almost intact while the religion changed. Then again, the culture might well have changed phenomenally and yet remarkably little change was manifest in the religious structure. It could probably be shown that sometimes a culture died because of the handicaps of its religious structure, and again it might equally be true that a culture survived because of the dynamics of its religious institutions. In short, the relations between the religious customs and the balance of a culture is far from simple. Religion

(1) Cannot be said to be a simple product of a culture in any specifically predictable way such that a specific kind of the religion is the product of certain particular aspects of the balance of the culture pattern. Certainly it is not a simple product of some single factor such as the basic economics of the culture.

(2) Nor is it a product of any predictable evolutionary process.

(3) Religious customs are not necessarily smoothly integrated with the balance of a culture: they might even be seriously at loggerheads.

(4) Furthermore, religions are not necessarily always socially constructive factors in the culture.

(5) As for its relation to the political or power structure of a society, it might well be found to vary from complete control of such political power as exists to conflict up to and including open warfare. In between it might support, or withhold support from a political power structure, or be almost completely indifferent to it.

On the other hand, it is safe to expect

(1) That a religion is likely to reflect the chief concerns, problems, frustrations, and aspirations of a culture.

(2) That the magico-religious practices and expectations will in general be not too incompatible with the rest of the culture.

(3) That they will also tend to be "colored" by practical necessities, or that compromises with practical considerations will be apparent.

(4) That religious practices are likely to be modified by dra-

matic discoveries or events such as local volcanic activity, the fall of meteorites, a new drug, etc.

(5) That religions are frequently greatly influenced by personalities, their idiosyncrasies and innovations.

(6) That cult and belief are likely to have a slow rate of change where the total culture is subjected to relatively few changes or pressures.

(7) That the form and content of a religion can be expected to show a relatively rapid rate of change where it is introduced into an alien culture or where its native scene is subjected to great stresses and rapid changes.

(8) That fortuitous culture contacts may at times have dramatic consequences in religious as well as secular matters.

Yet apart from the historical transfer of functions from the generally "religious" to the generally "secular" which has marked the accumulation of secular or scientific knowledge in the west, it would be difficult to point to any general direction that the evolution of religion has taken, or even to any specific beliefs or theories that religious beliefs have converged toward, or even that there were any dependable criteria of what constituted "higher" as opposed to "lower religions." Secular sophistication has forced revisions in animistic notions generally, wherever it has occurred. The fallacy in all assertions of the similarity of all "low" religions, and the similarity of all "high" religions[12] is just that the judgment of what is high and what is low is purely subjective, and the similarity of the "low" is simply a function of the fact that what was already similar was put into that classification. Similarly with the characteristics of the "high" religions. The statement, "—the supreme believers worship the same Supreme God everywhere"[13] reveals only that by definition, "supreme" believers are those that worship a supreme God!

One might well ask, where is the evidence that the worship of one supreme god is so superior to the worship of several gods?—that is unless one takes the position that it is difficult enough to furnish proof of the existence of one god, and that each additional god assumed to exist would simply double the problem faced. If the reduction in numbers of deities of itself has merit, then why are not those religions in which no gods whatever are worshipped the "highest" of all? As Ducasse[14] has well pointed out, the evidence for one god is no better than that for the existence of a dozen, and perhaps even not as good.

An amusing lapse in logic is to be found in practically all attempts to justify any particular faith or belief. The lack of evidence for the belief may well be conceded, but that concession is at once minimized by the assertion, probably a correct one, that there also is no specific evidence that this particular belief is false. The effect created, psychologically, by such a juxtaposition of statements is that of equating the probability of such a belief or proposition as being true or false, that is, giving it a 50-50 chance of being true. Nothing could be more erroneous. The statistical probability of any proposition being true or false is not 50-50; it is more nearly one against infinity. True propositions are few and far between. In the absence of specific evidence for the truth of any proposition the odds are slim indeed that it is true. The skeptic who rejects out of hand any and all beliefs, particularly those whose nature is such that it is impossible to obtain the usual sort of evidence that produces computable probabilities, is acting on sound statistical grounds. Believers of all sorts, both before and after Pascal, have been fond of pretending that their particular faith or belief, even without evidence, had a 50-50 prospect of being true. This is the serious defect in statments such as this one in Ducasse:[15]

"This means that earnest atheism at least, no less than theism, is a species of faith not of knowledge—negative instead of an affirmative faith."

Rejecting any belief has far greater probabilities on its side, in the absence of any evidence, than has the acceptance of such belief. And only those with some fond and specific belief to justify can possibly fail to grasp this very important principle.

Precisely what the historical or psychological processes are that have favored in some areas or in some times the idea of but one god rather than a variety of them, is rather

difficult to guess with any degree of confidence. Certain it
is that all the current monotheisms still show plenty of traces
of the more numerous personalities or entities once presumed
to exist or somehow fused into a single entity. Actually the
insistence on the single deity seems to be a conclusion drawn
by experts and virtuosos in religious or ceremonial matters,
rather than something emerging out of the practical devout observances of the run of the mill communicant and believer. The
believer continues to address his pleas to the old deities, whether
they are assimilated as mere "saints" or as part of a mystical
trinity-that-is-one. If your author had to make a guess at the
factors tending to bring this state of affairs about he would
cautiously advance the suggestion that this reductive evolution stemmed from the rivalry of the respective priesthoods of
the various separate deities. The efficiency resulting from a
reduction of the effort spent in devout observances might
have had some long-run survival value in a culture, but such
effects probably were limited to the gain in common attitudes
and values that make for group cohesion and unity.

The psychoanalytic formulae seem to unlock all mysteries,
at least to the satisfaction of psychoanalysts, and motivation
behind monotheism apparently offers the Initiates no great
difficulty:

"Devotion to monotheism is diagnosed as a rarefaction of
anal erotism since it occurs in persons who seek to combat
unconscious cloacal tendencies. Parsimony becomes a theological
passion in the monotheist in that he saves time and expense in
worshipping only one god, and anal erotic sublimation shows
itself in the obstinacy of the monotheist. Laws, rituals, symbols
all display a passion for symmetry in monotheism."[16]

To which the only fitting comment can be: *caveat emptor!*

Even more frustrating must be any attempt at arriving at
anything like a clear idea of just exactly what this God is that
is spelled locally with a capital "G." Every militant atheist,
looking for water for his mill should acquire a copy of "My
Idea of God," edited by J. F. Newton[17] which contains essays
on the subject written by fifteen or more men, learned in the
subtleties of their respective creeds. The nearest thing to agree-

ment on this very important matter would seem to be a response of "yes" to the verbally put question, "Do you believe in God?", from all these men, with the possible exception of the Unitarian for whom gods are but concrete symbols of the Great Reality which is too abstract for the ordinary mind to grasp. Another asks us to believe in a God whose nature is such that no mortal mind can grasp it. Some hand out the official dogma that is their creed. For some, God has an objective existence, independently of man. For another, God is evolution. Then in another chapter, God is that intelligent spirit who is accomplishing the good. God is creator for some, but only of the spiritual universe for another. God is personal for some; for another it is "misleading to speak of God as personal." For another, God is a spirit standing in the same relation to the world as that in which the individual spirit stands to the body! Such spirit it identified with the personal "will." Anyone aware of the serious limitations in the power of the "will" over the body must come away from such a theory with a much chastened conception of Omnipotence! God is infinite and changeless for one; growing and finite for another. Then again, God stands for indestructible belief in something that cannot be defined!

Well, it is a free country, for which we had better be grateful! The dogmatists would dearly love to "use the secular arm" to force us into conformity. Happily but few of these ideas about the supernatural will any longer directly interfere with research into, let us say arterio-sclerosis, even if the constellations of ideas that go with some of them may well interfere seriously with constructive efforts at solving social problems, or otherwise discourage the scientific spirit.

The number of different gods believed in may have been considerably reduced during the last few millennia in western civilization; but the number of different conceptions can only indicate that an increasing knowledge of the nature of man and his universe makes it more and more difficult to retain or justify the naive anthropomorphic conception of a god or gods that has come to us out of the past. The believer is driven to embrace more and more abstract, attenuated, and incidentally meaningless ideas in order to be able to retain any belief in such a symbol. They are meaningless in the sense that they are incapable of contributing anything to the organization or the understanding of the facts of any part of human behavior or experience. Some hold that such fictions are critically and vitally important to a culture. But one looks in vain for any substantiating evidence for such assertions. Rare indeed, and then only for limited periods at best, are any fictions superior to any facts.

CHAPTER VII

LEARNING AND RELIGION

The Origins of Religion as Problems in
The Psychology of Learning.

Most theorizing as the the nature or origin of religion proceeds from assumptions of a highly questionable sort. Some of these are about human nature, its instinctive religiosity, its innate piety, or man's religious "sense." Modern psychology provides emphatic negatives for such lightly assumed entities. But most of the fallacious assumptions are in the area of what is presumed to be true of religious beliefs and practices everywhere. If there is to be some single entity, "Religion" that is universal, some universal evidence or manifestations must be found to justify the assumption. Accurate anthropological evidence has slowly been accumulating and what may once have seemed to be universal to man on the basis of knowledge of a few groups is now often definitely known not to be. There follows herewith a list of some of the more commonly assumed "universalities" of man in his religious proclivities. In each case, the question of its universality is raised and the answer provided.

1. Do all languages have either an exact equivalent or even a reasonable approximation to our term "religion?" The answer is definitely NOT.
2. Do all peoples believe in the existence of a god or gods? No.
3. Then do they all believe in the existence of spiritual agents of some sort? No.
4. Is a "hereafter" everywhere believed in? No.

5. Where "hereafters" are believed in, are they universally assumed to be desirable places, or an improvement over the mundane abode? No.

6. Is the belief in personal immortality everywhere accepted? No.

7. If some individuals are believed to have personal immortality, does it then follow that all persons are presumed to be immortal? No.

8. If men are believed to be immortal, are women also conceded to be? No.

9. If it is believed that spirits exist, are these presumed to be immortal? No.

10. Is it everywhere believed that man has a soul? No.

11. Do supernaturals, if believed in, universally have high moral characteristics assigned to them? No.

12. Is a sharp line always drawn between the "sacred" and the "secular?" No.

13. Does every religion have a cosmology? No.

14. Is it everywhere assumed that the universe is run by "personal" agencies of some sort? No.

15. Where personal agencies are believed to "run" the universe, are they universally presumed to be of high moral character? No.

16. Do all people pray at some time, to something? No.

17. Are sacrifices universally made to anything at some or any time? No.

18. Where prayers, rituals, or sacrifices are made, are they always assumed or believed to be more or less effective for some ends or purposes? No.

19. Where both exist, is religion generally distinguished from magic? No.

20. Is the "spiritual" necessarily linked with the "ethical"? No.

21. Does there appear to be any limitation on the variety or diversity of things worshipped? No.

22. Do all societies have some sort of specialized priest, medicine man, or shaman? No.

These are some of the frustrating contradictions that confront the earnest seeker who tries to answer some of the recurrent questions about that intriguing subject: religion. Any theory as to the universality of, or the nature of, or the origin of religion must somehow take cognizance of the embarrassing realities that are provided by the diversity of cultures that have at one time existed, or still do exist here on this planet. The things presumed to be universal to man generally prove to be but social norms in a very limited culture area. But surely, there must be something universal in human practices or beliefs that provides the "core" of the "religious!" Read widely and you will find almost as many different things presumed to be that core as there are authors venturing into the field. Turn to the detailed accounts of precisely what the very many different groups of people do, say they do, or believe with or without acting upon those beliefs, and you can be assured of finding generous exceptions to anything presumed by anyone to be "universal" in this area.

But surely some common denominators of attitudes or behavior must exist, if only one define them broadly enough, and here seems to be about the very best that this poor seeker can turn up:

1. Everywhere one will find beliefs or ideas held that are not based upon empirical or statistical evidence. These ideas or beliefs may or may not be acted upon, and may involve purely "secular" matters only.

2. Everywhere, regular, habitual, and predictable ways of meeting the unpredictable, the impossible, or the uncontrollable, are developed, if they are momentous. With this as the criterion, magic or religion might perhaps then be said to be universal to man everywhere. Any such acts as have no practical or obvious mechanical function are likely to be classed as ritual, or ceremonial, or religious—by us!

3. Appreciative attitudes toward certain kinds of conduct or "values" are certain to appear. If these have an obvious mechanical or practical function they call for no special comment. If they seem to have significance only vis-à-vis a mythology of some sort we may well call them magical, moral, or religious, depending upon our traditional criteria in that distinction.

4. Disapproving and avoidant attitudes toward some objects or activities are also certain to appear. Again, if these have some demonstrable and direct practical function they call for no comment, they are presumed to be "logical." If we cannot find a practical basis, or some demonstrable grounds for their existence we will probably call them taboos, unless we ourselves happened to be observing an almost identical avoidance, in which case would probably refer the act to our religious beliefs, or to our standard of "morals."

Universals beyond this point would have to be sought in the physiological functions of life itself, of eating, digesting, reproducing, keeping warm, and dying. But do not look for them in the manner in which these needs are met; endless variety and variations are the rule. Specialization of role and function for different individuals begins in even the smallest groups; but many of these, and even some larger ones, do not have specialized priests, shamans, or medicine men. When they do appear they are most likely to take over jurisdiction in the areas of the four above-mentioned universals. And, when a full-time specialist takes over in an area there is rather likely to be an extensive proliferation of activities, observances, and functions. These fellows are likely to find ways and means of amplifying their functions and increasing their importance in the group. Religion, as we know it, is as much the product of these specialists as is the music we hear a product of individual composers. They might fasten upon some particular area or function and make it the all-important center around which the entire culture might seem to be given organization and significance. Another area might be relatively neglected. Almost the entire life of a group might well be given such meticulous regimentation or ritualization, or such processes might elsewhere be limited to but a small segment of the total pattern, or even be entirely absent.

It should therefore be apparent why there can be no simple criterion of just exactly with what "religion" must be concerned. There is nothing to prevent anyone from marking off a group of motives or practices and saying, "this is religion," but any such criterion would leave whole sections of the populace without any.

What remains then, as a practical problem for inquiry is precisely how any beliefs, practices, rituals, or cults of whatever sort are acquired. This problem is recognized, and conveniently disposed of, in practically all systems of organized religion by means of the supplementary myth of specific instructions in these correct procedures at the hands of the creator gods themselves or other personal culture heroes who gave the specific instructions or set a firm example. Or, some unquestionably reliable prophet is assumed to have gotten the specific instructions at first hand. Now it must not be forgotten that such venerable instructions, whether oral or in written form, cover a host of matters which in this secular age are no longer subsumed under the "religious" category. Thus, Old Testament chapters will be found to supply with a blanket confidence specific and approved instructions in the matter of burnt offerings, bubonic plague, adultery, nutrition, or specific or general guilt feelings.[1] The more scientifically enlightened cultures have of course developed newer and presumably more effective procedures for plague, leprosy, and to some extent for nutritional matters than are to be found in even the shrewdest of the ancient mythologies or folklore. But the question still remains, how are such rules, practices, codes, or beliefs acquired in the first place? The penalty for rejecting the convenient belief of their supernatural or contra-natural origin is simply that one is then confronted with the question of how they originated in human behavior. Some individual at some time, or even perhaps several different individuals at widely separate times and places, must have introduced, however trifling, some specific variation in previous procedures. In short, it must then be assumed that all such cultural manifestations are the products of many and varied trial and error processes of an all too human sort in a not too familiar but at least materially ponderable world. The difficulties involved in assuming that such "religious" acts are the product of or the manifestations of, a special religious "instinct" will not be reviewed here. There remains then the other alternative, namely to find the answers to our questions in the psychology of habit, broadly interpreted to include all forms of learning, association, forgetting, "conditioning" or whatever principles might be presumed to be operating in the production of variations in human behavior. We are left with no other option.

That man has learned, and still learns, "by trial and error" is perhaps one of the few unquestioned truisms. But there is hardly a more bitterly disputed question today than the adequacy of that descriptive concept for all human discovery, unless it is the quarrel over just *how* this trial and error process results in learning. Both questions are still heatedly fought over. If man has some higher-level tricks other than learning by trial and error, what are they? A favorite answer with some psychologists is "insight." Man, they say, and even some animals, have this insight, an "ah-ha" reaction in which a discovery or solution is suddenly made, perhaps covertly before it is demonstrated overtly. But even casual inquiry into the past experience of the insightful person reveals all too clearly the earlier learned units that constituted that particular "insight." And again, how are we to distinguish the bad theory, the "bum hunch," the sudden illumination that failed to illumine from one that proved fruitful? Subjectively they seem equally valid and genuine when they appear. We are tempted to say "insight" when a frustrated ape suddenly dashes to a romote cage and fetches a stick with which he retrieves the bananas lying outside his immediate cage. But when this same ape having learned to reach the fruit in his cage by climbing on top of a pyramid of boxes under the bait, now tries to climb up on a lone box *while* holding it up at eye level, in the absence of all but the one box for his pyramid, we laugh at his ignoring of the first law of gravitation but omit any mention of "insight"! In short, it seems that an "insight" occurs in any situation in which the application of previously acquired skills results in a fairly prompt solution. If past habits fail to work or even seem to interfere with the working out of a new solution no one would use the term insight to describe the event. Some psychologists even deny that such phenomena belong in the learning category.[2] But an embarrassing fact is not disposed of simply by a trick of taxonomy, and both man and beast can acquire a pattern of maladjustive as well as of adjustive behavior in a given situation. The burden of proof is upon those who hold that the processes are of a fundamentally different sort. If they are not, then such logic would demand that the acquisition of almost any undesirable habits must be of a very different stripe from any habituation that constitutes an improvment. Such logic would come perilously close to the sage observations one formerly encountered in textbooks on "moral philosophy": "Good habits alone have to be cultivated; bad habits grow of themselves like weeds." The author of that text I have long forgotten, but I distinctly recall that it had a copyright date of 1917! Value judgments of action must not be confused with their casual explanations; and a particular case that proves embarrassing to one's theory is not disposed of by the postulations of more unknowns.

But even if we grant for the sake of the argument that man perhaps at least at times learns a "correct" response or solution of a problem "by insight," what are we to say by way of explanation of the cases in which the final habit acquired in a given situation cannot by any stretch of the imagination be called a "solution"? What "rewards" have reenforced these persistent, stereotyped, perhaps even maladjustive habit patterns? When a series of acts has brought the animal to some food, or effected its release from a cage, or corrected any organic imbalance the "why" of such habit fixation *seems* obvious: somehow the reward seems to have fixated or reenforced the behavior pattern which led up to it. In terms of apparent numbers of adherents, this is the most generally approved learning theory of today.

But, unfortunately for such learning theory, this concept is completely useless in the field of the psychology of religion, if the core problem of that field is conceded to be the question of the whys and hows of religious behavior. Because even if one could somehow surmount the difficulties of finding evidence that rewards, goals, or end results or purposes somehow fixate the habit series that led up to them, what would one turn to in cases of behavior patterns where admittedly there no longer is any question whatever of the causal efficacy, where the most earnest convictions fail to produce even the faintest trace of statistical warrant that the activities in question have contributed to a goal, a purpose, or a "success"? And, rest assured, the modern, more sophisticated religions, those that have somehow had to learn to coexist with a rapidly developing scientific materialism, have not been unaware of this dilemma confronting their techniques and postulates. Many have learned to bow out gracefully from fields in which materialistic devices have made palpable improvements over chance. They have learned to frown severely upon the application of their techniques in situations where the statistical odds are stacked too solidly against them; in fact one of the chief zones of offense between different religions lies precisely in the question of which areas of events are presumed amenable to coercion by distinctively "religious" techniques. Most of the offense generated in western readers by customs such as are described in Katherine Mayo's "Mother India" derives from this source.

But if the behavior called "religious" is not the direct expression of an instinct, if it is not understandable in terms of its successes, rewards or purposes, where can we turn for insight and understanding? Well, to begin with, before any acts or activities can become any part of any habit pattern, religious or otherwise, they must be "available" as Maier and others have it: they must be present in the response patterns of the individuals, either as inborn reactions or as combined in habit patterns, themselves the product of associative or conditioning processes. It could hardly be otherwise; but failure to note this obvious fact has made some religious behavior seem monstrous or enigmatic to people unfamiliar with such variations. That gods are so frequently treated as super parents is no doubt not unrelated to the fact that each of us acquired predictable behavior adjustments toward parents long before coming to grapple with cosmic questions. Kings and gods are frequently addressed in somewhat similar terms. If a child learns that certain techniques of approach are effective in having requests granted or needs filled by parents, here then is a pattern of behavior "available" for use in other situations of stress. Thus it is that about the only safe generalizations that can be made about attitudes taken by people toward their gods is simply that these attitudes are rather likely to be somewhat akin to those generally found effective in the social relations in that particular society. So the patterns have varied from the extremely circumspect treatment of their god by the Hebrews who at times did not even dare breathe his name, to the threatening, cursing, reviling, and even "killing" of a god as practiced by the Kwakiutl, and with the very human, "horizontal" gods of the old Greeks with whom man's relationship might best be described as "democratic," somewhere in between. Anthropological data illustrate beautifully the range and variety of conduct one would expect on purely psychological grounds.

One might well wonder then that there does come to be predictability or uniformity, even in one particular culture, if we are dealing with what seems to be solely a habit phenomenon. To this the obvious answer is that there is indeed much variability, even within each culture, as well as from one culture to another. Radin tells us that even primitive cultures have, and always have had, their individual skeptics. And some of the Plains Indians did not hesitate to change their super-naturals in cases where a convincing run of impotence could be charged to them. There is then to be found no single, simple entity that is "primitive religion"; rather a great variety of ways of meeting various needs, situations, or crises. These ways are not classified by these people as "religious" or "secular." That dichotomy is left for us to make. Any activities whose causal efficacy is clearly discernible in terms of a convincing mechanical sequence are of course thought of by us as purely secular. Should we discern in the rest of their activities any evidence that control was being attempted by appeal or entreaty directed to more or less personalized animistic agencies we are almost certain to classify the activities as "religious." If, however, there appear in any activities the remotest suspicions that they are designed to, or are expected to *coerce* such agencies into complying with the will of the practitioner then they will no doubt be rated as "magic."

But magical or religious, it is precisely these activities that are a challenge to the psychologist. To any form of teleological interpretation they constitute an enigma, as well as to any form of "reenforcement" learning theory. As activities they are unlikely to be wholly unique in the repertory of behavior; rather are they likely to be part of the "available," i.e. past, habit patterns of the individual. But how can they persist? How survive? How become part of amazingly stable behavior patterns? To begin with, there is no known neurological mechanism that can make it possible for a successful act per se to reinforce the habits that led up that that act or success. Goals *to be* reached, or purposes *to be* served in no known way determine the activities of the striving individual; those activities are a product of his inborn equipment, his past habits, and present stimuli, internal and external, acting on the individual at the time in question. Such activities may or may not be effective in solving the problem, attaining the "goal" or in facilitating the homeostatic adjustive mechanisms of the striving individual. So long as an individual remains alive that alone testifies to a reasonable degree of overall success in the maintenance of the organic regulatory mechanisms. But such success is not necessarily the product of the activity of the organism; that might well have been unrelated to the outcome. Such actions could have been wholly unrelated to the causal processes that were effective and yet be fixated as a "habit." *The activities in question need only have been going on when the situation changed, when the problem solved itself, or the individual was removed from the situation.* Thus, long ago Thorndike's cat learned to scratch its ear as a "means" of escape from a cage. The experimenter had simply opened the door as soon as the cat had scratched. This scratching became the cat's habit, not because it was the most "recent" act of the cat, perhaps by a few seconds of time; this scratching habit was simply *not in turn inhibited by the cat's practicing of some other response in that particular situation,* so it remained the cat's "habit of escape" when next it was placed in the same cage.

The same point is perhaps even better illustrated in a recent experiment by Skinner.[3] Pigeons were placed into cages that had arbitrarily timed food release mechanisms which opened after the elapse of an exact number of minutes, regardless of what the birds, or the experimenter, were doing. Skinner reported that the birds become "superstitious"! The ground for that facetious observation was simply this: the pigeons showed a strong tendency to fixate as habits whatever activity they happened to have been engaged in when the release functioned! But it is wholly unnecessary to anthropomorphize; these pigeons acquired these habits in precisely the same manner that Thorndike's cat had learned to scratch its ear. The activity last practiced in a particular situation has a high probability of recurring *in the same situation* since it has not been displaced by the practicing of some other responses in that same, highly specific situation. It must be remembered however that the variety of "superstitious" habits that could become the final habits of these pigeons is strictly limited to the available activity patterns in the repertory of the experimental animals. By original structure, and by habit factors, each animal arrives in the experimental situation with some well-practiced activity patterns rather likely to be called out at almost any time or place. The odds strongly favor the probability that when the door opens the most recently practiced act will be one of these that is already high in relative frequency of occurrence. The next trial will find the probability even higher. Animals have each their own distinctive "personalities" which consist of precisely these quite predictable behavior probabilities. Just as Guthrie and Horton[4] found that among their cats were biters, clawers, rubbers, rollers, etc., whose habit patterns upon arrival in the experimental situation obviously stacked the cards in favor of particular modes of egress, so it is a safe bet that similar preestablished habit patterns helped to determine the specific "superstition" of the particular pigeon.

Yet it is readily seen that where there is a rivalry of response tendencies of relatively equal strength, the *fact* of postremity, as it has been called by Voeks,[5] namely of the last practiced response in the prediction of succeeding activities begins to loom large. Take, for example, the familiar error of attempting to unlock the house door with the office key, or vice versa. The Freudians have long seen in such errors damning indictments that the attempt to open the house door with the office key subtly reveals a preference for staying downtown and making love to the office secretary, rather than coming home as a dutiful husband should. The reverse error presumably implies deep dissatisfaction with the job or a strong wish to remain at home, tied to the apron-strings of the wife who is of course a mother-image. A little careful observation will probably reveal far sim-

pler factors at work. Long days at the office with consequent
frequent use of the office key are likely to find one attempting to
unlock the apartment with the office key, particularly if one
is distracted as in conversation while approaching the door. I
have never tried to *lock* the house door with the office key.
This error is made highly improbable by the simple fact that
the office door has a snap lock so its key is never used for locking purposes, and also because it was the house key that was
last used when I come to select a key for locking that door.
Where rival activities have had about equal amounts of practice
in a particular situation then postremity is indeed a potent
determinant.

What light does this account of animal and human learning,
first clearly formulated by Professor Guthrie[6] cast on the problem of magic and religion? What is the relation, the similarity,
that exists between the habit acquisitions of cats, rats, and pigeons, and what man acquires in the way of cultural traditions,
folkways, and magical or religious practices? The answer is very
simply this: a sound account of behavior should fit equally well
man or beast, cat or pigeon, practical as well as magical or
religious behavior. When we have solved a practical problem,
or worked out a sequence of behavior that has a visible achievement to its credit we are not likely to question the details of
how that habit was acquired. The end result, the purposes
served are eloquent enough reasons that fully "account" for the
existence of the habit pattern. We simply note that a given
purpose obviously called for a particular method of achievement.
But this is undoubtedly bad science. Unfortunately that is apparent to only those few curious people who are interested in instrumental knowledge, in the movements actually made on the way
to a goal rather than merely in the fact of the attainment of the
goal itself. And it is this sort of a psychology that is obviously
needed if we are to throw any light at all upon behavior that is
rigidly fixed, and persisted in, in spite of every known type
of evidence that the results aimed at, the goals or purposes
strvien for, are in no way causally related to the magical, religious, or ritualistic practices in question.

Your cultural determinist sees here no problem whatever.

The present generation of people practicing certain rites or accepting certain beliefs simply learned these habits from the people about them, principally their elders, while they were children. This is of course largely and practically true. But not exactly. Slight changes do occur, innovations appear at times, and these events are habit changes in some individual at some time. Culture is human behavior. An element of culture is a pattern of human behavior and a cultural change is a change in the habits of particular people at some time. Before any activity could become "culture" it had to be established as the habit of some individual or individuals. The activities which a culture acquires that have practical, identifiable consequences seem to demand no particular explanation, no general or blanket "theory of the origin of practical, instrumental activities." But when we come to examine our cultures and find therein activities whose practical consequences are brazenly at variance with our otherwise generally recognized principles of causality, such activities quite understandably call for an explanation. These things seem so unusual that there must be a different "explanation" for them in contrast with what passes for "explanations" of our more practical or prosaic activities. The completely provincial person of course never questions his particular way of life and belief. The demand for explanations follows on the heels of some considerable contact with a variety of cultures, where each is found to contain its recognizable quota of similarly puzzling activities that do not fit into the principles of our workaday world. Actually, a truly scientific explanation of behavior should be as adequate for our practical behavior as for the magico-religious. Any resort to a different kind of explanation for a different segment of animal or human behavior is but an eloquent admission that what had passed for "explanations" of other aspects of that organism's behavior was hopelessly inadequate. The same can confidently be said for the various learning theories whose proponents are driven to distinguishing from two to a half-dozen different "kinds" of learning, for each of which a separate theory or "explanation" is then offered.

Viewed as human habits, the common denominator of all

religion, magic, or ceremonial behavior whatever is simply this: in contrast to all activities which we class as "practical" or "secular" here is a class of activities whose causal efficacy, if any, is assumed to lies outside the realm of familiar mechanical sequence. To the "reenforcement" psychologists they must constitute an enigma because they produce no practical successes, or satisfactions, which in the opinions of these men provide or produce their reenforcement. And yet, there they are, firmly fixed, probably more so, than almost any habit patterns most people have. How is that possible? Theories that obviously fail to fit the facts of their material are just bad theories. The simple facts of learning are just that success or failure of an act in solving a problem have directly nothing whatever to do with the elimination or retention of that act as a habit. What on the other hand, is critically important is this: what activity was the person engaged in when the situation changed, the need was gratified, the desire fulfilled, or even when the individual *ceased* to desire for whatever reason. For with a recurrence of any of these needs or drives it is the activities last engaged in under similar circumstances that will again be elicited. This activity need have had nothing whatever to do with actual physical resolution of the situation; it need only have been going on, like the activities of Skinner's "superstitious" pigeons, when the situation changes, to again appear as the expected habit when the original problem is faced.

The heated quarrel over the differences between magic and religion that has usually been able to account for at least a couple of chapters in almost any book on the origin of religion need not detain us long at this point. Nor will the "failure of magic" theory of the origin of religion. It need but be remembered that the lack of a causal effectiveness in an activity is no bar to its retention as a final habit in a frustrating situation whose distinguishing characteristic is just that the current habit equipment of the animal or man does not include a pattern capable of overcoming the frustration. That is to say, the pattern of motivation *as it stands* cannot be effectively resolved by intervention on the part of the frustrated individual. Indeed the drive or motive in the individual will not and cannot remain a constant. Hungers can become more intense or time may dull them. Fears and apprehension might be exaggerated or diminished. And each of these changes *within the individual* in effect changes the situation, the pattern, the relation of the individual to his world. And any magic, religion, ceremonial, cult, or prayers by their effects upon the individual thus change, and often profoundly, the entire situation. Your literally realistic materialist, confronted with people praying for rain or for surcease from a plague gives a contemptuous snort at such naiveté. But he fails to attach sufficient importance to *the effect of the prayers upon the praying people themselves.*

Now precisely what effects do prayers generally have upon communicants and how do they acquire the capacity or power of eliciting them? Typically, the parent teaches the prayer to the child at an age when its correct repetition is something of an intellectual feat for which the child is warmly praised. This first step in the learning or "conditioning" processes provides the general linkage of saying the prayer with social approval, the reactions following on the heels of having done the good or the meritorious. One begins a meal, the table groaning with food ready to consume, with a prayer for "the daily bread," and lo! the eating, the satisfaction of the hunger, the removal of the internal irritations or distresses of hunger follow. By the processes of simple conditioning, the activities which preceded the actual eating, in this case the saying of the prayers, come to call out in the communicant part of the total reactions of relaxation and satisfaction they so frequently have preceded because they constituted the activities last engaged in when hungry. Similarly with the prayers said upon retiring; if the uttering of the prayer has long enough been followed by no activity other than sleeping the prayer may well end the activities that constitute worry or apprehension and bring sleep to a poor bedeviled mortal. For similar psychological "reasons" one may fall asleep more quickly in the presence of the familiar stimuli provided by the familiar bed. But if for some reason a pattern of worry and insomnia has been acquired in that bed, a shift to different surroundings might aid in breaking such a handicapping habit. However, if the difficulties originally giving rise to the worries have not been removed it is rather more likely that one will shortly become an expert worrier in any bed!

But, it will be objected, what happens when the prayed-for fails to materialize? Notice that with few exceptions indeed, the individuals who persist in praying are those who acquired the habit of praying early in life, when they began by praying for the food already there, the sleep that had already effectively "sanded" their eyes. Such an individual, praying under great emotional stress for the unattainable, need only continue such prayers until the emotional stress, by sheer fatigue or exhaustion finally exhausts itself, as all emotional states must in time do. This relief from emotional stress then occurs *while the prayers are still being said*. Hence, when emotional stress recurs the odds favor the prayers as the most likely reaction since that is what the individual was doing when last the distress was present. The praying persists as a habit simply because that was what was practiced under distress and nothing else. The greater the variety of circumstances under which prayer alone was resorted to the more likely it is that it will be elicited and persisted in. And, on the basis of the processes called by the Russian experimenters "higher order conditioning" (or "secondary reenforcement" by the theorists who assume it is the "reward" that fixates the steps of behavior leading up to it) the activity of praying itself comes to speed up the process of emotional equilibrium formerly completely dependent upon regulatory organic processes alone. In this way, prayers come to have important emotional effects upon those who practice them. By virtue of the conditioning process, the saying of prayers can early induce the emotional states or resignations that once waited upon a favorable turn of events or upon the exhaustion of states of grief or frustration. This is, of necessity, true also of ritual activities other than prayer. In the Chinese "Book of Rites" (3-4 centuries B.C.) we find the following: "The due regulation of the emotions is the function of a set ceremonial."

If the prayers induce a feeling of hope and confidence apprehensions are thereby relieved, the activity of praying itself, in "filling" time thereby makes time pass more quickly, subjectively; and that is of course the only way we experience time! In the normal course of events rains usually do fall, plagues run their course, and even if the crops are lost or the illness carries away many individuals of critical importance, *in the end* either the crises are resolved in the material world or the individual finally adjusts himself to the loss of crops or family, which he must by one means or another anyhow. *And whatever activities were concomitants of this adjustive process that finally ended the stresses will again be the habits called out the next time similar crises arise.* We laugh at the heathen who continues to pray to his idols time and time again after they have "let him down" as we see it, or who continues to work his magic in the face of repeated failure. Probably a little introspection will disclose the fact that the difference between his beliefs and ours is simply that we have learned not to risk the confidence we have in our rites by their application in just such situations. Within the limits of the general compatibility of any activity, beliefs, or ideas with basic structure of a personality, it makes practically no difference what sort of terminal concomitants there are for emotional attachment to fasten upon. The combat pilot who could not even contemplate going on a mission without wearing a particular sweater was as surprised subjectively by the irrational attachment as was any non-combatant. It was not the product of an act of logic; he just *found* the attachment there. And there you have the psychological essence of all magic and all fetishism. Another combat pilot found that once when the "going got really rough" he extemporized a verbal recital that was obviously concocted out of prayer neglected since early childhood plus some very special details of the immediate situation. Much to his surprise he found himself saying the almost identical words in successive "tight spots." Being a practical realist he noted that this recital calmed and steadied him so it is now "standard procedure" as he puts it! I shall be content to leave to the theologians and the metaphysicians the subtle differences between the indispensable knitted jacket and the recital which has become "standard procedure" for the colonel in critical situations. Psychologically, the methods of their acquisition are identical. The uncanny similarity of such fixations to the escape routines acquired by cats in a puzzle box is hardly a chance phenomenon. As described by Guthrie[7]: "Evident from the very first were startling repetitions of previous behavior.—The outstanding feature of the series of escapes was a strong tendency for *escape routines* to be repeated with high fidelity." And again—"In some cases long series of movements—a triple tour of the periphery of the cage including numerous stops—would be repeated in detail." Not only the very last movement preceding escape becomes attached to the situation *but whole series of responses leading up to the last activities* become part of the total response pattern. This is an item of very great significance for understanding the historical acquisition of significant discoveries as well as for magic and ceremonial or ritual.

As has been previously emphasized in this chapter, a sound psychology should be equally significant in behavior wherever found. Let us turn for the moment to some primitive techniques whose causal efficacy rests upon something more than just distraction or social or individual emotional reenforcement of activity. Take, for example, a "native" formula or recipe for poisoning arrows such as is to be found in the Amazon valley or in Africa. These processes fit exactly the basic picture of the character of trial-and-error as seen in the above illustrations. The formula in use is conspicuous for its retention of an amazing number of steps that have no essential relation to the final effectiveness of the poison. There may well be a dozen or more absolutely worthless ingredients that seem to have remained in the brew much as Guthrie's cat retained its triple tour of the cage. Note: the important, the significant, the truly causal steps must be "fixed" in the habit series by precisely the same processes, psychologically, as are the ritual, the ceremonial, the magical. These people have no knowledge of what we would call the "essential" ingredient in these brews. Instead they have a firmly fixed routine, each part of which is to them as important as any other. This they "know" and follow faithfully. That particular sequence of steps ended the series, it got the results. When starting out to get the same results the same steps exactly were again taken. The controlled test of each separate ingredient is a very late development indeed.

It is of course true that the activities to which the contemporary world is likely to apply the term "magic" will be found to involve more or less overt manipulation of material objects. This fact is no doubt responsible for the theory held in some parts that magic was the progenitor of science while animism evolved into religion. And there just is no denying that science could only develop in a manipulative, trial-and-error tradition. But at any given historical time there is a decided limit to the elements or ingredients that are available for manipulation in any trial and error process. At any such time one might, for all practical purposes, classify all human problems as soluble within the current realm of possibilities, or as insoluble. So long as the problems are soluble, the premium, the obvious advantage lies in a continued trial and error in the realm of practical effort. But many phenomena lie wholly outside this realm of possible mechanical intervention. With them, the long run wisdom lies in *not* attempting the impossible, in the husbanding of energies, in preventing the emotional tensions of the moment from producing social disorder. The seasonal changes cannot be hastened; the rains cannot be made to fall or cease falling (at least not until recently!), the dragon cannot be prevented from swallowing the sun in an eclipse, no known medicament is effective in the disease that threatens. The question now becomes simply this for man: what kind of activities will he engage in during such periods of crisis? It is obvious that the odds are strongly against a resolution or solution coming at the precise moment that any brief, unusual, or frantic activity was in progress. The odds strongly favor familiar, well-practiced activities of long duration, already "available" in Maier's terminology, as well established patterns of activity of that particular person or group. It is activities that can be carried on for long stretches of time at a very modest rate of energy expenditure that have some considerable cards stacked in their favor. But this is far from the only factor involved. The psychological, subjective duration of unfilled time under tension introduces factors making for behavior of another sort. Such tensions can be broken by a resort to dramatic activity;

and, organized religions well illustrate the application of both principles. "Primitive" cultures, and modern, freely illustrate the application of both devices and various degrees of their institutionalization. They might well be designated as the techniques of entreaty or resignation, and of ceremonial or orgy. The fundamental nature of the learning process favors their acquisition if only they are persisted in long enough. For be it remembered, the activity in question need not at all "cause" success; it needs but to have been the activity engaged in when either the crisis is resolved in the material world or the desire itself has been exhausted, or reconciliation to failure or defeat was itself emotionally accepted by the individual. The same learning process will fixate entreaty or orgy equally well. The term "orgy" as used here implies merely any sort of activity involving a relatively high energy expenditure on the part of the communicants, as in sacrifice or ceremonial, in contrast with the activities designated as "entreaty" of which the distinguishing character is simply that the persisted-in activity involves a minimum of overt action and might well be limited to verbal-symbolic or minimal activities. Excluded from the concept of "orgy" are of course all activities that could by any stretch of the imagination be construed as directed toward or grappling with factors seen as material determinants in the situation.

Psychologically, these devices of resignation and orgy stand in a complementary relationship to one another. Persisting in either one for any considerable time stacks the cards in favor of a shift to the other. A period of prolonged inhibition of overt activity generally leaves the organism in a physiological state favoring the initiation of overt action of some sort, and vice versa. In fact, both activities frequently constitute a larger, organized social whole in a pattern making full use of both devices. But it is apparent that in what passes today as the "higher" cultures there has been an unquestioned over-all trend toward the keeping of orgiastic activities well within bounds. These activities depend for their effectiveness upon their capacity to distract and "fill" time effectively, that is, to make events seem to move more rapidly, subjectively, by the activity and distraction techniques. But there is the rub! The best of distractions will pall in time. The keenest excitements become commonplace with repetition. Hence the need for more and more dramtaic performances. There is no doubt but that animal sacrifice functioned in that role. But as animals pall the ante is raised to more and different creatures. A human victim is no doubt very effective, for a time. But that sort of logic can lead to the astronomical numbers of victims such as the Aztec priestcraft resorted to in times of crisis.[8] Many cultures give evidence of a violent reaction at some time against such devices. The drama of it might well have left only traces of a figurative or symbolic sort in the surviving rituals. Thus the orgy techniques might be found to have survived only in elaborate ceremonials and processions with images, tableaux, pageantry, etc., with a basic reliance upon the varied forms of entreaty or resignation, to wit: activities, attitudes, postural sets, or Einstellungen, of a sort that can long be maintained with a minimum of energy expenditure and hence likely to be the last directed effort or the last activity in process when the situation changes. Hence its probable retention as a more or less permanent habit. An additional factor making for this result has been well described by Maier. In his observations on animals subjected to insoluble problem situations he found an apparent paradox, namely that the habits fixated by the animals in situations without any solutions, without any reward, were far more specific and stereotyped than those formed where there was a solution. Hamilton[9] made similar observations in regard to both men and animals almost forty years ago. In other words, habits of a very definite sort are formed where no reward ends a situation, where the frustration and conflict persist without any solution. Here the animals develop a "—degree of stereotypy that perhaps exceeds in specificity the execution of responses developed or maintained under ordinary learning conditions where reward is given in connection with the response," as Maier puts it. And again: "The fixation they develop in an insoluble series is more persistent than the response they develop in a reward series."[10] In short it is precisely a condition of frustration that best produces a ritualization of behavior. The habits practiced under pronounced emotional tension are most recalcitrant to measures designed to change them. This is probably but an extreme instance of what is a commonplace in all learning, namely that a word shouted out aloud is more resistant to forgetting than one barely mumbled. By the time such a reaction has been many times practiced in a variety of situations it is almost extinction-proof and will be elicited even in situations differing to some considerable extent from those in which it was originally acquired. Institutionalized religions then supplement these mechanisms of the fixation of stereotyped behavior with a variety of social sanctions and reenforcement mechanisms. In fact, they provide time-tested and socially acceptable patterns of behavior which are already drilled into the individual and ready to function before frustration is encountered. Yet even where such patterns of behavior are not socially provided, each individual quickly enough develops his own individualized activity patterns under conditions of stress, frustration, and defeat.

Thus it is readily seen how the stage is set for a rivalry between techniques and the vested interests gravitating around each. In the absence of an effective secular medicine, for example, where there was nothing to do but to wait out the homeostatic mechanisms of the human body in overcoming the illness, entreaty or resignation techniques were no doubt highly effective as judged by subjective appraisal. In comparison to the therapeutic enthusiasms of the early secular medicine with their blood-letting, leeching, and purging, the most convinced secularist of today could hardly help but choose the soothing of a murmured prayer or an innocuous anointing in preference. There was indeed a long period of trial and error therapy before man's clumsy efforts had a respectable statistical superiority over the general entreaty, resignation, and orgy[11] technique. But for the long pull, the period of painful trial and error had to be endured in the interests of the empirical and deductive techniques, if we were ever to have a scientific medicine. The inevitability of that logic was however not always as apparent as it now seems to us. To revert for a moment to the problem of methods of therapy, let us note the complex problems it presented in the matter of the choice of effective techniques. Let it not be forgotten that the situation is complicated by the fact that, but for a very small

fraction of instances indeed, man always did recover from illnesses regardless, or perhaps more properly, in spite of what was
done to effect a cure. Between the hopes of the patient and the
effects of suggestion in general, most any sort of hocus-pocus or
quackery could offer convincing competition to whatever devices
the oldest profession, the priestcraft, might have evolved. Witness the competition offered to scientific medicine even today
by an assorted crew of Christian "Scientists," Chiropractors,
Faith Healers, Hydrotherapists, etc. Small wonder then that
the mediaeval priesthood tended to give short shrift to their
secular competitors equipped with what were at best dubious
improvements, statistically, over the high percentage of automatic recoveries *which tended to be credited to whatever device
had been employed. Belief, faith, and confidence attach to whatever activity was last engaged in* much as a cat or pigeon fixates
as a habit the activities it was engaged in when escape or food
were provided. The responses last practiced in such a situation
will reappear when the situation recurs. C. G. Jung quite correctly notes that religion does not derive from theological arguments or spiritual insights. He notes instead a tendency to the
recurrence of childhood habits and even older reflex reactions.
These do indeed frequently appear in religious and ritual behavior. But so do an astounding variety of other activities. The
essential psychological insight into religion is the process by
which these fantastic varieties of behavior have become the fixed
"religions" of various peoples. There are neither activities nor
motives that are universal or unique to religious behavior, only
a common habit psychology operating to fixate practically any
behavior that somehow is persisted in until the situation changes.
This same process fixates impartially the magical, the "religious,"
the sacred, the profane, the scientific, the ritualistic, the causally
effective, the ridiculously useless. It may fixate as a habit some
action originally learned as a child, a response once wrung out
under similar emotional stress, or anything else that psychotic
abnormality or individual idiosyncrasy might provoke. Yes, it
may; and viewing religious and magical behavior widely, it is
apparent that somewhere, or sometime, all these possibilities,
and more, have been realized.

Thus it is that the psychology of the processes of habit formation provides an understanding of the persistent linkage, historically, of pageantry, sacrifice, and orgiastic activities generally with the priesthood. Before they became stereotyped and fixed by a calendar, such performances were resorted to in times of crisis: when the rains were due, or overdue; or when the enemy needed defeating; for example the endless files of human victims sacrificed to the war god by the Mexicans in an effort to stave off defeat at the hands of Cortez. One might say today, "How could they do it? Didn't they know *that* couldn't defeat the Spaniard?" Yes indeed; the more insightful of the priesthood may well have suspected it, but meantime, there was the populace to be taken care of, for who can tell what might not occur to them when frustrated and rapidly losing confidence in their priests? Under such circumstances the price of failing to keep the multitude actively engaged may well be that of becoming its victim. Like Hitler in his Berlin bunker, they tend to postpone surrender far beyond the point of any possible hope from anything other than supernatural miracles. Ordinary "magic" is but a simple form of the same technique. No sharp demarcation is possible. Dramatic orgies, ordinary magic, entreaty, and resignation, all, when resorted to, are psychologically "in line" to be fixated as habits for any situation in which they are invoked, if they are persisted in until the situation is resolved. The first two of these have the advantage of drama, excitement and action; the second two are superior in the matter of economy of effort and hence compete quite effectively against the more dramatic orgiastic devices. Where they can be invoked or provided, the former would have the advantage as a device of mass control, once the dramatic action can be brought to the people. The latter would of necessity be superior where control would have to depend upon "built-in" activities that could be depended upon to control behavior when alone—"in his solitude" is the approved expression in current theological circles. Whatever substance there is to current theories of the "evolution of religion," or the "failure of magic" theory of the origin of religion, careful scrutiny will probably be able to find nothing more objective than a general historical trend in western civilization toward a reduction in emphasis upon orgiastic techniques and a concomitant increasing dependence upon entreaty and resignation. In fact, in the most "advanced" circles, entreaty in any form is suspect since it so often takes the form of a request to the gods to alter the order of events in favor of the communicant. In the "best" religious circles today, the only alterations in events that may legitimately be sought are in the personality of the communicant himself. For that purpose, "entreaty" may be resorted to. As it was eloquently put recently by Cattell:[12]

"The orisons of the devout, therefore, become relatively meaningless today except with respect to the subjective life of the individual or the people. Increasingly prayer retreats to the position of concerning itself with the improvement of the personality and the maintenance of personal or group morale. In this function, psychology cannot deny its efficiency, as a form of autosuggestion, but it may nevertheless ascribe to it the harmful tendency of suggestive practices to increase the individual's general suggestibility."

Just how effective such "religious" techniques will prove to be in the domain of personality improvement remains to be seen. The significant thing to point out however, is just that religion does not exist in a vacuum. It must not be forgotten that there is no *religion* that is a pure, unalloyed essence of some sort, detached from humans and their behavior, their needs, wishes, or desires. Rather, we meet certain situations, some particular needs, with behavior habits that we class as "religious." Our religions consist of particular habits of thought and actions that we have been taught to consider appropriate to certain particular situations. Given a particular situation we have a pattern of behavior that we feel to be correct and imperative. Any attempts at interference with these specific habits at once arouse the strongest of emotional reenforcements tending to perpetuate the familiar habit. In spite of contemporary protestations to the contrary, religious activity is never an end in itself: it is but a tool for the satisfaction of some drive or motive, or for somehow resolving a situation for which there is no known practical solution. Almost without exception, when any activities become freed from all uncontrollable hazards and variables they come to be completely secularized in the public mind. The era of the triumph of science has been rightly called the era of secularization. No other single concept expresses anywhere nearly as adequately the changes that have been wrought in the life and thinking of Western man during the past few centuries. His life has been secularized, namely freed, in large part from the rigid, stereotyped behavior characteristic of the adjustment patterns acquired by man and beast in situations where his best overt efforts come to naught and where instead he acquired and crystallized as a permanent habit pattern for these situations such activities, including attitudes of entreaty and resignation, as happened to persist until events resolved themselves, or until the fears, anxieties, worries, or desires of whatever sort ceased or exhausted themselves. The proper formula when prayers fail has long been "more prayers." Even the keenest desires and the strongest emotions finally do blunt themselves; the organic bases for such states cannot and do not last indefinitely. *And whatever activity had persisted until this state had been reached will be that person's habit pattern the next time a similar pattern of tensions arises.* And, like all activity patterns acquired under conditions of unresolved tensions, these will be characterized by rigidity, inflexibility, and emotionality.

The incredible and fantastic variety of magico-religious rites and practices has long astonished every inquirer that ever took the trouble to look beyond the norms of his own little social world. Sensibilities are outraged, but also intrigued. These heathen rites both attract and repel. The combination of familiar and repelling elements move us at one moment to say, "Do you call *that* Religion?" and on the other hand to assert the universal, instinctive, character of religious observance. They give us the mixed emotions that watching a well-trained chimpanzee gives a firm Fundamentalist. To attempt to derive an underlying "logic" from these varied activities is to court madness. The "logic" essential to, or apparently underlying the beliefs and practices in one culture seems preposterous when applied to the next. The search for a single, universal, underlying emotion or motive is equally frustrating. The emotional patterns and conduct appropriate to religious edifices and the priestly caste in this culture is approximated only in the dairy barn and with the cattle attendants among the Toda with their ritual cleansings, chants, and chastity. The varieties and variations are as numerous as are the recognizable variations in culture generally. Only a recognition of the fluid possibilities of an associationistic or conditioned reaction psychology can provide a "logic" for the prediction of specifically ritualistc acts—or for their control.

Consider for a moment the compulsive, almost paranoid attachment exhibited by all "believers" to their articles of faith, creeds, or, if you will, superstitions. Certainly such beliefs make a mockery of the statistics of probability which are presumed to guide "rational" conduct. The specific item of belief in question is a matter of no importance whatever. It might be the combat pilot's irrational insistence upon wearing his "lucky sweater" or trousers on each new mission; it might be the left hind foot of a graveyard rabbit that is held to assure success in a love quest; it might equally be a calm faith in the capacity of an orthodox prayer or sacrifice to pull one through whatever crisis is impending. Unless one insists that for his particular technique the normal laws of causality are held in abeyance, that this device actually induces an interference with the normal processes of the universe, these things too are but problems in the psychology of habit or learning. Cautious attempts at gaining insight into such matters by probing questions directed at believers reveal first of all a great reluctance to verbalize such matters. But it becomes apparent almost at once that a great deal of learning has taken place in the believer, specifically in the matter of the kinds of events and phenomena that seem to him to be amenable to such ritualistic control, and for which it is permissible to use such devices. These will generally be found to be situations in which there already exists a strong presumption of a successful outcome, or such extreme situations in which even straws must be grasped at. In short, the learning process quickly functions in the selection of situations in which the devices are to be employed. This alone improves the statistical aspects of the believing process. But habit processes seem upon close examination to have insidious characteristics that make them relatively immune to any statistical calculus. As Freud once wrote: "There exists in psychic life a repetition compulsion that goes beyond the pleasure principle." And again, "The Unconscious never forgets." A profound truth lies hidden behind these teleological and mystical statements. In simpler language it is just this: the effects of a habit once acquired are never completely eliminated. In that experimentally simple form of learning known as "conditioning" this principle is clearly demonstrable. Start with any conditioned reaction however acquired. It might be a salivary secretion conditioned to a bell after some fifty pairings of bell and food. Or it might equally well be a leg flexion conditioned by means of an electric shock to a distinctive sound and established with one pairing. Now repeatedly apply the newly potent stimulus without further pairing with the food or shock. The conditioned reaction will become weaker and finally disappear along about the tenth to the fifteenth stimulation. But just let some considerable time pass and the conditioned response is rather likely to reappear without any additional pairing. With other variations in the situation it again might reappear. Or better yet, pair the two original stimuli *once* more and your conditioned reaction reappears full strength. Hence the rabbit's foot can fail ignominiously a dozen times, only to have a single success reestablish to the full the original confidence in its potency. The competition between the various vested interest groups for the "first crack" at the conditioning processes in the young has then a very sound basis in the learning process. The persistence of the early acquired prejudices against particular racial or cultural fractions is similarly understandable. They illustrate processes fundamental in learning that fit neither insight nor reward nor purposive theories. For purposes of *control* of such reactions we know nothing else but to make use of the most exact descriptions we have of continguity or conditioning principles.

There is implied here no desire to minimize the role played by the social world of an individual in determining beliefs or practices. Most items of belief, sound or unsound, are socially acquired. Not only belief in the potency of the rabbit's foot but also the strictures as to the limitations of its efficacy are likely to be socially provided. The individual is even rather likely to deny having had recourse to magico-religious techniques, particularly in the case of their failure, unless their use in such a situation has at least a certain amount of social sanction. Here is unquestionably the psychological firing point behind the centrifugal tendencies with which organized religion has to contend. Once new items have somehow entered the structure of his beliefs the individual so equipped begins to demand social sanction and reenforcement for these variations. To the outsider the differences might well seem trifling but even a trifle can seriously disturb the equilibrium that constitutes a personality pattern. Enough similarly troubled inviduals can then constitute a new frame of reference, or a pattern of socially approved values or beliefs in which they can feel "at home." The alternative to these centrifugal forces in a world such as the modern, kept eternally in a ferment with new facts and new social pressures, is of course a strict regimentation of all accessible facts and beliefs. Any system of ideology or faith hoping to maintain itself in the face of such uncontrollable secular pressures would have to provide a complete system of educational influences in which the facts most glaringly at variance with the old belief structure would have to be given very careful interpretation and rephrasing. The attempts on the part of the Stalin political machine to prevent its ideological undermining at the hands of the geneticists is a case in point. Numerous similar instances are to be found of course, much closer to home.

Once established, the chief effect of all ritualistic habits whatever is that of producing attitudes of calm, quiet, confidence in the outcome of whatever events are in question. Certainly there are at least some tribulations whose overcoming is probably facilitated by an emotional calm. And where persistent, ritualistic behavior keeps up confidence and effort of a more directly determining sort, as, for example, where men "Trust in God *and* keep their powder dry" there can be no question whatever of the indirect contributions of such rites, prayers, icons, or relics in the production of a desired outcome. Historically, of course, the sponsors of, or experts in whatever techniques seem to demonstrate a convincing efficacy in some important social dimension, have strongly tended to "throw their weight around," to extend their control over wider dimensions of the social scene, and to suppress rival techniques. Probably no craft or guild can claim a universal immunity to this temptation. Certainly the priestcraft is no exception to the general rule, even if it is at once necessary to concede that they have easily been outdone in this regard by the professional soldiery. But it should be noted, parenthetically, that in the past these two particular crafts have typically worked out a very effective *entente cordiale* in the overall control of the social structure. In the current scene both have effective rivals in the form of financiers, entrepreneurs, professional politicians, and labor leaders. Were they not such incurable individualists it is even possible that on some tomorrow in some culture the scientific workers might constitute such a pressure group. Up to now the "conflict between religion and science" has consisted almost entirely of pressures upon individual scientists by the organized priesthood. But that is a familiar story—and of no immediate concern. What was aimed at here is simply establishing a common denominator for all human behavior whether practical, ritual, magical, ceremonial, or religious, in the light of the contemporary learning theory that concerns itself with overt or covert acts or responses rather than with insights, goals, ideas, purposes, or other animistic or teleological concepts.

The reluctance of the priesthood to accept any such purely materialistic and secular analysis of this segment of human social phenomena is naturally quite understandable. With McDougall, I quite agree that a final abandonment of animism leaves but little outside the domains of science. The assumptions underlying this inquiry into the psychology of religious origins are simply this: that the term "religion" as a universal, as a noun, is a dubious semantic entity. The particulars to which it has been applied have been entirely too diverse and historically fluid. An enormous variety of human behavior has been so characterized, but it had at least this common denominator: it was always human behavior. And it has been as just that and nothing more that it is being dealt with here.

It must then be apparent that to speak of "THE origin of religion," as though it were a single specific entity that had a specific and definite origin in some one particular motive, act, problem, or situation, is to talk nonsense. A functional analysis of human social behavior will reveal an astounding array of activities other than the simple, direct, mechanical, materialistic if you will, motions and effort necessary to satisfy needs or fulfill purposes. And all these superfluous activities are potentially ritualistic. "Man does not live by bread alone" as it has been sagely put in other aspects of human motivation. An entire activity pattern that was followed by any more or less complete restructuring of the situation tends to be preserved and repeated when the situation recurs in which it was somehow called out. Ritualistic as well as successful behavior thus tends to be repeated, not only the essential mechanical details but the entire preceding routine pattern, if it was persisted in until the situation was resolved. Thus an endless variety of situations have given and will continue to give rise to habit patterns that are not materially effective. Now much of such mechanically unessential activity has the very real function of supplying the maintaining stimuli, the self-provided cues which keep the individual properly oriented, timed, and persistent in his activities. In any scientific sense such activities are non-essential, but practically they may be very important indeed. Practically and functionally these *habit patterns gave man predictable behavior for situations that were themselves unpredictable.* Excepting of course what man did by way of mechanical and material intervention in such situations, exactly what he did by way of keeping his own behavior predictable varied enormously and it did not much matter exactly what was done. It could only not be in too great conflict with the basic habit systems of the rest of the personalities, his own and those of his fellows. Hence the almost infinite variety of behaviors variously identified as magical, religious, fetishistic, ceremonial, or ritualistic. And, let it not be forgotten, the more frustrating the situation, the more rigid, persistent, and unchanging the habits acquired, and in effect "frozen" there. But in the history of their acquisition, in the fundamental nature of their effectiveness, these activities cannot be *objectively* distinguished, regardless of what great gulfs may seem to separate them subjectively.

I said a moment ago that the magico-religious provided man with predictable behavior in situations that were themselves unpredictable. More accurately stated what happens is this: in certain kinds of unpredictable or uncontrollable situations man actually acquires quite predictable behavior which we then call variously magic or religion, ceremonial or ritual. And this is often a very important step in an effective adjustment to such situations. Calm familiarity must precede the capacity for objective observation. As to just whose pattern of behavior in such situations is to provide the norms for a social group—that question can have no different answer from what can be said in general of the influence of any one particular individual upon the rest of the group. As in every field of endeavor there are virtuosos and there are unimaginative duffers; there are initiators and followers, but even the meekest follower colors in some part the social whole by his capacity to follow the pace set by the innovator. But there are innovators in other fields and there are those that turn up different methods for achieving a variety of goals. Rival techniques thus appear. And if not by this means, then contacts with other cultures provide glimpses of other, perhaps more effective, perhaps only more dramatic ways of doing things. By one means or another, piecemeal or by revolutionary change sparked by a conqueror, new ways of doing things are introduced, old ways discarded. Discarded ways are then given a distinctive designation or classification. It bears repeating here that the term "magic" honors the skills of the old Persian priesthood, locally known as magi. Lynn Thorndike[13] tells us that the term came into general use for the special rites and skills of all foreign specialists in priestly functions and also for the older practices indigenous to an area after they had been officially displaced by some different system, usually at the hands of a conqueror. Today's religion, tomorrow's magic! No system of practices or beliefs in regard to one aspect of life is wholly untouched by the facts and principles accepted in the rest of the culture. In the western world religious beliefs have in recent centuries been under an almost continuous pressure due to the accumulation of exact, instrumental knowledge that could not help but displace the older ritual techniques. And, if we define as magic all discarded beliefs and practices, then and only then is one warranted in holding that religion evolved out of magic. What has in fact taken place is that practical, instrumental knowledge has made superfluous older traditions for meeting particular situations, many of which had effects only upon the practitioners by increasing their patience, supplying a calm confidence, or quieting fears or apprehensions. Important as these are, they cannot be expected to compete with specific controls of the situations themselves. And it is the developments in this field of instrumental control that have proved effective competition for any and all rival techniques. The evolution of both religion and magic has for the most part been a cumulative abandonment of fields invaded by the experimental method. It is however unfortunately true that the acquisition of "ritually effective" behavior habits then strongly tends to inhibit and discourage the pursuit of other, more directly efficacious approaches to the problems in question, and the experts in these older methods then are likely to oppose any competing or rivaling specialists.

There is no sound basis for assuming that at any time in the past some special set of conditions obtained, or that man reacted in some unique way to some aspects of his environment. New patterns of "religious" behavior appear today at irregular intervals in both primitive and "modern" societies. Their roots in the past as well as their points of departure in the present are all too obvious. Typically the radius of influence of such an innovator is small indeed. At the other extreme lies the epoch maker who leaves his mark across the millennia. Is there any good reason for assuming that it was not ever thus? It is when similar behavior patterns are adopted by social groups of greater or less size, adding social facilitation and group pressure to beliefs and conduct observances that we recognize the characteristics of a full-blown religion. The accumulation of material paraphernalia and the development of a class of specialists who come to live by, for, and on their ritualistic functions completes the process of institutionalization. But such bedazzling proliferations must not be permitted to obscure the psychological fundamentals of their being and origin.

CHAPTER VIII

BELIEF AND FAITH

"At your age I managed to believe six impossible things before breakfast."
—The White Queen, to Alice.

The Psychology of Belief

If experiment and probability are the distinctive stuff of science, belief and faith can truly be said to be the bases of religion and supernaturalism generally. Viewed as behavior, beliefs are almost if indeed not entirely verbal. That is, they are response tendencies attached to verbal statements either spoken by someone else or by the believer himself. Many beliefs remain almost exclusively in the verbal realm; nothing else is ever done about them. Most people, for example believe that "breathing exercises" are somehow valuable, but if they take one somewhat deeper or longer breath after having verbally expressed this belief that is probably about the average amount of non-verbal behavior attached to this belief. Similarly, most people believe that savages have keener senses than have the "civilized" races, and that ostriches hide their heads in the sand when pursued or attacked. Were we actually to compare the sensory acuity of assorted peoples we would shortly be set right on this matter. If we were dependent for our dinners of ostrich drumsticks upon captured ostriches we would quickly be disabused about another belief. But as things stand we can, and do, retain such beliefs, purely as verbal behavior. The beliefs involve no other actions whatever. Failing to keep company with savages or ostriches, we acquire no other habits of response in regard to such spoken words.

Beliefs are acquired by two principal processes: from first-hand encounter with various aspects of the universe, and from the behavior, overt and verbal, of our fellows. Both are very effective learning devices. The child quickly learns to accept at face value the "beliefs" taught him by the adults in his surroundings. Resistance to commands to overt action develops rather early; bitter medicines, painful needles, onerous tasks quickly enough produce a profound negative suggestibility in the young. It is usually quite some time later, if at all, that the young begin to question the area of verbal beliefs, or the practices of the prestiged members of his groups, particularly those beliefs that require nothing further than a reiteration of the belief, verbally. In fact, a verbal belief can persist long after all corresponding overt behavior or action has dropped out or disappeared. Verbal habits tend to outlive habits of overt action.

Beliefs tend to become systematized, to become part of a large variety of other beliefs and practices, all of which are likely to reenforce the original belief, so that any change now in any part of the belief structure would necessitate disturbing reappraisals of a great variety of facts and situations. This is particularly true in the area of verbalized beliefs. Overt actions tend better to adjust to the pragmatic details of the specific situation. The too conspicuous gaps between professed verbal beliefs and actual overt practice usually come to be bridged by a few supplementary verbal rationalizations, socially acceptable or emotionally acceptable explanations of our conduct.

In the area of secular facts there is a general expectation that the strength of a belief is, or should be, a function of the validity of the evidence available. The rational animal, or soul, that man likes to think himself, rather demands it. The psychological processes of the acquisition of beliefs have, however, quite other laws and determinants. The basic process is associative and not necessarily rational or logical as popularly presumed. In its simplest and most easily understood form it is best illustrated by the experiments in the conditioned reaction, which are far from being as simple as they are popularly thought to be. Probably the best way to state what takes place in such conditioning is just that whatever cues or stimuli happen to be present when man or beast makes any given response for whatever cause or reason, such response will tend to recur when the same stimuli again are present. Of these cues, not the least important are the cues provided by the organism's own activity. The improvement in the predictability of such conditioned responses that comes with repeated training or practice is probably a function of the greater variety of self-provided cues that now have been acting when the original action arousers called out the response. When the individual is no longer dependent upon any cues other than those provided by his own organism we say, in the case of man, that he now "knows it by heart," although the heart probably contributes but few significant cues to the performance. This transfer of capacity to call out a response to cues other than the original arousers may result from a single pairing of the stimuli. Where there are many variables in the situation the process might well take much longer. At any event, we now have a situation where a predictable response is called out by a specific situation. (The term "situation" as here used means nothing other than all the stimuli of whatever sort acting in or on the organism at any particular time in question.) Specifically, given a particular situation, a predictable response is now forthcoming from our individual. The "predictable response" may be an overt movement, an internal glandular activation or inhibition, or it may be best described as thought or imagery, or a belief—a readiness to express a particular article of faith, such as "Thou shalt not kill," or "There is no God but Allah, and Mohammed is his messenger." The greater the variety of situations under which such a belief is expressed or reiterated, the more firmly fixed will the belief be. A greater variety of cues now has become associated or linked with that particular response. The more extensive the participation of the entire organism in the making of a response, the greater the prospects for its retention as a habit. If we were to shout out Mr. Pflatzenpumper's name directly upon being introduced, the chances of recalling that name at a later time are much better than if we but gave that name a dubious mumbling. A belief held in the face of strong arguments tending to discredit such a belief is then effectively resistant to ever stronger arguments. Psychologically the process is identical with the habits we form in regard to regular attendance at work. We go when it rains, when it is cold, when we have not had sufficient sleep, when minor household crises develop, when we are slightly ill, when we really should not leave the house, finally even when dangerous illnesses are upon us. Of course, the learning process can take the opposite turn, and we stay away for increasingly trifling reasons. With most work there are obvious limitations on the development of such a trend, but psychologically the process is identical with that operating in the formation of desirable habits, or approved beliefs. The processes involved in the firm fixation of a belief are identical with all other learning processes in their fundamental nature. Ceasing to believe too, is like dropping or breaking any other habit. It is the persistence of both beliefs and habits that has long intrigued the practical manipulators of human behavior.

Beliefs, like all habits, tend to persist, once established. If both the individual and the environment remain as they were when the belief was acquired the belief would probably persist indefinitely. A belief that must be acted upon fares badly in a changed or changing environment. But the logic of the retention of a belief is not at all statistical. A belief, once accepted, is not recognized, subjectively, as invalid when the statistics of its successes show no improvement above chance. The retention of a belief has, instead, the characteristics of a conditioned response being subjected to experimental extinction. The term "extinction" is really quite inappropriate, because all but the most extraordinary conditions at best succeed in producing what is better described as "inhibition," the temporary failure of the habitual response to appear. Conditioned salivation to a ringing bell, for example, will diminish in the volume of salivary secretions elicited by the bell, if there is a succession of ringings not followed by food for the animal. If persisted in, such stimulation finally results in no increase in salivation and may even be

pushed to the point where less than a normal flow of saliva
follows upon the sound of the bell. This process may require
from a dozen to twenty stimulations without food. But with a
single ringing of the bell followed by food, the conditioned
salivary response returns in full, and then again requires almost
as many stimulations not followed by feeding before the salivation is again inhibited. This seems to be about the state of affairs
with once established beliefs; the count of negative cases can
far exceed the score of the hits, and yet the belief is firmly held
to. When we say of such performances that 'we remember only
the cases where our prayers worked and forget the failures' we
are but trying to fit the facts of the case into our traditional
accounts of the human performance. Actually, the believer may
be completely aware of the statistical imbalance of his data, as
careful questioning can frequently ascertain, and yet continue
to repeat the verbal item of belief, and, more important, continue
to have the subjective and convincing feeling that the belief
is somehow correct in spite of the statistical discrepancy of the
objective data that the believer will not dispute. The first-estab-
lished belief enjoys precisely the kind of priority that the once-
established conditioned salivary response has over the statistically predominating negative cases that follow.

There is even good evidence from experimental conditioning
that the resistance of a habit to experimental extinction is increased by the introduction of trials in the learning or conditioning situation that are not nicely paired with "reward," "success"
or satisfactions of any sort. This process is referred to by many
contemporary psychologists as "partial reinforcement." A recent and extensive survey of the experimental work done on
this problem[1] has summed up this aspect of the question as
follows:[2]

"3. *Resistance to extinction*. The most striking effects of
partial reinforcement are apparent in response strength as measured by resistance to extinction. In almost every experiment,
large and significant differences in extinction favoring the groups
(of subjects) partially reinforced in conditioning over the 100%
ones were found. The practical implication of this principle for
maintaining behavior is obvious: Administer the reinforcing

stimulus in conditioning according to a partial schedule, and the behavior will be maintained for long periods in the absence of external support from primary reward."

This shows clearly why the failure of events to correspond to a belief, far from weakening it can contribute immensely to its strength, during the initial learning as well as in the further maintenance of such a belief. In the case of religious beliefs and faiths the original acquisition of them is usually a social learning of them as verbal affirmations or cult observances, seldom if ever, involving any objective demonstrations of the truth of the beliefs being acquired. Any weakening of such beliefs would then again be counteracted and faith in them restored by the original social process by which they were taught if such reinforcement were socially provided with reasonable frequency, even in the complete absence of any concrete demonstration of the truth of the item of belief in question. How else could, for example, beliefs in regard to events post-mortem otherwise survive? It would appear then that the persistence of beliefs, once established, the pride or despair of man, depending upon circumstances, is but a universal characteristic of the learning process in man and beast. And, as often in other traits, man outdistances the performances of the lower animals so markedly that some observers insist that the differences are qualitative rather than merely quantitative.

All this is quite as it should be, not on any simple theory of learning resulting from a summation of "bonds" formed by each practice reaction, but rather when learning is seen to be a process in which an increasingly important role is played by the cues provided by the organism itself. The organism "learns" to continue responding in a particular way even in the absence of the external cues upon which the habit was first dependent. One can teach an organism to persist in a particular pattern of response in the face of "failures" rather than success; the tolerance of an organism for "failures" can be systematically built up. What else, might one ask, is the process of building up "delayed" or "trace" conditioned reactions as the Russian experimenters call them, but the persistence of behavior based upon the organism's self-provided cues rather than upon immediate environmental cues? In these experiments there is a systematic stretching out of the time interval between the new cue and the original, perhaps inborn action-getting stimulus, until a delay of almost a half-hour is produced between the application of the conditioned stimulus and the appearance of the conditioned response. Such a reaction depends, however, upon a specific pattern of intervening activity on the part of the organism to provide the cues at precisely the correct moment. Any break in the practical immobility of the animal maintained during such a delay will ruin the nice timing of the delay period. It might seem paradoxical to speak of "immobility" as a pattern of intervening activity until it is remembered that maintaining immobility, or even a reasonable facsimile thereof is a difficult task indeed, as any recruit can eloquently testify in regard to standing "at attention." Acquiring a "belief" is learning to persist in a particular pattern of response in the face of evidences to the contrary and, in many cultures today, learning to continue in a particular pattern of behavior in the presence of people who behave quite otherwise, or who may well have conflicting or contradictory beliefs. But a belief acquired in such an environment is far more resistant to social erosion than one acquired without competition from rival beliefs. It is psychologically akin to the habits acquired where the training included unrewarded or negative cases as well as "successes." The naive Russian peasant who firmly believed that heaven was located but a short distance above the earth was a far readier convert to an atheistic materialism than was the urban dweller, already exposed to much of the "higher criticism" of his religion. An airplane flight on a clear day sufficed to destroy the peasant's belief in a heaven and the god that went with it.[3] Learning to obey specific commands and to carry out particular orders in the face of distraction and terror is a similar process, psychologically. We approve of the process, if it is our orders that are to be carried out. We applaud the persistence in a belief under contrary evidence and strong social pressure if we approve of the belief. We comment upon human mulishness and stupidity if evidence valid for us is rejected.

As we have seen, belief may be produced with varying

amounts and kinds of evidence. Then too, beliefs may consist of purely verbal formulae upon which but little, if any, action is predicated. More commonly, beliefs predict actions of some sort at some times. The tendency to act upon beliefs is commonly referred to as "conviction." When an individual's actions correspond closely with his expressed beliefs we say he is a man of strong convictions. The terms "belief" and "conviction" in themselves carry no connotation or implication of the merits of the evidence upon which they are based, but it is generally assumed that the evidence falls something short of providing convincing certainty, or the kind of probability that is termed "knowledge." The term "faith" differs somewhat from "belief" in meaning, although the terms are often used interchangeably. "Faith" commonly implies a belief, based upon varying amounts of evidence, but held with a firmness or intensity that is unrelated to the statistical validity or other rational criteria of the merits of the evidence. It is this emotional intensity of a belief, unrelated to the quality of the evidence for it that provides the distinguishing characteristics of "faith." So long as the faiths in question are those in good repute in our culture "Faith" is considered meritorious and praiseworthy. But the dubiousness of the evidence upon which such faith is based is quite generally recognized. Some anonymous schoolboy has long been given credit for a definition of faith which goes as follows: "Faith is when you believe something that you know ain't true."[4] It is the very real grain or more of truth in that apparent paradox that intrigues us and has kept the quotation, whether genuine or not, in circulation these sixty years since James used it, and who knows for how long before his time. Yet even if we retreat from the naive denotation of the schoolboy and define faith simply as belief whose firmness and content go beyond what any known evidence warrants, it is apparent that only the vested interests identified with some particular local faith could possibly find merit in it. When it is remembered that the *psychologically distinctive element of faith, namely its emotional intensity and firmness, is actually produced by lack of evidence and even more by conflicting and contradictory evidence,* the earnest seeker after truth learns to be doubly suspicious of his firmest beliefs and faiths; and, as did Charles Darwin, learn to carry a "notebook for negative cases." Otherwise the negative evidence, by a peculiar quirk of the learning process, can, under proper conditions, increase rather than diminish the strength of a belief, in exactly the same manner that habitual but unrewarded responses in animal experimentation can be made to contribute more to habit strength than the same number of well rewarded responses. This process is in all probability the unconscious source of the motives that produced the popular reversal in the old observation—"The exception proves (i.e., puts to the proof) the rule," so that now it is popularly believed that the discovery of an exception to a rule actually establishes the validity of that rule! What the exception is likely to do then is actually to increase the psychological "strength" of the belief in the rule. Should this more or less paradoxical account of the psychology of belief and faith be utterly unacceptable to the good reader, permit me but to suggest that he try his hand at accounting for a small sample of the many and varied beliefs and faiths that even a cursory glance at the field will reveal. Let him ask himself how even a low grade of common sense could somehow arrive at some of these fantastic beliefs and maintain them in the face of the most obvious evidence to the contrary, if it were not made possible by some underlying but non-rational process in our fundamental make-up.

Even the briefest glance at the variety of things worshipped will reveal an incredible list containing practically everything that the eye can see or the imagination invent. The rare, the unusual, vie with the commonplace for the adoration of the multitudes, and all get it, if only one looks around a bit. Stones, large and small, or varied sizes, shapes, contours, or colors, at some time or place become objects of veneration and worship. Aereolites are a favorite. Hills and mountains, with or without gods on them become sacred. Long before the West named it "Everest," it was Godess Mother of the Snows. Trees and plants without number, the latter particularly if they yielded a drug or narcotic that could change the subjective experience state of whoever consumed it, might be revered as god, spirit, or totem.

Any inclusive listing of animals worshipped would leave for

serious speculation and doubt only the question—"Is there any animal that is neither a totem nor worshipped somewhere?"

The traditional "Four Elements" are seldom neglected; as rain, winds, storms, volcanoes, soil, or means of warmth they figure everywhere.

Astronomical objects, sun, moon, planets, comets, star clusters, even individual stars might become the center of a cult, as is Polaris with the Mandeans who orient their temples and their worship on that particular star.

It is apparent that objects are worshipped because of their importance, real or imagined, to man. So too, man himself is frequently the direct object of worship, either specific and particular men or women in the flesh, or just mankind in general. They may be worshipped because they are beautiful or ugly, strong or weak, well or ill. They may be worshipped or killed because they are of multiple birth, or albino, idiotic, psychotic, or epileptic. The person worshipped may be ruler or slave, old or young. Hindu wives actually have a cult of husband worship, the husband's big toe coming in for especial attention.[5] Sometimes an accidently placed individual comes in for worship amounting practically to deification. "Not a century ago a tramp came to a Hindu village and fell asleep at a deserted shrine. When the villagers awoke they found him there asleep. Nothing could persuade them that he was not the god returned. He in turn awoke to find himself the object of worship; food, drink, attendance, reverence, all were his. Alarmed at first he protested that he was only a poor villager like themselves. But they would not believe him; rather they believed in him and he, finding the post an easy one, remained there ever afterwards and lived and died a god."[6]

Ancestors are a very common object of reverence, either the individual's particular ancestors, or just ancestors in general. Heroic fellows are frequently deified, in the flesh or postmortem, their reputed powers frequently increasing during the centuries.

Not only can men become gods, but gods can become men, as they do in both Finnish and Persian epics. Gods also hybrid-

ized with men as reported in Genesis 6:2 and 4, and presumably
confirmed in the New Testament account of the origin of Jesus.
There is still some considerable difference in theological opinion as to the genetic constitution of this particular hybrid, the
question at issue being that of the relative dominance of the
divine and the merely human genes in his makeup. In this dispute, no opinion whatever is ventured here.

Gods may have a ghostly or a non-ghostly origin. They may
be creative or destructive. Among the Gonds, bells become
minor gods by virtue of the fact that they have the power of
frighten away ghosts. Iron is a god to an African tribe that
smelts it and makes a good living out of it by trading. Gods
may start out as individual persons, or they might have a history of a progressive personalization of some natural object or
phenomenon. Gods may be mortal or immortal; in perpetual
good health or suffer from temporary or chronic illnesses: Isis
had an abscess on her breast; her son Hor suffered from dys-
entery and anal trouble; the sun god, Re, suffered from diseases
of the eye. Demons are credited with capacities to bring such
distress to gods.

Mortal man, like Gautama, might start out teaching that there
is no god and that man is not immortal, and end up revered
as an immortal god by some of his followers and believers.

Gods may be thought to be concerned with human conduct;
the concern may be with the meticulousness of ritual performance, or with its ethical significance. Or, as in the case with the
deified Budda, he is assumed to be indifferent to the ethical
implications of human action.[7]

Devils are frequently presumed to exist; they may be credited with a malign or merely a whimsical nature. Shiva, the de-
stroyer, seems devilish enough to Westerns but is commonly
classed as a god. Certainly he is worshipped enthusiastically
enough by multitudes. Perhaps we class him as a god because
of our reluctance to admit that devils might deserve such a
large following. The human taste is catholic enough in its objects of worship. Even an abridged mythology lists some five or
six hundred Greek and Roman supernaturals.

Nor does adopting one god to worship seem to decrease the chances of a variety of others to come in for a quota of rites or adulation. Perhaps quite the contrary. Gods to worship seem to proliferate. They are added to a roster quite easily, but once adopted are abandoned only rarely, particularly the specific cult of a god. Cults frequently remain intact but with a different god, or with a modified role for the old god, as in the case of the transformation of pagan deities into "saints" in Christianity. Fantastic lists of gods can be rolled up in a particular community:

"In one small community of India are worshipped the "mother-goddess of the threshing floor," Sodal Mata; the goddess of roads and steeps, Telia, to whom are offered libations of oil; a deified tree, Anjan Dea; the goddess of smallpox, Sitala (revered with heaps of stones to resemble pustules); Bhulat, a cowherd, probably an historical person, and Singaja, a man who lived three hundred years ago and is now a god remembered with an annual fair at his tomb in September; and besides all these and the usual gods of a fairly large pantheon, reverence is paid to a god called "Fifty-Six," Chappan Deo, who represents "the largest number of places to which a lost wife or child may have strayed," and is worshipped as a real divinity."[8]

Science vs. Dogma

The bases for believing in such a diversity of deities would hardly bear objective scrutiny. Acquiring such beliefs is probably a function of the psychology of the learning process operating in a particular cultural setting. The Westerner, confronted with so baffling a mixture of what he considers magic, superstition, ignorance, and religion recoils in horror, feeling that it cannot be possible that human intelligence can fall so low. It may not seem possible or reasonable, but there is the evidence. It should give us a feeling of emotional kinship with the farmer reputed to have reacted to his first sight of a giraffe with—"There ain't no such animal!" And let it chasten us to remember that the strongest attachment to beliefs is not found among primitives who have always taken a particular myth or explanation for granted. It is rather to be found in circles where the individual believer has held to his faith in the face of accumulating evidence against such faith. Such an individual becomes an expert in believing in the face of more and stronger evidence against his beliefs. The menace of these processes to sound knowledge has long been recognized, if indeed it has sometimes been lost sight of for a millennium or so. Hippocrates is credited with having said, "Science and Faith are two things: the first begets knowledge, the second ignorance." It took almost two thousand years before western European medicine reacquired that Hippocratic insight into the dangers of faith. Who among us would venture to calculate the cost in human suffering that long delay entailed! Charge, that, oh Cosmic Bookkeeper, to the debit account of Faith!

There is a quite understandable sensitivity on the part of the professional theologian on this question of the nature of faith. The charge that religion depends upon assumptions that are untrue bites uncomfortably close on many items. A recent writer observes: "Faith certainly is not 'believing things that ain't so,' but very often is just believing things that do not seem to be so, and always it is believing what cannot be proved to be so."[9] Just what has become of the beliefs and faiths of the past that proved preposterous he fails to indicate. They probably are disposed of as not having been a *true* faith. In the same volume, (p. 14) the author tells us that "The objective of religion ever has been the same, and ever is the same: to know the truth and to live by it. The expression of religion, exactly for that reason has to change continually, as day by day we learn a little more and are qualified to live a little better." Just what sources we are to depend upon for this truth, he fails to specify. If our source of truth is to be science and experiment then we have little room for *faith* as commonly defined. He seems reconciled to a continuing change in religion in this quotation. Such change could presumably have but two possible sources: the new in science, or some new revelations in which to have faith; but he fails to point out these limitations in the possibilities. A few pages further and we encounter the following:[10] "The realm of religion is the realm of faith, and specifically not that of demonstration." One wonders just how faith is to produce the ever new by which we become qualified day by day to live a little better! This good theologian is obviously confused and probably more than a bit worried. He is trying to reconcile science with faith and dogma, and they are simply not to be reconciled. A particular individual might indeed be an expert in scientific method in one area of inquiry and depend upon the faith and dogma of the past in another. Such an individual might be laboring under the delusion that he has reconciled scientific method with faith; but all he has done is to prevent them from coming into contact with each other. In so far as he is a good scientist he keeps clear of any and all dogma in any way relating to his field. Where he accepts dogma or any sort, just to that extent he is not a scientist.

It might well be not at all amiss to analyze sharply, and contrast scientific and dogmatic attitudes, point by point, to emphasize their profound incompatibility.

The Scientific	*The Dogmatic*
1. Certainties excluded as by definition impossible.	Certainties assumed, existence without them completely intolerable.
2. Assumptions and presuppositions consciously made, open and identified.	Assumptions and presuppositions disguised, repressed, or suppressed.
3. A virtue is made of flexibility in assumptions.	Blind and unquestioned faith held to be a virtue.
4. Taxonomy recognized as but a practical classificatory or mnemonic device.	Taxonomy held to be inherent in the nature of things themselves.
5. The occurrence of exceptions points up the limitations of any rule.	Exceptions thought somehow to reenforce the validity of any rule.

6. All bare "Authority" regarded with extreme suspicion; empirical data always preferred.

Great fondness for "Authority," unquestioned revelations, sacred writ, etc.

7. All Laws, Theories, or hypotheses tentatively accepted as generalizations valid over limited areas.

Insistence that propositions be categorically either true or false.

8. Makes a virtue of tolerance for oppositional views or theories.

Intolerance of oppositional views.

9. Assumes that today's wisdom will tend to become obsolete.

Claims to have eternal truths today.

10. The "real" held to be quantifiable.

Ultimate reality unquantifiable.

11. Is but a means to practical, concrete goals.

Tends to become an end in itself.

Scientists and Religious Faith.

Many of the characteristics of dogma are a function of the fact that here we have attitudes, rules, and principles laid down by leaders, and calculated to maintain the strict discipline necessary to a surviving institution. But the acceptance or rejection of these two basic attitudes might well be to some extent a matter of their compatibility with other variables in the individual personality. Considerable research data seem to point in that direction.[11] Howells selected fifty students indicating a high degree of agreement with and belief in a group of orthodox opinions, for comparison with another fifty students showing a low degree of agreement with orthodox beliefs. His conservatives, in comparison to his radicals, showed up poorly in ability to withstand painful electrical shocks. Under threat of painful shocks for failure to improve in a motor skill, conservatives improved their efficiency considerably in comparison to the radicals or "unbelievers." Conservatives also succumbed decidedly more to suggestion, whether given orally by the experimenter or in printed form. In tests involving remembering, following directions, or solving maze problems, the radicals were significantly superior. So also in retention of high school learning, in university grades, and intelligence test scores. A study by the author[12] gave similar results on suggestibility and intelligence test scores. Many other studies on college students have confirmed these results on academic grades and intelligence test scores since that time.

This dilution of faith and dogma in the upper levels of intelligence is not a phenomenon of "immature minds" as it is frequently charged. Nor is there any evidence for the much publicized assertion that "the greatest of scientists are also the most devout believers." There is, in fact, considerable highly convincing evidence to the contrary. There is, for example, the study of Professor James H. Leuba.[13] Here is a study made on a respectable sample of American scientists and students in the year 1914, and repeated in 1933, confirming the earlier results. Leuba's criterion of religious faith was merely believing in any form of a personal god. He separated the scientists on the basis of their respective specialties, into physicists, biologists, sociologists, and psychologists. The eminence of each scientist was established by a system of ratings by fellow scientists in the same field. Leuba summed up his conclusions as follows: The largest percentage of believers in God and Immortality are to be found in:

1. The least eminent men in every branch of science.
2. Scientists of 1914 as against scientists of 1933.
3. Students of 1914 as against students of 1933.
4. Students in lower college classes as against upper class students.

A table can best present the differences between scientists in the various fields as well as the differences in degree of eminence as related to the incidence of belief in any form of a personal god:

PERCENTAGE OF BELIEVERS

Ratings by Fellow Scientists	Physicists	Sociologists	Biologists	Psychologists	All
Lesser	43	30	31	13	35
Greater	17	20	12	2	13
Greatest	—	5	—	—	—

It is interesting that the highest percentage of believers in a personal god is to be found among scientists dealing with inanimate matter, with those furthest removed from man as an organism in their fields of competence. If the relatively higher percentage of believers among sociologists is cause for comment, let it be remembered that no other academic field drew into itself so high a percentage of former divinity students in the decades after the turn of the century. They probably had, as several in this author's acquaintance put it, "retained their religion but parted company with theology." Particularly significant, it would seem, is the fact that it is among psychologists that the smallest percentage of believers is to be found. When it is remembered that it is the phenomena of the "mind," "soul," or "spirit" that have provided the basis for the animistic view of the world so congenial to most religions and are at the same time the prime object of study by the psychologists this fact cannot be lightly dismissed. When, in spite of the powerful pressures for social conformity in matters of belief, we find the scientists in this area of study illustrating or demonstrating Thomas Huxley's "—extension of matter and causation and the concomitant banishment of spirit and spontaneity," we cannot in all good scientific conscience ignore their opinions. Their conclusions demand the respectful attention we have at least in part learned to give the specialist when he speaks in the area of his professional competence. Yet there is hardly an area of knowledge, unless it be that of statesmanship, in which we are more reluctant to concede the specialist the mastery of his skills. Privately, we all consider ourselves sound psychologists and statesmen. Or perhaps we consider such matters as the nature of mind and spirit to be matters of "good common sense," a quantity in which no one rates himself as being below average, and hence there is no expert opinion to respect. Here it must be remembered that strong motives are not lacking for conformity on the part of the psychologist, or any other scientist for that matter. Should some scientist take time or trouble to write some article refuting some item of popular belief in the area of religion it is doubtful that he would find a publisher. But let any scientist of consequence in any field, however remote from the phenomena of the human equation, reiterate any of the old items of belief, or provide a variant on an old rationalization in support of such item of faith, and he will make the headlines and receive generous checks from the publishers. It is without question the excellent press such efforts achieve that has created a popular impression of the piety of scientists completely at variance with the actual facts of the case which can be ascertained only by means of studies such as those of Leuba. A more recent study[14] points in a similar direction. Twenty-two theoretical and experimental physicists, judged "eminent" by their peers, reported but little interest in the church. If this item made the popular press or "condensing" magazines it evaded my vigilant eye. To quote Roe:

"Of religious sentiment mention was made by very few and my impression is that probably only one of the group has more than a vague feeling of the sort, and I doubt that his is very developed."[15] And again:[16] "Only a very few of this group are church goers; perhaps not more than two of them are emotionally involved in an established church in any way."

On the other hand, no efforts by any psychologists have had a better press than have the studies purporting to report the operation of "extra-sensory" processes and other aids and supports to animistic theory, whose statistical validity, even as claimed, would be laughed out of court without even a trial were it a formula for a vaccine or even a new "cold cure."

A sample of the sort of thing that finds a ready market in the popular press is an article by a physicist in a recent issue of a mass-circulation magazine entitled "Can a Scientist Believe in God?" Such questions come to be asked precisely be-

cause there is no small amount of evidence accumulating that
scientists increasingly do nothing of the kind. But it has certainly not yet reached the stage where the discovery of a scientist professing some dilute form of religious belief fulfills the
"man bites dog" criterion of the newsworthy. *Of course* any
one particular scientist might believe anything! A scientist, after
all, generally has training in but a few narrow fields at best.
One might plunge into the mysteries and complexities of nuclear physics and leave completely untouched such beliefs as
one had previously accumulated in "human nature," dietetics,
the gold standard, the New Deal, "one's immortal soul," cannibalism, or the Immaculate Conception. Yes, one might. But by
and large, there is considerable generalization of the fundamental principles of the scientific method. There develops in the
average scientist a respect for data and conclusions derived
from the kinds of experiments and the statistical methods he
himself employs to such good effect. The average scientist acquires a knowledge of, and a respect for, other specialists
making honest attempts to apply the same methods of getting
at facts he himself has learned to trust. The too obvious gaps
between traditional beliefs and the facts emerging from scientific research cannot help but become apparent. The obvious
logic, that if the traditionally "infallible" sacred texts are wrong
in their astronomy and their biology, should not the rest of their
content be equally suspect, does finally dawn upon at least
some earnest "souls." But not upon many. Like Rhine and
Ducasse,[17] whose faith in telepathists and "mediums" was not
shaken by catching them at dubious trickery, your typical "believer" in a sacred text will readily concede you that the astronomy it contains is childish, its cosmology infantile, its geography
ridiculous, and its dietetics and materia-medica in no way
superior to that of any culture at a similar level of technological
development, but he will insist that these same texts will contain the very last word, even The Divinely Inspired Word, in
matters of the ethics of conduct! At this point a logic-tight cur-
tain falls, and the practices and standards of conduct they
happened to have acquired in childhood become not only laws
of nature but of the god they had simultaneously been led to

believe had ordained such behavior standards. Thus, our physicist:

"When I am trying to work out a problem of right and wrong, then God is a clear and unambiguous voice, an unfailing source of moral guidance. I do not in the least understand how these things happen; but I know perfectly well, if I listen to this voice, what is the right thing to do. I have many times been uncertain which course of action would best serve a certain *practical* purpose; but I cannot think of a single instance in my life when I asked what was the really *right* thing to do and the answer was not forthcoming."[18]

It seems incredible that at this date there still are literate people who are yet so completely innocent of what has transpired in the areas of anthropology and psychology since the days of John Locke that they have no idea where such conceptions of right and wrong come from. Failure to recognize in this day and age that such a "clear and unambiguous voice" is nothing other than the values of a particular culture, uncritically accepted by a child, and no wiser than the parents or parsons who did the indoctrinating, is to forever brand oneself as unfit to provide intelligent ethical counsel in the world today. It is precisely such "clear and unambiguous voice" that sanctions everything man has ever done, from cannibalism to cautery, from crusade to pogrom, from construction to destruction. If the values were but taught early enough they provided the "clear and unambiguous voice," upon which men have acted, wisely or unwisely. Happily, we are beginning to produce a generation of critical people that has become extremely suspicious of precisely such unquestioned and unverbalized judgments and values. They have been shocked into awareness that, like Shaw's barbarian,[19] they have confused the manners and customs of their little island with the laws of nature. From such a chastened position, there is hope for the development of a functional ethics that has prospects for being something more than a long-faced sanction for whatever the past has made traditional. Who knows, with more attention to objective facts and less to the voices of the past, perhaps we can improve upon punitive measures in controlling drug addiction, and can come to prefer birth-control and curettage to unwanted or unprovided-for children, or bastardy. But first, the "clear and unambiguous voices" that most people give ear to, will have to be muted or their content radically transformed. Such "voices" are no divine mystery; they are a historically determined product, and no wiser than the crude perceptive powers man had in the long ago.

The current high repute of verifiable, statistical fact is a relatively recent product. Before the last two hundred years or so an empirical fact frequently got but short shrift when confronted with some accepted item of faith. There was a time, not too long past, when a dissection that failed to show things as they were given in Galen or some other venerated "authority" was itself presumed to be somehow in error. "Authority" just was not questioned. Typical is the frequently quoted biographer of St. Thomas who spoke warmly of a time "—when men doubted less and hence were nearer the truth." Today it seems hardly possible that man ever could echo such sentiments. But among the faithful of many a religion there is a special virtue that goes with believing even the most preposterous miracle or tradition. It has often been felt that there is no special merit in believing the possible; the test of a true faith is to believe the impossible! In the atmosphere of medieval Europe facts were not nearly as important as the acceptance of a particular belief. No wonder: sticking to a stubborn fact, no matter how well substantiated, might well cost you your neck. It was always safe to echo any official faith. Under such circumstances any fact, no matter how obvious would quickly become the worst of bad taste, and facts in general, at least in certain areas, could become downright evil. Given similar circumstances, it could happen to any of us! The heresy-hunting epidemics in the United States following each of the two world wars should make this process familiar enough to anyone who has lived through such a period. It may well be that the "wickedness" of any belief, opinion, or even fact derives from the social consequences of its expression. When evil consequences follow upon the heels of the expression of an opinion, that alone provides the emotional value judgment of "evil." The

eighth planet that exists millions of miles away can do you no
harm if you deny its existence. But assert that there is one
among people who consider such assertion to be an evil and
dire consequences are not far behind. There is a popular illusion that belief precedes its verbal assertion. The reverse is
probably far more often the case; we come to believe what we
have only said often enough. We make "believers" simply by
starting them out early enough in repeating the words we
ultimately want them to "believe," and by showing social dis-
approval of, or providing punishment for any contrary expression. Far from being an obstacle, vagueness of any belief is
definitely an asset, both in its initial acquisition and its retention in the face of logic or evidence to the contrary. The vague
is unlikely to be in conflict with past verbal habits or memories
in general, and is therefore more acceptable initially. Once
acquired it is much less vulnerable to any possible logical analysis or embarrassing fact. It is cetainly the relatively vaguer
theistic beliefs that have survived in good repute into the current scientific era which has stripped the supernatural of so
much of its role and function.

Scientific method, as a source of ideas worthy of belief, is
hardly two hundred years old. And look at the magnificent
structure that it has raised! A religious faith less than ten times
that age would have to be set down as a relative upstart, a
Johnny-come-lately. Yet with all their age and venerability,
what have such faiths achieved? For the most part, spawned a
motley crew of dissident and warring sects whose sole contribution to mankind has at best been a slight variation in the
traditional devices for arousing and assuaging feelings of guilt
over matters of ritual, rather than of the empirical bases of
conduct. The application of scientific method has indeed raised
new issues and confronted man with new problems. The Believers are fond of reminding us of this aspect of the consequences of scientific empiricism. But it should be emphasized
here that the solution of such problems as arise is typically far
more a problem in combating the efforts of the ritualists in
preventing the solution of such problems than it is a lack of
knowledge of what to do, or how to do it. Science did indeed

create a population problem when it learned how to eliminate the black death, small pox, and diphtheria. But the only obstacle in the way of the solution of that problem is the ritualists and the attitudes they have deliberately cultivated during the past millennia.

Another consoling device the ritualists have recourse to is that of placing a heavy emphasis upon things that scientific method has not yet achieved. Their theme song is "Science Can't—." These gentlemen and ladies are not one bit impressed by what *ritualism* has NOT achieved in six or sixty thousand years. It would seem that as a matter of fact nothing is, or should be, expected of devout observances or ritual of whatever sort, other than perhaps that "peace of mind (or soul)" which in effect paralyzes human initiative and action. But it would seem that of the achievements of science such people know nothing but a few whoppers of what scientific method has *not* thus far managed to master in its paltry two hundred years of more or less self-conscious existence. Typical of such are, "But science cannot create LIFE"; "Science can't repeal the law of gravity"; or "Science knows nothing about things of the Spirit," this last limitation being meant to imply that by definition it couldn't possibly learn anything about the phenomena such people choose to designate as "spirit"; that such things transcend that vulgar, material realm in which scientific method might operate. What this point of view generally implies is that there is a profound, metaphysical gulf that separates the logico-empirical or scientific from the value-judgmental, the ethical. One might well wonder just what the basis in fact is for such a separation. Cannot value judgments and ethical standards in men be made practically to order, even within the framework of ordinary social relations? Certainly the justification offered by religious machinery practically everywhere for its existence is that it is deterministically creating or making them in those whom it indoctrinates. They can hardly deny the existence of a cake while at the same time busily eating it!

Yet, there are those who hold that the realm of religious faith does transcend relatively mundane phenomena such as the value-judgmental. Stace, for example,[20] writes:

"The religious impulse in men *is* the hunger for the impossible, the unattainable, the inconceivable—or at least for that which is these things in the world of time. And anything which is less than this is not religion—though it may be some very admirable thing such as morality."

This comes dangerously close to agreeing with the contention of Herbert Spencer when in the first few pages of his "First Principles" he assigned to religion the entire domain of the Unknowable! At any event, it points up the implied or expressed contention of practically all spokesmen for the "religious," namely, that there must be and are facts or truths outside of or beyond those apprehended by the conceptions or methods of science. If there is a common denominator to the religious beliefs that survive in cultures alongside of the scientific method and technology, this is it. It is their universal and persistent illusion. They insist that they do know a lot about this Unknowable, or have a childish faith that some person, or even an institution, is authoritatively informed about it. Such knowledge is presumed to be arrived at by methods other than those involving the channels of the familiar senses. Nor is it subject to the usual critical logic applicable when ordinary matters of fact are at issue. This kind of knowledge is assumed to come to at least some men by way of a direct and uniquely "religious" experience.

The Role of Belief in Religion.

One of the commonest fallacies encountered among laymen is the opinion or the assertion that they adhere to their religions "because of" their particular beliefs. Certainly the particular beliefs they subscribe to seem to be central in their thinking and analysis of just what their religion consists. Belief seems to come first, to have that priority in time and in reason. Nor should this error of analysis occasion surprise because the same error is common among even scholars and experts in the field who have obviously given considerable time and thought to the question. W. J. Goode[21] has this to say:

"It is no strain on faith to believe that there was a beginning to religion, that there was a time when our ape-like cousins-far-removed began to believe. This occurrence, or occurrences, was a definite point in history—definite, unknown, and unknowable. The data are not available and they will not appear."

This statement obviously implies that religion began with a belief of some sort, however stupid or primitive. It conveys the idea that at some time, somewhere, perhaps an ape-man assuming the posture of Rodin's "Thinker" began to think something as follows: 'This earth is an incredibly large and wondrous place; it obviously must have been created by an even more awesome being or agent. Therefore I shall begin offering him the best slice of venison so that he will be favorably disposed toward me.' Something akin to this he seems to presume started "religion"! Any notion that thinking, however muddy, must have preceded and given rise to what we recognize as religion has quite some hurdles to clear before it could be seriously entertained. Did a similar thought process, however crude, also precede all magic? The evidence from modern psychology of learning is all against it. We find, instead, that while we frequently meet situations with old habits, sometimes successfully, our successful responses in really strange and unfamiliar problems are not preceded by any form of logic or reasoning. Instead we find that we have made responses that come as a surprise to us and which may even give us trouble in duplicating. Alfred Loisy[22] comes close to a recognition of the true role of reasoning processes or beliefs in the origin of religion when he writes as follows:

"—religion is not a childish explanation of the world since the religions that exist or have existed have always had a cult before having a cosmogony."

That lucid and scholarly professor of Sanskrit and philogy, E. Washburn Hopkins[23] observes:

"Historically, man worshipped first and enquired later what he was worshipping." Professor James Leuba writes somewhere in his "Psychology of Religious Mysticism" as follows:

"Religion is not so much thought out as danced out."

Exactly! "Religious" beliefs or ideas, cosmological, agricultural, or therapeutic, have always followed along behind the overt practices. These actual practices are the result of the operation of stimulus-response and associative learning processes. They were not preceded by a verbal or rational "logic." A little excursion into the area of things actually believed, not by hypothetical ape-men but by members of the genus Homo should here be illuminating. Let us take, for example, the whimsical practice of cutting off a finger joint, usually a self-inflicted mutilation. Cro-Magnon man apparently did it since the human hands that appear in drawings on cave walls sometimes show this mutilation. Of course we cannot ask him what belief he had that prompted him to make this sacrifice, but within historical times some half-dozen tribes still knew the practice. Now if belief about something momentous provided a logic that said "cut off a finger joint" there should be something like agreement in regard to the circumstances or conditions that called for this minor amputation. But what do we find? In one tribe it is the accepted device to use as an aid in obtaining a vision. Great store is put on visions in this culture; they are the nearest thing they have to what corresponds to both religion and vocational guidance in our culture. A vision is necessary to a young man if he is to have a convincingly authoritative start in life. In some half-dozen tribes the practice is resorted to by an individual during some sort of a group crisis or period of tension, such as awaiting the appearance of a run of salmon, or during a period of game shortage, or drought, or excessive precipitation, or during a disease epidemic. What logic of belief could ever prompt such similarities of acts? So far as these peoples have been reported on there is no discernible agreement as to how the causal process operates in these cases. But they seem convinced that the act "helps." Of course it "helps," it provides action and excitement and distraction, thereby "filling" time psychologically, which subjectively makes time pass more quickly and hence in terms of experience seems to "cause" the desired results. No form of belief could dictate such a line of conduct; even to verbalize what actually happens in such a situation tends to destroy such belief as might cling to it. Such a course of conduct had to be hit upon by accident and fixated as unreasoned acts in a behavior series. A bona-fide accident or combat might well have set the pattern in most cases. No antecedent "belief" in advance of the act or accident could invent a supporting logic for so unprecedented an act. An interesting variant is provided by a New Guinea tribe in which the groom at a wedding chops off an index finger of his newly acquired bride. What kind of a belief could dream up that in advance of the act itself? Even a crude logic should grasp the fact that it was certainly no advantage thus to handicap a working partner! But once some dramatic accident, or an outburst of emotion of some sort on the part of some highly prestiged person, has set the pattern it might well survive. There are plenty of historical records of the setting of such precedents, and they are not necessarily intelligent procedures either. It is a safe bet, however, that inquiry would discover a whole host of "beliefs" among these people, presumably providing the "reasons" and motives for such customs.

The role of belief and faith in religion can then be summed up something as follows: The traditional, the historical religions are popularly believed by their communicants to have been a structure which followed upon the development of particular beliefs. "I believe, therefore I act," appears to be the developmental sequence, both historically for the religion itself, and also for the individual. Actually, the acts themselves frequently are hold-overs from some previous pattern of life and with which an entirely different "faith" was identified. The Christian celebrations of Christ's birthday on the old festival of the day of the new sun directly after the winter solstice observed hundreds of years before Christ as Mithra's birthday, is a case in point. The celebrations long antedate current belief. Long before the crucifixion, fish was eaten on Friday, Freya's day. The approved "belief" at the time in regard to the practice was that it was constructively helpful in the areas of Freya's special concern, namely, reproduction. It is a safe bet that these old European pagans enjoyed both fish and reproduction! Their linkage in ritual and ceremonial is probably as fortuitous as the American eating of turkey and cranberry sauce at Thanksgiving time. How could it well be otherwise? What special logic could come up with a formula like this: "because Christ was crucified on one particular day of the week we will eat fish rather than meat on that day?" Is eating fish rather than meat a form of penance? Perhaps for some in this well-fed day in some countries, but the reader need not be reminded that for the great bulk of the citizens of Christendom in the days before rapid transit and refrigeration fish on any day of the week would be in the nature of a gastronomic treat! Positively anything else might, with equally good logic, be substituted. But the current practices have true determinants or antecedents, like the Thanksgiving turkey.

Traditional beliefs, then, tend to be in the nature of what Pareto calls "derivations," namely, theories, justifications, ideologies; in short, rationalizations or socially or morally acceptable "explanations" of our behavior, rather than historical or deterministic accounts of just how it happened that we are behaving in this particular way. Such rationalizations almost without exception are developed after the acts or customs have long been established, in fact, it is when they begin to come under fire that there is likely to be a spate of such verbal justifications and defenses. The importance of such justifications in the habit equipment of the believer must not be discounted. In a world that prides itself on its increasing reasonableness and rationality every item of practice and belief can expect to find itself under critical fire. Any practice or custom left without it ideological outposts would be vulnerable indeed, particularly in the contemporary world where experimentally based beliefs frequently do initiate large scale action. Increasingly we expect a genuine logic for our acts, and it had better be good or else rival behavior patterns will offer serious competition. Belief and faith can well expect an increasing competition from experimentally based logic.

Of the psychological processes involved in belief, no overall evaluational judgment is possible. What is significant in each particular belief is its relation to action. The same belief-processes that supply calm and patience and confidence to the individual in a situation where there is nothing to be done except await the outcome of events beyond control, can discourage the highly essential trail-and-error that is the necessary prelude to any advance on the frontier of knowledge and skill.

The blind faith that keeps the communicant repeating the same prayers or rituals during a crisis can also keep an experimenter with a "hunch" making endless and fruitless trials till perhaps a six hundred and sixth trial does mark a significant gain. It might be said that in general the faith that keeps an individual at a repetitive ritual can at best tide that individual over a crisis, and at worst lead to the forbidding of anything other than that particular ritual for all sorts of crises and situations that actually cry out for empirical innovation and trial and error. The most glaring instance of such misapplication of faith and belief in Christendom is the long record of opposition to scientific and therapeutic innovations during almost the entire history of Christianity. Still, it must not be implied that this shortcoming is unique to this faith. The best period of Indian medicine coincided with the rise of Buddhism when the traditions and prestige of orthodoxy were so badly shaken that innovators had a chance against entrenched orthodoxy. In his appraisal of the medicine of ancient Egypt, Dr. Victor Robinson[24] has this to say:

"Was antiquity's tribute to Egypt justified? Must we confirm or reverse the verdict? Authors yet unborn will some day add books, to those already existing on the remarkable state of medical knowledge among the Egyptians. But the most surprising aspect of the matter is that a people so capable, should have produced a medicine so barren. Egyptian medicine was non-progressive, and since it could not advance, it went backward with the centuries. The earlier papyri contain more medicine and less magic, while in later scrolls the incantations are predominant.—Since all wisdom was contained in the forty-two books of Hermes Trismegistus, the priest-physician could not question or modify the sacred writing: no blame attached to the practitioner if the patient died according to the hermetic rules, but if he deviated from the prescribed regulations and the case terminated fatally, then his own life was forfeit. The Priest-physician was a hybrid that could not survive; the priest conquered the physician, and medicine succumbed in the enfolding arms of magic."

Lest anyone assume that priests have a corner on such

obtuseness and addiction to rule and ritual, consider the following episode that occurred about 1936, almost a decade after Dr. Robinson wrote the above, in a large hospital in a large metropolitan area, probably better supplied with competent medical personnel than any other area in the world. A victim of an accident was brought to this hospital where the receiving interne quickly recognized a concussion with a simple skull fracture. The patient was unconscious and his reflexes indicated increasing cerebral pressure. A spinal fluid pressure reading indicated pressures at, if indeed not above, the point of critical danger. By all symptoms, the man was dying. The interne, not yet too respectful of the contemporary equivalent of the books of Hermes Trismegistus, saved the patient's life by quickly having his skull shaved, laying bare the skull at the fracture and, by prying apart the fractured bones, allowed the accumulating blood from the brain hemorrhage to escape, thus bringing down the internal brain-pressure which in but a matter of minutes more would certainly have killed the patient. Transfusions and other emergency action then pulled the patient through. One might expect that such swift diagnosis and prompt, efficient measure should have merited praise and commendation when the senior neural surgeons arrived next day to review what had been done to the patients. Not so! What the interne actually got was a reprimand for "*compounding a fracture.*" He could have allowed the patient to die a dozen times, if he had died *according to rule.* But to save his life meant a reprimand if a rule in the book had been violated in doing it![25] Well, we have progressed a bit at that from the times of ancient Egypt. We no longer kill the deviant physician. Still, if with a saved life to his credit he still rated a reprimand, what indeed might not have happened to him, had the patient died? One dreads even to contemplate such an eventuality!

A hesitance to deviate from the rules of orthodoxy is probably still costing us plenty in similar areas and circumstances. Reading the account of the death of President Franklin D. Roosevelt as reported in the press made at least this reader feel that prompt if a bit unorthodox action might well have saved the man. He had his physician at his side. He reported terrific headache and visual failure, suggesting at once a cerebral hemorrhage in the occipital area. Even a primitive neurological examination could have quickly confirmed that location if it were indeed there. And with a life in the balance desperate chances are in order. In these days of anti-biotics even crude, extemporary surgery is not to be dreaded too much. At least some attempt could have been made to keep that pressure from building up to the point of death. If upon opening the skull the hemorrhage persisted, other measure of an emergency sort would give the patient a fighting chance. At least your author hopes that when his turn comes for a cerebral hemorrhage that an ingenious and not too orthodox interne is at hand who thinks only in terms of the mechanics of the problem; and "damn the traditions"!

Just what constitutes the circumstances conducive to learning and innovating in a given situation is indeed an interesting problem. Consider the Egyptians, for example: they removed the viscera from millions of bodies but during all that time learned apparently nothing about anatomy or pathology in the process. And what a golden opportunity to learn that was, even under the limitations laid down by the traditions to be observed in embalming! The medieval inquisitors in Europe too, tore bodies apart, tore out tongues and hearts and slaughtered thousands in heresy hunts but learned nothing about anatomy or pathology. It is probably true that had they been motivated by a zeal for knowledge they would have been neither inquisitors nor heresy hunters! At least this is certain: the worst atmosphere for learning anything excepting new punishments for heretics, is that provided by unshakable belief and faith of any sort. In the world of knowledge, any faith or belief beyond what will provoke persistent and enthusiastic search or manipulation in the pursuit of fact is probably no asset. Any faith that sparks nothing but a repetitive ritualism can at best be but an emotional crutch supporting an individual during a crisis, and there is always the danger that the emotional crutch is applied where heresy, heterodoxy, and empiricism should have a free hand.

The Need to Believe.

An opinion popular in some circles has it that the individual absolutely must have an organized system of faith of some kind; that he must have an explanation of some sort for the enigmas of the cosmos, that he cannot perpetually face an "X" or an unknown and become reconciled to it. As it is commonly put, "You have to believe something."

Piaget's studies[26] in recorded conversations of children when not playing up to their elders certainly seemed to indicate that the typical reaction for a child confronted with a question is to give an answer, an "explanation" of some sort. A child might indeed admit not knowing something himself, but this sample of children's conversations seemed to indicate that in the child below the age of 14 it is of course assumed that all things are known. Seldom, before age 14, did his records show a child saying, "they do not know," or "that is not known," or "no one knows about that yet." Before that age, and often enough after, the most preposterous nonsense suffices as an "explanation"; the important thing seems to be that there must be something offered as an explanation, just what is offered or presented seems to be a matter of no moment to the child. Anything seems to satisfy him.

The question that now arises is this: is this attitude on the part of young children in the matter of demanded "explanations" in any way revealing of an innate need for a feeling of certainty about its universe as is commonly claimed? The author has had this question under consideration and observation for a number of years and can report with confidence that the source of this attitude on the part of the average child is not far or long to be sought. The children learn it from their parents. Most parents feel, apparently, that they have to give answers or explanations even where probably no answer is known. They give spurious answers or teleological explanations of phenomena about which nothing is known. Thus it is that the child gets the impression that there is an answer to all questions, that the answers really are known even if they are not. Of course a child can acquire the habit of expecting answers to everything! But he can also learn, without in any way disturbing him, that there are plenty of questions to which the answers are not known.

Even if a child's own parents refrain from supplying it with an arbitrary roster of items that must be believed, it will no doubt encounter other children who have been thus indoctrinated and hence are likely to pass on to their playmates this confident wisdom. At a very young age, before having been introduced either to radio listening or devout observances of any sort, one of the author's children came to the dinner table after a period of play with other children, and unburdened himself of the following query:

"Is it true, (pause) that when you die, (pause) and if you have been good, (pause) that you get to go to a castle up in the sky, where you meet the Lone Ranger?"

Naturally, I could only inform the child that I had never encountered exactly that particular belief, but that it did not differ too markedly from a great variety of beliefs he would no doubt in time encounter. The boy was not at all perturbed that beliefs varied greatly, and that it was not at all incumbent upon him to accept any one belief arbitrarily. Nor has he been made uneasy since by this variety of beliefs although he has had long and friendly associations with companions of at least two dozen different faiths, covering practically the entire range of the world's major religions. He does not feel any compulsion or pressure whatever to "believe more than he can prove" as is so confidently asserted by some that one must. Mortimer Ostow and Ben Ami Scharfstein,[27] for example, write as follows:

"The particular metaphors in which we define our experiences always change, but there never is any change in the need of society to enlist the conscience of its members, or of the individual to believe more than he can prove."

They continue, on the same page:

"Believing is almost as necessary to humans as eating. What is believed is of course not necessarily useful, any more than what is eaten is always nourishing. But belief is essential to the efficient functioning of the human organism, and this belief is more than the elementary faith, implicit in all the actions of a sane man, that effect follows cause, that there are other persons besides himself, and that he can distinguish between his dreaming and his waking life. We have the need to believe, and it is futile to think that many of us can be happy though thoroughly skeptical."

Come, come, gentlemen, just what must one believe? There is no such thing as "belief" in the abstract; a belief without content is like Lewis Carroll's famous grin minus the grinning Cheshire cat. What kind of super-rationalism is this we are being fed, that pretends that there is no action without prior "belief" to spark it and give it a conscious motive? I have news for you: beliefs are rationalizations we manage to dig up to provide excuses or a rationale for habits we have long had and practiced. You do not make an Episcopalian by first selecting a person and indoctrinating him with the famous thirty-nine articles of faith; you send him to church as a child where he learns the proper behavior for an Episcopalian before he probably can count to thirty-nine. Or, as an adult, one might learn the advantages, financial or social, of joining the church that the "right" people already attended, and then brush up a bit on its doctrine. Even the organized church did not begin with the articles; they were formulated after its organization.

And what kind of thorough skepticism is it that at best but a few could manage to live with? And how do we know it? Have you any data on large numbers of citizens brought up as skeptics from childhood in much the same manner that most of us are given some specific faith? And have these fellows in later life surrendered and rushed wildly into Methodism, Shinto, devil-worship, or whatever happened to be lying around at the moment of their break? True, there are cases of skeptics abandoning their doubts and returning to the religions of their childhood. But then too, there are cases, far less well publicized, of people on their deathbeds, refusing the last rites of their church with the remark that it was high time they ceased being hypocrites, having lost their erstwhile beliefs long since!

Of course, every stable society must somehow manage to socialize its members, to have them internalize the values of the group. But where is the evidence that this calls for believing more than can be proved? The obvious importance of and the advantages of orderly social existence is not something that cannot be proved. It can quickly be made apparent to even the dimmest wit that can manage to add two and two and come up with an answer no more than 50% off the correct result.

One might also wonder, just what belief is necessary to the efficient functioning of the human organism? Since our authors have failed to specify what must be believed for that purpose, shall we guess? I take it that no problem is involved here with things that can be proved, or for which there is some plausible evidence. What is held to be necessary is to believe something that cannot be proved. Come, come! Whose list of unprovables? That of, let us say, the orthodox Hindu? Of a Fundamentalist from the Bible and Jim Crow belt? Of the Egyptians of the time of Amenhotep II? Ridiculous? Of course. Even relatively young children can be introduced to the concepts of probability as opposed to certainty; after which "certainties" of all sorts can make them acutely uncomfortable. As for expecting them to believe anything for which there is no evidence—that becomes a challenge to their imaginations; they will promptly invite you to believe a real whopper. They can learn deterministic explanations; and where the complexity of a phenomenon goes beyond them they at least are reconciled to the fact that the determinants are there, even if in a quite complex system or relationships. To teach a child that the events of life with its accidents, illnesses, and deaths are part of a moral order is to invite conflict and personality disorganization at a later date. But emotional safety lies in an early introduction to the true nature of the determining factors in events. Conduct can then be guided by sound statistical probabilities and objective social determinants. Unless you teach them to expect "certainties," children will never expect them; in fact, once introduced to probability they will be as shy of certainties as the devil is reputed to be of holy water.

Any belief that any individual holds and upon which a secondary structure of belief is built, will naturally be missed if it is given a thorough and dramatic destruction, and it is to be

expected that attitudinal and behavior changes might be expected to follow. But the commonly assumed dangers supposed to follow from the loss of an item of belief are probably
exaggerated. The destruction of the divine authority of the 10
Commandments would probably not be followed in anyone by
an orgy of murder, theft, and parricide. Our behavior stems
largely from the cues provided by the specific situations; easily
the best guess as to what will be done by anyone in any situation always is just this: what ever the person last did in that
same situation. Yet it would be sound council to avoid the
teaching of any belief as an absolute verity. Probability is in
the end a far safer foundation; probability and as many of the
objective determinants in the situation as can be identified.
The organization of a personality should be built around elements and items far more stable than social fictions. Social
fictions should always be taught for what they are, namely
variables rather than absolutes. No discredited social fiction
can then disorganize a personality.

Faith as an Active Causal Agent

"Faith" is often thought of as an agent of some subtle sort
that can violate the usual order of events in nature and which,
if invoked or expressed by proper prayers or rituals can "move
mountains," cure otherwise incurable illnesses, or even raise
the dead. Any such power, if its reputed batting average were
to stand up under statistical scrutiny, would be of such transcendent importance that no culture could neglect or fail to
make use of it to the full, if it would hope for survival in competition with cultures that were cashing in on such power
sources.

An examination of the beliefs in regard to such faith and its
potency will readily reveal considerable variability as to its
nature, sources, and application. The primordial belief seems
to have been that there were particular individuals who somehow possessed unusual powers to work wonders, to get results
far beyond the capacities of the run of the mill layman. Such
were the wonder-working magi, medicine men, and priests of

all sorts. A reading of any one of the synoptic gospels will quickly reveal the role played by such minor miracles in the reputation of any prophet of whom the populace was wont to ask—"What miracles hath he wrought?" "Hath he healed the sick?" etc. before rendering him full acceptance. What is interesting to note in regard to this healing is that there is an increasing emphasis upon the role played by the belief or faith of the patient in achieving the cure, as when Jesus says to the cured woman: "Daughter, thy faith hath made thee whole." (Mark 5:34). Here is a recognition that the therapeutic process is in some way a function of events going on in the patient, in this case the faith in the physically present miracle-worker. But, as with all primitive magic, the unusual potency in the miracle-worker seems capable of transference to articles used by him, to appointed substitutes or vicars, or to persons specially taught or prepared for the role, or hair, bones, excreta, or nail-parings of the wonder-worker, much of which would fall into Frazer's classifications of homeopathic or contagious magic. For these wonder-workings, the most important single factor seems to be the matter of the prestige of the operator, no matter of what the initial powers, potency, or superiority consist. A few dramatic performances and achievements directly under the eyes of the patients are of course very effective. The dramatic discarding of crutches after a "laying-on of hands" by the healer, or at a shrine, is well-nigh irresistible. But prestige can have other bases. The good National Geographic Magazine[28] reported, for example, that in Tibet the Muli King lives in a house with the embalmed mummies of his ancestors, and that the King's excrement is molded into pills, gilded and dispensed among the peasants to prevent illness. Who is to set a worth upon the feeling of confidence in the peasant following upon so potent a prophylatic? What black night of illness or hypochondria might it not make bearable? A few dramatic demonstrations of apparent miracles will quickly give almost anyone or anything an effective prestige. But other power symbols have their potency, too. One needs but remember how long the king's touch "cured" scrofula in England. During the brief but dramatic period when Hitler was in power in Germany some Nazi psychiatrists and psychotherapists found they could make effective use of a blind and blanket "faith" in the Fuehrer as a therapeutic device, much in the manner that authentic relics of Buddha or nails of the "true cross" produce similar results, each in its own respective areas of prestige.

How, in all honesty, is one to separate the apparent therapeutic powers of such bones of saints, royal touch or excrement, select passages read from the Christian Bible with or without supplementary passages from "Science and Health with Key to the Scriptures," the nine-day Navaho healing ceremony, or any other shamanistic performance, from contemporary psychoanalytic or psychotherapeutic procedures, shock and drug therapies of course being excluded? With all due respect to the differences between these techniques, there is no denying that the similarities are indeed profound. To begin with, all depend at least in large part upon faith and confidence in the procedures for such satisfaction or success as the patient might report. Then in no case does the practitioner or therapist dare commit himself to a time-schedule during which favorable results can be promised. Thirdly, the ailments thus treated are of such a nature that for all those in which successes of some sort are claimed there frequently is a spontaneous remission of symptoms in the absence of any systematic therapy whatever, and fourthly, for none of these systems has there been anything like an application of scientific controls and statistical analyses of results. In the eyes of the devotees, converts, believers, or adherents to each of these techniques their efficacy is obvious and unquestioned, not in the least because all systems "cash in" on the very high percentage of cases in which the various homeostatic and regulatory processes of the body have, with time, set themselves aright, perhaps in spite of the innovations the organisms have been subjected to during the varied therapeutic processes and attempts. *Whatever activities were being engaged in when improvement was noted, or had been carried out conspicuously in between, will get the credit for the "cure."* Any activity that entailed the expenditure of some considerable sums of money, even if it occupied but a small fraction of the total elapsed time, yet the economics of which continued to loom large in the patients' reckoning over the period, is almost certain to get credit for the amelioration of the distress. Christian "Science" practitioners and psychoanalysts agree at least on the importance of the fee in bringing about a "cure." This writer has no evidence whatever on the efficacy of fees in the therapeutic process. But he is highly confident that a sizable fee will stack the cards in favor of the treatment getting credit for the "cure" when there is an improvement, whatever may have brought it about.

It would be easy indeed to oversimplify this problem of the efficacy of any and all forms of psychotherapy, using that expression now as a generic term covering all forms of amelioration of distress by methods other than drugs, nutrition, "shock," or surgery. Many a knotty question is involved here, not the least of which is the problem of the relation of all forms of habit, or learning, to physiology. At the extremes of, say, a broken leg on the one hand and speaking a language on the other, these phenomena seem clearly to be questions of physiology and of habit respectively. But already problems in physiotherapy seem to be a border-line phenomenon between neurological, physiological, and habit questions, as illustrated by the problem of restoration of function after damage to the central nervous system. And yet in popular belief, even the matter of the healing of a broken leg has its minority of some 5% in a recent sample by the author that holds that strong faith might well do a swift job of healing it. Since any and all habits, if we are not to revert to animism, must have a basis in some sort of biochemical changes in the organism, the practical question in regard to any psychosomatic illness can only be this: to what extent is this but a disturbance of those normally reversible states that form the bases of habits? Or, one might put it this way: what success can we claim in treating this disorder by the methods of habit modification? And let such success as we pretend or claim be based upon a hard-headed system of controlled experiments and sound statistical analyses of the results. Any therapeutic powers that might be chargeable to "faith" would presumably have to function in the area of such processes as were not amenable to habit modification, or where they showed a clear superiority to such, and where other regulatory or homeostatic activities were ruled out.

It is of course difficult to evaluate the miracles worked by "faith" during the distant past, with or without the active presence of particular miracle-workers. It is significant to note that the "Miracles" traditionally ascribed to saints and saviors of the past tend to lie in the area of meteorology with its fickle moods, or that of the ills the flesh is heir to. Of the former, it is a safe bet that our contemporary cloud-seeders could show something in the way of improvement over chance that would give serious competition to even the most potent miracle-worker or to any faith linked to whatever virtue. The same cannot be said with equal confidence for modern psychotherapy in comparison with the powers of faith. In one of Freud's letters there is the admission that his phychoanalytic techniques had at that time not yet attained to the level of therapeutic success achieved by the bones of the saints with the faithful. The excessive modesty of the great, one might, say, but Freud was hardly conspicuous for his modesty. He seems rather to have agreed with Frank Harris that "modesty is the fig-leaf of mediocrity!" The separation of fact from fiction in the entire area is far from a simple task.

Stripped of their esoteric terminology and such cult characteristics as they have acquired, there yet remains to psychoanalysis, and psychosomatics generally, a certain amount of objective substance. That core of fact is just that the homeostatic or regulatory functions of the organism are, at least in some individuals, subject to modifications in their operation that strongly suggest at least some aspects of learning or habit processes. The experimental invasion of such visceral functions by Pavlovian conditioning processes has been pretty well established. Some of these experimentally induced "neuroses" or "psychosomatic disorders" do have a convincing resemblance to certain very disturbing or distressing human symptoms. Since there appears to be nothing too convincingly constant in the environmental conditions giving rise to such disorders it would seem to indicate that Freud was on the right track when, early in his study of hysteria, he came to the conclusion that this was

a disorder having profound organic bases in the individual. A
recent and excellently designed and executed study in England[29] using both homozygous and fraternal twins as well as
definitely neurotic children, seems to warrant the conclusion
that approximately 80% of the individual differences in the
neurotic factor are due to the operation of hereditary factors.
Yet such evidence as there is for the operation in at least some
cases of something akin to a habit factor in the acquisition of
some rather dramatic disorders, or their amelioration, has put
the miraculous "cures" traditionally ascribed to sacred personages in a different light for some people, even if they are highly
skeptical that any contra-natural forces or agencies were at
work in the cases recounted in sacred traditions. It has strength-
ened a suspicion, long indigenous, that it is "faith" that has perhaps as yet unguessed powers. This general suspicion is well
put by Stace:[30]

"We are coming to know a little more about the powerful
effects of unusual psychological states on the physical organism.
Faith may well be one of these powerfully working psychological states. We are still woefully ignorant of such matters."

Here is revealed, even in the sophisticated scholar, a readiness to accept evidences of miracles out of mind and faith.
Certainly any evidence offered should be given a most careful,
and critical weighing, but in the layman one finds it more or
less taken for granted that faith does work miracles, particularly in matters of personal health. Really convincing and conclusive evidence in this matter is very difficult to obtain. Even
the skeptical and critical observer is confronted with some particularly baffling complexities in even such cases as he has
himself under direct observation. Let us say he has charge of a
critical case; it seems nip and tuck whether life or death will
win. He notices that in spite of critical and dangerous symptoms the patient nonetheless wishes strongly to recover and has
unquestioned confidence that he will. He must then concede
that the confidence the patient registers might well be a function of the as yet intact "vital reserves" of the patient, the same
factors that produce this energy of attitude may also spark a
recovery. He knows too that illnesses differ greatly in their

effects upon the subjective feeling state, the euphoric-depressive balance. With some illnesses the patient dies, still confidently asserting that he will recover and hardly ever feeling very ill, subjectively. There are other disease conditions that probably have never killed anyone, but which induce such keen and intense agony and depression that the patient actually comes to fear that death will never come to end his suffering! He may well beg earnestly to be put out of his misery. Strong emotion might mobilize the last ounce of energy out of the adrenals, but rare indeed must be the cases where that tipped the scales critically and favorably. The layman all too readily perceives the "will to live" in the patient and assumes that "he just would not let himself die," that the purely mental "will" drove the body to a recovery! He might even confidently express the opinion that the patient will survive against the learned judgment of the attending physician. Or be convinced a patient "hasn't a chance" against a reasonably favorable prognosis from the doctor. Common sense just is not expert in any area of specialization. But it is frequently enthusiastically and uncritically opinionated.

The expectation that "faith" can work miracles in areas that on the face of them involve obvious physiological damage is to be found only in people of the lowest cultural strata today, or at best temporarily during acute personal crises in the somewhat higher levels. But when the malfunction does not involve gross structural or obvious physiological deficiencies faith and psychotherapy might well find themselves in competition in many cases. When no *known* physiological or biochemical basis exists for any disorder or behavior or function, we are driven, willy-nilly, to resort to other devices. Such disorders have had, in the past, animistic designations of some sort or other. Hippocrates records one of the early dissatisfactions with such taxonomy in his essay on epilepsy, then called the "sacred disease," as follows:

"I am about to discuss the disease called sacred. It is not, in my opinion, any more divine or more sacred than other diseases, but has a natural cause, and its supposed divine origin is due to men's inexperience, and to their wonder at its peculiar character."[31]

Currently we no longer designate such unknown disorders "sacred," but they are designated as "mental," as "disorders of the mind," or phenomena of the "unconscious," all terms designating nothing more objective or specific than does Hippocrates' term—whatever it was—that the translators render as "sacred." What we practically do with such disorders is to assume that, lacking a known structural base, they are to be approached as though they were amenable to some form of habit changing. Suppose it were true, as it indeed probably is, that some basic chemical imbalance lies at the bottom of the disorder, as now seems to be the case with the "sacred" disease of Hippocrates' time, that knowledge is of little avail in the case now before us. We might, of course, be stepping up our research in that area if we did not insist on spending billions in deliberate attempts at style obsolescence in clothing, automobiles, and recreational activity generally, but for the particular person suffering from, for example, schizophrenia, it is cold comfort to tell him that the familial incidence of that ailment is some ten times chance. It is a bit too late for him to change grand-fathers; and because the current crop of patients can make but little use of the genetic facts of the inheritance of certain disabilities, the entire psychiatric fraternity tends on the whole to pooh-pooh even unimpeachable evidence for the operation of hereditary factors in the etiology of behavior disorders. Such genetic factors, however lightly they might load the cards, are none the less valuable clues as to where attacks on the disorder are to be made; they are to be sought in the domain of biochemistry rather than on the analyst's couch. But such research and its possible clues are too far in the future; the patient wants results at once, or at least the hope of immediate alleviation of his ills. So the attempt must be made to provide the miracles.

The question at issue in the area of religion is this: what kind of "miracles" are there in this area, if any; and, if none, what is the true nature of the processes involved? Precisely

what is the role and power of "faith?" Are the effects of faith
in the supernatural any different from those which result from
faith in some secular therapist or system of therapy? Here it
must be reported with regret that there is a complete absence
of anything even remotely resembling the collecting of the kind
of data that could by any stretch of the imagination resemble
even a plausible sampling of cases. How indeed can one compare the efficacy of faith as a therapeutic agent against secular
techniques where nothing like controlled experiments have ever
been performed aiming at the comparative evaluation of the
various secular systems of "mental" therapy, nor even any convincing figures on cases left completely without treatment as
compared to those receiving treatment? It is assumed, today,
that there no longer is an issue over faith vs. vaccination in
smallpox, nor faith vs. penicillin in the treatment of syphilis,
etc. and that the "live" issue remains in the area of illnesses for
which no material therapy has as yet been devised. Certainly
there have been no comparative studies on the relative efficacy
of the saints and deities of the various religious cults and systems. The nearest thing to a statistic in the entire area that your
author can recall is having seen some time in the past a study
of the average ages at death of the members of the various
faiths and occupational groups. Certainly there was nothing in
those figures suggesting that any one occupation of cultural
fraction was privy to any significant techniques. Christian Scientists, for example, seemed to fall a bit short of their unilluminated contemporaries in average life-span; but they did tie the
objects of their contempt, the secular doctors of medicine! Don't
rush in with "explanations" that the doctors dug their graves
early, heroically trying to keep the rest of us alive; they yet
outlived the average common laborer by a good margin. It is
most likely a problem of the factors directing and channeling
interests. Medical students have been found to have had on an
average more personal medical history of illnesses requiring
rather extensive treatment. Any such history correlates negatively with longevity. Factors like that do operate to direct interest. Dr. Anne Roe, for example, found that of a large sample
of eminent biologists recently studied forty percent had lost

a parent before age ten. We are unaware that such factors channel our interests, but they probably do. Similar factors also probably operate in determining who becomes or remains a Christian Scientist! A surprisingly large number of them have a long history of "functional" disorders, i.e., disorders with no known organic basis, as one can learn at any Wedesnday night session.

As has been said, significant data on the comparative value of the various and varied "faith" cures and "mental" treatments are non-existent. If historical precedents have any value one might safely conclude that the role of faith in "mental" diseases will in the long run prove to have been not too different from its role in the treatment of the more obvious ills of the flesh in the pre-scientific era. That role is, at this stage of history largely misunderstood, and, as almost always, the facts are not of the sort that paint a clear-cut villain on the one hand, and shining virtue on the other. The facts of life are far too complex to be found to coincide with a simple moral judgement. It is beyond dispute that in the history of western European medicine the vested interests identified with therapy by faith in the operation of some divine animistic principle which was to be appealed to in prayer and trusted implicitly, frequently discouraged the introduction and the discovery of a secular knowledge dealing with the mechanics of health and disease. And it is equally true that this vested interest had, in the long run to be pushed out of this critically vital area. But, should we wonder why the conflict was so long a dubious battle, an examination of the psychological realities of the struggle will make clear its history. To ask first, what genuine specifics had the secular medical treatments evolved down to the 19th century and the answer is, few enough. But what was general in these secular treatments were hosts of concoctions whose sole claim to distinction now seems to have been their evil taste or smell. Then there were those really dangerous and enduring fads, the purgings, bleedings, cauteries, and vomitings that with time find fewer and fewer occasion for use and which were once practically standard treatment for every sort of disorder. Viewing that period of history from the vantage point of today one would have been well advised at that time, given the choice of the treatments by faith and prayer as opposed to the standard secular treatments, and assuming possible illness at random, to have elected to survive with the aid of the prayers and faith. Just imagine the consequences of administering a purge to a patient with an infected appendix! That would finish his last chance for possible survival. If one had faith in the prayers they would at least have helped to quiet apprehension and husband energies to combat the disease processes. A bleeding would no doubt weaken one in the struggle for survival in all but a few rare instances of excessively high blood-pressure. With the built-in homeostatic mechanisms of the body almost certain to restore normality of functions in all but a small minority of illnesses anyhow, it is easy to see that any superiority of secular techniques would of necessity be limited to their application in very specific illnesses, as for example the administration of quinine once it was introduced into Europe. It is significant to note that this drug was rather quickly adopted by the clergy and came shortly to be known as "Jesuit Powders." Not even a powerful organization could long hold out against so dramatically effective a specific. The simple truth is just that an enormous amount of secular knowledge had to be accumulated before that knowledge had a practical worth showing a significant improvement over faith and prayers, which at least had the negative virtue of not adding to the stresses already provided by the illness. There was a long wait between the discovery of the physiology of the absorption of oxygen in the lungs, for example, and the development of effective therapy for illnesses of the respiratory tract! In between, some predictable behavior for the situation had to be acquired. The determinants of such behavior are purely matters in the psychology of habit. We tend to repeat what we last did in a similar situation. The administering of quinine in fevers not of a malarial origin is a case in point, and is "logical" enough on the basis of its dramatic success in some fevers. "Fever" is fever, until a whole lot more has been learned about micro-organisms. Any other magic or ritual is similarly learned. And if persisted in until recovery takes place or until the situation has been altered, even by the death of the patient, the same ritual or treatment or prayers will still be the best bet as to what will be done in a similar situation when it arises. The prayers are psychologically on an even footing with the quinine or any other therapeutic agent in this matter. The persistence of a habit, a faith, or a belief is not contingent upon the effectiveness of these habits or beliefs; it is but a function of what the individual somehow practices doing in those situations, either in overt act or in belief.

Apart from a few minority cults where ritualistic techniques are still invoked against all illnesses, it is in behavior deviations of all sorts that the techniques once standard practice in all illnesses still find systematic application. It is here that the value of "faith" still warrants examination and appraisal.

It is the characteristic of a large fraction of behavior deviations, even of those having a profound organic bases, that they overlap in their nature and character with behavior that is the product of variations in the ordinary range of the learning process. Psychopathic behavior, and even the major psychoses can develop directly under the eyes of one's fellow citizens without the abnormality being apprehended until some very special law or taboo is violated. The associates of such a person adjust progressively to increasingly deviant behavior, even to the point of producing those fantastic cases of folie à deux, the dual madness, in which an otherwise normal individual has come to take over completely the delusionary system and values of a psychotic, unaware of its abnormality. The world has recently experienced the same phenomenon on a gigantic scale where obviously abnormal rulers of monolithic states have turned their particular irrationalities into social norms. This should have a sobering effect upon serious students of social phenomena, and force them to realize that the perennially made error of social theorists has been that of underestimating the varieties of social patterns that can develop and even survive for long periods, if indeed not indefinitely. So long as any behavior deviations are not linked suspiciously with organic cycles or symptoms of some sort we will continue to consider them as modifiable like any other behaviors that can be corrected if objectionable. The situation is something of a forced option; at the present state of our knowledge there is little else to be done.

Without at the moment raising the embarrassing question of the nature of the successes claimed for these variously modified habit-changing techniques it should be remembered at the outset that the styles and fashions in these forms of "therapy" are subject to considerable change over the years. Such devices must always be nicely attuned not only to the general cultural scene, but more specifically to the individual "patient," the latter particularly in a culture that allows considerable latitude in the development of the individual, or where specialization of interest and function and education have produced more than a modicum of skepticism in regard to long-accepted mythologies that might otherwise function effectively as integrating mechanisms in the personality. Bones and relics of saints provide effective devices for individuals early and long indoctrinated with recitals of the powers of these wonder-workers. Given the proper background of a non-authoritarian church, fresh social revolutionary traditions, and a culture in which there was a growing familiarity with the term "science" if not with its spirit and content, and add a dash of New England transcendentalism and you have a certain percentage of the citizenry for whom Christian "Science" makes psychological sense if not scientific logic. Similarly, it was the discovery of so potent an "invisible" force as electricity and magnetism that gave substance and plausibility to the "animal magnetism" and suggestion therapies in the early 19th. century, and even the late 18th. The same period saw the rise to fame and fortune of Perkins and his bi-metallic "tractors" as therapeutic devices. These paired metal rods obviously drew their inspiration and prestige from the then recently publicized voltaic cell, the wonders of which left a populace open to suggestive effects emanating from anything seemingly embodying the same principle. Similarly, psychoanalysis in all its forms and modifications is a product of the Zeitgeist: a reaction against Pauline and Victorian prudery, a reconciliation of man to his physiological, his animal nature, and the slow extension of the inquiring attitude even into the domain of human motivation. The result is a method of emotional reeducation, more conspicuous for its dramatic consistency than for scientific methodology.

As it has been pointed out before in these pages, the evidence for the efficacy of any and all of these devices for breaking old emotional habits or establishing new ones is of a highly dubious sort, regardless of the nature of the supposedly effective forces presumed to be at work. There is at this date no basis for the making of invidious comparisons, one against the other. The "effectiveness" of any system is always a function of its overall compatibility with cultural background and the personality idiosyncrasies of the person involved, and of course too, the nature of the problem requiring attention. Such "effectiveness" as here implied makes no demands other than that the individual receiving the "treatment" should report improvement of some significant sort, wholly apart from any social evidences of success. The piles of crutches and braces accumulating at shrines for the most part have been found to mean customers for the vendors and makers of orthopedic appliances. Many a chronically painful condition is not reacted to during the excitement and hope provoked by presence at the holy spot, much like the cut knuckles ignored by the boy during the excitement of the combat. Far fewer are the cases where the mechanical aids are permanently discarded without impairment of comfort or function. But they do occur on occasion. Inquiry into these cases usually reveals a history about as follows: the handicapping condition may well have long been under treatment, including major surgery, but normal function or use had not been restored. The normal time for the recovery of function may well have long since elapsed. The delay might have been a function of slower than average regenerative processes, or the tissue regeneration may have long been complete, only a *habit of invalidism has survived.* In such cases, cues provided usually by the body itself have become conditioned to call out the pain of discomfort formerly the product of the injury or illness. The breaking up of such "habits" seems to take place best under conditions of strong and genuine excitement. Similar are the "habits" of not responding to a given modality of sensory stimulation as in hysterical or functional deafness or blindness. A famous shrine or a "healer" with a large social following, or a high-priced psychiatrist frequently provide the conditions under which such habits are successfully broken. One might well wonder why some individuals turn up with such functional disabilities, or the capacity for such unusual habits while others do not under what seem to be similar conditions. Organic and hereditary factors seem to be involved. Even Freud thought hysteria to be an organically based illness. At any rate successes in treating such behavior disorders are far from 100% by any method. There is reported to be in existence in New York a rather exclusive club, membership being limited to people who have spent at least five thousand dollars on a particular "analyst" and at the end of that much money are no worse than they were before starting "treatment." Let it not be implied that the bones of the saints have all the failures to their credit! Without question, it is in just this area that religious faith as a therapeutic device comes nearest to holding its own in competition with the proliferating secular systems and theories. But the things attempted by the methods of "faith" are themselves subject to refinement and adjustment to the general temper of the times. This pressure exerted upon religion, tending to move it in the general directions and trends taken by the secular world is beautifully illustrated by a recent work by Dr. Karl Stern, a devout Catholic, who makes a heroic attempt[32] to synthesize Freud and Catholicism, and to make the synthesis fit into the general temper of the times.

New and bizarre variants on the general technique of resolving crises or illnesses by some form of "faith" technique are continually appearing. Rarely does one catch on. Dozens of innovators at one time or another feel moved to demonstrate just how it should be done. But seldom is one of them heard about outside of his own little circle, if indeed he got as far as to have a little private circle of followers. Even those that do "catch on" are likely to be very much dated and limited in geographical appeal; and almost all look foolish in a generation. Some of the more successful ones bear a more careful analysis. Certainly the most epoch-making one among the secular systems of the past century is psychoanalysis in all its variant forms. The "devils" of the witchcraft days have here been replaced by unconscious conflicts and complexes which inhabit us instead, the evidence for their presence being perhaps even the presence on the skin of a "devil's claw" or anaesthetic patch of the witchcraft days, but more commonly irrational hates, fears, compulsions, or other disabling or embarrassing misfunctioning of the body. The theory assumes that these untoward reactions were acquired through some sort of unconscious but nonetheless effective *motivational* process, and all the more effective precisely because it was unconscious. These motivational processes are held to consist largely of the action tendencies strongly suppressed or inhibited by the proper moral code of the culture. In practice, the therapy depends for its success upon highly racy and spicy interpretations of the motives (unconscious) of the patient, which paint a breathtakingly shocking picture of the individual; shocking, that is, in terms of conventional morality. Where a patient's troubles gravitate around such emotional problems it is rather likely that such a process, tending to put the individual at ease toward his own shortcomings, will have a balancing effect upon his emotions. After having been convinced by the analyst that he is filled with autoerotic, analerotic, homosexual, and incestuous urges, he will no doubt feel much less distressed, if that is his trouble, over "the law of the flesh" as St. Paul called it, in his own behavior tendencies. Such spicy verbalizing can have the result of making it easier to break some kinds of bad habits of emotional response. One might call it an "emotional" shock therapy. This necessity to provide such strong verbal shock leads to the development of some bizarre theories—to be used in therapy, of course. A sexually-frigid woman, for example will be told by some therapists that her frigidity is caused by her desire to revenge herself against men for her own lack of a male sex organ! That is teleology grafted to Baron Muenchhausen! If such "explanation" then cures the frigidity it will be held as a proven theory! Negative cases or failures can be overlooked or forgotten.

Against such competition there is no reason to suppose that

faith in official religious "miracles" or in Christian Science will be displaced at any phenomenal rate. Certainly there are millions of persons, nurtured in a gentle, if a bit unrealistic atmosphere, for whom simple miracles that can be hoped and prayed for will be far more congenial and probably equally effective.

The writer had better plead guilty to an increasing skepticism in regard to the "purely functional" or "purely mental" character of a large fraction of behavior disorders. When no organic basis is found for a disorder, the verdict should be supplemented with a loud "as yet." Some of us can still recall the time when there were theories of the "functional origin" and bases of general paralysis, in the days before Wassermann tests! It seems probable in the light of current research that the next decades will see a considerable retreat from many of the present extreme environmentalistic positions and find promising fields for research based upon genetic and physiological variables. There is excellent evidence for the existence of genetically controlled patterns of alcohol consumption in rats and other animals.[33] The area of the purely "functional" can confidently be expected to contract, and with that goes a reduction in precisely that area in which faith competes on most nearly even terms with professedly deterministic procedures. Even psychoanalysis is at bottom deterministic in spite of its menagerie of ghostly, teleological agents!

The Duty, Right, and Will to Believe.

Ruling classes, cliques, or vested interests of whatever sort are quite understandably apprehensive about the stability of the sovereignty that they exercise. The more precarious their hold, the stronger the competing pressures or forces, the more do they fear the rise of uncontrollable trends that might threaten their prerogatives. In fact, anyone content with the status quo is likely to look askance at whatever in any way threatens its stability. Where an inefficient or unstable social pattern is highly dependent upon some social fictions or mythologies or ideologies it is to be expected that the greatest zeal will be manifested in their maintenance. Heresy hunts thrive in an atmosphere of apprehension and uncertainty; they would be laughed out of court in a culture that was full of confidence in itself. Apprehension brings a demand for a rigid conformity. If a behavior trend is to be controlled, no exception can be permitted; conformity must be enforced. Beliefs and ideas are as much behavior as any overt act. The ruthless and single-minded Japanese ruling class recognized this clearly when they outlawed and punished "seditious thoughts." They had no illusions as to the nature of their assignment. Beliefs and ideas then can become "immoral," and it can become a moral duty to have the correct ideas or have the right beliefs. I recall a fundamentalistic parson threatening his congregation with hell-fire if they refused to believe the text of Genesis literally. Given the secular power, that fellow would have resorted to rack, boots, wheel, and boiling oil to enforce the belief. Apparently the only limits on the devices for producing "conformity" are the limitations of human ingenuity in things mechanical or thermal. Certainly the limits are not set by compassion or the "milk of human kindness." If one is to survive under such conditions it becomes truly "moral" to conform, even in one's innermost thoughts; for heretic hunters are expert in detecting the earmarks and signs that betray repressed and inhibited action tendencies. They can easily distinguish that faint bulge in the cheek while one puts the pinch of incense in the flame, and can intuitively distinguish premature anti-fascism from the correct kind. Where there is apprehension in any area of human relations there will be zeal to enforce conformity; in belief as well as in behavior. Beliefs and thoughts are potentially dangerous to any established order. Sovereign forces can be expected to be fully aware of this and to act upon it. The dangers inherent in beliefs that are not kept strictly under control, as well as the advantages in a free play of beliefs and ideas, have long provided man with a dilemma. Just where can we tolerate freedom in belief? In religious beliefs and the free expression thereof? That will be found to be championed enthusiastically by religious minorities who generally change their tunes when they become, or already are, majorities. Can we have it in armies? In political life during wartime? It would certainly

have been fine if the *German* citizen could have expressed his
beliefs freely during all the last war; a lot of casualties would
have been spared all around. But of course we could not tolerate a lot of loose and irresponsible talk or journalism during
wartime, a "hot" war. But how about a "cold" war? How about
a period of internal crisis incident to revolutionary changes in
the social pattern? Just what were these "Alien and Sedition
Acts" that have been pilloried in the history books ever since?
The entire subject of "belief" in all its aspects and relations
is momentous indeed.

The cumulative experience of at least western Europeans
under the pressures exerted by the varied priestly castes in controlling beliefs brought in time a demand for the ending of
such pressures. Freedom of belief in religious matters has a wide
popular support, except of course for freedom from any religious belief. Popular moral judgment has it that "you ought
to believe something." An extensive survey of public attitudes
in 1955 found that 60% of the public was opposed to allowing
public speeches against churches and religion.[34] The right to
beliefs and the free expression thereof is still a delicate and
fragile structure even in the freest and most stable of societies,
even in the area of the "supernatural" or the beliefs about it,
let alone in really momentous and critical issues, such as those
involving our habitual modes of making a living,—or having
it made for us. The same survey found almost one-third of
the American public opposed to allowing an advocate of government ownership of big industries to speak in public!

The question of belief in palpably demonstrable facts seldom arises. Even the rustic who is reported to have disbelieved
his own eyes on the giraffe would have succumbed rather
quickly if transported to the veldt or wherever it is that these
periscopically equipped creatures roam. It is the beliefs about
matters that cannot be demonstrated that have caused all the
speculations about belief and believing. Firmly fixed beliefs
in an area that cannot be demonstrated are commonly called
faith. Official, or socially accepted "faiths" have frequently become somewhat anachronistic or obsolete in the face of later
discoveries, but are yet adhered to, officially or formally. During

such a period of "lag" an individual might well subscribe to the official belief, and yet "know better." Such a conflict provides the emotional "punch" that finds humor in faith defined as believing what isn't true, and which has caused some serious students of religion to assert that there are significant psychological differences between our religious beliefs and the beliefs acquired in the workaday world. The theological and philosophical literature of Christendom provides eloquent evidence that the official beliefs have not always ben accepted easily and without struggle. This was not because the beliefs of Christianity were any more preposterous or inherently incredible than those of the other major religions; it was rather because during this period the dynamically active culture in which Christianity found itself was expanding explosively, both geographically and technologically, thereby, often unwittingly, destroying the bases of credence in many of its previous items of faith.

A growing body of knowledge, no longer under control of the priestly caste, confronted European religions with a situation such as had not previously confronted any official system of "wisdom." The development of secular knowledge with its demonstrable exactness was really something new in the world. The official beliefs in many cultures are not items that are taken too literally; often there is even no great concern as to whether, for example, a cosmological myth is literally true or not. It is simply the story they tell. As with contemporary primitive cultures, there is no great concern about the literal truth of the tale. That is just their particular story that fills the gap. It might be well known that an adjacent tribe told a quite different tale, but that is no cause for alarm, wonder, or resentment. Their concern for veracity was often limited to concern about the exact and verbatim repetition of the familiar story, of which the dramatic consistency was of far more import than its historical truth which no one could really know. But if the traditional story is faithfully and accurately told, that is a matter of serious moment and concern. Once attention is centered upon the instrumental accuracy of knowledge or belief a whole new criterion of truth comes into being. Such an attitude is rather likely to develop where many cultural fractions or splinters are in active contact. Each culture has developed a variety of practical, instrumental knowledge that tends to be quantitative in character, and dependable. Such knowledge, far from conflicting with similar knowledge from another culture is rather likely to supplement, expand, enrich, or multiply it. The proliferation of the practical technology of Western Europe had no other basis than this. The general acceptance of Christianity as a system of beliefs in western Europe coincided with the spread of a much enriched technology which was the chief vehicle upon which the Christian faith rode into Europe, much as the contemporary missionary "sells" his Christianity as a concomitant or adjunct to his medicines, surgery, and improved technology generally. Christianity had the problem of keeping itself believed in at the same time that the cultural scene in which it functioned was destroying the habits of thought that permitted it to pass muster. The ontological, cosmological, and teleological arguments for the existence of God are monuments to the fact that the traditional bases for belief no longer sufficed a thinking, well informed person. A member of a primitive culture needs no such elaborate rationalizations for his belief; he has it, almost automatically, and holds it without too much emotional heat because he has not been made emotionally sensitive to the contradictions inherent in it. His practices involve no elaborate verbal rationale. That is why he can, as has the Mexican and other American Indian, accept the verbal formulae of the missionary—and add them to his old and familiar practices. I still have a vivid recollection of the shocked expression on the face of a New York Catholic when confronted with an offering of grain in a rural Mexican church!

The efforts of Pascal to find valid reasons for believing where the sort of evidence necessary for any secular belief is absent, have proven to be a delight to philosophers down the centuries. Similar sentiments are frequently echoed by people who surely never have heard of him. Questions as to the legitimacy of believing on the basis of slender evidence are answered with "What can I lose?", which indeed embodies the essence of Pascal's logic. The ritual duties or observances themselves are smoothly habitual, even if the logic about the supernatural is a bit incongruous with the general principles of secular evidence. But the implication is clear: there is at least a slim chance that the traditional story about things post-mortem is true, in which case it is just too bad if you deviated from the ritual rules. There is your possible finite loss pitted against a possible infinite gain! It is easy indeed to find satisfactory verbal defenses for continuing to do what we long have practiced.

Where an individual has encountered but one belief that constitutes for him a living option, and then weighs the evidences against its being true, his "psychological mathematics" of probability seem to give the belief a 50-50 chance of being true, if the evidence seems equivocal or not strongly enough against the belief to cause him to abandon it. The thousand and one other existing beliefs, and the many times that number of theoretically possible beliefs, simply do not exist for him as live factors. He examines his belief, and even if he questions it, reacts as if it had an even coin-toss chance of being true. But already the first uncertainty, namely the probability of *any* revealed faith being true rather than none, just does not exist for the average believer. As for the rival revealed faiths, it would seem that no criterion of human reason, logic, or experience could be applied in determining which is the one true revelation. Revelations must be accepted "whole hog" or not at all. The instant human experience, wisdom, or logic are drawn upon, human wisdom is set up as a judge of revelation, and as its criterion. In such an event, revelation becomes an obvious human product. And if anything is to be a human product, the most dependable methods must be used in creating that product, namely the scientific. Any attempt to select out of any revealed content those elements which are true and to reject the counterfeit involves the same contradictions. What kind of transcendent wisdom is this from which mortal man can hand-pick and cull? Here the position of the simple fundamentalist of whatever creed is at least lacking in self-deceit. "If there is any transcendent wisdom I want no "higher critic," a mere mortal, to mess around with it and substitute his judgment," says the fundamentalist.

The brilliant William James grappled with the problem of

belief in an essay which he entitled "The Will to Believe," but which he should have called "The Will to Believe in Protestant Christianity." It is to be strongly recommended to any believer who might begin to doubt that he had adequate grounds for continuing in his belief. It will be a delightful balm to whoever wants to still his doubts and go on believing. To strengthen the case for belief he identifies the hypotheses and hunches which actually motivate concrete research, and give birth to ingenuity in techniques for getting at facts, with the beliefs of religious faith. It is obvious that theories and hypotheses have proved to be powerful motivating factors in the quest for new facts. But how can James or anyone else identify such emotional confidence with the blind faith in an area where evidence is by definition impossible of attainment? The one serves as a stimulant to inquiry; the other effectively ends inquiry and marks the entry of the believer into an "as if" land. The only faith that can help create a fact is a faith that stimulates concrete action in an area where at least something can be tried or observed. The individual who does not happen to have a religion he already believes but who would like to cash in on the gains to be got from belief now has even a worse problem at hand, namely how can he evaluate in an area where by definition no evidence is to be had, no facts obtainable? He cannot help but observe that in some 98% of the cases the belief confessed by an individual is one that an all too deterministic process in his environment provided for him; be it monkeys, snakes, the sun, or Polaris that is believed in and worshipped. And he can follow the advice of the professional theologian by starting out to act as if he had accepted a given belief and shortly the subjective experience of belief will appear. Any such acceptance of a belief without evidence can only result in a forgetting of negative evidence and a succumbing to the pressures for belief provided by a particular culture. Even a shadowy awareness of the number and variety of different beliefs accepted without the kind of evidence which we demand for practical, secular judgments should give anyone pause. Once aware that his particular set of social pressures is determining his belief-acceptance in precisely the same way in which the offerer of human sacrifice acquires his belief one might well wonder what kind of a mathematics of probability it is that the believer accepts. The genuineness of any revelation can never be questioned by any mortal mind; that mortal mind is a product of the conditioning or learning history it has fortuituously been subject to. These have provided Pascal's "reasons the heart has which reason does not know." Once even one grain of human judgment is permitted in the balance the entire problem must be conceded a problem for human wisdom and ingenuity to solve; and in such solutions there is no room for revelations of any kind. If "willing" to believe implies making verbal statements of what is being accepted, and engaging in overt practices corresponding to the verbal formulae, it is obvious that a "will to believe" shortly has an individual acting and thinking predictably like other individuals behaving in the same pattern. It might well produce many desirable social or subjective consequences in the individual. But one thing it cannot do, and that is produce truth of the objectively verifiable kind.

Believers confronted with evidence casting serious doubts upon their faiths frequently reject such evidence with a claim of some abstract "right to my own opinion or belief." Unless they result in overt action of some sort beliefs are relatively innocuous and are in most quarters an unquestioned "right." Even delusions are tolerated unless they result in anti-social conduct. Actually, such resort to a "right" to an opinion is indicative of but one thing, namely that the believer is aware of the inadequacy of his bases for belief but is nonetheless persisting in it. What he is in fact demanding is a subjective, psychological capacity to continue believing in the face of contrary evidence. And he has it—we all do! And the only sign of the increasing difficulty we may have in holding such a belief might well be an increasing ferocity toward avowed non-believers!

Confronted with options on which there is no evidence, James, in common with most believers, acts as if any proposition had a 50-50 chance of being true. Practically an infinite number of false propositions can be made for every possible true one, even in an area where simple facts are available. What boots it, one might well ask, to acquire a belief in areas such as those described by James as "genuine options that cannot be decided on intellectual grounds," unless such belief is in the nature of a program of action for discovering some factual data in that area. Any belief would make increasingly improbable the perceptive grasp of evidence were it somehow to manifest itself. James berates the scientists who seem reluctant to accept or even examine the "evidence" in regard to the phenomena of "telepathy," referring specifically to some unnamed and already then dead biologist who favored the suppression of any evidence, even were it to appear, that tended to "undo the uniformity of nature." We can join enthusiastically with James in denouncing anyone afraid of any evidence. However, James then goes on to say,[35] "But if this very man had been shown something which as a scientist he might *do* with telepathy, he might not only have examined the evidence, but even have found it good enough." To which can only be added, yes indeed! Any evidence *that has instrumental value* has these days little chance indeed of being left a neglected wallflower at the scientific dance! And if that evidence pointed only remotely in the direction of the animistic view of the nature of life, mind, or nature it would have no need to worry about an adequate supply of press-agents. Let anyone demonstrate bona fide telepathic powers and he would be invaluable to statesmen in diplomatic conferences, to business executives in important negotiations and high finance generally. When anyone's extra-sensory perceptive powers begin to wreck faro and roulette tables, we can all begin to make pilgrimages to the fountain-heads of such wisdom; and make no mistake, if and when that happens the rush will be on.

But James will not be remembered for a persistent and consistent defense of any particular position, but rather for effectively verbalizing many of the common-sense convictions of his time and doing his best to outline their limitations. He could express convincingly his convictions of the moment but was perfectly capable of expressing a contradictory opinion shortly after. Where he could say:[36] "There is but one indefectibly certain truth, and that is the truth that pyrrhonistic scepticism itself leaves standing,—the truth that the present phenomenon of consciousness exists," he could, not too long thereafter write an entire essay[37] seriously questioning this "indefectibly certain truth" and in effect come to a conclusion exactly the opposite. All of which is perfectly consistent with his own expectations in regard to his convictions.[38]

The conflict James has within his own beliefs is probably best revealed by the following passage:[39]

"This feeling, forced on us we know not whence, that by obstinately believing that there are gods (although not to do so would be so easy both for our logic and our life) we are doing the universe the deepest service we can, seems part of the living essence of the religious hypothesis."

Can it be that James knew nothing of the role played by early indoctrination of the child in the family and the culture generally that he pleads that we know not whence the feeling that it is virtuous to believe in the gods? And surely James knew enough of Buddhism to know that at least Hinayana Buddhism is atheistic but yet religious and "spiritual." What he actually should say is this—'against my best logic I continue to believe in gods, but I have no idea why it seems virtuous to do so'!

Of such is the "Will to Believe"!

The Structure of Religious Fictions.

Said Ludwig Feuerbach long ago: "Anthropology is the secret of theology. God is man worshipping himself. The Trinity is the human family deified." Madonna worship was presumably included with the Trinity by this scorner of things theological, and with that added to Christianity the similarity of the heavenly family to the mundane is probably not just a chance product. Many since Feuerbach, and probably also before, have made the same observations in regard to the all-too-human character of deities. Kipling, in his poem, "Evarra and his Gods" portrays a somewhat different determining factor that he thought gave the specific character and personality to the different gods, and added the gloomy reflection that once having constructed a god after a particular fashion man then declares war to the death on any and all who would make them otherwise. Certainly the jehads, the crusades, the "Thirty Years' War" and the "Hundred Years' War" are eloquent testimony to the truth of his observation. But not necessarily: until the recent geographical separation of Pakistan from India there was a relatively long stretch of "live and let live" in that peninsula. The followers of Gautama too, seem never to have slaughtered each other nor those outside the fold over matters of doctrine.

If there is One omnipotent god, he certainly has a macabre sense of humor in making so many different followers of so many different gods and then, apparently as the whim moves him, setting these varied followers at each others' throats! But the evidence is far better that gods are local or piecemeal products, each with his own historical determinants, but human, all too human, every one of them. Freud and his motley crew of deviationists and followers have certainly provided us with highly dramatic versions of the process by which man constructs his religions and gods, even if they are on the face of them more in the vein of a Baron Muenchhausen tale than in the manner and spirit of science. Freud must early have become obsessed with the theme of parricide. Long ago, in the dim, distant past of the race, he held, some sons slew their father over the possession of the females in the family group. Such an event is of itself not at all improbable, but in Freud's thinking this was One Big Event that occurred in the direct family line of all of us. Not only that, but by some as yet unknown but of necessity Super-Neo-Lamarckian mechanism of inheritance, all of us still inherit, deep down in the Unconscious of course, some shadowy memory of this event, and, which is even more miraculous, we somehow inherit the emotional remorse these young rascals were smitten with, directly they had done the terrible deed! As every reader of Totem and Taboo recalls, it was this remorse that caused these murderous ancestors of ours to set up the incest taboo, thus denying themselves the very wenches for whom they had committed the murder.[40] Then, since they had also polished off the old fellow in a cannibalistic feast, they commemorated their forswearing of such diet by setting up a totemic animal whose eating was tabooed in symbolic denial.

As for the repercussions of all this in religion, the "thou shalt not kill" commandment stems from the irresistible emotional reaction against the murder of the primal father who all along has been the prototype of God, according to Freud.[41]

Everett Dean Martin[43] also assumes the universality of this feeling of a need for a redemption from sin, and sees this playing the critical role in the making of religion. Again the key role is played by the father figure which is the prototype out of which the idea of a god is created. How a religion could arise among people like the Trobriand Islanders is a bit difficult to imagine, since there the father is at most a benevolent playfellow and never wields any authority over his children. At any event, under this theory, religion is largely an expression of a regression to a sheltered infantilism, a dependence upon a super-parent, and probably indicates a failure to develop a satisfactory love life. Kimball Young[44] examined a large sample of Protestant Christian hymns and analyzed them for essential subject matter. He found that 33% of them had the infantile return theme and 25% the future reward motive, against a mere 8% each for sinfulness and exaltation in religion. In his "Psychological Frontiers of Society," [45] Kardiner gives the same idea a somewhat different twist:

"The superego is based on affection, not hatred; on delegated and not enforced authority. The strongest factor in its establishment is good parental care, the relief and not the creation of painful tensions. This acts as an incentive to accept discipline in order to perpetuate the boons of the past. The fear of loss of them is the greatest threat to the security of the child. Hence the child is able to renounce important gratifications in order to preserve the magical powers of the parent. It is this constellation which is projected on the deity and is the cornerstone of all religions."

The expression "all religions" is dangerously inclusive, as everyone should know by now. But if man is not to get his habits of thought and his habits of perceiving from his past experience, where could he get them? And if, during the formative years of childhood one has trust and confidence in what is for the child's needs, practical omnipotence in a parent, there is then in us such a pattern of responses, ready to be touched off by situations bearing only a small fraction of essential resemblance to the original. Such is the nature of the conditioning of reactions in humans. So it should cause no surprise if some gods bear a suspicious resemblance to parents or other family units or structures. If animals are potent figures in early life, supernaturals might well be clothed in such forms or symbols. Anything else, impressive for any possible detail, might elsewhere be invoked. Heavenly bodies, trees, stones, anything that for any reason induces or once induced emotional reactions of any considerable intensity or uniqueness might be, and probably has been somewhere, drawn upon. In India there is even a solemn cult organized around a bottle of whiskey![46] Not too preposterous after all! We need but ask how we came to apply the term "spirits" to all concoctions containing a generous percentage of ethyl alcohol? The precise psychological factors operating to favor one identification or another are probably not too significant. Naturally it is the universally operating factors that most frequently color the characteristics ascribed to supernaturals: the family structure and relations, conspicuous details of the cosmos, of geography, of meteorology, outstanding personalities, dramatic events of all sorts, diseases, plagues, catastrophes, important plants and animals. The only serious question that remains is just this: is there, in fact, anything under the sun or even beyond it, that has not been apotheosized?

The details of the precise history of the derivation and acquisition of the ideas and beliefs currently in good repute in the Jewish-Christian tradition cannot be gone into in any detail in a work of this kind. For those in whom there survives even a remote trace of suspicion that this particular tradition is in any way unique or original and not derived from far older notions and cultures, Professor Homer W. Smith's highly informative and readable "Man and his Gods," published by Little, Brown and Company, Boston, 1952, is earnestly recommended. The scientific research into the history of this particular tradition has made the traditional beliefs in this field as obsolete as the Origin of Species made the special creation hypothesis, and

Professor Smith has done an excellent job of getting this work into brief and readable form.

It must never be forgotten that the entire theory of the existence of gods and of a "divine" or contranatural order of reality is not a hypothesis made necessary in the light of the contemporary scientific world view. All these ideas, on the contrary, are a heritage from the pre-scientific past when the only knowledge man had was of the order of the crude empiricisms of his workaday world. This empirical knowledge of man expanded, with time, to produce today's majestic and dramatic scientific knowledge. Strangely enough, this empirical knowledge long ago became separated from the speculative, later called "religious" ideas, which have come down to us out of the past relatively unchanged. We have hung on to them, usually in the face of serious flaws in their logical structure, as judged by the standards of the growing scientific system of knowledge. It was the tenacious adherence to some of these older notions about the nature of reality, which were at the same time increasingly meaningless in the problems of the material world, that with time demanded an end to the single Universe in which man long lived where there was no duality of natural as opposed to the supernatural. Thus there survives, alongside of the natural order, (the world of measurable, objective phenomena coming rapidly under human control), what is variously referred to as "the divine," the "supernatural," or even the "eternal" order of reality, where, by definition man's scientific knowledge is entirely meaningless, and instead we find here that many of the ancient notions of reality and causality are still presumed to be operative. Of this latter order of reality, it is commonly held that man cannot possibly have any knowledge other than that obtained by means of the mystical, or religious experience or "vision." This process is presumed not to involve any of the ordinary channels or methods of obtaining knowledge. Instead, at least some humans can have the direct experience of the eternal order of things in mystical states or visions. These phenomena will be explored in greater detail in the next chapter. Meanwhile it can be stated that the mystical experience, if had today, presumably confirms previously "revealed" insights that there are divine beings of some sort who are given credit for having created, variously, the world, or the entire universe. Particularly when but one god is presumed to exist, this one is frequently characterized as being an "infinite mind." This makes of such agencies an interesting whimsy indeed. If the term "mind" has any objective reference at all it must refer to certain activity of very much finite and mortal man, specifically to the continually changing subjective experience state. Whatever changes cannot avoid being very much finite. An "infinite mind" would then of necessity be nothing other than a contradiction of terms, and any such god but a semantic contradiction. It has taken man a long time to learn that he must demand of his words that they have definite objective references.

The various characterizations man has sought to apply to his gods have caused him no end of trouble. Is a god absolutely good? Then he must be powerless or else his standards of ethics are hopelessly different from man's. Do his powers transcend human logic? Then he must be able to construct square circles! And if not, then he must be bound by the same logic that limits man. All of which provides a feast day for a semanticist! Such questions are as embarrassing to theology today as they were when David Hume asked them in the 18th century. No wonder that there is a strong tendency today to assert that the divine order owes no allegiance whatever to the earthbound logic of science. Let us now see what luck man has had in getting reasonably reliable information about this divine or eternal order of reality.

Chapter IX

THE RELIGIOUS EXPERIENCE—MYSTICISM

The Subjective Experience State and Religion

It may have been purely coincidental, but the fact remains that the 19th century increase of interest in the religious experience did coincide with the decline in the scientific confidence in rationality as an explanatory principle in human behavior, as well as with the gradual decline in the general acceptability of religious belief as something that could be logically or "rationally" justified. Just as many psychologists began to pursue the reality of things psychological in the world of "experience," so too, it was in the world of the specifically "religious" experience that the reality of religion and the religious came to be sought. Thus, William James, in explaining his broad, general aims in writing his classical "Varieties of Religious Experience" had this to say:

"—first, to defend—"experience" against "philosophy" as being the real backbone of the world's religious life. I mean prayer, guidance, and all that sort of thing immediately and privately felt, as against high and noble general views of our destiny and the world's meaning: and second, to make the hearer and reader believe, what I myself invincibly do believe, that, although all the special manifestations of religion may have been absurd (I mean its creeds and theories) yet the life of it as a whole is mankind's most important function."[1]

Now it must be recalled that James rejected the classical introspectionism with its discrete sensations, images, and ideas, and replaced them with the conception of a continuous process, the stream of consciousness. Even though James later rejected the idea of consciousness as an entity[2] there was a mystagogical or panpsychistic streak in James which made him see individual conscious processes as part of a cosmic consciousness from which fitful influences might leak in through weak spots in the normal circumscribed and adaptive consciousness. It is in this area that he found the sources for religious experiences, the possibilities for "psychic" phenomena, ie. "psychic research," and the exploration of the conscious state through drug intoxication. Always, there was to him the possibility that the individual conscious processes might be directly influenced by that "more spiritual universe."

Perhaps that is as close as James could come to what is popularly assumed in practically all "revealed" religions, namely, that at least at one time their own particular god could, and did, act directly upon the very human mind or minds of the prophets or founders of that particular faith. That such action is still currently presumed to be possible is apparently not even questioned in some faiths. To quote from a textbook with a 1948 copyright:

"In the beginning of this chapter we have attempted to point out the reality of the Divine Being and the fact that He can and does act upon the mind of man. Hence any attempt to analyze religious experience without due attention to the divine action of God upon the soul is to omit from the analysis that which is of greatest importance."[3]

Just how the supernatural acts upon the human mind or conscious experience, and just how such action is to be recognized is a matter of considerable moment. In sacred traditions the supernaturals apparently spoke in very unequivocal language to their earthly vicars so that these could pass on the messages with considerable confidence. But at present there seems to be much doubt even in the minds of the experts in such matters. James rejected the idea that there was a specific religious sentiment, a specific and unique content to consciousness that could be identified as religious. Nor was there a characteristic psychological process which serves as a sign of the religious experience, it must be identified by a group of characteristics. Jung defines the religious experience as that of being seized by a power outside of ourselves which is not the product of an act of will. Hence it must come out of the "unconscious" which for Jung is already a more or less "religious" entity. Freud, on the other hand, considers a feeling of powerlessness to be the opposite of a religious feeling, which is instead a feeling of independence and an awareness of one's powers.

The German philosophers have long been grappling with the problem of just how the "mind" comes by its religious content. Kant did not include "the religious" in his list of a-priori categories. To him, religion was but a recognition that our duties were commands from God. But beginning with Friedrich E. R. Schleiermacher (1768-1834) and Jacob Friedrich Fries (1773-1843) there seem to have been a general agreement that somehow the human mind could, and on occasion did, manage an intimate glimpse into an eternal reality of some sort. Fries puts it this way:

"Die Erkenntnis durch reines Gefuehl nenne ich Ahndung des Ewigen im Endlichen. Ein Gegenstand unseres Wissens und unsrer Anschauung wird nur das Einzelne und Endliche in der Natur: fuer den Glauben hingegen koennen wir das Ewige nur durch die Idee des Nicht-Endlichen denken, wir denken uns nur die Aufhebung der Schranken des endlichen Seins fuer das ewige Sein, ohne eine positive Vorstellung des Ewigen. ——Eine positive Vorstellung des Ewigen haben wir unmittelbar garnicht, aber durch die Vereinigung des Wissens und Glaubens in demselben Bewustsein entsteht die Ueberzeugung dasz das Endliche nur eine Erscheinung des Ewigen sei, und daraus ein Gefuehl der Anerkennung des Ewigen im Endlichen, welches wir Ahndung nennen."[4]

It is from passages such as these that the German language gets its bad reputation for incomprehensibility, and it may well be true that no small part of Fries' reputation for profundity in theological matters derives from the ambiguity of language he uses to state his position. But if this passage asserts anything it says, in brief, that he defines "Ahndung" as the recognition through (or by) pure experience (or feeling) of the Eternal in the Finite. Also, that we can grasp the concept of the Eternal only by way of that of the Finite. Lacking a positive concept of the Eternal, we none-the-less achieve the conviction that the Finite is but a manifestation of the Eternal by way of a unification of knowledge and belief in the same or identical consciousness. It is out of this that arises the feeling (or experience) which recognizes the eternal in the Finite, which he calls Ahndung. Elsewhere[5] Fries also defines "Ahndung"[6] as being just a faculty of divining the "objective teleology" of the world.

For Schleiermacher the specific and unique religious experience was subjectively a feeling of absolute dependence. It is thus that the innate consciousnes of the Deity manifests itself; not through ideas, which he holds are foreign to religion. Fries, and Rudolph Otto after him, assert that the "religious" constitutes a fundamental category of the mind, much after the manner of the Kantian categories which did not thus honor the religious. Otto, who elaborated upon Fries' ideas, named this category "The Holy" and held that it was not to be equated with absolute good. Instead, the Holy is a unique, original feeling-response, which can be in itself ethically neutral, and non-rational. But its distinct qualities are best characterized by the term "numinous," which could not be further defined, but could be analyzed into "elements." Such numinous experiences do not consist of feeling alone, but also exhibit, or include, a category of immediate apprehension and valuation. Subjectively, it is a creature feeling. "It is the emotion of a creature abased and overwhelmed by its own nothingness in contrast to that which is supreme above all creatures."[7] The "numinous" might also be described as the experience of the supremely mysterious, which is both tremendous and fascinating,—wholly other. Such experience is not a rational knowing process, apparently, and Otto insists that God cannot be rationally known. Things holy, can only be subjectively experienced.

But exactly what is the "holy"? Wach,[8] after having defined the religious experience as the experience of the holy, says: "We agree with another philosopher of religion, D. M. Edwards, who contends that the "holy" is not so much a fourth value to be added to the Good, the True, and the Beautiful as it is the matrix from which they are derived, their common form and origin." And again:[9]

"Religious experience being fundamental, constitutes the basis for communion of a most intimate character, boring deep into the bedrock of impulses, emotions, and thoughts which are common to all men. This subjective religion has at all times proved potent enough to unite and integrate people who are otherwise widely separated by differences in descent, profession, wealth, or rank. A study of the social status of those who followed the prophets, teachers, and founders of religion will reveal the surprising social heterogeneity of the motley groups who became as one when united in a common religious experience."

Just how the subjective, evaluational states or feelings become translated into any sort of bases for guidance or action is not too clear from the writings of these devotees of the religious experience. That the mental processes operating in matters religious differ from those that are valid in scientific thinking was recognized even by Hegel who held that the cognitive processes operating in science and philosophy are "Begriffe," that is to say specific concepts, while those operating in religious processes are "Vorstellungen," which is probably well translated as "images," or imaginative representations. Here as with Bergson's "intuition" validity is claimed without the usual logical or experiential bases. Where such intuition operates it presumably supplies an authoritative basis for belief.

Such sentiments may well be religion, and they frequently are poetical. But they cannot be confused with scientific understanding. But the acceptance of religious belief has never waited upon either scientific proof or understanding and this is quite as it should be—in theological opinion. "Certainly it would be a mistake to hold that the truth of all religious beliefs should be rationally demonstrated before they are accepted and acted upon," as it has been quite frankly put.[10] In competition with the scientific point of view and methodology, there is but little for religion to do but frankly retreat into mysticism, particularly where the reality of religion is looked for in the subjective religious experience. On the face of the problem, there seems no valid basis for separating the individual religious experience from perhaps more dramatic forms of the mystical states of "consciousness," ascribed to certain virtuosos in this field. As William James put it, "(the) personal religious experience has its root and center in mystical states of consciousness."[11]

What is known as mystical philosophy has always held that behind the world of sense, or beyond space and time there is a transcendental type of reality inaccessible to ordinary experience, but still existent and, in fact, the ultimate REALITY. This ultimate reality is reputedly revealed through a special mode of knowledge, which is distinct from perceptual and ideational cognition, and is superior to them. Such claims have long been made in primitive societies for a variety of trances and revelations, and Plato's conception of the "nous" is not too far removed from them. Mysticism further claims that the mind or soul of man is either identical with or at least very closely akin to ultimate reality, a doctrine reminiscent of the Judaistic doctrine that the human spirit or essence returned to god at the death of the individual. Similar ideas are found in a wide variety of mystical doctrines, in some of which extremely whimsical ideas are held, such as that of the denial of the objective world and the disappearance of the individual personality (soul) into a unity with ultimate reality or a god that is everything; a pantheism without a cosmos. If there is a common denominator to these mysticisms it is that they all take a dim view of the natural, material, objective world, which they insist is illusory and evanescent, and of which they aim somehow to get rid. The basis in reality of all of them is simply the experiences of the mystical conscious state which is presumed to furnish a direct knowledge of reality. The content of that state proves upon examination to be all too obviously a product of the normal learning processes the individual has been subjected to in his cultural pattern, including the current mystical doctines. Such a brooding upon the pattern of beliefs available in his culture can at best yield a limited number of modifications and recombinations, or possibly elaborations and extensions of certain minor elements. At any rate, whatever is long contemplated can acquire a hallucinatory clarity and vividness in the subjective experience of the mystic that is then only with difficulty distinguished from objective reality. But no great innovations are to be expected: the Christian mystic remains a Christian; the Hindu remains a Hindu, and the Buddhist and Mohammedan too, remain what they were. One will look in vain for the "great mystic" as envisoned by Bergson:[12]

"The great mystic is to be conceived as an individual being, capable of transcending the limitations imposed on the species by its material nature, thus continuing and extending the divine action." Plotinus, he held was one! It is probably far safer to assume that at this distance in time we no longer have available the cultural influences in which Plotinus developed, the ideas and influences he was subjected to, and which no doubt conditioned and produced his interpretations of mystical reality. But Bergson thinks of mysticism as "a leap beyond nature," a "dynamic religion."

All this from the subjective, mystical state. But just what is this state like? How is it to be recognized? The lucid and articulate William James has given us one of the best accounts of it. His sources were the writings left by the more verbal and literate of the mystics, plus perhaps something out of his own, first-hand experience.[13] Such states are marked (1) by their ineffability; they are more a matter of feeling than of intellect; they seem to defy verbalization of expression. (2) They have a noetic quality, they create an impression of deep insight, and seem authoritative long after they have disappeared. (3) They are transient, they last but a limited time, at best one-half to a full hour. (4) They are characterized by the passivity the individual experiences while the state lasts. The personal "will" seems to be completely in abeyance, once such a state is initiated. Some pages on (op. cit., pp. 422-423) James adds the following:

"Mystical states usually are, and have a right to be absolutely authoritative over the individuals to whom they come.— They break down the authority of non-mystical or rationalistic consciousness, based upon the understanding and the senses alone. They open out the possibility of other orders of truth."

We will not raise the question of just what is meant by 'the right they have to be absolutely authoritative,' but there is no doubt that it is these mystical experiences that have provided the bases for all the "revealed" religions. For the communicants of these faiths, they are indeed "authoritative." But what of the conditions and circumstances of their appearance? The evidence seems to be that the communicant has a long period of incubation of ideas, during which time he goes again and again over the problem that becomes almost an obsession. The rather sudden "illumination," the "great Light" seems to come much after the manner of new insights to discoverers and inventors in the fields of mathematics, science, or invention. The constructive thoughts suddenly appear, not the product of conscious, rational sequences as in our ordinary thinking. The typical report indicates that the "flash" or new idea-sequence comes during moments that could only be described as passive, rather than actively conscious.[14] It is interesting to note that in human trial-and-error problems it has often been observed that in much the same way the responses that effect the solution are not preceded by conscious, or rational, decisions in situations where something really different from our past knowledge or habits must be developed or organized. Solutions to such problems must of necessity be violations of our old habits, and the conscious processes seem to be particularly resistant to such innovations. Some such discovery seems to have motivated the deliberate cultivation of passive states in oriental rites and mysticism. Whether or not such deliberately cultivated "passivity" has anything like a convincing record of achievement to its credit remains to be seen.

There are apparently decided limits to the achievements that can emerge from such passive states, and really creative products emerge from them only under very specific conditions. The searcher or thinker must long have been grappling with some problem, during which period he must have literally soaked himself with everything even remotely relevant that is available. Then there must be the period during which these elements or details of the puzzle have been "tossed around," played with, arranged and rearranged in the vain hope of a solution. But the sought-for pattern or solution evades the conscious seeking processes which the thinker brings to bear on the problem. Then, sometimes, better rarely, in either a completely "passive" or inactive state, or while toying with some trifling idea, a solution suddenly appears in a surprising flash of clarity, and without any volitional effort. Sir William Hamilton reports that his quaternions came to him in this manner. A period of insomnia resulting from coffee drinking produced Poincaré's Fuchsian functions, and many poets including Goethe and Coleridge reported such flashes of creativity; the latter, alas! reporting that on one occasion the untimely arrival of some unwelcome guest prevented him from capturing all that the flash-vision had brought. Periods experienced as "exalted creativity" frequently prove to be sad disappointments, particularly if the condition of exaltation was contributed to by alcohol. Much nonsense too, has been produced during what seemed to have been periods of inspiration. Even dream states, sometimes if but rarely, make significant contributions. A story is frequently told of the archaeologist working on some forgotten language in vain. But he continues to saturate himself with every bit of available information about the people and the times that produced this challenging problem, recurrently concentrating most heavily on a large tablet bearing a lengthy inscription, presumably relating to a monarch who played an important role with the people whose language he is trying to decipher. Yet he fails; till one night in a dream the monarch appears at the tablet and reads off a translation in a language the archaeologist knows. The resulting excitement awakened him and by quickly writing down everything he could recall of the dreamed "translation" he solves the puzzle of the language in a relatively short time.

Such a story is delightfully mysterious and supernatural. But note, such a dream could occur only to an individual who is deeply involved in some specific problem or topic. It would seem that the "inspirations" obtained by the earnest fasters and seekers after guidance in the wildernesses were of a similar character. What such "prophets" emerge with from their retreats are but slightly restructured or recombined patterns of whatever it was they took with them: some minor variant on some issue of rather limited concern. Far rarer are the revelations such as those that came under the Bo tree, and which were obviously a violent reaction against the supernaturalism gone wild that was the Hinduism out of which Buddhism emerged.

Yet, these mystical states, like any other source of information, will have to justify themselves by their product. It is not enough for the mystic to report that in this state he experiences the "wholly other," that he is "in tune with the infinite." or that he has transcended all earthly limitations, etc. There are a variety of drugs and narcotics that produce precisely such subjective states and experiences, and are, in fact, closely linked with the origins or the practices of many a religion. Even to the eyes of the sympathetic James the obvious kinship of much of the experience and behavior of the mystic to psychopathology was apparent. No amount of sophistry or blindness could possibly disguise that fact. James made no attempts whatever to do so. Instead he insisted that pathological or not, truths of importance had come out of such mystical states, since the great leaders and innovators of religion showed similar idiosyncrasies. Furthermore, James denounced as "medical materialism" any attempt to discredit out of hand any ideas or values simply because there was somewhere about their origin a suspicion of psychopathology. He saw no reason why a somewhat elevated temperature might not be more productive of truth than the normal. And, one might well add, what else is there, what other bases are there to be found for religion once ritual and tradition have lost their compelling significance? Professor James Leuba[15] has done a much fuller job in documenting the evidence for psychopathology in an overwhelming number of religious mystics, particularly the Christian, largely because the documentary records on these are so readily available. But again it may well be that it is in such troubled individuals that perceptive processes might develop that are impossible for the healthy minded Philistine. At any rate, religion no longer has any other option. It is the religious experience to which it must look. As so aptly put by Professor Stace:[16]

"But in India it is not thought impossible that atheism may

be as profoundly religious as theism, nor is atheism regarded by religious men as in itself unspiritual. This is extremely hard for a westerner to understand.—He does not see that the essence of religion lies in religious *experience,* and not in any belief at all, and that all so-called religious beliefs or doctrines are merely theories about the religious experience." (Italics as in Stace.)

Certainly the "revealed" religions cannot in any way object to this diagnosis of their nature. Without exception, the revealed faith is the product of the interpretations put upon their own experiences by the founders. Without exception, a great illumination, or a first-hand conversation with a god, or a unique enlightenment under a Bo tree is the basis for the new dispensation, the new way of life, belief, and faith. This meant a battle with orthodoxy, as it was with Buddha, Christ, and Mohammed, to put them in chronological order. But in time the social movements launched by these founders on the basis of their religious experiences, became the institutional norm over larger or smaller geographical areas. This does not end the era of experiences; a leader might well continue to have or to create such inspirations whenever they were opportune. Such leadership too, tends to set the pattern for the "experiences" of the faithful, the followers. Private experiences lending themselves too readily to heterodox interpretations are almost universally discouraged by fair means or foul in most going religious concerns. Those confirming men in the proper faith or the proper path are likely to be accepted as authoritative or genuine. Ways of rewarding the faithful are devised.

Cultures differ greatly in the matter of the use made of the unusual subjective states. They may well be denied any place or function in the culture, as among the Zuñi. They may be central in the nearest thing they have in their culture to "religion" and vocational guidance, as they are among the Crow Indians. The Zuñi frown upon any manifestations of disturbed or abnormal emotional states. There is no place made for anything other than the placid, calm demeanor that is their ideal and standard of human conduct. With the Crow the vision is elevated to a place of high honor and respect. The adolescent was expected to seek a vision to provide guidance in the selection of a social role or occupation. Visions, more exactly, hallucinations, were induced by days of exposure, fasting, thirst, and sleeplessness. If that did not induce a "vision" a finger joint would be cut off as a sacrifice to the agencies that granted visions. The vision would be interpreted, either by the suppliant himself or by elder advisors as to its meaning for vocational selection. This was their nearest approach to the "supernatural," the most intimate relation reached with any such agency.

When a Crow Indian, or anyone else for that matter, has induced serious disturbances in his metabolism with exposure, thirst, fasting, and perhaps blood-letting, we are not at all mystified that he should experience hallucinations. Such abnormal subjective experiences provide us with no great mystery; nor do we expect great things from them. If the adolescent Crow gets a "hunch" out of such a "vision" we are ready to point out that the contents of such visions are culturally determined to some considerable extent, and that any validity that they might have by way of significant vocational guidance would at best be something after the manner in which clues to motivation and personality can be extracted out of the perception of ink-blots. Latent wishes, desires, or evaluational attitudes are presumed to have been reflected or revealed in the content of the visions.

But what now, when an individual experiences hallucinations, or "visions" if you prefer, without any such deliberate insults to his physiology? If we have strong attitudes of faith and belief toward some particular "revelations" experienced by the founders or the prophets of our special "faith," we are rather apt to overlook the interesting little detail that again and again such founders and prophets practiced exposure to the elements, fasts, thirsts, and lonely vigils as deliberately cultivated devices for attaining visions, guidance, or communings with spirits or gods. It was apparently standard practice with Biblical characters and prophets. But not all visions by any means had to be invoked with such heroic aids. Mystical experiences seem to come to some individuals without any extraordinary preludes or preparations.

In the less sophisticated cultures, mystical states, if they play any significant role in the culture, are rather more than likely to be of the drug-induced sort. Hardly a substance known to primitive cultures with conspicuous effects upon the mental state but what it has been incorporated into ritual or traditional use by some people somewhere. Alcohol, opium, hemp, coca, poisonous mushrooms or herbs, snake venom, anything and everything capable of inducing vivid modifications of the normal state of subjective experience, has been incorporated into the magico-religious customs of some people, somewhere. It is more than likely that the unusual, the abnormal if you will, conscious state, however induced, has been the most frequent source of the concept of the supernatural, the transcendent, the spiritual, and the godly.

Ideas, visions, beliefs, or practices, based upon such experiences are, with here and there notable exceptions, given authoritative status that removes them from competition with the prosaic principles and procedures upon which ordinary knowledge is dependent for warrant and justification. When William James said that such mystical sources are, and have a right to be, authoritative over ordinary kinds of knowledge he at least put into black and white what many of the world's cultures have long been doing, regardless of the sources of the mystical states, be they the products of fasts, drugs, epileptic seizures, hypnosis or auto-hypnosis. Incidentally, the Yoga of Patanjali recognize the similarity between the condition secured by the Yoga practices and that produced by drugs.

Professor James Leuba[17] has given us a most careful and scholarly study of the mystical state and the mystics, both major and minor. A careful reading of his work is imperative for all who prefer any kind of factual data to any kind of blind faith. As William James long ago conceded[18] the evidence for the significant part played by pathology in the lives of the major mystics is as good as any evidence can be at this distance in time, and it points to hysteria. These mystics did not lead, and were apparently incapable of leading, normal lives. Not one of them led a normal sex life, nor was it because of a lack of opportunity. Like all too many of today's cases of hysteria, they were simply incapable of making a normal adjustment in their sexual lives, in spite of the usual opportunity so to do. Some were cold, sexually, to human contacts, but capable of frequent attacks of erotomania. Yet it must not be thought that mysticism is to be interpreted purely as frustrated sexuality. These hysterics simply messed up their sex lives to much the same degree that they were incapable of normal life adjustments .

Their mystical states themselves varied widely in frequency, "depth," content, and method of inducement or excitation. With some they had many of the earmarks of epileptoid seizures, and apparently entirely unrelated to any volitional initiation on the part of the mystic. Others used devices strongly akin to the practices of the yogin, with their modifications in the normal course of visceral functions. There are those who deliberately cultivate these abnormal states of experience and can initiate them almost at will. The commonest techniques used strongly suggest the methods of inducing a hypnotic state, the so-called auto-hypnosis, probably the conditioning to self-provided cues of rather complex functional disturbances of the normal bodily activity, with highly variable effects on the conscious or experience state of the individual. Your ordinary hysterical patient too, is rather likely to make a good hypnotic subject! Many of these "grand" mystics knew precisely how to induce the trance or hypnoidal states in themselves. With some it was a device for creating a desirable phantasy world. A former colleague found that during the first world war he could hypnotize some of his follow-soldiers in the trenches, thereby giving them for a half-hour the surcease of a vivid and "real" visit" to home, loved ones, or safety. Many of these mystics had simply learned the trick of providing precisely the right auto-suggestive cues that would similarly send them into a "heavenly" ecstasy for varying periods, typically of the duration of the more familiar hypnotic trance, which may or may not be conscious, unconscious, or selectively one or the other. Names, even their own, or prayers, or names of saints or deities frequently played an important role in the particular sequence of activities that could induce the mystic state.

Yet no matter how humble or suspicious the origins or concomitants of the mystical state may be, such matters alone cannot provide the bases for an evaluation of it. In terms of his contemporary social, ethical, or religious norms, the mystic, for the most part, tends to be a conformist. He accepts without question the values of his culture; and the greatest source, apparently, of the emotional conflicts the mystic seems to battle is his own shortcomings in his attempts to live up to the highest ideals of the group. Far scarcer, historically, are the mystics whose conflicts can not be resolved in the framework of the old culture pattern, and who bend their efforts toward the remaking of at least some of its institutions, frequently the religious. Here are your strident-voiced innovators, striving to make their own particular message convincing. The inner voices that speak so emphatically and clearly for them, far more often strike no responsive chord in others. Only very seldom in history do innovations find acceptability beyond a small circle of people similarly moved by time and circumstance to echo the innovator's insights, or find them congenial.

Probably little is to be gained from any elaborate attempt to separate the ordinary religious experience from mysticism, if indeed they can be separated. Certainly as a philosophy, or metaphysics, mysticism generally implies a fairly specific doctrine, and the true mystic is offended at any use of the term implying merely a careless assumption of causal relations or a general fuzziness or haziness of logic. As a matter of fact, most description of the mystical state corresponds closely to descriptions of the religious experience and it is commonly assumed that they are more or less identical. Certainly the western religions have no corner on them. Here, for example is the way the state is observed or described in Egypt:[19]

"Mysticism can be defined as an interrelated series of specific states of consciousness that can be studied through introspection. It goes through three stages, the first being preparedness, which is characterized by fear, anxiety, sorrow, and vagueness; the second developing a tendency to mysticism which

the author calls "emotions of mysticism"; this leads into the
final stage of resolving this confusion by following the tenets
of a mystic order. The life of the mystic is a constant struggle
between his desires and the supreme spiritual values to which
he aspires. This struggle is resolved by the voluntary inhibition
of these desires which the mystic suppresses and then sub-
limates through his striving for spiritual perception. The head
of the order plays a role akin to that of a psychotherapist."

With due regard for general cultural differences, it is easily
apparent that what is here being described is a blood-brother
to our old friend the religious experience. This Egyptian thinks
of it as mysticism. For the mystic, the mystical state of experience derives its validity from the assumption that in this state
the distinction between subject and object is transcended, that
the experience is God for the Christian mystic or Nirvana for
the Buddhist. As aptly stated by Professor Gordon Allport:[20]

"The ordinary processes of knowing, like desiring and valu-
ing, require the separation of the self (the subject) from the
object of knowledge, desire or value. Such separation is inimical
to the unity that religion affirms—".

Well—perhaps some religions so affirm, but probably *all*
mysticism does!

Stace[21] similarly defines it as follows:

"The foundation of this relation—(between mysticism and
love)—lies in the fact that in the mystic vision all distinctions
and therefore the distinction between one man and another are
transcended. There is for him no such distinction between an
'I' and a 'you' as would cause him to seek something for the
'I' and deny it to the 'you,' to hate another while loving himself,
to cause pain to another while grasping at pleasure for himself.
He lives in all men and all men live in him. His desire, his love,
therefore, is not for himself but for all men. It is this which
makes mysticism the source of the moral life and provides the
religious foundation of ethics."

Should one wonder just how these mystical processes work,
let us turn again to Professor Stace.[22]

"All men, or at least all sensitive men, are mystics in some
degree. There is a mystical side of human nature just as there

is a rational side. I do not mean merely that we are potential mystics in the sense that we theoretically could, by living a life which is a practical impossibility for most of us, achieve the mystic consciousness. That would indeed be next to useless. I mean that we have the mystic consciousness now, although in most of us it shines only dimly. This is proved by the fact that, as with poetry, the utterances of the saint or the mystic call up a response in us, however faint it may be. Something in us answers back to his words, as also something answers back to the words of the poet. Why has the phrase of Plotinus, "a flight of the alone to the Alone," become famous and echoed down the ages? Why has it fascinated generations of men? It is not mere nonsense to men who, though they do not claim ever to have had anything which they would call a recognizable "mystical experience," yet possess spiritually sensitive minds. It must be that it stirs in them some depth of the waters of the soul which is ordinarily hidden, and which, by these words, is, if but for an instant, drawn up to, or near, the surface."

Now what can the prosaic scientist say in the face of such poetry? Simply that some people, including probably all mystics, just love their mysteries and prefer them to prosaic, instrumental knowledge. One wonders, have these mystics heard nothing of what has gone on in the realm of experiments with the conditioned responses, particularly to verbal cues? Have they never heard of the variety of things perceived in ink blots? These reactions to poetical sentiments, or let us say specifically to words like "alone" are not something out of some transcendental realm beyond space and time; they are the simple products of the conditioning process operating on verbal cues. With absolute control of the influences operating on an individual it would be possible to attach any emotional reaction desired to any words, situations, or even ideas. That such reactions have a naturalistic, a deterministic, yes, even a "materialistic" history in their production does not make them any less potent in their effects upon human behavior. And such conditioned emotional reactions to verbal cues are emphatically "real" and not nonsense, since they constitute the "triggers" that determine what are called "values" or evaluational attitudes, as well as "subjective experiences." But to build a whole realm of transcendent reality upon phenomena of human behavior that can be produced experimentally can only appear ridiculous in the eyes of all who have seen the logic of Occam's razor, or who have been impressed with the capacity man has shown for some thousands of years to deceive himself with his own verbal noises.

One would think that these addicts of mysticism had never even heard of the salivation of Pavlov's dog conditioned to a bell, not to mention the dramatic experiments on the conditioning of visceral effectors generally, or of trace conditioning, or of higher-order conditionings, or of conditioning to self-provided cues, or of conditioned inhibitions, of conditioned electrical activity in muscles and brain, almost any one of which would provide the bases not only for a naturalistic theory of these "mystical" functions but for naturalistic and instrumental programs of action in the production and control of specific reactions, be they physical or ever so "spiritual." Rare indeed is the child that has not a history of complex emotional states conditioned to the word "alone," regardless of what language he spoke. With a little practice, almost anyone would be capable of considerable proficiency in reporting on the precise details of the internal or subjective "experiences" induced by this or any other word. There is, after all, no great mystery about "introspection," nor does it have any transcendental significance or validity. As has been shown by Max[23] the introspective report of events is far from being the most sensitive indicator of organic processes in the body, and, if they achieved nothing else, the Freudians certainly have put sufficient emphasis upon the completely unconscious character of the major portion of the determinants of human behavior. Obviously inadequate as the determiner of the behavior of an individual human being, the mystic now expects us to accept the simple fact that the individual can give an admittedly incomplete and spotty account of some of the activities going on in his body as an earnest of the nature of true or "ultimate reality," whatever that childish concept can refer to in this day of the chastened scientific probability that even the most accurate knowledge is now known to be. The "Mystic Consciousness" has all the earmarks of a bad noun constructed out of a perfectly good adjective.

As with all individual differences, there are to be expected great variations in the richness and variety of the "subjective" life, namely the readiness with which elaborate feeling states or imagery are conditioned to socially or self-provided cues. When some of the reputedly high-powered mystics provide us convincingly with short-cuts to something of genuine, instrumental value, the things that eliminate the worries, pains, and tribulations, and provide the leisure requisite to the cultivation of the more "spiritual" aspects of life I shall be the very first to burn incense at their shrines, to pray and pay for lessons in how to attain the inward light or the "Higher Reality." But as of now, the most that seems to emerge out of this "cosmic mentality" is a few minor variations on the local animism or supernaturalism. But few new theological ideas emerge out of mystical states; they are brought to them by the mystic. And a great variety of drugs will bring to anyone subjective experiences apparently indistinguishable from the mystical states achieved by exceptional individuals, who usually are well supplied with the earmarks of pathology.

There are today, and apparently there have long been, those who have been dissatisfied with the painful, pedestrian path to significant knowledge or wisdom by way of specific sense data, laborious trial and error, tentative hypotheses, and controlled experiment. For such it has been all too easy to believe in the possibility of a sudden influx of certainty from divine inspiration or other unimpeachable sources, enabling them to attain to "higher truths" with no greater involvement of effort than that necessary to still their few remaining critical qualms. To permit themselves the luxury of such phantasies they have postulated an entire realm of "higher reality" to which, by definition, reason could not possibly attain, but to which their mystical techniques gave them direct access. This has been going on a long time. The old Hindus were at it, apparently thousands of years before such practitioners developed in the west. Might a Philistine be permitted to ask at this juncture, what, other than private phantasy-worlds for the initiated, have been the fruits of such transcendent wisdom? It is not knowledge of such stripe that lifted man to the enviable state where yesterday's impossibilities are today's commonplaces, and where he has doubled his sojourn here and removed an imposing fraction of the pains and indignities life formerly provided for him. Today's mystics are repeating the empty phrases of those of yesteryear while they pursue their mystical states much after the manner of the drug addicts that no doubt were their earlier version at the beginning of the traditions of mysticism. Some of today's crop have merely learned how to induce similar subjective states by means of a variety of modifications of the techniques of self-hypnosis. There is more than a suspicion of pathology about such states; the great bulk of mankind experiences them only under conditions of serious physiological disturbance, where we have learned to put them into their proper category of the pathological.

The Religious Revival and Conversion

The particular pattern taken by the religious life in a given area is of necessity a function of the peculiar historical and cultural factors operating at the critical times in history when a relatively dynamic pattern emerges where there had previously been but a loose structure, or none. The circuit-riding preachers, bringing organized religion to the frontier settlers beyond the Alleganies created, in the process, considerably modified religious customs. Much has been written about this period and this process.[24] The widely scattered settlers, having lived quite some time without benefit of regular religious shepherding, but recalling it vividly from their pre-frontier days, succumbed to the combined influence of the exhorting preachers and the heightened emotion induced by the unfamiliar crowd situation in the "revival" meeting. Note the term, "revival"; it points to the fact of the previous ordered and institutionalized religious beliefs and practices these people knew before their frontier days. The older generation had their religious beliefs "revived"; the younger ones with no previous contact with institutional religion, became "converted," "felt the power," "accepted the spirit," or "came to Jesus." There the precedent developed for the expectation of religious conversion as an earnest toward the assumption of adult demeanor and responsibilities. A survey made around the turn of the century in a middle-western state indicated that upward of 90% of all adults had experienced such a "conversion," and it was long assumed to be an inseparable concomitant of adolescence.

Professor E. D. Starbuck[25] describes the state of things in the academic study of religion as found by him in the period 1890-1893. "One leading university listed a course in the history of religion and announced that the object of the course was to show that the Christian religion was the only one capable of rational justification"! But he began his researches into the conversion phenomena and by 1894-95 reported to a graduate seminar on his findings. These he interpreted as pointing to the similarity of the conversion process to habit breaking, re-centering a dissociated personality, and Prince's split personality phenomena.[26] He also reported his findings on the piling up of conversions at puberty. The discussion of his report was opened by one whom he identifies as Edward Borncamp, who, face white with emotion, said "It's all a lie!"[27]

These studies of Starbuck have become classics in their field. They were heavily drawn upon by James for his famous "Varieties of Religious Experience." They have supplied us with what is probably the most reliable account of the religious life of the American Protestant of the period just before the turn of the century. The picture of the conversion experience that emerges is something as follows: before conversion the individual reports a sense of incompleteness and imperfection, with much time spent in brooding and introspection. The predominant mood is one of depression, blanketed by a sense of sin. There is much anxiety about a future life and what it holds for him, and a feeling of distress at the doubts he has about the truth and validity of the faith. Then comes the "conversion," which tends to center statistically around adolescense, the female average being a year younger. In terms of today's norms for adolescence Starbuck's figures would seem to indicate a quite late adolescence as the norm; but such things might shift in a half-century, what with the dramatic change in the American diet in that time. At any event, after the conversion they reported a feeling of happy relief, and a sense of pardon and a feeling of certainty about things here and hereafter.

Now the question is this: is this a unique consequence of the Christian faith or is it a product of the social situation? During the American economic depression of the thirties a similar study was made on the young joiners of the Communist party, the data being gathered in much the same way. The general picture, both before and after this sort of "conversion" is indistinguishable from the process and effects of religious conversion, according to these findings.[28] This will no doubt add conviction to the opinions of those who already are convinced that Communism is a religion, a verdict shared by such men as former Dean Edgar Furniss of Yale University Graduate School[29] and John Dewey,[30] but such conviction will not add much light to the conversion phenomenon, be it religious or political. It may be to the point to report here that a survey on the frequency of such religious conversions as was made by Starbuck and in the same general area but made some thirty years later showed a decline in the frequency to something around twenty percent as against the over ninety percent of the earlier period. Apparently there is such a thing as a pattern of such behavior, set in the culture. The spectacular conversions, such as were made in public at revival meetings on the frontier, and the technique of which is still to some extent preserved by the inheritors of the traditions of D. L. Moody, Billy Sunday, and Charles G. Finney, and of which the current representative is the South's gift to religion, Billy Graham, are today relatively rare, particularly outside of Protestant circles. It is not that there have been lacking evangelistic parsons to carry on the tradition; small-scale "revival" exhorters have been continuously active in the country since the formula was first discovered. They have simply not "caught on" with sufficient success to become exportable beyond a very limited area. The phenomenon of wholesale conversions is on the wane. The frontier revivalist won his souls back to religion against no competition; the frontier was simply an intellectual as well as a religious vacuum into which the childhood faith of the frontiersmen readily returned or was "revived." Those who drop away from religion in the world of today find themselves in no such void. The silver-tongued exhorters draw large crowds but their ratio of converts to audience is small indeed.

A still more recent statistical survey made at Harvard and Radcliffe colleges[31] reported that the crisis type of conversion experience had been experienced by only seven percent of the male sample, and by but nine percent of the females. This low percentage is no doubt at least in part a function of the generally lower degree of piety in college students. The geographical origins of the individuals reporting these experiences would probably be the areas where such religious crises are still rather commonplace.

But the revival tradition is not yet dead in the United States, even if it no longer seems a part of the usual or accepted way of life. Minor outbreaks of revivalism still occur, particularly in the American middle-west where that culture trait was once best established. The New York Times of February 10, 1950 carried a United Press despatch of the previous day, from Wheaton, Illinois, describing such an occurrence:

"A spontaneous mass confession by 1,500 students of Wheaton College passed the twenty-four-hour mark tonight and showed no sign of a let-up.

All classes were suspended at the Liberal Arts School as the men and women students and their 150 teachers jammed into Pierce Memorial Chapel to proclaim their faith and confess their sins.

Many students are training for religious life at the nondenominational college, which has a graduate theology school, but many others are liberal arts students.

The demonstration had been going on since 7 p.m. last night when a few students went to the platform at a routine evangelical meeting to "testify" and the confessions developed into a mass movement.

All last night and through today the students kept up a steady stream to the platform, leaving only occasionally to get a bite to eat or some sleep.

Some were bold in their confessions, some hesitant and some tearful. One tall red-haired youth rose to say that he gave a diamond ring to his girl 'that the Lord picked out for me.'

'But I had one difficulty in telling whether I loved the girl or the Lord the most,' he said. 'Well, I got that straight with her this afternoon. The Lord comes first.'

Almost all confessed wrongs against some person—their teachers, parents, friends or sweethearts—and named the offended party.

Now and then as the confessions went on the students called a halt, opened the windows to air the chapel and sang hymns until the admissions resumed.

Throughout the meeting the boys and girls sat together on the wooden seats of the chapel, dressed in sweaters, blue jeans and other conventional campus wear. Members of the football and basketball teams were among the confessors.

Authorities of the school, which was founded in 1860 and opens its doors to students of some thirty denominations, made no move to stop the demonstration.

'We will let it run its course,' they said.

One girl said she had cheated even in Bible Class. A music student confessed that she had been singing for her own pleasure rather than 'the glory of God.' Others said they had been guilty of cheating, lying and many other forms of wrong-doing.

But one girl went to the platform and said she thought her fellow-students were 'silly to give testimony,' because she hated insincerity and couldn't believe that all were sincere. Then she asked forgiveness for doubting their sincerity.

The students had gathered at the chapel last night for another service in the school's 'evangelistic week.'

Dr. J. Raymond Edman, president of the college, rose to ask if there was any one who would 'like to give a word of testimony or praise on the blessings of this week.'

The students arose immediately and began pouring out their faith. Others rose and the hours passed as the testimonials continued.

All night long the unprecedented demonstration went on. Today more and more students packed into the chapel until all standing room was gone and the crowd overflowed into the balcony and an auxiliary chapel in the basement.

A few tried to go to classes today but there were not enough students or faculty members on hand and the classrooms were forgotten."

Such an event is at best a pale, a polite, and a restrained version of the lusty, zestful, and uninhibited revivals that were its progenitors a century ago. When one remembers that almost anything becomes an adequate excuse for breaking up the routine of class attendance, and that if a small fraction of the student body is in a mood to supply the dramatics of such mass confession, certainly the rest are willing to play the part of amused or interested spectators. But here at mid-century, such events are rare enough so that they are definitely newsworthy. Note that the atmosphere at the school had been prepared for such attitudes and behavior by an authorized "evangelistic week," and professional or expert revival preachers were already on the campus. Obviously, the local traditions include just such behavior phenomena, and their occurrence almost anywhere but on a college campus would never have called for comment. The colleges at which such an event could transpire in 1950 are relatively few in number.

The psychologist, Raymond B. Cattell[32] sums up the conversion phenomenon as follows:

"Most of the early studies of the psychology of religion were perhaps unduly concerned with the spectacular phenomena of sudden religious conversion. We now know that such experiences are comparatively rare, associated with some degree of temperamental abnormality, confined almost entirely to the age of adolescence, and prone to occur only in certain types of religious culture. Generally its explanation seems to be that the upsurging of sexual emotion at adolescence is met by the powerful inhibitions of a culture which attaches a strong sense of guilt to sexual expression. Increasing conflict between actual sexual expression or unconscious wishes on the one hand and the forces of repression on the other, causes an intolerable strain of anxiety and guilt, from which pressure the individual may unexpectedly escape by the solution of renouncing the goal of sexual pleasure or the right to individual self-assertion. At the cost of sublimation—converting sexuality into love of his fellows, and self-assertion into vicarious self-assertion through God—he thereby obtains peace of mind. To explain the process in terms of psychological forces is not to belittle its importance to society, for whether the process be sudden or gradual, it constitutes in moderation a desirable adjustment in civilization. It would be better still if brought about without recourse to illusory ideas."

With the addition of a few comments on the role played by the economic inadequacy of the adolescent and the fact that all too often opportunities for effective economic effort on the part of the adolescent are also contingent upon conforming to the conduct standards of his culture, this summary by Professor Cattell seems pretty much to the point. But any conclusions on the nature of such processes must in the end be validated against detailed individual life-history and personality studies, admittedly difficult to make. Documents, if genuine and the spontaneous product of the subjects under observation or study, are valuable. The following letter, written by a sixteen-year old adolescent to an older brother who had already left home because of conflicts over religion and education in a family that was attempting to maintain a level of piety somewhat in excess of the local norm, may well be illuminating. Only the names of persons and places have been changed.

Lanesville, U.S.A.
Jan. 15, 1923

Fellow Citizen:

Well how goes it, I hope its hard. But I'm glad you left for since your thoughtless criticisms have left me I've had a great experience. I'm saved. Now don't go & let Olaf read that & laugh & scorn. Probably you do think oh he don't know any better, but think on fair one. God is only taking you thru what your going thru for a purpose. I'll tell you I've had experience of every kind of life this fall. After you left, I attended all public dances in Avon & in Laneville. Drank wine etc. I was popular among a certain crowd. But what good—none—. I met your friends, Ada Farmer & Lucy Hamilton. Shes most crazy over me But thank God I'm thru that stuff now and Austin I can't tell you how happy it makes me feel. Not me alone but Dad & Mother & Uncle Pete & Susan. I'll tell you Uncle Pete is a good scout. Hes one of the most liked men of Falls City. I strutt around with him & live high on his Rep.

Austin I can't begin to tell you how happy I am. Why I don't pride myself but Ive sure won a rep around Falls City & Laneville. To begin with Mother & Dad think the world of me & consequently I've got a light suit & light coat & patent leather oxfords that make people look for blocks at me. Please remember this is not bragging, only facts, C. Honestly I have it wonderful. Why here I am in a Mansion. Wanting nothing why dad & mother give me anything I ask for. Absolutely I don't need to ask for it Pa comes & asks me if I need it. (spending money) you C. business has been fine & I get spending money whenever I want it. Mother & I went to Falls City Sat. & I got face powder, Face Cream & oh anything I want. oh yes, most important of all I got a swell gold ring with a green square ameythist (sp.) set in it. Just saw it & asked ma for money to get it with. Why Austin I'm in heaven on earth. I can't tell you how nice I have it. Ive gone to the Falls to Church all fall. for last couple mo. you C it about killed mother when I went to dances & they heard of wine. Boy I sure can dance swell zowy. All the girls awaited a dance with me. Lucy Hamilton's a nice girl but not nice enuf for me. I'll tell you ole man I'm traveling in class, C. Well then I settled down when it hurt ma so. But didn't change to a christian until a few days ago. Dad let me take the car up to the City often over Fri-nite Sat. & Sun. I went with a classy girl up there. Pretty, oh Boy. Uncle Pete knew her well & thot the world of her. Hence the couple. Well I went to see Pres. of Skelly, Pres. of Mountain Mills, & every big man in the City—introducing myself as Rev. P. S. Youngs nephew. Well I wish you could of heard what Jim Wilson (owner of Wilsons Dept. store.) said about me I'm going to put initials on his car. The great man that he is. to think that he'd look at me & he gave me the biggest blow-up to Uncle Peter that you ever heard of. I'll tell you when I'm in Falls City I go among Class, C. Boys its a great life around here. Every one happy (*now*.) Ill tell you how I became converted. I decided to put god to a test. I have felt miserable I couldn't believe there was a god. & eternal life. *So the* other nite as I was watching the Avon-Laneville Basket Ball game (The hardest of the season) I decided to put god to a test. Three quarters of the game was played. Score 22 to 20 in favor of Laneville. I prayed to Jesus & said. Now I want to know if theres a God. I said if there is why during this last quarter Avon's won't make a basket & Laneville will. Austin during that last quarter, Laneville scored 12 points & Avon 0. and at the last Laneville's second team were put in. oh I was so disgusted when they went in. I tho't well now heres where it all goes & what do you think Avon's wonderful team didnt make a basket off of our 2nd team even tho' they shot about 7 or 8 times. How about that??? thats enuf for me. Austin theres a God. I've tested him that way several times now & it *always* works. (now what do you think?) You know yourself that if you thot there really was a Divine God who offers eternal life that you'd be willing to accept that eternal life for a few moments of life on this earth.

I told Mother & Dad the other nite of my test & told them that I expected to go thru Jones & Smith Bible Institute & then become the greatest Evangelist that this country has ever known. You may laugh me to scorn. Go on you *fool*. If you could know how happy I am in the Lord to-nite why you'd come home rite now. Austin your turn is coming & "The Hofer Brothers" you & I are going to be the greatest Evangelists ever known. You may laugh, scorn *but you C*. I'll tell you Austin I've got some pep & something to back it up. I'll bet you $100. that inside of two months I'm the most popular kid at Jones. You C. I can do anything that I want to. I've got enuf will power to become Pres. of old U.S. at age of 45 if I want to. But my lifes mission is to be a Billy Sunday the 2nd. only more wonderful. Laff you in-

fadel but you C. Some day Ill be richer than Billy Sunday
is & hes worth Millions. Altho he started out poor. Someday
you & I will be The greatest Evangelists ever known. *You C.*
I told mother & Dad that the other nite. & you ought to
have seen the look on your mothers face. Simply *wonderful*
But its all going to come true. Austin if you want to be
happy, absolutely happy why give in to God. & you & I go
to Jones together next Semester. What say. Ive got a few
things to ask you. Now be sincere about these questions &
think for yourself *once* & quit letting other men do your
thinking. 1. If there is a God would you like to know it?
If your honest, you must answer yes. 2. If you tho't there
was a God would you be willing to pay the price to find out
for sure that there is a God, a eternal life? If your a *man* &
Half way fair you'll say yes? 3. If there is a God, would you
like to be living the way you are? If your an honest thinker
you'll say *no.*

All rite now be fair you said yes to the 2nd question. I
heard you So do this. In spite of Gus & Olaf. You live a
christian life for a few days. Start rite now & pray & act
as tho' you were a christian. Pray to Jesus & tell him your
going to be fair & give him a chance & pray that if there is
a God that he show you some way within the next few days.
Put him to a test of some sort. Try him out. & if your half
way fair Austin you'll do this. Now the folks told me not to
tell you this. But Austin if you give in to God why you & I
can go to Jones together the 2nd Sem. Now don't just say
you believe and bluff so that you can get to go, but be a
man give God a chance Do what I have asked you to & you
& I room together at Jones inside of two weeks. 2nd Semest
starts Jan. 29. but it matters not if your a week or two late.
But of course I don't want you to tell the folks you've become a Christian & that your going to be a christian worker
with me unless its true. Austin if you want to do the right
thing the manly thing. Give God a chance & become converted & The folks will send us both to Jones. Now they
told me not to tell you this But you C. Mother thinks that
her prayers will soon all be answered & then if you become

converted why she wanted to have that as a surprise for
you (going to Jones). But of course if you don't believe in
God why go on you fool & C. how far you get. I'll guarantee
that the name of Frank Hofer will be more known all over
the world, more than the name of Austin Hofer. *You'll C.*
But if you'll be anywhere near-decent & give God a chance
why you'll share my fame cause we'll be "Hofer Brothers"
evangelism for the Lord. Now Austin quit your laughing &
scorning & think a little about this. Give God a chance or
I won't even think you deserve the name of Fellow Citizen.
But Austin you've got good qualitys about you & I believe
your man enuf to give God a chance. Im hoping that my
brother still has that many brains. Well if you do it remember its happiness we'll go to Jones together & I'll make
you popular if you can't make yourself that way. Well now
I'll tell you about Bessies Vacation in Laneville.

When she came home she was changed why kid shes
not the same girl. Why shes got the most spunk & Pep of
anyone I ever seen. From what I heard, shes the most popular girl at Jones. She has some swell rich fellows out there
& when she came home she had planned not to give me a
stand but I acted as tho she was the littlest imp that ever
occured & she sort of took to me. Well the result was I was
with her till after twelve bells 11 out of 14 nites that she
spent in Laneville during Xmas season. Why man shes the
most changed you ever seen. She had promised a Jones guy
not to let anyone else kiss her & I soon broke that. I wish
you could of seen her when I told her I was going to Jones,
Last half. Why man never in my life have I experienced such
a thrill. She pretty nearly went crazy. & to think shes the
most popuar girl out there. Guess that makes me feel proud
eh! to think I could influence her like that. Well she told me
she loved me more than all those men put together 50 times.
So I gets big headed & thinks to me self. You little Devil
I want you to realize what kind of man you got. I'll tell you
I did too. I just wanted to see how crazy I could make her
over me. So one nite I said "Bessie I'm going to California
instead of to Jones & she cried for three hours so I didn't

get to leave till one O'clock. Now don't let Olaf read this I don't want that infadel spreading this in Laneville C.C. *I mean it*. I couldn't get her to stop then before I left, she kissed me & smiled for me. Well that was Saturday nite & Sunday was their last day here & we (all our family) were invited to Asters for Sunday dinner. Cause Mr. & Mrs. Aster tho't I wouldn't look at Bess when she came home cause I had so many other higher class friends in the city. Bess was thinking she wouldn't bother with anyone like me. So I suspicioned that & at the end she cried & cried cause she didn't want to go back to Jones. Boys its a thrill, zoowy. I'll tell you thats more than you could make a girl do for you.

Gertrude Halsey falls all over me every time I c her. Nancy Ross who goes to Falls City business College cried over me right in front of ma the other day cause I hadn't been to C. her for a month. Shes a swell dame to wears a big diamond ring. that she got for graduation. Her home is in Winston & she went home over vacation C. She sent me a $5.00 tic for Xmas present. She stays in Falls City all the time. Shes beautiful & has red hair. What makes her like me huh! I'll tell you the secret I dress *swell* & walk around as if I were John D. himself. & when I'm with her I act as tho' she was the most miserable little wretch that ever happened.

Well the next sunday or the next day after Bess cried over me why she didn't come to church. I asked Aster the trouble (I knowing what it was) & he said "I don't know she has cried all morn." When we went down to dinner she was no place to be found. Well I looked her up & found her in a corner crying. So I jollyed her up & told her I wouldn't go to California & she kissed me (On her own accord remember) (cause I wouldn't lower my-self to kiss any girl) and smiled for me & was all rite for a hour or so. Then when the folks went home at 4:00 I stayed & talked to her for a long time & she left that nite on the seven O'clock car, as happy in me as I am in God. She promised to be absolutely true to me till I got there & she said that if I went to California instead of coming to Jones to see my

little Sheba why she'd take her money & go way away where
no one knew her & start life over again. Hows that sound
Huh? Its all true. By Jinks show me the girl that I can't
make her cry over me in a short time. If I can make girls
that daffy why surely I can win souls by the thousands. So
can you if you get over your crazy ways. Come on brother.
Give God a chance & you & I will put our names on the
Maps.

Hofer Bros. "Evangelism of the World" Our Motto,
what do you say ole man. How about it. Can you say no
to God? This is a pretty mixed up letter cause I'm all
excited & nervous. Too much writing but I know I'll be paid
for it by receiving a letter saying you've changed. Saying
your ready to bring your Prodigal old personage back from
its wanderings.

Oh boy I took Oscar & Mildred Mason, Lester & Rose &
Bess & myself to Arcaria to a Basket B. game & on to Falls
City in the Buick one nite, Bess & I went skating several
times. & I taught her how to skate. I never saw anyone learn
so quick in my life. Shes a swell skater now. All my fault
too. I'll tell you I think a lot of her. But I don't want her
to find out to much of it. I don't want to get to serious yet.
Save that till I'm older. But I'll vouch that shes the girl I
marry. She'll travel with you & I in our Evangelism campaigns & you'll have a nice little wife too. I don't know
why I say "little" so much but guess its cause I call Bess
My little *something* so much. When I wrote the first letter
after she got back to Jones last week. I started out by saying, "well Hows my little Sheba coming. Wonder if she
still loves someone back in Laneville who misses her oh
just an awful lot. I bet that baked her. In fact I know it did
cause the next letter I got why she felt so proud when I said
my little Sheba as If I a king & she a little damsel. Well
Love is fun, ain't it, especially when everything comes your
way. I got another letter from her is A.M. But I ain't going
to answer it. Leave her sweat. If she wants me she must
learn to appreciate every thing that I send When I get off

of the train at Jones I'm going to have a swell package for her & she'll be there to meet me. Then I'll say, Hello Bess. Hows my little Sheba. Her sheik brought her a little package that she mustn't open for two days, C. Won't that melt her heart. Zoowy. She'll fall all over me, oof, oof.

Prof. Dawson a big gun is coming in his car to meet me too. Won't those college kids look when they see me in Company with Prof. Dawson & Bessie. I'll have won a to be worshipped reputation rite then from the start eh! You C Uncle Pete know him very well & he's the reason I'm in with Dawson. Tomorrow is tues. last day of real school. Wed. Thurs. & Fri. Semester exams. Then I have a weeks vacation *cause* Semester at Jones starts week later. I leave Laneville week from Fri. & stop at Dayton at Clara's for over Fri. nite & Sat. Sat nite I leave for Jones & ride all nite, arriving at 7:50 A.M. Hot Dog. But Don't spose I'll have it as nice as I do here. Not as nice a house etc. But I'll be in a new community where it'll be fun to set new girls on their ears, & whats more & best. I'll be with Bessie. Zoowy. Love is fun. A Thrill in every move. Won't I fell proud when I rob her away from all those college guys about 20 to 25 years old. Can you feature that. I can. easy simple well my pen, it hath begun to scratch. My pile of paper it hath shrunk to its utmost depths My brain It could guide the pen forever but my eyes they are fastly falling.

Pa says I have to go & talk to Randall. Supt. here fore I leave. Oh he thinks the sun rises & sets on me. It'll break his heart when I leave so I must explain. I've got canned twice this year had to go to a school board meeting to get back. Randall says I have more power over that school than he. He said when I'm bad the rest are. When I'm good the rest are.

Trusting that you will be the Lords in a short time I am
Sincerely your fellow Citizen
Frank

I'm taking Caesar its AWFUL.

P. S. *Ans. soon* & give the more serious of the serious parts of this letter. A few moments of your own tho'ts. You never think for yourself. When do you? All you do is read other peoples tho'ts expressed in words of untruth & beauty.

Frank

Like it or not ,here we have a picture of the adolescent mind in the raw. The pressures making for approved social conformity are clearly depicted, along with the advantages such conformity entails. So too are the individual, egotistic, and biological motivations. There is the conflict engendered by incompatibility of the two resulting patterns of motivation. There is the local conception of a personal god directing and planning the events that befall the individual, the naive confidence that the correct ritual appeals will bring supernatural intervention in the emotionally salient events in mundane affairs. Here we have, eloquently depicted, the nature of the siren call of both the socially approved motives and the biological-egotistical. There is even evidence of not quite successful attempts at a repression from the conscious processes of the socially disapproved motives.

Here we have the obvious contractual relationship between man and the god he worships at the moment. Such a god is expected to provide victory in basketball games, and satisfactions in life generally; in short, a powerful aid to be acquired at but the cost of a few ritual gestures. The god has "delivered the goods," and so he is "believed in." By such crude devices are the gods made acceptable to the young. "Payment" to the gods, in the form of credits in the account of rituals and sacrifices in advance of needed services follows along subjectively and psychologically, even if not openly, as it has tended to in so many systems of organized religion. Certainly this seems to have been the attitude of the ancient Romans toward their gods.[33]

But above all, the letter reveals the character of the individual drives and motives that are somehow to be socialized, and for which the kind of religious teaching that was provided, and the morality it sponsored, were obviously inadequate for this particular personality. As observed elsewhere,[34] there is some evidence that attempts at maintaining in the family a degree of piety in considerable excess of the social norm may well be a significant factor contributing to a complete abandonment of religious belief in favor of an agnosticism or atheism. Certainly this family provides confirmatory evidence in that but one child retained anything even approximating the parental degree of piety, one retained a piety more nearly the general social norm of the area, two have abandoned religion completely and are emotionally indifferent or distinterested, while two could best be described as having some considerable degree of hostility toward animism and contranaturalism of all sorts.

It is apparent at once that in the main, Professor Cattell's theoretical summary fits the psychological facts of the motivation and mechanics of this case of the conversion process pretty well. The classical picture of pre-conversion apprehension, worry, and doubt are there, as well as the joyous relief after taking the step. Most conspicuous of all is of course the role played by the social approval of the world of the adolescent. But the conversion process had a job on its hands with this young man. Was it able to keep him renouncing the goals of sexual pleasures and self-assertive satisfactions which this young fellow already sees can be linked with financial competence and success? No pretense is made that this letter is in any way typical, or even that the writer of it is an "average" adolescent. He obviously was anything but that. But he wrote with an almost complete lack of inhibitions, and that is what gives the document its value. Should it be objected that this youth was neither typical nor representative of adolescents one could safely assert that his religious experience is yet far closer to average than are those of the religious virtuosos or great mystics. Did he rival or outdo Billy Sunday? In making money, yes, but hardly in "saving souls." Here his future was far more nearly a challenge to the prowess of Jacques Casanova. His career in the theological seminary was short-lived, terminated at the urgent request of the faculty. Did he marry that girl he vowed he would? Indeed he did, but it was an unstable union! As was to be expected, once out from under financial dependence upon his family and with the economic resources to gratify his biological and social urges, all dependence upon religious devices ceased completely. The intensity of motivation that caused the writing of a letter of this length, and such high emotionality could almost be guaranteed to find its applications and rewards in the field of business enterprise where he has indeed equalled the millions he beleived Billy Sunday to have amassed in those happy days before heavy income taxes.

It will be argued by the devout that this young man never was "truly religious," that he did not have a true conversion, etc. That is probably a matter of semantics. Certainly there was a period, however brief, when he was convinced of the superiority of the behavior pattern advised by his elders and the respectable social elements and when he felt the joys of the "saved." But there were other drives, and time away from the watchful eye of representatives of the godly path, and the years were the "Roaring Twenties" during which the automobile was coming into its own as a transformer of the mores. What is actually atypical about this case is just that organized religion "lost" him, in spite of having gotten there first!

Now for the Hindu, the religious reality is also in the private, subjective ecstatic state; a flash of certitude arriving in the midst of deep meditation. But far from being an adolescent phenomenon, this is expected later in life, after the completion of the normal cycle of expected activities involving (1) being an earnest student of things spiritual; (2) being a married man and householder; (3) being for some time a hermit; and (4) a period as a mendicant holy man. Here the "illumination" was expected at the end of the cycle of desire. It would seem that the belief or the philosophy here adopted merely reflected the probable cycle of physiological growth, maturity, and decline, where the ideal striven for actually is that statistical norm of involution where the decline in physical vigor is reflected in the passing of conscious desire. Such an "illumination" seems to be, or to mark the process of being reconciled to one's end and passing. The factors making for such a doctrine and such precedents can easily be appreciated, particularly in a culture whose medical techniques and way of life result in an increasing percentage of the population surviving into the age where such involutional processes anticipate the end of life for so many. We have paid but little attention to the private emotional storms, struggles and conflicts that mark this phase of life for the old. A detailed and complete picture of the process would probably have many points in common with the more familiar picture of adolescent "Sturn und Drang" that in the American scene was long presumed to be the only possible time for the religious conversion, illumination, or mystical state. The religious experience is apparently as much the product of a learning process in a specific social situation as is any other element of culture.

CHAPTER X

PRIESTHOOD—THE WORLD'S OLDEST PROFESSION

The world has long enjoyed the facetious characterization of soldiers and campfollowers as 'the world's two oldest professions.' When bad political leadership has bungled us into another war it no doubt consoles us a bit at the moment to recall that wars and their attendant social mischief are no invention of ours. But, as with many a popular belief, the facts in the case are at considerable variance with the tradition. Even a cursory examination of the anthropological and ethnological literature makes it apparent that this priority in the professions must go to the medicine man, the angakok, the shaman, the priest, the parson, or whatever name is assigned to this expert in the extraordinary, this performer of the impossible, this fount of knowledge about the Unknown and the perhaps unknowable! Yes, just what name are we to assign to this profession? Were the whole subject not so charged with emotion almost any name would do. But what name will be acceptable as generic for the whole group? If we were to borrow the specific name of some group for their specialist that would perhaps unwittingly but none the less actually tend to color the entire profession with the perhaps peculiar idiosyncrasies of that one kind of specialist. The term 'medicine man' would thus automatically identify all religion with therapeutic quackery; were we to borrow the Chukchee term 'shaman,' that could hardly help but identify religion, unconsciously perhaps but none the less certainly, with possession by demons and epileptoid seizures. The term 'Brahman' would tend to identify religion with a privileged caste, in western ears, and to eastern ears it would no doubt sound libelous to dignify some illiterate functionary with the 'Brahman,' much as it would appear to our ears to call them all priests, parsons, or rabbis! And, in view of the fantastic variety of such specialists and functions, this sensitivity is quite understandable. Still, some common term must be hit upon in the interests of economy in communication. Brevity and wide usage would seem to favor the term 'priest' as a generic term for the entire profession. Unless otherwise specifically indicated the term will always be used in this broad, general sense.

The development of professions is but a small part of the general process of the division of labor, of a specialization of functions with by and large a resultant general increase of efficiency in human effort. Far from being an exception to the general rule, the priesthood, as had already been suggested, was probably an early form of specialization in most if not necessarily all cultures. What, might one well ask, are the determining factors making for this specialization of function?

How does any individual come to play a particular role, assume some specific function, or dominate some aspect or segment of his social group? Even a cursory review of the evidence bearing on this question will reveal an astounding variability in the factors determining the selection of a person for a particular social role, be it that of priest, military leader, or scapegoat. Widely surveyed, the world will probably provide instances of all possible criteria of selection. Obvious fitness would seem to stack the cards strongly in favor of any one individual filling a particular role and it certainly does so very frequently. It is a safe bet that a leader of warriors will be no mean fighter in person; but even this is not without generous exception. Such a position might well be fixed by lot or by heredity. One might expect, for example, that the role of artist would be assigned an individual on the basis of performance criteria of some sort, as it no doubt usually is. But remember Dr. Mead's Mountain Arapesh among whom the role of artist is assigned arbitrarily to anyone born with his navel cord wrapped around his neck, and their criterion of art is very simply that which such a person produces or creates! Some

Polynesian and some African tribes assign roles by social compulsion, even those of medicine man (priest) or diviner. Special physical assets or defects are sometimes the bases of role assignment, as for example the Chukchee shaman's epileptic seizures. A dramatic single performance in some activity might result in a permanent role assignment. Democratic societies frequently illustrate the assignment of roles of one sort on the basis of effective performance in another, perhaps quite unrelated, field of function, as when army generals are thrust into the roles of statesmen.

Far from being exceptional, the selection of personnel for the priesthood will be found to illustrate as varied bases for selection as can any other profession or specialty of social function. This might well mean a long, onerous, or painful apprenticeship, involving serious or ceremonial hazards. Often enough the priest must be a deviant. He might be of either sex or even of dubious intersex status. His unusual role might derive from his fits, trances, or hallucinations. He might be an albino, a monorchid, a homosexual, or have crossed eyes. He might practice chastity or dietary idiosyncrasies. A psychotic state might well cast one in the role. So too could almost any illness. This might well be followed by an abandonment of the occupation with recovery. The neophyte priest may first be compelled to serve an apprenticeship, or, in more complex societies undergo formalized education. But then again elsewhere much more importance might be attached to the personal 'call' the individual felt for entering the profession, much as it is today in some Protestant sects. The formal preparations for the functions of the priest are often very similar to those required of anyone entering upon any dangerous or strenuous endeavor demanding ferocity or courage, such as preparation for leading war parties or hunting dangerous game. This sometimes calls for the violation of the strongest taboos, such as incest with mother, daughter, or nearest female relative.

There are apparently no functions necessarily those of the priest. He may or may not concern himself with healing, meteorology, agriculture, food supplies, enemies and warfare. Interestingly enough, it often happens that if the regularly recognized priests ignore some such field or do not consider it a proper sphere of activity, it may become the province of some 'expert' who might achieve a certain amount of social recognition of his expertness. But not necessarily to the point where such recognition is embodied in a name or title. On the other hand, if the more or less official priesthood long neglects an area of life in which there is demand for priestly services an unofficial or "bootleg" ritualism or magic is very likely to develop. Thus, there were the mystery cults that existed outside of and apart from the official state religion of the Athenians and there is good evidence that a similar condition existed among the Maya, the Aztec, and the Inca peoples. Even in Christendom such aberrant groups and practices frequently appear and often enough acquire permanent institutional form. It is precisely this varied character of the functions and concerns of the priesthood in the various cultures that makes it difficult to find a single name or term that can express a common denominator because such common denominators as exist are not readily definable in objective terms.

What about the power and prestige status of the priest? Nothing could be more uncertain, since it varies from the theocracy on one hand in which the chief priest is also the absolute secular ruler, to a situation in which the priest lives on the very border-lines of respectability or legality vis à vis the secular state machinery, as he has recently in some states during periods of social revolution, and until some new power status or relationship is developed between the state machinery and the priestly caste. On a smaller scale precisely this type of battle has been fought out in many a tribe where medicine-man and warrior chief had their jurisdictional disputes. Typical, however, in long stable societies is a condition of mutually acceptable and useful division of power along some currently workable lines. Too many complex problems face a society and the survival odds favor the cooperative arrangement. Chief and priest are each unquestioned in their respective zones of authority or of power. The cooperation may even reach the point of the priesthood serving in an elaborate espionage system; many a humble tribe illustrating on a small scale the state of affairs between church and state in prerevolutionary Russia. Yet one must not underestimate the varieties of roles of the priesthood nor the degrees of respect in which they might be held. The Kwakiutl of British Columbia illustrate an interesting state of affairs in regard to theirs. The general attitude toward their priests is that their profession is a very hazardous way of getting prerogatives without inheriting or buying them. One might become a shaman by being put away in a hut in the woods when ill. Upon recovery one could claim that the supernaturals had cured one, at the same time having been given instructions for, and being initiated into the priesthood and the status change marked by giving the neophyte a new name. The secular validation of the title would then be achieved by a distribution of property. As a priest you could then charge whatever the market would bear in the way of fees for a variety of services, including the cure of diseases, where a large fee would be demanded of a case that on the face of things seemed relatively hopeless; the large fee compensating for the loss of prestige suffered in the event of a failure to cure. These priests used trickery, confederates, and assistants, much after the manner of the contemporary vaudeville magician. But to be found out was fatal; it would mean a loss of prestige which was worse than death. Since the prime social motivation of this people is in prestige contests, it is in these that priestly prerogatives are primarily used. Rival priests might and do engage in contests in which the looser might either die of shame or hire a "goon squad" to kill his rival; a safe enough move since there was no social penalty for killing a shaman or priest. He is "on his own" and if his extraordinary powers are not sufficiently vigilant to save his neck, that is only a serious reflection on his powers. The local definition of priestly power is 'that which makes it easy to obtain property.'

Distance seems to lend enchantment and add to the reputation of these specialists. A large percentage of Westerners believe that the priests of India or Arabia have fantastic powers at their command enabling them to defy ordinary mundane laws. Reputedly they can toss a rope up in the air and then climb up on it, walk through fire without being singed, cease to breathe for hours and survive, etc. This high repute of distant magicians is to be found almost everywhere. The priests of ancient Iran, the magi, were famous far beyond their borders. Even when in ancient Rome and later in Christendom they were held to have been evil practitioners their skills and capacities were not questioned.

When any skill or capacity or function of any individual comes to be the means whereby he lives, a significant "corner" in social relations has been turned. This is not meant in any narrow economic sense unless prestige factors and agreeable ego inflation be classed as economic motivators. When any such role or function comes to provide any considerable body of satisfaction it can be expected shortly to take on the characteristics of a vested interest. Thorstein Veblen somewhere defined a vested interest as 'a traditional or hereditary right to something for nothing' and it is not being questioned here that vested interests of that sort exist in a variety of cultures. However, as used here, the term "vested interest" is a far less sinister concept. It implies nothing beyond habitual expectations based upon role relationships in which there may well be a minimum of exploitive relationship in the picture. The psychological essence of such a vested interest would consist of habitual modes of response in particular situations with the expected reluctance to adopting different procedures, and the familiar emotional reenforcement that greets any factor interfering with our old habits of response. Such reactions are not at all dependent upon a threat to a vested interest of an economic sort; in fact, the reluctance and resistance can be expected even where the change is patently on the side of the economic interests of the individual. In this sense everyone has a "vested interest" in his habitual mode of life. The obvious implication of this is that even the threat to any traditional or familiar expectations will be reacted to adversely. Hardly a change of any sort in our familiar world, however benign, but what it interferes with the traditional expectations of some group or individual. Let even some wonder drug appear, keeping alive people that normally died, and you leave a lot of morticians wondering how they are going to meet the payments on the new Cadillac. The organized undertakers did not try to outlaw the use of these drugs, but they were none the less keenly aware of their economic consequences. Anesthetics did not fare quite so well. Some New England divine is often quoted as having preached against the use of chloroform in the following terms:

"Chloroform is a decoy of Satan, apparently offering itself to bless women; but in the end it will harden society and rob God of the deep earnest cries which arise in time of trouble, for help."

There can be not even the shadow of a doubt but that the parson is here stating a profound truth, for here was a situation in which the priest could readily see that he was being, if not completely displaced, then most certainly relegated to a much less important role. It was probably not a conscious conclusion, logically arrived at. The assumption of identity of interests of God and priest is probably wholly unconscious, and now that we are completely reconciled to a secular medicine this objection on the part of the priest seems to us in bad taste and presumptuous, to state it mildly. But there is no denying that here is one more situation in which we do not 'turn to God' for help. And the priest is as much a victim of technological job loss as is the cobbler displaced by the products of the United Shoe Machinery Corporation. It would be naive not to expect technologically displaced individuals to oppose any such innovations.

Frazer somewhere expresses the opinion that the wizards are the oldest organized class in history. In his Magical Origin of Kings[1] he cites many instances of tribes living in a simple hunting economy in which leadership is exercised by persons depending heavily upon the techniques commonly associated with magic, wizardy, or priestly functions. This is nothing to be surprised at since the problem of leadership is one of establishing and maintaining ascendance-submissive relationships, and we well know that such attitudes can be based on a great variety of factors or devices and combinations thereof. To expect any leader narrowly to limit himself to but one class of devices is to libel human versatility. There is no reason why a chief might not add to his prowess with a spear his apparent ability to communicate with some great Unseen as a device for keeping his group in a proper submissive relation. And the evidence is that precisely this is of frequent occurrence. While historically the statistical odds have favored the survival, in the top position of the power hierarchy, of the military commander —note the frequency with which army generals step into the office of President in the banana republics and elsewhere even today—yet there are enough instances of the priest-king in history to make an impressive showing and to make clear why it is that in so many long stable societies a modus vivendi has been worked out that in effect is a sharing of power by priest and warrior, by "church" and "state." Each represents and commands fairly effective means of social control. They could fight and sometimes have, for social control or political power. One is tempted to speculate upon the limitations inherent in each, as well as the advantages. It would seem that where a priesthood controls the formation of early attitudes, beliefs, and ideologies of a citizenry, it then constitutes a very efficient instrument for social control, internally or domestically. The state machinery of force, however, talks a language that is understood universally and not only on the home grounds. Perhaps that is why so many surviving societies, particularly those subject to close contact with rival cultures, have this dual machinery of social control. At any event, whatever the power structure that an organized priesthood has achieved, whatever vested interests are involved, the organized relationships tend to perpetuate themselves. The organization tends to provide ready made roles of no mean prestige for those able and willing to compete for them. Pareto saw it as the "persistence of aggregates."

Just as art is a product of individual artists, as science is the work of individual scientists, so too is religion the product of individual leaders and innovators in this field. True, each innovator is subjected to the limitations laid down by the social scene in which he functions and which in part created him. But each individual in turn becomes something of a dynamic center of innovation. There is thus creative leadership and innovation in religious leaders as well as in scientists and artists. All too often religion is treated as if it were not just such a human product. It must never be forgotten that it has the same humble origins as the rest of our human institutions; that it is a product of the 'human, all too human,' to borrow an expression from old Nietzsche. And what kind of fellows have these magicians, wizards, shamans, or priests been? Paul Radin, in his Primitive Religion, its Nature & Origin,[2] claims that abnormal traits are universal to the priesthood. Since the term "abnormal" is used to mean anything from the psychopathic to the merely statistically atypical in human behavior this is a safe enough generalization. It would no doubt be far safer to assert that in each culture there would be found operating certain convergent factors that stacked the cards in favor of a particular kind of personality entering the profession. It would furthermore be an even safer bet to distinguish between the personality characteristics of religious *innovators* and the run of the mill, routine *conformists* of any period of time. Probably the safest generalization of all is that the priesthood has constituted the intelligentsia of most human societies over a long period of history.

It must be remembered, of course, that there have been societies that have lacked anything that might properly be called a priesthood, anything having the functions traditionally thought of as priestly. Rohde[3] who has made a most impressively thorough study of the ancient Greek civilization of Homeric times comes to the conclusion that they had no priesthood with a monopoly of instruction or an exclusive knowledge of the details of ritual and the methods of controlling the behavior of spirits. And down into the Athenian "Golden Age" the Greek State "religion" had no organized priesthood, no scriptures of any sort, and no theology. The temple priests were chosen by lot or by public election, for life or for a limited term, and no special sacerdotal character was presumed or required of the candidates. The office was sometimes even sold to the highest bidder.[4] Their function was simply to see that certain traditional ceremonies were carried out in the traditional manner in which they "honored their Gods" but this did not involve any particular set of dogmas. Similarly, in old China there was no priesthood at all. Public ceremonials were a state function, carried out under the direction of masters of rites who knew the traditional and proper ceremonials. These societies were, however, not lacking in a true intelligentsia. In the Homeric world this role was filled by the poet and the singer, and from what survives of their work it is apparent that they had a completely secular outlook, even in religious matters, and their attitudes clearly anticipated the later philosophic traditions and objectivity of the Golden Age. And, if they had their intelligentsia outside of their ceremonial life which was purely secular, it is most illuminating to note that alongside of the official state ceremonies and apart from their poets and thinkers, and largely ignored by all the really "nice" people of the time there existed the mystery cults, among them the Dionysos cult mentioned in Homer, as well as the Eleusinian, Orphic, and others, participation in which was purely voluntary. These cults specialized in inducing "mania" with wild music and dancing to the point of exhaustion, possibly with the aid of wine. Or, a ceremonial animal might be slain and eaten raw during the height of the excitement. Amusingly enough, the mystical theories of the nature of the individual taught by these cults was finally taken up by none other than Plato in Athens; and they are still with us! Similarly, the lack of an official priesthood in China did not prevent the flourishing of a motley assortment of magicians and tricksters of all sorts. No wonder; even a society with a well-entrenched priesthood and expert heresy hunters is kept busy keeping the communicants in line. There are centrifugal forces making for behavior deviations in even the most stable of societies, let alone in those undergoing any considerable restructuring.

It would seem then that there is a strong tendency to the recurrence of a peculiar but insistent demand in a populace for entertaining rituals, cults, performances, or promises, and if the recognized intellectual leaders or priesthood fail to provide it there apparently are plenty of individuals who will. In ancient Greece, Rome, Mexico, and Peru spontaneous and unofficial cults developed or existed outside of the official ceremonials that apparently satisfied the sophisticates in their respective societies but not the masses. Here, as in all free economies, there is a strong tendency to give the customers what they want. And as in a market economy, the demand can first be shrewdly created, the variations in this process being limited only by the ingenuity of the individual in sensing a ready demand or in creating it perhaps even against considerable initial resistance. Wherever there exist such strong centrifugal tendencies making for diverse cults and ceremonials there tend also to appear certain authoritarian tendencies, moves to restrict competition, to keep the field under control. The obvious superiority in social competition of the group with a stable ideology and effective symbolic control devices has favored the survival of those groups having an efficient machinery for maintaining such uniformity. And the more a social structure became complex, thereby producing people with diverse interests, equipment, and degree of sophistication in relevant matters, the greater the need for an effective machinery for maintaining uniformity since it is precisely under such social conditions that the centrifugal, splintering forces are greatest. No wonder then that secular and military leadership has found it expedient to establish an entente cordiale with a priestly machinery that could "deliver the goods." The relationship was usually symbiotic since the priesthood could and frequently has made effective use of the "secular arm" in disposing of rival technicians in the "spiritual" arts. Such is clearly still the state of affairs in those countries whose laws give "favored status" to some one organized priesthood.

So, while on the one hand there are forces and factors making for a stable, well-organized priesthood as part of a stable social order, it is also apparent that circumstances and conditions can arise making for behavior shifts and social instability tending to produce changes in the character of the needs, material and psychological, for which social leadership must make provision. Under such conditions a vigilant institution or vested interest can, and probably will, move to incorporate such new tendencies into the framework of its services. Note how today, for example, where the conditions of work and employment have produced a certain amount of militant, not to say belligerent, common interest attitudes on the part of employees, vis à vis their employers, the best organized of the current priesthood is hastening to make itself the champion of these sentiments, all within safe and sane limits, of course. The price of failing to take such steps would of necessity be that of large defections from the ranks of the faithful in a society in which there is something approaching a free market in the field of ideas, and where there is no lack of potential leadership seeking to crystallize human ideologies around new norms. Once such allegiance is lost it is recoverable only with great difficulty as witnessed in France today.[5] Under the impact of a dynamic technology, events even in the spiritual domain are likely to be subject to swift pulsations, and prove trying indeed to any ideology rooted in a frozen past. And who could be expected to come to the rescue of such ideologies if not the particular individuals with a vested interest in them? The well-paid state functionaries in charge of the official rituals in the Greek state could well afford to, and apparently did, ignore the proliferating mystery cults. Elsewhere, a rival shaman, "hitting below the belt" with alien ideas and tricks, might well become a menace that in self defense would have to be liquidated, much as the official church found a genuine menace in Huguenot, Waldensian, and Albigensian heresies. Where power structures patently become vulnerable, vigilance and action are called for. The first responsibility of any power structure is to maintain itself. Not until that is assured can an organization undertake anything constructive. Even the best of sovereigns must first of all establish effective social predictability and maintain it. Perhaps it is on the basis of this criterion that the British business men, themselves having suffered uncounted financial loss at the hands of the current Chinese government, were quoted in the New York Times (June 27, 1954) as rating it the best government China had ever had, referring no doubt to their own memory spans in so judging.

The long-run criterion of the efficiency of a power structure, however, is the constructive results achieved beyond the mere maintaining of itself in power. In competition with rival power structures this Chinese state will stand or fall on the strength of what it achieves above and beyond its mere self perpetuation. Similarly with the power structure developed by any priesthood. To survive, it must not only maintain its own privileged position, but it must also deliver significant service in the workaday world of its communicants against the competition of power structures such as labor unions, political parties, and in the future perhaps even from militant specialists in scientific methodology, all groups not handicapped by having too long been identified with the limitations stemming from yesteryear's bad errors and misconceptions.

It is at this point that a very special dilemma confronts the organized priesthood in its efforts to revitalize its "services" to its communicants. The instant it descends into the market-place to swing into action in behalf of some good cause the adversaries with which it finds itself embroiled hasten to denounce this abandonment of the traditional priestly role. In truth, such stepping out of character on the part of the priesthood is fraught with danger. In the face of social conflict or controversy they must either join one side of the quarrel or else discover some new and ingenious third course of action. Since the odds run strongly against the latter alternative, to champion the cause of one of the parties to a controversy means at once the alienation of the other. This can become very embarrassing, as in the current disputes between employer and employee interests. And yet the issues are so burning to the participants that in the heat of the battle they take sharp note of exactly where support and opposition come from. Hence there are always sharp pressures tending to bring the priesthood into the struggle on the side of the numerically greater masses among their communicants. This can have disastrous consequences, as recently in France where a considerable number of priests took jobs in industry in order to build common ground with the members of the group they hoped to influence. Imagine the shocks suffered by the higher echelons of the priesthood when they found that a not inconsiderable fraction of these deadly earnest workers in the Lord's vineyards abandoned completely their sacerdotal roles and went over, body and soul into the ranks of the atheistic arch-enemy: the left-wing political parties,

thereby providing in addition eloquent testimony to the determining role played, even in matters of the Spirit, by material,
environmental determinants.

But any appraisal of the role and function of the priesthood
made from the current scene would certainly fail to do historical justice to their hardy social progenitors of the past. For it
must be clearly recognized that up until a relative yesterday
the evolution of the priesthood has been the evolution of the
intelligentsia, the thinkers, the seekers, the empiricists, even
the innovators that the human race has produced. They were
the daring fellows who attempted the impossible and then delivered at least a reasonable facsimile thereof. Their social role
was such that of necessity they had to develop a certain objectivity toward, and insight into, the mysteries and processes
that baffled and frustrated the ordinary citizen. Once casting
himself in the role of controlling forces and possessing powers
beyond those of the ordinary mortal we have the source of a
motivation to venture beyond into the unknown. Here we
have the drive necessary for extensive trial and error, for the
agonizing search for a clue to the solution of some significant
problem. It is not at all necessary to assume that it was of
necessity always a matter of direct economic motivation on the
part of these primitive wonder-workers. With economic needs
at a simple level it is obvious that motives of prestige and
human sympathy are indeed frequently dominant. In fact, motivation for effective achievement is present in everyone, with
or without direct economic reward. But specific social pressures
acting upon an individual already cast in the role of minor
miracle worker raises motivation far above that of the passive,
well-meaning level. The priest here becomes the victim of a
bitter dialectic. Once he has a dramatic achievement to his
credit his failure to perform the next miracle that is demanded
is likely to be looked upon as some form of conscious with-
drawal of efficiency, if indeed not outright sabotage and malice.
Here we have the wonder-worker confronted with an ugly
dilemma: either he must reveal the deterministic sequence responsible for his success if he has such, or he must stretch the
miracle to cover the subsequent demands. No wonder then

that many a priest discovered the alibi of insidious counter-forces, usually presumed to be manipulated by evil fellows beyond the immediate area of local sovereignty. This process has at times reached such heights of tragic whimsy that in one series of islands in a typhoon zone the natives wage aggressive war on each other, always against the wind, i.e. on the island tribe immediately to windward of them; their priests having assured them that the powerful priests of the island to windward whose magic they could not counter, were deliberately aiming these destructive storms at them.

Yet, in all cultures, everywhere, many significant discoveries were made. And who could make them, if not the relatively intelligent, well-motivated individual already cast in the social role of which the impossible was expected? Who could make a discovery if not the man with a particular problem thrust into his lap? Who indeed makes discoveries today other than individuals similarly placed? At times the prestige of these specialists was indeed great. Andrew Lang[6] thinks the evidence is good that medicine men really pretend, and are believed to, exercise all the powers ever attributed to gods. It is a safe bet that such a state of affairs is to be found somewhere. Herbert Spencer somewhere makes the claim that gods developed out of medicine men, and again a faithful search of the evidence would probably find instances of a deified priest of some kind. Jesus is probably a case in point. The difficulty with much of the older anthropology and social theory generally was a quite understandable zeal to force all of human society into one historical pattern, to underestimate the diversity of possible social patterns and their courses of development. But for the most part the systematic attempts at an understanding of religion have almost completely neglected the role played by the priesthood in the evolution and development of the entire religious edifice. They have dealt with it as if it were some pure Platonic essence unrelated to the individual, organic behavior of the individuals who initiated, and developed it; exactly as science is the product of the activities of the very real individual personalities who made the separate discoveries. Were one to ask at this point just what the difference was between priest and scientist one would have to hedge by pointing out that your primitive innovator was both proto-scientist as well as proto-priest. The critical distinction, psychologically, between the tasks of the two embryo specialists was that the priest was handicapped by being saddled with the necessity of "delivering the goods" in a satisfactory manner for his communicants with his skills and devices to meet immediate, practical needs. He had to satisfy his customers in their needs and crises whenever they occurred. While the scientist had no objection to the practical application of his knowledge yet the basic pattern of his motivation had no such narrow limitations. It was facts that he was pursuing, and he was not dependent upon immediate, psychologically acceptable results for his status as was the priest, or whoever was playing the role of the manipulator of very special forces. First hand observers of the parts played by the medicine man or priest in primitive society agree that these fellows are first of all shrewd manipulators of human behavior, experts in the area of suggestion, and in understanding human motivation. For the most part too they have excellent insight into their own capacities and limitations and are not taken in by their own performances. Frequently they have a considerable body of practical knowledge of a surgical or therapeutic sort as well as a crude materia medica. Now these discoveries had to be made by someone; the effects and consequences had to be observed; the heroic first trials made. Who made those first desperate trials? Who first observed the slight improvement of symptoms that went with or followed on the heels of a particular desperate trial? Of all the varied vegetable and animal products in the world, how was it ever discovered that a heroic quantity of cinchona leaves relieved the symptoms of malaria? Even a small amount of quinine crystals scraped out of the grooves in the bark of the tree would have had a far more potent effect. But it was probably under the assurance of some desperate empiricist that enough leaves were tried. Often the toxic or therapeutic agent was a carefully guarded secret, and most often of the priestly caste if there was one, or of the individual tribal medicine man. Understandably, there was here plenty of motivation to discover significant skills, and also to keep the skills under control in the interests of future gain or prestige. There would then also be a concomitant motivation to publicize successes, cover up or rationalize failures or limitations in skill, and to keep out rival or competing systems or practitioners.

It is the operation of the altogether probable and human tendency on the part of the specialist to capitalize in one way or another on his skill or knowledge that has provided the ammunition for those who have sought to dismiss religion as entirely the product of the machinations of a priestly caste for their own emolument. That a similar charge is not levelled against all the various specialists developed by civilization is no doubt due to the fact of the relatively imponderable character of the priest's services at the time in history when the priest has been successively shorn of his more objective functions by a succession of skilled technicians specializing in some one aspect of what was once a broad priestly area. Yet, lest anyone suspect that this libel on the priesthood is of recent origin, say for example with the publication of Upton Sinclair's "Profits of Religion" sometime during the second decade of the present century, let it be noted that as early as the sixth century, B.C. heterodox Hindus were already claiming that all religions were but inventions of the priests for their own profit![6a] The same theory has appeared, apparently independently, at various times in western Europe. It would be ridiculous to deny of course, that, conditions in the market for such services permitting, the priesthood has not at times displayed all the evils of any other monopolistic function. It is to be reasonably doubted, for example, that the Hebrew god himself contributed the section of early Hebrew law quoting their god as saying "No man shall see my face empty handed." Such a sentiment is far more reminiscent of old Chinese legal tradition where one could not hope to obtain even an audience with a magistrate let alone justice from him unless one first presented him with a staff whose value represented a reasonable cut in the substance at issue. It would be easy to ransack any period of history and turn up plenty of instances of pecuniary and power abuses on the part of the priesthood, from the lowliest savage culture to the highest. When we find that a Polynesian priest might some fine morning confront a citizen with the information that in a vision he had caught the fellow's spirit or double in various and sundry taboo violations which only the priest could undo— for a fee—we feel that we have encountered a new high in rackets. A perusal of the Sinclair[7] volume, previously referred to, will reveal a generous assortment of contemporary instances that betoken no deterioration in the general reluctance to "give a sucker an even break." This expertness of the priesthood in undoing the evil consequences of ritual or taboo violations for a fee has been a socially dangerous skill indeed. Man has been notoriously deficient in his ability to distinguish irrational taboo violations from socially harmful remissness; and where the violation of an archaic taboo thus readily is put on a fee basis, serious ethical and anti-social practices tend to slip in under the same tent or even be put on an advance sale basis. "Selling Indulgences" was once a battle cry, not easily forgotten in western Europe.

Yet it is all too easy to misunderstand and even libel the institution of the fee for the priestly services. Beyond the obvious advantage to the priest that follows from a system of fees there is the not insignificant effect of such paying upon the communicant himself that must not be overlooked. Where the nature of the priestly services are such that they involve any aspect of suggestion, auto suggestion, or psychotherapy of any sort, or of distraction, or of the reconciliation of the individual to the inevitable—to God's will, as it is put in some cultures, there the payment of a fee of sufficient size to constitute something of an emotional impact upon the fee payer is a vital aspect of the ameliorative process. There is something about fee-paying that prepares the individual to accept the advice or dictates of the person to whom the fee is paid. No doubt it has no more complex basis than the neutralizing of one emotion by another, but effective it is. It is interesting to note that both Christian Science practitioners and psychoanalysts agree on the effective therapeutic role played by the paying of the fee to the therapist, in the case of the former it is a later discovery after Mrs. Eddy's initial attempt at founding a system of faith that should be free from the encumbrances of a professional priesthood, which in this cult reentered by the back door under the title of "healer" or "reader," but of course with a considerably reduced area of function and authority. Certainly the efficacy of such a device as the nine day healing ceremonial of the Navahos is of a similar kidney. Such a ceremonial can practically be guaranteed to bankrupt all but the most opulent, and it stimulates great activity in the immediate family of the patient and to that extent acts as an effective counterpoise to the grief and fear produced by the illness. It certainly distracts, and thereby shortens "psychologically" the time of tension, and is no doubt worth its cost. Even the most orthodox of medical practitioners has at least been aided in rationalizing a stiff fee by what seem to be equally legitimate observations of their efficacy as therapeutic agents.

It is interesting to note how frequently latter day religious innovators have striven to eliminate a professional priesthood from their new order, or at least to minimize the abuses that professionalism with its vested interests frequently brings in its train. Certainly the Christ of the Gospels was eloquent enough in his denunciations of the contemporary priesthood. The Mormons eliminated a professional priesthood from any ceremonial roles, but even they find themselves driven to producing an "educator" class requiring years of secular education and then occupied full time in teaching, no doubt to meet the competition provided by the well schooled gentile teachers in the higher learning. The Quakers have probably been most conspicuously successful in remaining free from religious professionalism, and keeping to a minimum the size of the roster of those whose primary source of economic sustenance is an institutional role. Not without reason has suspicion fastened itself upon those individuals who come to have an economic vested interest in priestly services. Where such work must demand the undivided attention of an individual it is a rather logical development. But, aware of the concomitant difficulties, note how, for example the Mormons draft the services of an individual for a limited period of years: after which he returns to secular life. The relative advantages and difficulties of the full-time as opposed to the part time priest are not too different from a similar dilemma confronting us with the soldiery. The full-time, professional soldier has his merits. But the abuses that are likely to accompany him has made many a society institute the part-time soldier, whose major focus never ceases to be civilian and who could with difficulty develop a zeal for soldiery for its own sake, or tolerate a state too much under the thumbs of the military.

The abuses of a well-entrenched priesthood have apparently been focal in the minds of the founders of new cults. It is interesting to note how many of these begin under a leadership that refuses to assume the traditional powers and prerogatives of the priest and instead makes yeoman efforts to set up a secular machinery that can forever dispense with what so readily becomes an independent vested interest. It is the classic pattern of the revolt against "institutionalized" religion; as witnessed by Albigenses, Huguenots, Mennonites, Dunkards, Dukubhors, Mormons, Quakers,[8] Christian "Scientists," and Jehovah's Witnesses.[9] But where individual and familial interests begin to rival the institutional, the disadvantages of the leaderless state begin to manifest themselves. Just as with secular organizations, the one with the paid secretary-treasurer tends to outstrip the ones without.

"Religion," as we know it today then must be recognized as in large part the products of one of the earliest specializations that evolved in the division of labor, of the professionalizing of functions that followed on the heels of a recognition of the existence of significant differences in individual capacity and function. The particular skills constituting the equipment of these primitive specialists, and the social areas in which they function are indeed enormously variable. It is probably safe to assert that there is hardly to be found a function or skill or service not somewhere the prerogative of the priesthood, or again elsewhere not in the hands of a specialist of a priestly sort. It is, for example, common to have an important role assigned to a priest in matters of life, health, and family affairs. Yet such was not the case in the old Hindu culture where the family functioned without the assistance of a priest in matters such as weddings, birth, and health generally. Nor is there to be discovered any regular progression of functions with changes in the general cultural level. Naturally, rain-making functions in the priesthood will not be found where rainfall does not constitute a vital part of the local economy. The functions of the priesthood will of necessity reflect local concerns and problems. And with a shift in the basic economy there is likely to be a shift in the area of uncertainty in which typically the priesthood finds its role. Radin's theory of totemism as a defense against the shaman with the appearance of an agricultural economy at least recognizes the likelihood of a shift in priestly function with a change in the basic economy. But the most significant shift in the priestly functions derives from the progressive secularization of a culture; where specific skills are preempted by individuals making no pretense to especial competence outside the area of their specialty, or, where a considerable body of erstwhile esoteric knowledge or insight that might well have provided the bases for an impressive skill, has, so to speak, gone into the public domain.

There can be no question, however, but that there has been a dramatic and overall reduction of both prestige and area of functioning of the priesthood during the span of time now of record in human affairs. This decline has not gone unnoticed, least of all by the priesthood itself which is frequently eloquent in its denunciations of a process that has reduced it to what must seem, in contrast to its previous glory, a sorry state indeed. Naturally enough they have seen it as convincing evidence of a serious moral decline of mankind, unless of course it is the decline of some rival priesthood that is being observed. Yet there has been but little detailed analysis of the precise process that has constituted this decline, perhaps because it is more easily bemoaned in its totality and without detailed dissection. For the most part this decline has been a wholly fortuitous by-product of the perfection of a wide variety of specific secular skills, and not the result of any systematic and motivated attack on the priesthood as such. Much the same process has been at work on the ancient crafts of the barber and the philosopher. Some rival technician developed knowledge or skills sufficiently instrumental to undercut some pre-

vious practitioner and displace him. Take the case of the
barber, by way of example. Here was a fellow who by virtue
of his skills and tools fulfilled some of the requirements for the
job of surgeon sufficiently well so that for long he functioned
in what seems today to have been a strange dual capacity. But
it had its own historical logic. Here he was, the one man in the
community with a knife really sharp enough for the effective
cutting of human tissue with a minimum of pain, and, as a
cynic might add, he had frequently enough cut his customers
while shaving them so as not to be disconcerted at the sight of
flowing blood: One might say that the barber was both "instrumentally" and emotionally prepared for the job of surgeon
and so the role fell to him. But when the "physickers" began
to make a serious study of anatomy and physiology they soon
developed here a set of skills of such complexity that the mere
matter of acquiring sharp tools and learning to keep them
sharp, and the cultivation of a certain amount of fortitude at
the sight of flowing blood were simple skills indeed to add to
their repertoire. And so it was that time ran out on the barbers,
in their role of surgeons, that is. A very similar fate has over-
taken the philosophers. Time was when anyone with a modicum of perceptive capacity and a bit of idle curiosity as to the
nature of things could shortly acquire what was, relatively, an
impressive amount of general knowledge. But as successive
areas that were readily empirically explorable became the special domain of astronomers, physicists, chemists, biologists, etc.,
there was a decreasing area of competence remaining to those
individuals who preferred arm-chair contemplation of problems
to their empirical investigation. Their traditional speculations
in the fields of metaphysics and epistemology, having no
sounder bases in objective reality than those of the professional
theologians, could make no headway against the animism so
essential to western theology. Philosophers were in effect, reduced for long to the ignominious role of handmaidens to the
theological machinery which was well buttressed by its alliance
with the powers of the state and by its control of the educational process. Today, where experimental psychology has made
relatively meaningless the classical metaphysics and epistemol-

ogy which so long provided a bone of contention with the theologians and gave philosophers something of an excuse for existence, there is little left for them but to rehash the classical disputes in the same terms in which they have traditionally been fought, making no use of the findings of modern psychology which have in effect made their unquestioned, fundamental assumptions meaningless. Since such rehashing is almost certain to seem anachronistic to anyone with even a smattering acquaintance with contemporary psychology there is of necessity a decidedly limited marketability for such verbal skills. No wonder then that the contemporary academic philosophers are to be found heavily involved in aesthetics and social ethics, or even dabbling in current social movements, sometimes with disastrous consequences both to themselves and to traditional academic objectivity. The events of the past few hundred years in the development of science have indeed left our philosophers victims of a technological obsolescence.

Essentially a similar processes has been operative in the area of the competence of the priesthood. Over increasingly large segments of the populace, gone are the days when the priest was the only recourse in illness. A myriad of specialists have convincingly made a role for themselves in this area. Even at a death where formerly the chief functionary of an institutionally recognized sort was the officiating parson and where an adequate coffin was fabricated by one obliging neighbor and a few more dug the grave, we now have coffin makers, coroners, organized morticians, and even the grave-diggers' union to contend with, as a result of which the fee collected by the officiating parson is picayune in comparison with the bill rendered by the groups that have only recently cut themselves in, sometimes on the flimsiest of grounds, on what formerly was entirely the domain of the priesthood. Similarly in area after area, function after function, special skills or rival vested interests have seriously eroded their historic backlog of functions. Adverse weather that once drew upon the priest for his special intervention now represents an interesting transition zone. Here a long period of observation of weather finally made possible an era of prediction sufficiently effective to establish even in the lay mind generally deterministic attitudes toward its causality. To this determinism the public is generally reconciled during normal weather variations. But the extreme variations reaching the outer limits of the probability curve and seriously threatening some vital aspect of human affairs are likely to cause a reversion to older techniques, and the priest with prayers and sacrifice is again called upon. Just within the past few years, and in the world's largest metropolitan area, with cloud masses being seeded with silver iodide crystals and solid carbon dioxide, organized prayers for rain were provided by the priesthood of a variety of faiths. Among the laymen there was then considerable difference of opinion as to which device had been effective and responsible for the subsequent rains. It should be added parenthetically however, that farmers whose hay crops deteriorated seriously during these rains, and the resort owners whose expected guests remained at home entered suit against the city for hiring the rainmakers with their cloud seeding devices and not against the priesthood responsible for the organized sessions of prayer.[10] Where once many an organized priesthood depended largely upon their skills as astronomers for their prestige and prerogatives, as in Egypt, Babylon, and Yucatan, in the Western Civilizations that subject was, until relatively recently, a sleeping dog that the priesthood preferred to leave lie, for they were all too keenly aware of the fact that far from having made any recent contributions to knowledge in that area they had been somewhat excessively resistant to the recognition of the validity of the findings of the secular specialists that had taken up where an older priesthood had once discovered much that was new and important. Today, however, the subject is relatively non-controversial, and some sectarian institutions of higher learning are actively promoting study and research in this area, finding it a safe one in which to demonstrate that "Religion and Science are not incompatible."

Perhaps most interesting of all the current jurisdictional disputes is that concerning the field variously called "mental health," "mental hygiene," or personality adjustment, now the scene of a three-cornered struggle for dominance between the medical profession, the professional psychologists, and the clergy. This is a particularly fascinating bit of rivalry and deserves a careful analysis. As already pointed out there has been a progressive pirating of functions from the priesthood by a variety of specialists, but the development of secular medical specialists has been particularly interesting because in the process the doctor has tended to acquire much of the awe for his person and skills traditionally reserved for the priest in the period before the development of secular specialists. This is without question a function of the medical man's effective and sometimes dramatic contests with death itself, a skill attributed to or claimed by a large fraction of the classical priesthood. Into this contest the priest brings his traditional and prestiged role of spokesman for the contranatural, the awesome powers of "Eternity." The medical doctor brings the well-earned awe of the secular powers that deliver almost on schedule many of the miracles on rare occasion demonstrated by the priesthood of old.[11] The psychologist has the advantages that generally accrue to scientifically directed research specific to the problems at hand. One of the interesting aspects of this contest is the fact that there was in this case a somewhat belated recognition on the part of the contemporary priesthood that they were in effect losing jurisdiction in an area in which they had long been serving. Contemporary theological training is hastening more effectively to arm its products for effective competition in this field by emphasizing all branches of psychology, and in particular the areas of personality structure and conflict, and of course sufficient understanding of abnormal behavior to recognize the out and out psychotics and to shuttle them back into the hands of the psychiatrist. There are still some sections of the priesthood who do not concede the area of mental health to medicine. The semantics of their position is something as follows: "Mental" phenomena are blanketed with the concept "soul," and in this sphere this priesthood claims competence. In a large metropolitan city there was recently a period of open warfare between the priestly administrators and the secularly trained psychiatrists attached to a hospital, over the question of where authority lay in matters of mental pathology. The higher ranks of the clergy however shortly intervened and, as far as public knowledge is concerned, the matter was effectively hushed up. But the sniping, both from the pulpit and the public lecture platform and press continues on occasion between some brands of the clergy and particular schools of psychotherapy.

Intelligently to follow this three cornered struggle with a view to forseeing its general direction of development and outcome calls for a considerable insight into the nature of the difficulties involved in these personality disorders or troubles. The ancient dichotomy of mind or "soul" versus "body" still effectively rides herd on much of our thinking in this area. The intricacies of the historical development of psychiatry are too tedious for a complete review at this point, but by and large any aberrations of behavior for which predictable physical correlates could be found were not considered "mental." But where these clear-cut bodily aspects were not apparent it has been traditionally assumed that a mere "mind twist" of some sort was involved. Such cases then constituted a very "touchy" question because the mind (read "soul") was, and still is, frequently held to be linked closely to the stuffs of which gods are composed and hence are definitely of the clerical rather than secular domain. Such dichotomies seem clear cut, obvious, and simple to those whose sources of information do not transcend the current "common sense" or mediaeval scholasticism. In this day of expanding knowledge of hormonal and endocrine imbalance, of metabolic processes generally, such thinking is indeed of the Dark Ages. Where profound deterioration of erstwhile completely normal personalities is clearly linked with the effects of a single dominant gene as in Huntington's Chorea, or where behavior aberrations occur with almost clockwork regularity, unrelated to any discernible "mental" event, even common sense balks at animistic explanations, and physical causes are presumed. But today's jurisdictional disputes center in a more complex area that obviously fits neither of the old formulae. It is the field of "functional disorders," of "mental health," or "mental hygiene," an area in which the problems encountered seem but minor deviations from normal behavior, but which have in the past been variously seen as "character defects," "moral weaknesses," or "bad habits" and of which the manifestations were not clearly related to bodily processes of any known sort. These disapproved behaviors are variously labeled "hysterias," "neurasthenias," "psychoneuroses," "psychopathic personalities"; or the individual might even be described as suffering from "conflict," "complexes" of various sorts, or as being simply "maladjusted." There is a very strong penchant in the mental hygiene fraternity for referring all and sundry of these disorders to some aspect or other of the environment, a quite understandable bent in view of our colossal ignorance of the finer elements of physiological processes involved in these areas, and for the simple reason that the behavior disorders here involved are closely akin in apparent origin and nature to habit processes. Then too, one might well ask how else is one to handle these cases? It must not be forgotten that the symptoms of these disorders are all well within the range of ordinary habit variations. They manifest themselves as variations in logic, emotionality, or motivation, and literally tempt one to try to "reform" them. Sometimes they even date from some particular traumatic episode in which the reactions made were well within the normal range but of which the persistence and duration go beyond ordinary bounds. With no sharply specific disease entity diagnosed, with no specific therapy known having the statistical respectability or efficacy comparable with that of contemporary chemotherapy of some germ diseases, the treatment of these disorders is of necessity limited to what must be at bottom some form of *habit* therapy, that is, the disorder must be assumed to be in the nature of an undesirable habit, and the therapy an effective way of disposing of it. The psychologist, the priest, and the psychiatrist must then be exponents of what can at most be different techniques in regard to habit control.

It must not be assumed here that the phenomena of habit are all too sharply separated by any great metaphysical gulf from purely "organic" phenomena. Unless one is to revert to some form of mystical metaphysics he will be compelled to recognize that any learning process must at bottom be incorporated as subtle but none the less real organic changes in the learner, probably largely in the brain cortex, and yet not necessarily limited to the central nervous system. It must also be recognized that where behavior processes or habits take the form of modified visceral functions one must expect that persistent habits can produce cumulative organic effects after the manner of emotional tensions and their role in the etiology of gastric ulcers. Certainly it would be reckless to overlook the possibility of this sort of circularity in emotional reactions playing a significant role in the genesis of the personality disorders here under discussion. But be that as it may, the fact remains that lacking any more detailed understanding as to what is accomplished by the various systems of therapy we are compelled to assume that they are but varying devices for inducing changes in the habit systems of the personality under treatment.

Viewed then, as utilizing varied techniques of habit making and unmaking, how is one to uncover the common denominators in the learning process utilized by all therapists, whether priest, psychiatrist, or psychologist? And why should there be differences in the first place? And how are these differences perpetuated? If one considers the early therapeutic traditions that antedate the institutional separation of priest and medical doctor it becomes apparent that the specifics available to this early practitioner were few indeed, far fewer than his capacity for making differentiating diagnoses of familiar ailments. The treatment formula for the great bulk of ailments was then limited to distractive, confidence-giving devices, and the varied forms of suggestion therapy, all of which are in effect operations on the habit systems of the patients. The chief weapon in his therapeutic armament was the patients' confidence in the potency of the extraordinary or "supernatural" powers the priest was presumably privy to. But as fast as secular medicine identified specifically, and provided secular therapy of an effective sort for any particular condition, there was a rapid shift of such illnesses to the domain of the secular doctor. In fact the active organization of medical men into pressure groups shortly gave them an effective "corner" on therapeutic services of all sorts, with the exception of all matters involving the "soul." But they are still trying to blanket the field completely, as witness the current efforts of the medical profession of a very populous eastern American state to have laws enacted giving them complete jurisdiction over therapy of all sorts, whether of body or mind. This brought together against them a coalition of the clergy and their materialistic arch-enemies the psychologists! As it has been well said before, "politics makes strange bedfellows."

It is a safe bet that in the long run the great bulk of what passes contemporarily for the "mind" and its illnesses will be found to be largely a matter of subtle physiological processes in all the areas now diagnosed as psychoses, neurasthenias, psychoneuroses, or neuroses, and a sound medicine is bound to inherit them in the long run. Ironically enough, such a materialistic point of view is anathema to large sections of the medical profession whose insight into, and understanding of things psychological is of a very primitive level as witnessed by the large percentage of them that turned to the dubious metaphysics of the various "analytic" schools, Freudian and otherwise, in grappling with behavior manifestations as varied as social revolutions, folkways, and neuroses. Yet psychologists need have no fear that such an eventuality would leave them wholesale victims of a technological obsolescence; for the aforementioned deviations in behavior represent but a small fraction of human behavior variabilities in the populace, normal and abnormal. It is in the realm of practical certainty that the processes that make us crooks, Communists, columnists, congressmen, Republicans, or scholars and gentlemen are primarily in the domain of habit, and in this area there are no serious challenges to the psychologist. And there can be no question but that the really serious human problems lie in this area. At this stage of the development of knowledge about such matters it is a practical impossibility to separate all "pathology" of the "mind" from its normal workings. Hence the fundamental logic behind assigning problems involving physiological pathology to those presumably learned in this area, and leaving to experts in the problems of behavior the patients of whom we know only that their behavior is aberrant and that no known non-habit techniques are applicable . . . Indeed this should not in any way discourage research in bio-chemistry, endocrinology, shock therapy, dietetics, chemotherapy or anything else that might possibly lead to significant discovery. There is no danger that the psychologists will deprive these researchers of materials upon which to try their experiments.

But to revert to the question of the different techniques in therapy of the three claimants to the field of psychotherapy: we have reviewed the historical process that determined the character of the therapy available to any priesthood. Their devices were selected because of their effectiveness on a people of a particular culture. It is then obvious that such devices as a priesthood uses must undergo revision as the ideas, beliefs, and concepts of their flocks evolve. One might well ask, is it not true that at least the *successful* medical men have used essentially similar devices in addition to such other therapeutic agents as they might have possessed? The answer is, indeed they always have, particularly in any area where medical services are for a fee and the doctor must keep the customers coming! This largely unorganized and very unsystematic tradition is but part of the traditional "bedside manner" of the doctor, and for long medical training left that to the individual practitioner to develop in his own way. Even formal psychiatric training was meagre enough until the medical schools were driven to it by the dramatics of the various analytic "schools," from whom they were shortly "borrowing" a variety of currently effective devices. It must be remembered that to be effective, any psychotherapeutic device must be culturally compatible with the idea structure and background of the patients on whom the devices are to be effective. Relics and bones of saints can only be effective as suggestive device or emotional "spark point" with which unconscious but none the less real habits are broken or reorganized, on people who have long been taught to believe that such things can be effective when ritually correct use is made of them. The powerful emotions elicited by symbols of the supernatural can function as habit reorganizing devices in functional disorders if any are present. In much the same way the highly spicy conversations in regard to the strongly tabooed functions and drives of sex were found to be quite effective on the products of Victorian prudery by the psychoanalytic schools of therapists. But Freud himself modestly conceded at one point in his career that his analytic methods still fell short of the degree of effectiveness that the bones of saints had on the Faithful. This admission was most certainly not for public consumption by his patients, for skepticism in the patient is fatal in this type of therapy.

The practical therapist then sensibly tailors the garment to the man, carefully surveying his personality and then selecting therapeutic techniques calculated to be effective with the personality in question. Thus we find ministers of the Gospel surreptitiously reading Freud, Adler, and Jung, especially the latter, and psychiatrists and some psychologists showing, for the first time in years, some interest in the psychology of religion. The net result is that the techniques of therapy employed by all are much the same, with far greater variation between individual therapists than between psychiatrists, priests, or psychologists as such. They are all busy borrowing from one another. It may well be that the psychologists as a group tend to make more use of testing devices of all sorts in their primary study of the individual because their training has generally been such as to bias them in favor of devices having some sort of statistical respectability. But testing at the hands of a competent psychologist is becoming routine procedure for many psychiatrists before any attempts at therapy.

Small wonder then that today's priesthood is hastening to equip itself with whatever latter day secular scientists have dug up in the way of comprehension and understanding of current social and personality dilemmas and problems, since tradition had cast them in the role of confessor, whether officially sanctioned by their church organization or not, and, as a member of the clergy recently put it to the author:

"I spend most of my working time trying to function as a psychologist or a psychiatrist and I cannot honestly continue doing so without seeing to it that I am thoroughly equipped. It is not that I want to play at being a psychiatrist. I only want to be sure that the parishoners that come to me for help get the very best help possible. I want to spend my working time as far as possible only with those whom I happen to be best placed to help. I want to be able to identify the kind of problem I should not attempt to handle, and know to whom I should send them for help of the right kind."

And who, might one ask, would like to be too certain in advance as to just what kind of help a given individual would need? A well-meaning pastor, without a vested interest of an obvious sort but with sufficient understanding to separate out the individuals needing specialized care from those requiring intelligent and expert counseling, and knowing where to send them for specialized services is indeed a desirable goal. This could easily replace rivalling vested interests with intelligent team work. There can be no question but what the priest occupies a position that has strategic advantages from the standpoint of the institutions of religion. At all but the very top levels or sophistication it is to the priest that the bedeviled or troubled individual turns. It might well be true that today there are other specialists far better equipped to diagnose or treat personality complications than the priest, but he it is to whom a large fraction of the populace first turns. The practical problem is that of not permitting such hisorical accidents to stand in the way of the adoption of better techniques if available, as they sometimes do. There is, by way of example, the sad case of our frozen water pipes! Tradition has long linked pipes with plumbers, so when our pipes freeze we call a plumber. But alas! This poor chap is in all likelihood prevented from giving you the swift, safe, and cheap pipe thawing service that modern technology has provided in the form of a high-frequency electrical thawing device which opens the most stubborn pipes frozen in the most inaccessible places in a matter of minutes. And why? Simply because he is in all likelihood not a licensed electrician and hence not permitted to sell the services of such a device! Instead he must laboriously use a dangerous blowtorch, thereby running a very live danger of setting your domicile on fire. Or he may even tear open walls to get at these pipes if the matter is urgent and you cannot afford to be without water until a change in the weather reveals if your pipes have burst or not and thus either locates the job for the plumber or saves you from calling one. It is asking too much, however, to expect the plumber to refer you to an electrician when you call in to have your frozen pipes thawed! Let it be hoped that the priesthood of all persuasions sees to it that it does not stand in the position of obstructionist to newer insights in regard to the nature of the "soul"! It remains to be seen if the burdens of dogma prove too serious a handicap to the scientific objectivity that is the first and greatest need in this field. Certainly the psychological character of the priestly task has had increasing recognition. Not too unusual in the literature is the following:[12]

"The church provides group therapy to heal guilt and isolation, to set men free to strive for goals in company with others. The aim of the church is to save souls, and religious conversion, like psychosis, is an earnest attempt to solve an inner conflict. But the church has offered treatment without diagnosis. ——Ministers need clinical training——must apply scientific method to the field of religious experience."

This is typical of the clear warnings that scientific method is invading the area of the principal remaining function of the priesthood. Certainly it would be highly dangerous for any organized group to retain illusions as to precisely what the nature of its functions and services is. The entire cultural complex in which it hopes to function must be grasped realistically. Their services must serve a vital need in the total pattern. Where there is a lively competition for the time, energy, and support of a populace there is likely to be a ruthless turnover in favor of the culture elements most closely related to immediate practical needs. Any institution that depends upon needs and demands for services which it must itself create against the competition of a lively and diversifying culture can be safely predicted a reduced significance and importance for the future. Where a religion is increasingly a thing separate from the basic cultural pattern it must in effect set up a rival pattern within a culture by the maintenance of separate educative machinery for the young, separate recreational facilities, even separate pressure groups such as labor unions, veterans' associations, and political parties; in short it must supply the individual with a parochialism from the cradle to the grave. Such a process tends to consume the energy margins available for exploration and discovery in a sterile struggle that at best but serves to maintain and preserve the institution.

The elementary factor that any priesthood is confronted with in contemporary society is simply that of a reduced prestige for its role. Today the priesthood is confronted with a myriad of proliferating and competing roles, as well or better rewarded, whose functions are clear-cut and not a thing apart from the dominant secular pattern. Where once the priest was the only learned man there now thrive a host of specialists whose pursuit does not so effectively compel them to fight a constant battle with the events of the present to make them fit the old infallibilities and certainties. That there should then be a difficulty in the recruiting of candidates for holy orders, both in number and quality, is no surprise. Where such candidacy requires in addition a serious frustration of normal biological drives and functions in a day when modern technology has effectively routed the Malthusian spectre and put biology under control, it is not at all to be wondered at that items such as the following are to be found in the press as was the following in the New York Times of Feb. 2, 1948. Quoting a sermon that stressed the shortage of aspirants to the religious life this paper reported as follows:

"We must face the fact that the church is not receiving a sufficient number of vocations. We are not getting sufficient workers for the work that is ours."

A letter from an even higher church authority was also read which appealed to parents to encourage and help their children to answer God's call to the religious life, and asked young men and women prayerfully to consider vocations to the priesthood, brotherhoods and sisterhoods. Thus have the mighty fallen! Imagine Hollywood having to plead with girls to become movie players! Or the medical colleges having to plead with young men to come in and become doctors! The simple fact is that in any population there is a decided limit to the number or reasonably normal, and able, individuals who will be willing to deviate thus extensively from the ordinary norms of biological and social life, in times such as this with the secular life offering such obvious advantages. In the long run no institution can transcend the quality and calibre of the men who compose or constitute it. Where the secular life is demonstrably full and satisfying, and the economics of it not too improbable, there must be modifications in the requirements of the priestly role if it is to remain attractive to the calibre of individual that can confidently count on successfully competing in the secular world. Yet such processes are slow in their operation. Given the present cultural diversity, particularly in the area of living standards, and the still sizable population shifts from one area to another, there will probably not be any sudden or dramatic dearth of candidates since for large masses of the population the role of priest still represents a peak in their levels of aspiration. Only in the areas most favored economically or educationally, or where social revolutions have destroyed traditional value structures, has the priestly role fallen from its former glory. But the overall historical direction is clear.

While there is no question but what the primary role of the priest is that of stabilizing, ritualizing, conserving, and defending the ways and traditions of the past it must not be forgotten that from their ranks have also frequently sprung the prophets, the innovators, even the revolutionaries and discoverers. This was certainly true when the priestly functions ranged over the entire field of human problems at the most primitive cultural levels, when the priest was more or less a law unto himself in his relatively small group, and when he was best motivated and best equipped to venture into the unknown. Here he was again and again an effective innovator and pace setter. Who but he could have the prestige, the insight and understanding? Who could best judge the true nature of the forces he dealt with and manipulated? No wonder then that from among the ranks of the priests have sprung at least some of the prophets that have at times given their priesthoods a much-needed overhauling, forcing them into the innovations that were necessary if they were not to be completely displaced. William James who was by temperament favorably inclined toward the innovator, saw the history of organized religion as a periodic and recurrent revolt by prophets and innovators against a largely futile and probably corrupt priesthood. This picture may well be not too far from the facts in those culture areas where there has been profound and rapid change in the basic structure of human relations, usually correlated with extensive technological innovations, and where, far from playing a vital, directing, and innovating role in a society, the priesthood was wasting its substance in a futile defense of a past in which it had vested interests, usually of a rather obvious sort. The exact status and historical function of any priesthood in any particular culture is necessarily a matter of considerable complexity. In brief, it involves the entire power structure of that society, the relationship obtaining between this structure and the priesthood, and the character of the competing societies with which it is contiguous and contemporary. The significance of its role is always a function of the specific scene in which it is operating. Blanket, evaluative judgments in advance are meaningless.

The "separation of the church and the state" must not be thought of as a permanent state of affairs involving stability and finality. Rather it is an uneasy state of truce in a continually on-going, pull devil-pull deacon contest. In the overall picture, viewed broadly and historically, the long-term secular tendencies seem unavoidable and inescapable. But that does not prevent the priesthood from giving a good account of itself in what must in the long run be rear guard actions. Like all good strategists, they frequently show that they know that the best defense is an offense.

During the past decade the priesthood seems to have lost ground in this perennial contest in eastern and central Europe and the Balkans, in Tibet, and perhaps in Belgium where the struggle is currently in a fairly acute phase. The contest in many areas is still a dubious battle. In Western Germany, France and the U. S. A. they have made small but significant gains, as they also seem to be making in Mexico after having suffered a serious set-back there some thirty years ago. In most places the struggle centers around the matter of the control of the educational machinery, the church dignitaries making their bids for martyrdom on that issue in the east European and Balkan states. In a dictatorial society the priesthood has the choice of playing along with the state or party "line" or shutting up shop. Czarist Russia had such a priesthood, and the Soviets seem well on the way to producing a priestly strain with which they can arrange an effective symbiotic relationship. Similar processes seem to be under way in all areas under Communist control. In China where there was no indigenous priesthood to speak of, the missionary fraternity from abroad is given short shrift.

In western Germany, the detaching of the predominantly Protestant east has left a state strongly under church influence with its consequent repercussions in internal and external policy. In France the inept and corrupt state machinery has found itself unable even to maintain its secular educational services so that the church seems to be taking over by default. In Belgium where already a significant fraction of the educational process was under priestly control the balance of power among the democratic voters seems to have decided to call a halt in the process.

An interesting process is under way in the more democratic states, those in which the national policy must extract a modicum of consent from the electorate, and where, by the same token, the state cannot turn a wholly deaf ear to popular clamor. There the priesthood is taking advantage of the current ill repute of communism to link it with godlessness, making the assumption that they are necessarily but two sides of the same coin, and conveniently forgetting that until wrecked by Spanish conquest the Peruvian empire was a communistic theocracy! (Again the error of under-estimating the variety of social patterns that might well exist!) With sufficient repetition of this assertion of identity by the priesthood, aware of the menace to them of a "godless" social order, and by those elements in the population most apprehensive of change in the economic order, the layman, particularly in the United States, is in an apprehensive dither over this twin menace. The resulting abnormal rapport between "church" and "state" has reached a point where it is threatening the traditional American separation of these two institutions. With any opposition to the aims of the clergy quickly branded as "communism," the vote-sensitive legislators have forgotten their constitution and jammed a local god into the schoolchild's pledge of allegiance and an assertion of trust in that same god on all the units of monetary exchange to be issued in the land. It is to be hoped that the Supreme Court will not be unmindful of its traditional duties when some earnest citizen, more mindful of the propaganda uses to which such moves can be put to by our enemies in the Orient, carries that legislation up to it for final judgment. The local god has too long been identified by the enemy propaganda, if not in the experience of the Oriental, with their current propaganda bugaboo, "Foreign Imperialism" to make this a wise move at precisely a time in history when we are denouncing our enemies for *their* attacks upon religious freedom. Too many of our citizens erroneously assume that because they believe their god to be omnipresent the rest of the world shares that belief. Whether we like it or not, for a large fraction of the world, "religious freedom" means also the right not to have a religion. That right, the local priesthood is putting to serious question, and in jeopardy.

It is of course not assumed here that the general "secular trend" in the church-state equilibrium is of necessity an unmixed blessing. There were periods in history when the advantage has been with the culture that could mobilize swiftly and act effectively as a unit, uninhibited by dissenters or doubting Thomases. The difficulty then is simply that the mobilizers and wielders of such power tend to become laws unto themselves. At such times there is much merit to be seen in the development of some other force to serve as a counterpoise. The organized priesthood has frequently served in that role but it has also not been reluctant to assume both roles, or to reduce the secular arm to the level of a lackey. A nice, undisputed equilibrium between such potential rivals may only mean a complete lack of interference with each others' villainies or absurdities. State machinery has stood unconcernedly by while a priesthood has persisted in wasting the human substance in cannibalism, human sacrifice, widow-burning, infanticide, erotic debauches, or taboos that depleted the biological strength of the group. The priesthood has stood by and even blessed the state in its incredible, criminal, and even suicidal programs without an organized or official protest. And both have at times vied with each other in a racketeering exploitation of their subjects.

The undeniable advantage of a completely democratic control machinery lies not in its superior wisdom but in its capacity to call a halt somewhere short of catastrophe, to displace any power-machinery that proves too frustrating. But even this has limits in the matter of advantages: a directing organization might sometimes be well advised to carry out a program in the face of continual opposition from the populace. It is notorious in history that the abuses characteristic of one system tend to give rise to conditions that set up the other. Look for dictatorships to appear where democratic rule and direction has been inept; look for democratic trends where dictatorships have long impressed their shortcomings on a populace. Similarly with the alternate cycles of Church vs. State power. The long term survival of any principle of organization will depend upon the quality of its fruits, its human product. Stability need not necessarily be incompatible with intelligent innovation, and an intelligent control machinery, secular or sacred, must assume the responsibility of not only giving intelligent direction and leadership but of preparing the populace for that direction and that leadership. It must set workable goals upon which it can get the constructive cooperation of the group. It must promote functional, workable programs. Mundane problems are difficult enough without complicating them with considerations that by definition transcend human experience and knowledge. The leadership offered by the priesthood is handicapped by the fact that it promotes as having cosmic importance that which is all too frequently but a thinly disguised vested interest of the clergy.

Nor is there any "natural" division of the affairs of this world for once and for all into those which are the Lord's and those which are Caesar's as the New Testament injunction has it. That too obviously depends upon the fortuitous boundary lines laid down in each particular culture some time during its

past. Those lines are usually the lines marking an uneasy truce
in a power struggle. The "things that are Caesar's" run to a
quite different count whenever and wherever there is a new
Caesar. It is the frequent invocation of this dictum as a precedent for leaving a social, political, or economic power-balance
undisturbed that has given some warrant to the theory that
religion is primarily an opiate for the masses. There just is no
denying that it has functioned in precisely this capacity, at some
times and places in human history. But there have been times
too, when rightly or wrongly it has fed the fires of revolt. . . .
Meantime, the church has on occasion suffered at the hands of
some of its well-meaning but apparently naive advocates, as
witness the following "defense" at the hands of Roger Babson
the business soothsayer, writing for the Inter-church World
Movement in 1920:

"What is our real security for the stocks, bonds, mortgages,
deeds and other investments which we own?—The value
of our investments depends not on the strength of our banks,
but rather upon the strength of our churches. The underpaid
preachers of the nation are the men upon whom we really
are depending rather than the well-paid lawyers, bankers, and
brokers. The religion of the community is really the bulwark
of our investments."

"For our own sakes, for our children's sakes, for the nation's
sake, let us businessmen get behind the churches and their
preachers! Never mind if they are not perfect, never mind if
their theology is out of date.—By all that we hold dear, let us
from this very day give more time, money and thought to the
churches of our city for upon these the value of all we own
ultimately depends."

If the ghost of Karl Marx was around at the time of the
release of this "defense" it no doubt said, "You took the words
right out of my mouth," or, "I could not have said it better
myself." (Who was it that said, "Protect me from my friends,
I'll take care of my enemies"?) It would be rather difficult to
ascertain with any accuracy just what percentage of the support of religious institutions is motivated by sentiments such
as the above of Mr. Babson. Probably no great fraction. It is no

doubt true in general, as the old proverb has it, that "he who pays the piper calls the tune," and certainly the religious institutions are not wholly exempt from that general principle. By putting the matter thus brazenly it is more than likely that Babson helped the church far more than the dollar value of the additional contributions his letter elicited.

It would seem that nothing in the way of factual data on the relations existing between power, wealth, and religion are at present available. But there is a problem here for those who feel that religion must have a very real and serious function in society. As an institution that merely puts the stamp of respectability upon whatever already exists, it has no significant future. When religions are in that phase they are stagnating. There are those who hold that when new directions of social development are indicated the old social and institutional leadership simply cannot be practically utilized.[13] It may well be that the entire make-up and tradition of the priestly caste is such that it will be unable to retain more than its present modicum of functional social leadership. Social crises are rather likely to be resolved at the expense of whatever dead wood there is in the social structure, and of this the priesthood is generally pretty well aware. Hence the general tendency of the priesthood to make common cause with other well-entrenched interests generally concerned with the maintenance of the status quo. Such a policy generally pays off well, excepting in cases where social revolution unseats the interests with which the priesthood has made common cause. When such happens, as it did in France in the 18th century, and in Russia relatively recently, the organized priesthood is set for a loss from which recovery is dubious and slow. On the other hand, where the priesthood has allied itself with aggressive forces, as it did in Ireland with the independence movement, and as it did recently in Spain, it frequently then enjoys a highly favored role and status. But if the social structure that results from such a marriage of forces is not viable or of reasonable efficiency, time and circumstances are rather prone to catch up with it. No institution can remain permanently at loggerheads with profound social trends and expect to retain its status. It can no longer be doubted that ours is the era of scientific method. There are inherent contradictions that prevent any priesthood claiming infallibility in anything from embracing the scientific method or of becoming its sponsors in any but highly limited areas. In fact, in its franker moods the more outspoken members of the priesthood frequently give testimony to this persistent hostility. On its Monday morning "sermon page" the New York Times of March 7, 1938 reported the then Msgr. Fulton J. Sheen as picturing man as a creature of God, on the point of annihilation from the five mortal wounds of Darwinism, Marxism, quantitative science, mobilization and the totalitarian state. Specifically quoting from the sermon, the Times reported as follows:

"By these five wounds man has lost his origin, God; his purpose, everlasting happiness; his superiority, his personality and his rights. In the face of these facts it is true to say that the world today is witnessing the greatest crucifixion since Calvary. Our greatest problem is, indeed, the forgotten man."

Such a sermon is indeed an interesting revelation on the workings of the theological mind. Note that Darwinism is no longer attacked as a factual error; its effects are, however, unmistakably bemoaned. Marxism, sandwiched in here between Darwinism and quantitative science, is promoted into a very good company indeed in this good theologian's attempts at the creation of an impressive line-up of villains for this religious rogues' gallery. But it is the presence of quantitative science in the line-up that should permanently cure or remove the last vestiges of the illusion to which all too many fall victim, namely, that science and at least the religion of this theologian are "perfectly reconciled." At the time this sermon was delivered. when it was the dictatorial states of Europe and Asia that were mobilizing and extending their totalitarian domains, and only the Western democratic powers not arming and mobilizing, one might well wonder at the motivation behind such pronouncements, particularly in view of the entente cordiale obviously existing between several of these totalitarian states and Msgr. Sheen's religious organization. Note too, the subtle phrase by which the economic "forgotten man" of the depression era is minimized as, against "mankind" in the abstract, suffering a ritual deprivation or insult. It is just such playing down of material needs by the priesthood and their emphases upon post-mortem goals that has provided some very real substance to the charge of religion functioning as an opiate. The charge has real and genuine substance whenever and wherever there is an attempt to substitute transcendent goals and purposes for measurable values in the here and now.

It is a serious error to fail to recognize that the priesthood constitutes a vested interest much like any other clique of special interests in society: indeed a very old one. And, like any other vested interest, it cannot even contemplate a social world in which it is to be deprived of any of its traditional or historical functions. Whatever may be necesary to maintain its role and status takes precedence, of necessity, over any and all other considerations, in precisely the same manner and for the same reasons as with any other special interest group. Any and all events that transpire are first of all evaluated from the standpoint of their effect upon "the institution," the traditional powers and prerogatives of its personnel. The organized priesthood in Europe fought secular medicine when it threatened the power and prestige of the church. Whenever any state function began to encroach upon areas traditionally hers, the church has reacted no differently than have the carpenters to a jurisdictional encroachment by the lathers. Since the organized church has long maintained charitable institutions it has quite consistently opposed any moves to put the state into the business of organized relief. Not until the depression of the nineteen thirties with the complete breakdown of private and religious charity in the face of economic crisis, did some of the more tightly organized churches cease their opposition to state welfare measures in the United States. As recently as November 7, 1955, a United Press despatch told of a bishop of a church charging the "so-called welfare state" with leading to the decline of religion in the United States, where the unemployed, the sick, the injured and the aged come to look to the state for support and security, instead of to the church and its gods. Quite correct, bishop! Even the earthworm can learn which turn of a maze leads to food and which to an electric shock. Man's limitations are, perhaps unfortunately, such that he comes to prefer food without blessings to blessings without food when the hunger drive attains to a given intensity. The reluctance of the religious machinery to get behind political pressures for such secular welfare moves has given further substance to the charge of religion as functioning socially in the role of an opiate.

Viewed broadly, human society has developed an increasingly diverse variety of specialized skills with which to meet the problems of life. These skills can most meaningfully be classified or dichotomized into two profoundly different ways: the first is that of a persistent, innovating trial and error approach that concentrates on attacks upon the reluctant or recalcitrant materials involved, with recombinations and variations in materials and manipulation. This has given contemporary man his scientific method and principles which have multiplied his powers beyond even the wildest dreams of the past, rivalling even the capacities formerly ascribed to his gods. It is this general method of meeting problems that has eclipsed almost completely that other way of behaving in the face of problems that we have previously referred to as involving symbolic entreaty, resignation, ceremonial, and orgy: all devices whose chief effects are upon man himself, and only remotely and indirectly upon man's problems, and then almost exclusively in the direction of tendencies to neglect or minimize any efforts at the direct frontal assault upon the practical mechanics of the source of his frustration. The specialists in the former of these two methods are our scientists; the specialists in the latter are the priesthood. The first group of specialists is increasingly talking a common, an international language; for good or ill they are producing what is culturally one world. The specialists in entreaty and orgy remain the sponsors of Omar's "two and seventy jarring sects," unified or united only in their opposition to secular science. They are the spokesmen for, and the specialists in techniques for which scientific method leaves them but a rapidly shrinking area in which they can yet pretend to function effectively. The doom of the priesthood was sealed when it chose the tempting path of meeting crises by working on man rather than on the baffling complexities of the material world that was the source of man's frustrations. They did their best to prevent man from learning about that material world; give them credit for having a sharp eye to the future of their own vested interests. They have long maintained a diminishing glory with rear-guard action and will no doubt long continue so to do. The historically minded, however cannot but ponder the question: Did Greece have her Golden Age in spite of not having, or because she had no priesthood?

CHAPTER XI

SOCIAL MOVEMENTS AND RELIGION

More than any other animal, man is always actively changing his environment. Then, in various ways, he himself changes to increase the likelihood that any equilibrium with that environment is likely to be of rather short duration. Human habituation generally manages to keep pace with minor and slow environmental changes, but swift and extensive changes are almost certain to be troublemakers. It is characteristic of some social habit adjustments that they must be made, if at all, by the simultaneous readjustment of the habits of a larger number of persons, either within the same group or in some other group with which it is closely involved in more or less well-established patterns of social interaction. It is then quite understandable that such changes as are contingent upon a more or less organized process are rather likely to lag, to become overdue, while the need for such change can be expected to reveal itself in varying amounts of social conflict, disorganization, and inefficiency, with an increasing percentage of the individuals showing evidences of frustration. It is under such circumstances that social movements arise.

There is no guarantee that social movements must take a constructive turn. They may well be stupid, unbelievably so. But behind every social movement, there is certain to be a social problem, or problems. A social problem can quite easily be defined as some state of affairs not being adequately or quickly enough met by such social machinery as exists; or perhaps more objectively defined, some habit systems somewhere are not changing as rapidly as they should be if the manifestations characteristic of social movements are to be avoided. A similar state of affairs might also arise from any factor tending to produce conflict in human relations, even if such factors existed only on the verbal, symbolic level, which then interfered with the normal functioning of the old social pattern. That is to say, it must not be assumed that there always exists any historical or moral necessity for a social change even if the outlines of a social movement do appear. But habit and custom being what they are, it is reasonably safe to assume that the existence of a social movement is eloquent testimony to the presence of a genuine social problem, even if this problem may exist only on the level of ideas, beliefs, hopes, or wishes of perhaps an unrealistic sort.

Social movements vary enormously in the extent of the behavior deviations that they sponsor. In a sense, any fad, style change, any craze might be called a social movement. And, one might insist that the *social problem* behind such vagaries of social behavior was a populace devoid of constructive channels of self-expression. At the other extreme are the social movements involving the rapid and drastic overhauling of some considerable segment of a social pattern and which by common consent are called revolutions. Careful study, however, of such rapid changes almost invariably reveals that the processes leading up to the sudden dramatic changes were long in incubating and perhaps even in the end might not necessarily have eventuated in precisely the form they took if some perhaps trifling factors had been modified, as by significant and effective action taken at critical moments by particular personalities. One thinks, for example, of what changes might well have been brought about in Germany and Russia by an opportune funeral or two before 1933. Social movements indeed vary, particularly in the matter of the specific activities or functions undergoing rapid change. Some of these changes involve matters commonly thought of as religious; in fact many social movements can be characterized as predominantly "religious" and every new religion represents a social movement of some sort, large or small, rapid or slow. Because western civilization was so long dominated by a religious social movement, many of the characteristics of such movements have come to be identified in the popular mind with "religion." So any reasonably effective social movement is likely to be called a "religion," even if in ends, aims, and ideology it might differ markedly from, and even be a deadly enemy of current religions. Such is the case with communism which is frequently called a "religion," naturally enough by people who are not too favorably impressed with the current role of religion in world affairs. It is with Catholic Christianity that communism is most commonly identified. Let us see what grounds we can find for this perceived similarity:

Both are millennial.

Both are evangelistic, with the emphasis upon action and results.

Both are catastrophic and revolutionary.

Both have personal, authoritative, and more or less deified founders: Jesus, Marx.

Both founders stemmed from the same culture pattern: the Jewish.

Both are apocalyptic and revelatory, and urge present sacrifices for future gains.

Both preach an unquestioned confidence in the truth of their creeds.

Their ideals are held with that deadly earnestness reserved for the sacred.

The doctrines of both are reduced to simple, confidence-giving creeds and concise shibboleths, teachable even to mediocre intelligences.

Both cultivate a distinctive terminology.

Both have sacred texts or writings: The Bible, Das Kapital.

The sacred texts of both are sufficiently ambiguous to serve as bases for elaborate prophecy.

The sacred texts of both are long, repetitious, and dull.

The rank and file of both seldom read these sacred texts.

"Authoritative" interpretations of the sacred texts are provided for the faithful as the need arises.

Both have adopted and use a distinctive symbol: the cross, the hammer & sickle.

Both avowedly aim to establish a universal brotherhood, a "brotherhood of man."

Both aimed their appeals at the poor, the disinherited, the suffering masses.

The early converts to both were definitely not of the "nice people."

Both symbolize their causes as a struggle in the name of super-personal entities: the Church, the Proletariat.

Both have identified a nuclear evil against which to crusade: The Devil, Capitalism.

Both firmly believe and preach the unquestioned superiority of their institutions over all others.

Both preach the unquestioned rightness of their aims and purposes.

Both teach the inevitability of the ultimate triumph of their causes.

Joining either of them, or being "converted" has similar effects on the personalities of the joiners or converts.

At some point in their history, both were militantly at war with rival contemporary creeds.

Both broke with a fairly systematic religious or philosophical background, Christianity from Judaism, Marx from the traditions of absolute idealism, Hegel, and the highly centralized German state.

Yet both carried with them much of the parent system:

Jehovah remained with the Christians; the "dialectics" and the emphasis upon state functions with Marxian communism.

Both demand the submergence of personal and familial interests in favor of those of the organizations: a celibate clergy for the Catholics; family needs must remain subservient to party needs with the Communist.

Both demand a priority in loyalty to the organization as against the family. Both set children against parents, brother against brother, at some period in their history.

Both insist upon absolute control over the individual in the indoctrination of the dogma or the "party line."

Both begin the indoctrination process at the earliest possible ages in children.

The savants and party hacks of both rewrite history to paint the glories of the new dispensation.

Both have made use of an Inquisition.

"The End Justifies the Means" has been the working philosophy of both at critical periods in their history.

Days of persecution have been known by both; and both have tasted the sweets of power.

Both have been singularly unsuccessful in making any headway in the cultures of their origin: a "converted" Jew is an anomaly, and communism has made but little headway in England, Germany, or in the industrial western Europe in which it was developed as a theory.

Both have been guilty of hostility to science. The war of the Church with science has lasted through the centuries. In spite of claims to being "scientific," Russian Communism since Lenin has not hesitated to coerce scientists into following a "party line" in their theory, research, and findings. It remains only to be seen if communistic states free from Stalinist control behave similarly.

Both have advocated and used force in spreading their "gospels."

There is a deadly similarity of organization:

Both have monolithic, dictatorial political structures, with all authority emanating from the apex of the pyramid of command in which:

> The Pope corresponds to the General Secretary of the Communist Party;
>
> The College of Cardinals to the Politburo;
>
> Being "Read out of the Party" corresponds to Excommunication; and,
>
> Moscow and Rome are the Holy Cities.

Both demand unquestioned discipline and obedience; and,

Both have at times taught the infallibility of their leader-

ship, which is with both a relatively recent doctrine:
Papal "infallibility" dates from 1870, and in communism
the leader cult began with Stalin.

There is even a fairly close equivalent in Russian Communism to the sainthood to which popes are often elevated
at death, if conclusions can be drawn on the basis of
so small a number of deceased leaders.

With so many parallels and similarities, surely there is something stacking the cards to produce a common denominator in
what on the face of things appear to be mortal enemies and
opposites. A little reflection might remind us that similarity
is no bar to conflict; in fact it increases the prospects of it in
many instances. Siblings can proverbially stage the most sanguinary battles: Is this similarity limited to precisely these two
movements? Since they are both products of the western world,
they no doubt have more residual similarities than would be
found in comparing an oriental and a western movement. Yet
even there, quite some similarities would be encountered, since
they are after all, social movements, and as such involve essentially the same phenomena of human behavior. The precise
items of behavior in question might indeed vary, but the common denominator of reactions to change would be there. Even
more significant in understanding their similarity is the fact
that both movements must be rated as "successful" as social
movements go. And successful movements, rated as such not
on any absolute scale of moral worth, but simply on the fact
of the numbers of their recruits and the wideness of their
geographical appeal, would be rather likely to exemplify more
of the general principles of their operation, and have in common the factors making for their success.[1]

Successful social movements are historically rare events.
For one movement that means an important change in the way
of life for a significant number of people over more than a
generation, there must be hundreds that produced nothing
more than a minor splinter or deviation from the old pattern,
and thousands that remained but a handful of people accepting
the advice or guidance of some particular individual who by

one device or another acquired prestige in the eyes of his fellows. The death of such a prestiged leader most often spells the end of that particular nucleus of social innovation. But then again the prestige of a dead leader can be exploited by astute followers who capitalize on his name and convert it into a symbol which can then be made to stand for whatever happens to be essential to any practical promotional program that power politics might demand. Such conversions have befallen the founders of practically all social movements, religious or secular, after their death. It is this process that has produced some of the paradoxical similarity between Christianity and Communism, in spite of the fact that the former movement was wholly concerned, in theory, with post-mortem affairs, and the other expressly limited to mundane concerns, which may explain its apparently greater acceptability in China. It is the practical problems involved in the large-scale changing of social behavior norms that demands and enforces the similarities in all social movements if they are to be successful. There are, after all, a limited number of ways by which the behavior of people can be controlled. A chain of command can be organized in only a limited number of ways. The devices by which conformity can be compelled are not legion, and successful social movements seem to have exhausted all the possibilities from systematic indoctrination and rewards to ingenious torture and dramatic execution in the name of the Prince of Peace, the classless society, or effective military discipline.

People are not easily broken away from their old habits. Even the most radical of revolutions, whether nominally involving sacred or secular matters, at best involves changes in but a few of all the habits acquired in a lifetime. Such a structure of dominant habits tends to maintain the entire pattern, to keep the behavior of the individual in its old groove. To break such habits of long standing calls for strategy. There are decided limits to what even the most effective machinery of coercive force can do. It is usually far more efficient to fire the masses with evangelistic zeal, sadistic hates, or the masochisms of martyrdom, or all three simultaneously. It is because these devices have so frequently been used by religious leaders and

religious movements that it seems to some the distinguishing
earmark of religion. One might call it the "excessive zeal"
theory of religion. Social movements concerned with gods, post-
mortem events, or the ritualization of conduct have certainly
had no corner on such zeal, but it has been often enough found
in them to provide the basis for such identification. It is largely
because of this characteristic that Communism is so frequently
spoken of as a "religion." Few indeed of the other common
denominators they have as social movements contribute to this
judgment. Yet their similarities as social movements involve
far more than just their excessive zeal.

The zealous phase of all successful social movements in
time seems to give way to a placid respectability. They frequently achieve at least some of the goals they set out to attain;
they acquire power and respectability. All too frequently such
a machinery seems unable to visualize or to perceive new goals
or programs of action. Religions tend to stagnate into an innocuous ritualism concerned at best with an isolated segment of private conflict resolution. The members of our "best"
churches would blush at the deadly earnestness of the Disciples.
Secular social movements too become innocuous and respectable
after having reached the limits of their expanding power; the
revolutionary elite they produce, apparently unable to maintain its dynamic leadership. Thus the stage is set for a new
social movement, whether secular or religious. At any event the
process is familiar enough. Pareto called the process the "Circulation of the Elite." An elite always rides to power on a new
social movement. Until it becomes a social movement, no religion is more than the deviant behavior of a particular individual or two, who might even be suspected of being a bit
abnormal. But deviant behavior and ideas are always turning up
in a lot of individuals. Of necessity but few of them launch full-
fledged social movements. It might well be a bit difficult to
write in advance the exact characteristics of, and the time of
the appearance of each new religion. But the process is no
mystery. Dissident offshoots are continually incubating; any
one of them might have the ingredients necessary for wider

acceptance. One wonders at passages such as the following occasionally encountered:[2]

"It is generally agreed that the emergence of a great new religious faith is one of the inexplicable mysteries which have accompanied the ascent of man and bears the most convincing testimony to the contingency and spontaneity of his spiritual history."

These days one might well wonder which of the great religions is such an inexplicable mystery in its origin. Judaism? It is an all too obvious product of the Mesopotamian and Babylonian and Cannanite culture complexes. Christianity? The recently discovered Dead Sea Codexes go a long way to closing the gap between Judaism and Christianity via the Essene sects. Buddhism? It was a reaction against the crippling complexities of Hinduism similar to the reaction of Moses against the complexities of Egyptian worship that left but little time over for anything else, and very similar to the sudden religious reform touched off in Egypt by Akhnaton the iconoclast who closed the temples of the old gods and proclaimed but one god, Aton, the sun god. Had he tended to his knitting in better fashion he might well have inaugurated something lasting. But his energy went into worshipping that one god with such concentration and zeal that he neglected to exercise his sovereignty effectively with the lamentable result that he lost his throne, and the once dispossessed priestcraft again took over. So there are plenty of precedents even for those few cases in which a new religion makes an heroic break with the past. In three different cases it is apparent that a leader of exceptional sagacity and skepticism balked at the excesses of futile ritualism. Moses apparently had the best luck, although the Golden Calves continued to plague him for a long time. Buddha too, had considerable success for a time in competing with the excessive Hindu concern over things post-mortem. His own area back-slid with time, but his ideas survived in the practices of other lands. Akhnaton, tackling perhaps even better entrenched vested interests had some considerable success but only for a short time. Are even these cases in any way mysterious? About as mysterious as the appearance anywhere of any sort of mechanical short-cut, and certainly no more mysterious in origin than is any "village atheist" or other religious deviant. Even the most revolutionary deviations or "new religions" impress one far more by their close similarity to the old than they give cause for wonder at the possible mystery of their genesis.

Like all social movement, new religions organize and crystallize around deviant personalities, exceptional individuals, creative geniuses, or, if one takes at face value the claims of their followers, specially created, divinely inspired, saints, prophets, gods, sons of gods, or Enlightened Ones, about whose make-up or origins there is frequently something unusual to mark them off from the run of the mill mortal. To claim for them a virgin birth is something not at all unusual, not because there is in all these cultures a sharing of the almost complete identification of sex with sin which characterizes Christianity, but simply as an unusual characteristic, not at all identified with sinlessness. This preoccupation with sexlessnes, ie, "sinlessness," has reached a point in some cults where a sexless origin is claimed even for the mother of the incarnate deity, which would be but a very minor miracle to accept and would certainly put a far weaker strain on one's credulity since the parthenogenetic activation of the mammalian egg has been experimentally performed in the laboratory and it is well known that a large variety of natural energy applications might well touch off such activation of an egg and cause it to develop into a full-blown individual without the aid of a male sperm. What is, in fact, more or less miraculous is that it does not happen at least on occasion, which it well might; but getting a cynical world to accept the fact of it is another matter. As before said, it would require only a relatively minor "miracle" such as a sudden elevation of the temperature, or just the right change in the salinity of the uterine fluids to activate an egg and start it on the gestational cycle. But such parthenogenetic process could only produce a female, since all eggs have the X or sex-determining chromosome, which, in an activated egg would be duplicated, and the result, as even every high school student of biology knows, would be a female. For a male to be produced by such a possible but rather improbable process, would require the superimposition of an even more improbable, if yet possible, "miracle" on top of the first. For it would require that in the activation process, which begins by each of the chromosomes duplicating itself in the egg, the X chromosome should for some reason fail to do so while all the others did. This is not at all impossible, just very improbable; yet similar accidents are not unknown in careful genetic experiments. Such an egg would then give rise to a male, if somehow activated by the processes already described. So no scientist worthy of the name would call "impossible" any such event as the appearance of a female child without the active cooperation of a father, nor even that of a male offspring. The only certainty in science is that there are no certainties. But the scientist witholds active belief until the probabilities run very high indeed. Therein he differs from the "believer." Then too, the scientist would hardly be impressed by, or take any exceptional stock in, anything said or done by an individual just because he might know or accept some evidence for such unusual genetic origin. In such a deviant he would be a bit suspicious of pathology.

But as before indicated, no social movement is launched without its dynamic, initiating personality at the nucleus of it. A social movement can get under way only if the concerns of some articulate and innovating individual somehow find a responsive chord in his fellows. The exact subject of these concerns can and does vary from area to area as well as with the times. Quite understandably, the social movements initiated reflect the general areas of conflict or concern in the culture at that particular time. Little enough is known in detail about the genesis of the many social movements, nor have they had the careful and detailed study that these variations in the social pattern richly deserve. A very interesting study has been made of the social movements developing in the state of California during the last one hundred years.[3]

In classifying these many colonies as "religious" or "politico-economic," some significant differences emerge. As is to be expected, most of these colonies had but a limited life-span. However, those classified as predominantly "religious" averaged about double the life of those designated politico-economic. This is the sort of a finding that stimulates curiosity. One might well conclude that it required the high emotional zeal of religious sanction to preserve an innovation in behavior in the face of outside social pressures. Then too, it might be thought that this country and this period in history are very tolerant of deviations in the field of religion; or that the religious segment of life is at best an innocuous ritualism and that even large scale innovations in this area would leave the life of the workaday world pretty much intact. Or, one might conclude that there is less ground for improvement in the area of the politico-economic which would practically guarantee failure to any innovation serious enough to demand a segregation of its practices from the general economy. Probably more relevant is the suggestion that the difference lies in the size and area essential to the effective functioning of even the most efficient of economic systems; that the theories underlying these experiments could not get a proper trial on so small a scale, while a single individual can long entertain the most bizarre beliefs so long as he does not allow them to conflict with his relations to other people. At any event, the social scientist has here an opportunity to study material of importance comparable to that of the anthropological variety offered by the world. Here is material from which much is to be learned.

With so many individual personalities at all times more or less in conflict with the behavior norms of their cultures there is no mystery about the source of the dissident leadership giving rise to social movements, whether of a predominantly religious or secular character. But the mortality rates of such dissidents is high indeed. They are confronted with all the inertia of habit, all the well-dug-in vested interests that tend to keep any and every social pattern reasonably stable. Where there are large land areas over which no effective sovereignty is exercised, or where there are considerable unexploited economic opportunities, deviants and variants, both religious and secular can and do on occasion appear and maintain themselves for longer or shorter time-spans. Witness the thriving of the Latter Day Saints in relative isolation in Utah, or the Perfectionists at

Oneida, for quite some time, even if in both cases outside pressures shortly compelled a certain amount of retrenchment in some of their areas of more significant deviation. But it is the establishment of any sort of deviation for however brief a time that marks the exceptional event. As with biological evolution, it is seldom indeed that an extensive mutation succeeds in establishing itself and surviving. It is the slow, barely perceptible, but cumulative changes that tend to determine the major trends of religious and cultural evolution. Yet dramatic revolutionary changes do sometimes take hold and survive, even to become shortly the dominant norm. Christianity was without doubt such a revolution. So is Russian Communism today. The only advantage that a revolutionary upstart of whatever stripe has is just that it can devise a program of conduct or action freed from some of the more anachronistic and handicapping of the traditions of conduct that tend to weight down even the most dynamic and progressive of cultures. It can start afresh with an ideology or a gospel that can take full advantage of such new understanding and insights as have accrued to man's stock of knowledge, completely freed from the dead hand of the past. Naturally enough, the prospects for the success of such a revolutionary deviation are in proportion to the extent that the parent culture is handicapped by the archaic, the inefficient, and the anachronistic in its make-up.

In the Western world, there is a strong tendency to think of religion as a more or less innocuous and isolated segment of the culture pattern, and as having but limited significance for the rest of the workaday world. And that, in truth, is precisely what religion has become for all practical purposes. The pattern of culture once dominated by Christianity, has undergone such fantastic proliferation in its technology and such drastic changes in the entire structure, that about the only aspect of it that is still recognizable is the traditional cult and ritual. Even the belief structure is now so changed that only the most naive believers can insist that it is still the same old belief. Cult, ritual, and belief no longer contribute anything significant to the organizational dynamics of that society. It is rather a ritual gesture of social respectability, incumbent upon

all individuals who stand sufficiently in the public eye so that
they would become a target for attack by the professional priesthood, should they fail to make minimal obeisances to some one
of the organized systems of supernaturalism. Lacking an official
or state religion, the priesthoods of the various creeds nonetheless make common cause against any who would flout them
collectively, or even profess allegiance to none of them. This
is at best a rear-guard action, an ignominious role for the
once mighty vicars of the Lord, many of whom resent with
every fiber of their being their currently low estate, and can
be depended upon to make use of every opportunity to improve
their status.

It was not ever thus. When Christianity spread over Europe,
it came, not only as belief and ritual but as part of a dynamic
social whole, a new way of social organization, and a largely
new and better technology including agriculture, animal husbandry, horticulture, architecture, and metallurgy. It was part
of a dynamic social movement, organized and designed to get
action, and it did! When collective action is called for, any
waiting upon democratic niceties is fatal. An effective chain
of command from an authoritative leadership is as essential
as is centralized command in military operations. The outline
of similarities so clearly apparent between communism and the
early Christian church comes pretty close to constituting a list
of essential techniques, devices, and organizational structure
necessary if a social structure is to be quickly and efficiently
remade. It is a pattern winnowed out by the trial and error of
history and found generally effective. It is a structure begotten
in conflict, and apparently capable of perpetuating itself from
one generation to the next if it keeps control of the educational
machinery to which the coming generations are exposed.

The social structure created by this organization began to
fare badly in western Europe when its too successful technology
created classes of people with interests incompatible with those
of the dominant priesthood. The Reformation marked the
passing of control of certain important social functions from
the priesthood to a secular machinery. Where the Reformation
reached, the priesthood was no longer the organizing nucleus

of the culture. Actually, the church had long ceased to provide
an imaginative ideology, a dynamic leadership in a program it
firmly believed in. It was at best defending its well-dug-in
position and privileges, but providing no new visions, no hopes
of a better life except post-mortem. Its traditions and organization provided no constructive social program. It could only
battle to liquidate the increasingly frequent heretics as they
appeared. The church machinery failed to see what the heretics
were seeking. It was no longer a fighting social movement; it
was but a well established vested interest that could imagine
nothing of greater importance than the maintaining of its privileged position and status. The basic organizational structure,
and its devices for capturing the imagination, the loyalties, and
the fighting energy of a following survive. It is a formula that
the leaders of other social movements can either copy or invent
independently. And they have, as the long list of similarities
between communism and the Catholic church eloquently testifies.

The effective launching of a social movement, whether
sacred or secular, calls for imaginative and effective leadership
backed by an efficient chain of command. Democratic sentiment is always outraged at the spectacle of what are "normally"
considered civilian affairs operated with military or quasi-mili-
tary methods and sanctions. Yet when a nucleus of zealots seizes
control of a society, the bulk of whose members are but reluctant dragons at best and prone to resist interruptions in their
familiar routines, the price of failing to establish a military
discipline is simply a reversion to the old familiar pattern of
life. "Dictatorship" is in essence but the application to civil life
of the routines and control techniques found effective in the
deadly earnestness that is warfare. The process is much the
same whether leadership is engaged in setting up new norms of
social behavior or if it is resisting strong tendencies in the
citizens to deviate from the traditional. Note the frequency with
which it is men trained in the military pattern that seek to solve
social and political problems by applying military techniques
and methods. If it is a workable pattern of social behavior that
has been initiated, routine habit factors shortly permit the

atrophy of the military machinery. There is no better measure of the residual friction in a social pattern than the extent of the machinery of force required in its maintenance.

When the new social pattern of behavior being set up by a more or less revolutionary machinery, whether predominantly priestly or secular in form, involves rather extensive invasions into the traditional behavior patterns of a people the odds increase that even to make a bid for the acceptance of the new will require a considerable machinery of force, and with it an effective chain of command. But almost any behavior pattern should in time be able to dispense with the arbitrary machinery of force and begin to govern by consent, with a consequent considerable reduction in the size of its coercive machinery. Any extensive retaining of dictatorial or coercive machinery during a time when no new institutions are being established or no significant social innovations being attempted might well raise the not unjustified suspicion that the populace is becoming restive under the current dispensation, and that the chief function of the dictatorial social structure and the machinery of coercion is that of preserving the vested interests of the ruling clique. If this is a reasonable conclusion in regard to political statesmanship it is even more so when the matters involved are purely in the domain of fact or logic. The very thought of an authoritative machinery dictating out of hand in questions of fact, or even where there exists a reasonable possibility of ascertaining facts, is anathema to the habits of thought produced by the impact of science and technology. Any attempt at the maintenance of authoritative dicatation other than that of the expert evaluation of evidence would seem to be prima facie evidence of a vested interest functioning defensively. To justify itself and its excessive maintenance costs, a dictatorial machinery must be "delivering the goods" in some social dimension. At worst, it must at least be providing some highly acceptable ideology making for constructive social organization or action. When it has become primarily an end in itself, expending its energies not in constructive social action but in the perpetuation and maintenance of its ritual and institutional machinery it can expect to be challenged by any group or class that can make any reasonable pretense to greater social usefulness.

Just as the authoritarian behavior habits of the military man make it highly probable that he will tend to meet problems with the habits of thought dominant in his past and the methods in which he is skilled, so too are we all the victims of the themes dominant in our up-bringing. Authoritarian parents tend to produce authoritarian children, even if those children are in active rebellion against those parents. The cultural backgrounds of the past and current generation of political dictators provides interesting material for speculation. Mussolini, Franco, Salazar, Hitler, Peron and almost without exception the Latin-American dictators were or are Roman Catholics, at least in their education and upbringing. And Stalin had considerable training for the priesthood of an equally dictatorial church. Confronted with such facts one is compelled at least to ask himself what kind of causal sequences are here suggested.

The possible options are not too numerous. Apart from the suggestion that it is authoritarianism that has bred more of the same, there is the possibility that it is in a culture long dominated by clerical authoritarianism that serious cultural lags and conflicts have developed. Certainly the cultural pattern dominated by Roman clericalism has been inimical to the scientific technology and the industrialization that is dependent upon it. Catholic scientists are so scarce that even high church dignitaries have been known to comment on it. No culture pattern today lacking the advantages of mechanical ingenuity applied to human needs while yet suffering from uneven distribution of such blessings through commercial relations with technologically advanced areas can be expected to be stable. Whether by chance or historical logic, it is the Roman Catholic Church that has long been dominant in many of these backward areas and can no more escape responsibility for that backwardness than the Republicans could, rightly or wrongly, avoid the odium of economic depression in the 1932 U. S. elections. Perhaps it was not just fortuitous chance that industrialization came first to the land that first threw off completely the Roman yoke. There are, after all, some incompatibles in cultural patterns.

There is no implication here that the Roman Catholic culture pattern has any corner on the general reluctance of the well-established to resist innovation. The old Chinese culture, almost completely devoid of a priesthood, nonetheless long resisted the encroachments of the western technology. That technology however, had such insidious appeal, as well as potent military pressure on its side, that China long suffered from the same uneven and disorganizing impact of it. Yet there are those who seem appalled at the apparently "religious" character of the current social movements in that relatively godless and priestless land, whose chief animus is that of redressing a too long existing technological imbalance.

The similarity of the belief and behavior processes in all social movements, whether religious or secular, has never been better illuminated than by Eric Hoffer in "The True Believer" (Harper & Brothers, 1951). Its reading cannot be too strongly urged.

CHAPTER XII

CONTEMPORARY MAGICO-RELIGIOUS
MANIFESTATIONS

Viewed strictly in terms of its scientifically defensible position, animism of all sorts has indeed fallen upon evil days. The
progress and extension of the scientific method has driven it
from a succession of erstwhile unassailable ramparts. Like
primitive peoples generally, the early church fathers thought
of souls and spirits and ghosts as composed of diffuse matter
or material of some sort. At the end of the second century A.D.
Tertullian could confidently hold that all that is real is body.
But when he specifically held that "the corporeality of God
does not detract from His sublimity" one can begin to detect
the trend away from the primitive monistic universe in which
materiality and reality were identical. Why else was he specifically motivated to enter such a denial? By the 5th Century
A.D., St. Augustine was already describing the soul as an "immaterial substance." The contemporary Catholic catechism expressly denies body to spirit, but the efficacy of spirit as an
effective agent is unquestioned in all contemporary theological
speculation or dogma. Generally, the entire area of the more
complex mental processes is claimed as the domain and function of the "spirit." Thus, for example, a Catholic writer holds
in an article on St. Thomas in Baldwin's Dictionary of Philosophy and Psychology: "The essential irreducibility of attention,
abstraction, comparison, reasoning, self-consciousness, and free
will to organic processes, such as those of the external senses,
the imagination and the sensuous memory, is the ground of

spirituality and immortality." Such specific designation of only
the "external senses" leads one to suspect that this devout
writer was not unaware of the very strong evidence of the role
played by *internal* senses in the higher mental processes. But
these internal senses still have no official recognition as existing
in these same theological circles; so they cannot be permitted
to influence his thinking in this matter.

Lay opinion can confidently be expected to be verbalized
in general conformity to contemporary religious indoctrination
since practically nowhere in the entire educational machinery
does the average student encounter any of the current scientific
researches into the question, nor any systematic presentation
of what might by any reasonable stretch of the imagination be
called a deterministic view of human behavior. Even most
teachers of college psychology prefer to take a "let sleeping
dogs lie" attitude toward the matter, in view of the vigilant,
entrenched, and organized theological machinery ready to call
to the attention of college administrative officers anything even
remotely resembling an attack upon, or disrespect for their
dogma or mythology, in public or private schools alike. The
author once sponsored a minor piece of research by an under-
graduate into the membership of an organization of atheists,
designed to throw some light into the various psychological and
sociological factors that entered into the making of the atheist.
Not by any stretch of the imagination could anything in the
study be interpreted as in any way sponsoring or approving of
either atheism in general or this organization in particular, no
more than a study of prostitution by a sociologist would imply
approval of that vice by the sociologist or his employing college. But some vigilant heresy hunters, the spiritual sons and
grandsons of those who forbade the study of the human anatomy, were right there, Johnny on the spot, to demand of the
college authorities that they stop such research activities. The
barbarians were apparently mollified by the administrators in
question when it was pointed out by them that the data obtained could be as useful to discredit such an organization as
to shed glory upon it. Similarly, a discussion once arose in a
class on the possibilities of parthenogenetic reproduction in

humans during which the author asserted that such was not at all impossible in the human species, merely relatively improbable, in any one particular case. A large fraction of the class thought it rather amusing when upon being questioned I disclaimed all knowledge or even opinion as to the role played by ghostly agents in such cases but instead held that one would have to concede the possibility of such occurrences without any intervention by supernatural agencies. A militant auxiliary of a religious organization in which considerable doctrinal importance is attached to this matter as an item of faith promptly denounced me to my college authorities for having ridiculed religious faith. We are probably not as far removed from the fires of the inquisition as we think. One might ask, has it ever occurred that an organization such as the American Association for the Advancement of Science has made formal protest when some member of the clergy has been guilty of out and out scientific error, or of an attack upon the methods and structure of the sciences? If such has ever occurred it has escaped my attention, and I can find no one who can recall any such happening. But the college administrator probably does not exist that would in such cases just remind the theologians to keep their noses out of areas in which they had no professional competence. In the first place the populace at large has no general understanding of scientific method, nor has it any respect for science except as a provider of minor miracles. As for being reconciled to a deterministic account of human behavior, that is rare indeed even among contemporary philosophers. So the college administrator must perforce mollify such vested interests as quite correctly find their entire position and function under scientific fire. The public educational institution is always responsive to organized political pressure, even of a minority group. "Don't make three friends if to do so will make one enemy" is still good political calculus. It would indeed have to be a well-endowed private institution that could afford to incur the wrath of organized contranaturalism, particularly in these days when opposition to it has been effectively identified in the popular mind with economic collectivism and practically all evils. Should one wonder why academic authorities find it so easy to mollify the vigilant theological would-be inquisitors it need but be remembered that administrative ability is in its essence largely a capacity for placating irate individuals. In this case the process is no doubt facilitated by the happy coincidence that college administrators rank considerably above the academic average in piety. They thus constitute an excellent buffer behind which scientific pursuits can thrive.

But, as before said, lay opinion is today far closer to theological doctrine than to scientific findings. Particularly in the area of psychology, general habits of thought and manners of speech tend to outweigh the effects and the logic of scientific findings. A recent sample taken by the author of upper-class college students, all with a minimum of a year's work in psychology, were probed on their reactions to the concept of "immaterial substance." Only 36% felt positively that the expression was meaningless and contradictory, another 23% thought similarly but did not feel so positive about it. 23% felt confident that the expression was valid and meaningful; another 18% accepted it but without feeling positive about it. A similar probe on the question of the belief that the purely non-material might have causal efficacy in or on the material world gave the following distribution of opinions: 34% felt confident that such was a possible and familiar course of events, another 17% agreed but without confidence. 32% confidently thought such to be completely impossible, another 16% agreed but lacked the confidence of certainty. "Mind" was held to be the non-material agent that had causal efficacy in the material world. Here we have in college upperclassmen, all with some training in contemporary psychology, still a majority, if indeed a slim one, agreeing with the traditional theological-philosophical metaphysics.

Meantime, the invasion of science into the bases of animism goes on apace. As I write this, I pause to glance over the Sunday Times and find[1] a report that botanists and biochemists at Washington University, St. Louis, Missouri have succeeded in splitting apart the molecule that is the tobacco mosaic virus and then resynthesizing it into something that behaves like a normal living virus. Even allowing for the gap that frequently exists between the report of even a good journalist and that of the scientists themselves as to just exactly what has been accomplished, it is at worst only a question of time before this will have been accomplished if this report should prove a bit premature, which it probably is not since significant intervening steps have been taken by others since the first crystallization of this virus by Stanley almost twenty years ago, and since essentially the same result was achieved by somewhat different methods in California a few months before. This constitutes probably the sharpest blow ever struck against the old dichotomy of the living as opposed to the non-living; far more impressive than the first artificial synthesis of an organic compound but little more than a century past. If one is to adhere to animism, the options which confront one here are not too numerous. One can take the familiar position of denying souls, or spirits, or animistic agents to viruses, or any living things below man. Or one can assert that the animistic "principle" of each virus molecule hastened back into the united structure with its resynthesis. Or, one can hold that the material, organic, synthesis simultaneously creates the animistic essence as an "emergent," a product that is more than a sum of its components. Or, one might dismiss animism completely as a hypothesis having no instrumental value whatever.

At any event, there can be no question but that any extension of a mechanism or a determinism into any of the phenomena of life will enormously weaken the position of animism everywhere. And, as McDougall aptly put it:[2]

"But while religion, superstition, and the hope of a life beyond the grave, have kept alive amongst us a variety of animistic beliefs—, modern science and philosophy have turned their backs upon Animism of every kind with constantly increasing decision; and the efforts of modern philosophy have been largely directed toward the ex-cogitation of a view of man and of the world which shall hold fast to the primacy and efficiency of mind or spirit, while rejecting the animistic conception of human personality. My prolonged puzzling over the psychophysical problem has inclined me to believe that these attempts cannot be successfully carried through, and that we must accept without reserve Professor Tylor's dictum that Animism "embodies the very essence of spiritualistic, as opposed to materialistic, philosophy," and that the deepest of all schisms is that which divides Animism from Materialism."

On page xiii of the same preface this author recognizes the dependence of beliefs in personal survival beyond bodily death upon the acceptance of animism and foresees the former disappearing with the latter. And he continues: "Nevertheless, I am in sympathy with the religious attitude toward life; and I should welcome the establishment of sure empirical foundations for the belief that human personality is not wholly destroyed by death. For, as was said above, I judge that this belief can only be kept alive if a proof of it, or at least a presumption in favor of it, can be furnished by the methods of empirical science."

This position of Professor McDougall's is very interesting. Where the theologians ask one to accept on faith their particular "revelations" or testimonies out of the past for a complete account of both the here and the hereafter, this scientist tells us we will have to look for empirical evidence for our beliefs, and in effect predicts that the long-run consequences of failure in empirical evidence will mean the abandonment of the religious metaphysics of animism, which eventuality he faces with foreboding. But what kind of evidence can we expect from the empirical sciences? Where are we to look for it? It is to be noted that at this level of sophistication it is no longer a question of testing a belief by asking favors of the gods involved, be it victory in a basket-ball game or, as in the year 1954 when the Hurricane Prevention Prayer Group of Miami, Florida, reported complete success in keeping all hurricanes away during that year, as reported by the Associated Press on October 29th. What is demanded by Professor McDougall is evidence that will stand up under critical inquiry for the survival of the personality beyond the death of the body that once produced that personality or at least "housed" it. Since the purported "evidence" submitted by those who make a profession of communicating with the dead fills but few indeed of the criteria of scientific evidence, McDougall, and most animistic philosophers too, apply their ingenuity in attemping to show that the activity of the living human demands somthing *more* than physical or material events, that the contemporary "materialism" is completely inadequate as an account of the activities of man. Today's attempts to defend the thesis of human survival must perforce claim that there is something more to man than the physical organism. And they must do it in the face of increasingly detailed and sophisticated insight into all aspects of human activity. Nonetheless, all the old favorites are trotted out, of which the assertion that an act of "will" is something more than, or other than a deterministic, stimulus-response process is the favorite. Out of the descriptive adjective "conscious," a noun "consciousness" is reified and a whole system of metaphysics built upon its dubious foundation.

Everything that psychologists have learned about symbolic and thought processes in the last twenty years is completely ignored. It is baldly asserted that the measurable processes, without which symbolic and thought processes simply do not take place, are not the "thoughts" themselves, thereby implying that "pure" thought takes place in a realm of pure "mind" somewhere, and is something "other than" the activities and processes that scientific methods have detected and identified. This is much like asserting that there yet is a realm of "real sunrises" in spite of the fact that a rotating earth is a more exact statement of what is actually going on. But the commonest device that permits the persistence of the old animisms or dualisms is that of limiting the role of sensory processes or "sense perception" to that involving the traditional "five senses." The vital role played by the kinesthetic senses is never mentioned. Here is a typical passage illustrating this neglect of the very senses without which anything even remotely resembling the higher mental processes would be impossible:

"The facts concerning which it (mathematics) seeks to make discoveries are not those which perceptual observation exhibits: nothing that the nose, the tongue, the eye, the ear, or the skin perceives is part of the subject matter of mathematics.—What the mathematicians must observe instead is the *concepts* which those (mathematical) symbols stand for, and the logical relations among those concepts. And, for observation of objects of this kind, sense perception is neither necessary nor practicable, nor indeed relevant at all."[3]

Such a statement could only be made by one completely innocent of any contact with the experimental findings in regard to the neurology and physiology of the fifteen or more senses rather than the traditional "five" with which the body is equipped, as well as with any of the recent work on the reactions and the activity that *are* symbolic or thought processes. For such philosophers, "concepts," "observations," and "relations" are by definition and by unquestioned assumptions denizens of a world apart from anything that objective science can ever hope to reach, except perhaps by a process of "introspection" which is at best a falling back upon old and familiar verbal habits and which can be depended upon to confirm past traditions in regard to the operation of "the mind." The modern concept of the individual as a largely self-stimulating, continually and dynamically active organism, whose "mental" powers are a function of very real and very much material and habitual response-patterns acquired painfully and laboriously over the years, is completely foreign to these mystics who talk today about human capacities in language that would still be perfectly intelligible to Plato or Aristotle, were they yet around. They are firm in their conviction that a "sunrise" is something *other than* our reactions to a rotating earth; that the bodily states or activities *invariably* present and measurable when we can or do report a "mental" event, but for which we frequently do not and cannot give "mental" reports when accurate apparatus convincingly reports their presence none the less, are something wholly different from the reactions we make when we report their presence, and that these "subjective" events provide the basis for the significant duality of mind and matter, of which the former constitutes an effective causal agency in the world of gram, centimeter, second, events, without itself having these characteristics! This is apparently the price we pay for being indoctrinated too early with the philosophical systems that were developed in the days before the development of a scientific account of human behavior, and it is precisely such archaic habits of thought that dominate current attempts at understanding the religious as well as the other segments of human behavior.

There have always been people who have not been happy over the painful, slow, laborious, and pedestrian dependence upon the testimony of the senses for their wishes, hopes, and beliefs. In the days before they were better understood as products of a 'heat-oppressed brain' as Macbeth put it, visions and hallucinations stood in high repute in many cultures, and many a civilization still today suffers under the dead hand of the hallucinations of men long gone. The wishes and hopes for authoritative wisdom have skipped lightly over the barriers of hard facts. Note how the process is at work even today in our thinking. For those largely verbalized aspects of our behavior, for the activities elicited under conditions of conflicting action tendencies and situations for which we do not possess any too well practiced or familiar reactions, we have designated the adjective "conscious." By reifying that modifier of nouns into a noun in its own right we have left a lot of cumbrous reality behind; "consciousness" now becomes an entity in and of itself. By the magic of words we can now easily think of a "consciousness" apart from the processes once merely characterized as "conscious" and from this it is but a short conceptual step to accepting the notion of completely non-material entities, minds, souls, or spirits, floating about in the universe, without their having lost the capacities for effective action their material progenitors had! It was learning a bit too much about gases and other forms of matter that drove us to this complete dematerialization of these semantic derivatives. Primitive peoples are not embarrassed with the wisdom that made this dematerialization necessary and can hence live in a "universe," in a single dimension of reality with such supernaturals as they might invent. But these disembodied entities which we have conveniently "freed" from the material limitations of the earthbound senses now invite even gayer flights of fancy. It becomes seemingly reasonable that such agencies should be capable of mental powers untrammeled by the pedestrian limitations of ordinary sense perception. And, surely enough, here come the apostles of Extra-Sensory Perception!

Were anyone to come along with claims that he could significantly improve upon chance in "perceiving" things or events not accessible to our conventional sense data and were making these claims in regard to really practical matters such as the identification of inaccessible objects, or the location of items such as gold-bearing rocks or gravels, lost wallets or jewelry, or even stolen automobiles, we would rather quickly put such a fellow to practical tests and even more practical use, could he make good on his claims. Instead, these practitioners of "Extra Sensory Perception" work in a very narrowly defined aea, an area that can best be described as the area of chance variability within sharply defined limits, supplemented by the usual aids from unconscious, and possibly even conscious deception. The motivation behind the interpretations and deceptions here encountered seems to derive from the hope of providing evidence that the universe is full of mysteries "that science can't explain," that there is more to the human mind and personality than the materialistic determinants of science. The high priest of this cult, the plant physiologist J. B. Rhine was not slow to point out what every hopeful reader of the literature of parapsychology recognizes at once, namely that the results claimed by these practitioners are favorable to the possibility of survival of personality after death.[4] There we have the motive and the explanation for the uncritical acceptance of research work as "scientific" in circles, which, on any problem involving evidence on more prosaic and mundane problems not involving this obsession in regard to personal survival beyond death, would reject it at once and in toto. On such evidence they would not even buy stock in a wild-cat Canadian uranium mine.

Belief in the validity of essentially the same sort of processes as are now designated as Extra Sensory Perception, ESP for short, are ancient. What is your dowser, or water-finding witch other than this? Interestingly enough this "art" survives in regard to underground water location precisely because wells are dug or drilled, for the most part, in areas where water has already been struck and where if one but drilled deeply enough the odds in favor of finding water are excellent, dowser or no dowser. Where industrially adequate amounts of water must be found it is now common practice to employ a geologist rather than the local dowser. Similarly in the finding of oil. One might well ask, why are these practitioners who claim extra-sensory powers of perception, or *for* whom our plant physiologist claims such powers, wasting their time guessing the designs on cards (with conveniently tell-tale clues discernible from their backs) when there is "oil to be spotted under them thar anti-clines," to paraphrase an old western idiom? If perceptions can be freed from dependence upon sense data, all that is necessary is to add a bit of such perceptive power to what the geologist can perceive in the rock strata and we will all come burning punk sticks before the shrines of ESP. Or, even more dramatically, and before audiences most likely to be quickly impressed, anticipate the fall of the dice or the ball's behavior on the roulette table with just an edge over the house percentage. The psychology department of a southern university recently had a phone call from a party who was highly indignant when she was told, "No, the department does not teach Extra Sensory Perception"! Even a modest but consistent demonstration of such prowess in but a few individuals would make such calls and such demands a commonplace. Lest we wonder why such fallacies retain a modicum of respectability in uninformed circles for so long a time, let us recall that astrology still has its devotees after some six thousand years without any confirmatory evidence, and a hundred or more years of faith without any experimental confirmation and with plenty of evidence to the contrary has not eliminated the faithful followers of the phrenologists. Table tipping too, still has its incurable devotees, and for the same reasons in human motivation: to get assurances in regard to some matters that are strongly in doubt but even more strongly desired. Evidences against dramatic beliefs or wishes simply do not make news. The New York Times recently featured a report on an article in the August 26, 1955 issue of Science by a chemist, Dr. George R. Price in the medical department of the University of Minnesota, which attacked the methods, pro-

cedures, and conclusions of the devotees of ESP. But the beliefs under attack were so newsworthy that the photograph
accompanying the news item was that of the plant physiologist
whose work was under attack. Lombroso's dramatic theories of
the physical stigmata of criminals were quickly challenged
and refuted by Goring. But who has ever heard of the latter?

Early in 1938 Professor Harold Gulliksen published a very
careful, scholarly and critical resume of the work in ESP that
was available up to that date.[5] In this summary it was pointed
out that the Rhine volume failed to describe at all clearly the
research methods used; that the statistical methods used tended
to overestimate the significance of the results; that the special
methods used could under proper conditions have their face
patterns and figures read from the backs as this writer can
testify to having seen done; that the subjects whose "extra-
sensory" powers were being tested on these cards were told
what cards actually were turned up successively, either one at
a time or in groups of five, so that, like any good card player,
they could deduce what was left from the cards already disposed of, and that the record sheets provided and copyrighted
by the promoters of ESP were so arranged as to increase the
possibility of favorable data in recording calls. In addition
there were in Rhine's work serious discrepancies between the
experimental "facts" as reported and his speculations about
these facts.

What fond belief and strong motivation will do to critical
judgment is beautifully described by Gulliksen in this same
article:[6]

"When dealing with the situation where results favorable to
ESP are found first and at a later date sensory cues are discovered, Rhine indulges in an unusual mode of reasoning. We
may illustrate this by reference to Lady, "the mind-reading
horse." Rhine reports observations on a telepathic horse. He
used various controls to eliminate gradually the cues given by
the owner. Later he found, on repeating the experiment with
the *same* controls, that the horse could no longer succeed in
demonstrating telepathic powers as she had formerly done,
when cues from the owner were gradually eliminated. Given

such data, many scientists would have concluded that the horse might have been responding to sensory cues even during the first experiment, when these cues were not noticed by the experimenter. Rhine says that these negative findings may be taken "as a check upon our earlier conclusions." "We were forced to conclude that the telepathic ability we earlier found the horse to possess has been now almost if not entirely lost." He also points out that if during the first experiment the horse had used "sensory cues she should have improved in training during the interval. Anyone familiar with animals knows that they may forget also."

"The unusual line of reasoning applied to the telepathic horse is stoutly defended *in principle* by Rhine. In discussing the Creary sisters, who were thought for a time to have extra-sensory powers and later were found to be attempting to signal to one another, he points out that the presence of trickery in their *later* tests is unjustifiably regarded as casting a doubt over their earlier successful results in telepathy.[7] He argues that "it is a poor kind of cheating which grows worse with practice." One might with equal justification retort that it is a poor kind of observation that doesn't increase in acuity as it proceeds, possibly discovering trickery not at first noticed."

One might well wonder what would suddenly motivate a pair of sisters such as these to begin trying to "improve" on their "extrasensory" powers with aids from their very ordinary, prosaic, and material senses! Unless one approached such a situation with prior bias in favor of the existence of extrasensory powers one would draw the same conclusions here as in the case of questions concerning the sources of previously displayed wealth for which there were no known sources, after having caught a man in a theft. One could give good odds that his previous splurges had been financed by similar devices.

But what of the evidence purporting to "prove" the operation of extra-sensory forces? In 1937 when Rhine published his "New Frontiers of the Mind," Gulliksen could find eight "confirmatory" studies, if the work if a Florida grammar school is counted, and also if the studies from one college giving an average of 5.5 correct card identifications against "chance" scores of 5. Nowhere but at Rhine's home base were averages as high as ten or fifteen out of twenty-five reported. In other "confirmatory" studies, even the "best" subjects averaged but seven or eight. Against these results, obtained under conditions not clearly specified, there were clear failures to confirm any such powers in subjects at six colleges and universities. And what about the conditions under which "positive" results are claimed? Let me again quote Professor Gulliksen now at Princeton University:[8]

"We have, when we consider all of the facts in the case, very marked limitations. This marvelous ESP ability is found primarily with a special deck of cards. It does not even seem to extend successfully to ordinary playing-cards, which would give some people a new leverage on bridge and poker. It is a "weak and delicate" ability that "fades" when subjected to hostility or doubt;[9] and even when carefully nurtured at the Duke Laboratory and not subjected to observation of doubting outsiders, it fades anyhow (New Frontiers, p. 97)."

Until convincing results can be obtained with really sound controls and with skeptical outsiders present, it is a far simpler hypothesis to assume that either deliberate or unconscious deception being practiced somewhere accounts for data that involve such a large element of chance, or rather the sort of data in which sheer guessing alone is bound to turn up occasional runs of successes that deviate more or less from theoretical or expected "chance." 5000 throws with 12 dice have yielded results differing significantly from chance expectation.[10] Such "runs" are the bane of research projects of all sorts.

John Mulholland reports[11] that he and Professor Pitkin prevailed upon the International Business Machines Corporation to run two hundred thousand cards through their machines, half white and half red, all cards being numbered with digits from 1 through 5, giving twenty thousand with each digit in the white cards and another twenty thousand with each digit in the red cards. The cards were then shuffled mechanically, one color at a time and run through the machine with a tape record of the number sequences as they occurred for the white and for the red cards. These two series then gave somthing approaching a "chance" series corresponding to the "exta-sensory perceiving" of Rhine's cards. Pure "chance" would have one correspondence between the two series in every five pairs. Some sequences of 32 figures failed to produce a matching pair. Runs of five matching pairs in sequence occurred well below the expected frequency and those of six successive matchings were as much above chance expectation as the sequences of five fell below. Runs with seven successive matchings came 59 percent more frequently than "chance," while the runs of eight occurred 780 percent more frequently than could be theoretically expected! The first forty thousand pairs produced three times as many runs of five as did the next sixty thousand! Here are "chance" differences large enough to demonstrate the fact that deviations from chance are to be expected and in themselves prove nothing except that they do not presuppose extra-sensory power on the part of the one card-series to anticipate the next.

Any number of events happen that on the face of them are highly improbable. Joe Doaks draws a horse in the Irish Sweepstakes. The odds against such a draw must be of the order of a quarter-million to one. But there it is, it has happened! It does not prove that there is anything wrong with the laws of probability, nor that the left hind foot of a graveyard rabbit caught by Joe in the dark of the moon made any contribution to the event. A few people always draw horses. With the Rhine cards, but not nearly so frequently with good old-fashioned playing cards for some subtle reason, *some* subjects, *for limited time periods,* make runs of correct calls that deviate considerably from chance expectation in some of the tests that have been reported. Similarly, other subjects have "runs" that produce more than the chance number of *incorrect* calls! We must overlook these subjects whose capacities one would have to call "extra-sensory illusory powers" if we are to claim that extra-sensory perception occurs. But with such standards of evidence one can "prove" the therapeutic efficacy of Bishop Berkeley's "tar water," "Christian Science," and Lydia E. Pinkham's Vegetable Compound. With no better evidence than has appeared, even from the "laboratories" claiming the greatest successes when *all* the data are included, those of the subjects that failed to produce results as well as those from the successful cases, not one penny would have been invested by hard-headed business men if the "evidence" in question were that of the improvement above "chance" of all cases upon which a vaccine had been tried. Before any layman even so much as hears about a new therapeutic device it has already had careful tests that would shame the methodology of the devotees of ESP. The more dramatic, surprising, or upsetting experimental results are, the more does an honest scientist check and double check his results. He passes on his directions to others to try. He seeks out flaws in the experimental techniques, he fights off publicity. Note the contrast with the procedures of the founders of ESP: results obtained without standardized procedures are publicized, select data are featured and emphasized, and the subject is at once commercialized. Small wonder then that the scientific world has by and large ignored the work, leaving its publicizing to the theologians and philosophers.

Professor C. Lockard Conley of the Johns Hopkins College of Medicine once related in a conversation that in testing for a rare blood type variant, thirteen of the first fourteen cases found were women! Continued testing, however, shortly evened up the sex ratio. Many a gambler has been impressed with the long runs of chance that have gone against him, if not by the runs that have gone his way! Yet if anyone honestly wanted to test "perceptive" powers where all sensory cues were ruled out and where such runs of lucky guesses were improbable, it would be a very simple matter indeed to devise materials that would be practically free both of chance hits and the errors of recording that tend to favor the count of hits. Why not use cards with completely unspecified content? The reason the "researchers" in ESP do not use such cards is quite simply that such procedures would quickly destroy all pretensions to perceptive powers of this sort. Instead, they continually prefer materials where "results" can be shown, as, for example, with supposedly random numbers. But when one human being makes up what he might assume to be "random" number series, it has been shown that such series are definitely not random, that our past habits with numbers, odd-even series, lucky numbers, trinities, and what not, tend to favor certain numbers and sequences, with the result that the "chance" arranging of series by an experimenter and the "chance" guessing by the subject result in statistically significant improvements over chance. When such sources of error were corrected for and truly random number series used, as well as large numbers of subjects, negative results were found, as one could safely predict in the first place.[12] With games of chance already so long with us, how could such unusual powers, as the devotees of ESP assert they now have discovered, been overlooked? The lucky possessors of such powers would long have cornered the world's goods. The devices that are presumed to identify individuals with extra-sensory powers also identify some individuals with a special penchant for making errors—for a while, at least. Probably for as long as the successful subjects retain their "powers," i.e. their long runs of successes. Always assuming, of course, that both conscious and unconscious deception and bad experimental methods are excluded.

One would think that even elementary familiarity with statistics and scientific method would protect one from accepting as sound evidence the output of the devotees of ESP. But where a prior conviction exists that the stuff of the universe that is describable, in gram, centimeter, second units is not all there is to it, and that these "other" forces or agencies have real and valid functions, even such shoddy goings-on are acceptable. They are grasped at like the proverbial drowning man reaching for a straw. Thus, the philosopher, Curt J. Ducasse, writes:[13] "That telepathy, or some other form of extra-sensory perception —sometimes occurs between living persons has been demonstrated by appropriate independent experiments:—." It is interesting to note that this "evidence" for ESP is cited in support of the plausibility of evidence for the existence of a life after the physical death of the body!

When it is remembered that the current vogue for extra-sensory phenomena was launched with a special pack of cards that could be read through their backs, that the experimental methods upon which the publicity for the work was based naively permitted the subject to profit by the knowledge of which cards had already been identified, that nowhere have data been published on tests of material in which the subjects had no notion whatever of what they were to "perceive," where they would really have to *perceive* rather than guess, one can but conclude that the hopes and wishes for immortality have again motivated many to "drown their honor in a shallow cup and sell their reputations for a song," as the realistic Omar put it long ago. Were one really desirous of testing for the presence of "extra-sensory" powers one would slip a few jokers, a few cards out of a game of "Authors" or "Pit" into the decks, if it must be cards that are used. It produces a wonderful crop of red faces—and rationalizations, in people who claim ESP powers! Just apply the sort of tests you would demand if you were to pay money for the services of someone claiming such unconventional prowess! But it seems that a childish compulsiveness comes over people when emotionally reinforced beliefs and wishes are involved, or even when confronted with a baffling problem. One thinks of the childish, repeating communication codes the military minds again and again construct and guard with elaborate care, only to have them broken because of their inherent limitations. Yet completely unbreakable codes can be produced by the million as rapidly as needed. It is apparent that our enemies were not using such codes in the recent war; and probably we were not either. We seem to develop specific habits and patterns of thought for particular problems that may be completely unrealistic. We can only, for example, think of punitive measures when faced, as we are, by the problem of the use of narcotics; and that in the face of examples set by other lands of far more intelligent and effective methods of meeting the menace of addiction.

Among the "evidences" taken seriously by believers in postmortem survival are those of the spectres, ghosts, or hallucinations, seen or experienced by otherwise sane individuals. Probably the most extensive examination of this question ever undertaken is described in Volume 10 of the Proceedings of the Society of Psychical Research, some time in 1894. This work was recently given a very favorable summarizing by Russell G. MacRobert, M. D. of 555 Park Avenue, New York, in the

Journal of Insurance Medicine, Volume V, No. 3, July, 1950. Dr. MacRobert feels that this British census of hallucinations established the following conclusions: (1) that at least British citizens with a frequency of no less than one in ten in sane and healthy individuals have experienced sensory hallucinations; (2) that these apparitions (hallucinations) of the sane are clearly distinguished from those of the insane; (3) that veridical (truth-telling) hallucinations in the form of apparitions of dying persons were found to occur with a frequency 440 times that which the laws of chance would allow, furthermore, that between deaths and apparitions of dying persons a connection exists which is not due to chance alone; and (4) that such veridical hallucinations establish the fact that the mind has a range of action which is not limited to the reach of the recognized channels of perception, and demonstrate the fact of influence of mind on mind through forces, factors or things outside the known laws of time and space.

Such conclusions might have been not too preposterous back in 1894, but they sound mediaeval in 1955, with the experimental work on conditioning of responses to self-provided cues familiar even to first year psychology students, and more specifically since experimental work has definitely established the ready conditioning of imagery. Professor Clarence Leuba of Antioch College[14] has provided the experimental bases for far simpler explanations of hallucinatory phenomena than the elaborate demonology of the Society for Psychical Research. Professor Leuba so conditioned his subjects that they were genuinely surprised and puzzled at the "sensations" conditioned in them by their own imagery or imaginative processes. The fortuitous linkages resulting from temporal contiguity in associative processes have been familiar phenomena since Aristotle's time. It is theoretically possible that almost any cue or cues might well become the conditioners eliciting previous reactions or compromises or combinations or mixtures of previous experiences. Such response processes may seem complex to the individual who does not know his literature of experimental conditioning, but let us just match it for simplicity with what one would otherwise have to asume by way of explanations of the phenomena in the ghostly realm. Let us say we have here the phenomenon of a vivid hallucination or apparition that is to be "explained." The hallucination is that of a fully clothed person. Strange, isn't it, that there are no apparitions of naked ghosts! Yet, as the hard-headed old observation has it, if ghosts have clothes, clothes too must have ghosts! Well, perhaps there has been a stray naked ghost seen, but they are admittedly scarce as the proverbial hens' teeth. But think of the complications this introduces into the metaphysics of the realm of ghosts! Not only must once-alive human personalities survive death, but wraith-like doubles of all their once-worn clothing too must survive, including all the myriad stockings discarded prematurely because of untimely "runs"! Either that, or else it will have to be assumed that a ghost has the power of creating for itself a suitable garb. But if that is the case, it is obvious that ghosts are an unimaginative lot; they are always seen in much the same garb as they affected while living. Now I submit, compared to such complications of theory the experimentally verifiable phenomena of conditioning or "association" if you prefer, are simplicity itself. There we know that just as in dreams the activity of brain and body can produce more or less real and at the same time more or less distorted images, memories, and even overt activity. Usually such things or processes do not intrude during the waking state. But a reverie, some perhaps not consciously reacted-to but still effective stimulus either from the environment or in the continuously dynamic activity of the living body, or fortuitous imagery of some sort might well have provided the cues that produced, among other effects, just the particular conditioned sensation or imagery that, in its particular context, was so startling. But in such an event, the hallucination would tend to have the characteristics of the objects as known in past experience. The "ghosts" would more than likely be dressed!

If further evidence were needed to confirm the naturalistic interpretations of such hallucinations or imagery one could not help but observe that any theory that sought to hold that it was actually "materialized" spirits that were being perceived would have to explain why such visions, hallucinations, or imagery, whether experienced during sleep or while awake, quite frequently include persons or things still living or existent. To make things worse, the living persons dreamed about or seen in visions can confidently assert that they recall nothing of the sort of activity experienced in these "visions." To get past such a difficulty, very complicated hypotheses indeed would have to be spun. The inanimate things experienced in such visions too, would have to be equipped with ghostly "doubles" if the ghost hypothesis were not to be left as full of holes as the proverbial sieve.

That dreams or visions sometimes anticipate events or reveal "facts" not otherwise known to the subject has long impressed susceptible individuals, particularly those who are looking for evidence confirmatory of animistic theories and of personal survival beyond death. It is visions more or less coincidental with the death of the person seen in the vision that have most fascinated the psychic researchers. The well-known British census on such visions examined this matter and came up with some startling conclusions. From the death-rate figures of the country they deduced the statistical prospects of any individual dying on a particular day. Their reports on visions were examined to find what percentage of all visions of persons were experienced within one day of the actual death of the person contacted in such a hallucination or "vision." They concluded that such coincidence exceeded chance expectancy by some 440 times! The committee came to the conclusion that "between deaths and apparitions of the dying person a connection exists which is not due to chance alone." "There are none so blind," as the old saying goes, "as those who will not see." Something is indeed loading these statistics, but does it necessarily point in the direction of spooky goings-on? Hardly. Such data as here presented mean nothing at all until broken down in detail. To begin with, these figures of coincidences include apparitions seen *before* the death of the individual identified in the apparition. One might wonder if this implies that even at the approach of death the spirit begins a few tentative journeys, calling upon old friends or relatives, without having recalled such a journey before dying. Then there is the little matter of the age distribution of the persons whose deaths "coincided," *give or take a day,* with their doubles having been seen, not to mention the little matter of the state of their health, usually known to those who have these visions, or see apparitions. Without corrections for these two factors, namely the matter of age and general life-expectancy as well as specific state of health or of the particular hazards of occupation as in the case of death premonitions of soldiers known to be in combat areas, such comparisons against "chance" are completely meaningless. One is also compelled to ask just what explains the apparitions identified as individuals that did not shortly die after having been thus caught off base, so to speak? Also, what reason is there for making a great distinction, as the psychical researchers did, between the visions seen while wide awake as against those experienced during sleep or dreams and in transition states between sleeping and waking? True, the dream phenomena are considerably more commonplace, but who has not heard of viridical, i.e. truth-telling dreams? Nor are the Freudian "interpreted" truths being referred to here; practically everyone has had or has heard of "dreams that came true," literally as well as figuratively. Yet these phenomena would then seem to constitute an entirely different realm of reality, presumably having far more naturalistic or deterministic causes or explanations than any hallucinations which occurred while the experiencer thought of himself as wide awake, normal, and presumably sober.

Another factor frequently overlooked by people who recount their dreams or visions is the little matter of the time of recall of these hallucinatory experiences. This author too, can relate dreams that were veridical. But the dream experience frequently is not recalled until the confirmatory event occurs. Then, suddenly the dream vision is recalled vividly, and one can then truly report: "Just about at the same time that the relative died I dreamed that he had died," although the dream may not have been recalled until the messenger boy was at the door with the telegram. These occurrences are not nearly so impressive when one is reminded that almost without exception these dreams are of deaths of persons the state of whose health is known to be precarious. Dreams or hallucinations revealing the deaths of anything other than soldiers known to be in active service, ill or aged persons, or of individuals whose deaths would be convenient for reasons of romance or finance, are rare indeed. Factors such as this which completely invalidate the raw statistics of frequency are so obvious that the only puzzle is why they are not at once apparent to everyone directly upon encountering the data which involve them. Such strictures on data tend to be overlooked by people who are already convinced that there is some special significance in such visions and that they tend to substantiate some fondly held beliefs.

Similar fallacies are to be found in all the evidence perennially offered for the existence of telepathic processes, or presumed powers of direct communication between individuals at a distance without any of the ordinary devices involving sensory processes. What is relied upon for "proof" of communicative processes is similarities or correspondences between what one subject "sent" and the other "received." Correspondences in excess of "chance" are frequently claimed, especially by pairs of experimenters who have long lived together or been in intimate association, as is the case with a famous novelist and his wife. Instead of working with unique materials which would really test the capacity of one "mind" to arouse predictable responses in another at a distance they prefer to communicate whatever sentiments or ideas that the moods of the moment may suggest when they happen to be separated. The similarities that turn up in their transcribed ideas are then ascribed to mental telepathy. This, of course, magnifies many times the type of error found in ESP experiments when supposedly "random" number series were used. It would be very strange if people after a long and congenial life together did not have many similarities in almost any sample of random thoughts. Such cultural limitations of the range of possibilities is encountered in much of the supposed evidence for "mental telepathy." A recent television program, supposedly tested the power of one mind to communicate directly with another. Three pairs of experimenters were shown, in each pair one person was to

"send," the other to "receive." The sender was to try to communicate directly to the other the content of a picture, which
the "receiver" was to draw. The nearest thing to recognizable
similarity of content that emerged from this test was something vaguely resembling a structure of some sort drawn by
one of the "receivers" where the picture to have been communicated did have as one part of its content a clear and conspicuous house, but not in the same location. The enthusiast
for telepathy who was putting on the demonstration claimed
a partial success. I kept tally of the next fifty pictures that came
into my line of vision; roughly one-third of them contained
houses or buildings. Even a rough check on the content of
sketches and painting will reveal a rather limited range of
subject matter. Sheer chance will show that much similarity in
sketches drawn, as these were, by young college student subjects. I'll be impressed when a Hottentot regularly duplicates
the non-representative sketch of a Greenwich Villager—and I'll
look sharply for some system of mirrors or signals that establishes effective communication between them, particularly if
they are "cashing in" on their success. A former student, now
a professor of psychology, with a confederate, put on a dramatic demonstration of telepathy before a class at Cornell
University, so convincing in fact that even after they had revealed the system of signaling in Morse code with ear-wiggles
some of the students still held to the theory that it was "telepathy" that was used![15]

Such are the current manifestations of the survivals of animistic habits of thought among the relatively literate and educated elements of the population. A comparison of this animism
with primitive or naive habits of thought reveals only a change
in the areas of phenomena in which the animistic preconceptions remain acceptable. The basic animistic idea itself survives
unchanged. That basic concept is, briefly put, the acceptability of a conception of causality that does not demand conformity to a calculus of "mechanical" or deterministic antecedents conforming in general to the concept of the conservation
of energy, but instead assuming the existence of processes of
causality after the manner of the popular, but erroneous, con-

ception of personal "will" or "volition," which basically assumes a non-material agency of some sort that is yet somehow effective in determining events and processes in the material world. Such "wills," "motives" or "powers" may be ascribed to anthropomorphic personalities of infinitely magnified power and potency, but of course assumed to be as non-material or "spiritual" as the powers which they wield. In fact, it is not at all unusual to assume an identity of the "personalities" and their "powers." The areas in which animistic agents intervene, and how frequently such intervention occurs, is much in dispute, and pretty much reflect the sophistication of the disputants. The relatively naive confidently seek and court intervention in the most trifling and deterministic of human and material problems. At the other end of the scale are those who look with horror at requests for animistic intervention in any mundane affairs *with the exception of* interventions in the matter of individual desires and motives or "will." It is interesting to note that these latter are for the most part rather well informed as to the causal processes involved in diseases, economic matters, and meteorology; but generally they reject a determinism in human behavior at some level: if not perhaps in matters of crime or delinquency, then assuredly in at least some creative activity; if not in saccharine popular verse, then in the writing of Hamlet! The last ditch fight is over the matter of human volition. Once that is surrendered there is no place for animism to retreat into. When the evidence for a determinism in human personality becomes embarrassingly convincing it is met with a moral judgment that it is "debasing the human spirit" or "reducing it to a mechanism." Actually, the extension of determinism to all of human behavior, to man's moral make-up, to his virtues as well as to his vices, his successes as well as his failures, far from paralyzing moral action cannot help but infuse this entire area with new life and new significance. No longer can we "pass the buck" to some inscrutable or transcendental agency. Every moral shortcoming of everyone will become a challenge to intelligent research and action. Every human failure, every disappointment will constitute a challenge to our ingenuity and our dedication.

An intelligent determinism has nothing in common with a
gloomy predestination, nor with idiotic doctrines such as that
of the Hindu Karma where ritualistic failures or oversights are
presumed to exact their obscene tolls. The deterministic picture
of man and the universe that emerges out of modern science
is instead one devoid of certainties as well as of impossibilities.
But above all, it is a world free from childish retributive processes and whims, of gods that behave like paranoid dictators,
of delusionary fantasies that promise the rewards of yesteryear's daydreams—post mortem. Instead, we are confronted
with a world in which for once we are in a position to grasp
some of the majestic dimensions of our ignorance. But it is not
an ignorance that begets despair; instead, it challenges us to
plan and carry out organized attacks upon it. This is a world
in which our every action has potentialities for unlimited consequences. It is a world that calls for innovating trial and error
rather than for the self-hypnosis of repetitive rituals. Only the
completely ignorant could complain that the deterministic
world as depicted by modern science was in any sense whatever an "oversimplification." Instead, it promises endless ave-
nues of discovery or at least the promise of such. But there
never was an animistic hypothesis that was not a serious oversimplification. Animistic hypotheses "solve" current enigmas or
problems by postulating even more complex entities that have
the additional handicap of forever being beyond the reach of
experimental procedures. And no animistic hypothesis has ever
had even the remotest instrumental use or significance.

But if animism still has its articulate spokesmen in philosophical, theological, and literary circles, and a nostalgic fringe
even in the life sciences, what is to be found at lay levels of the
population? A recent sample of several hundred students in
adult education courses which in general intelligence and level
of education run far above the population average, pictures
pretty well the expected lag of the layman behind the scholar
in assimilating the scientific point of view. Historians some
years hence will no doubt treasure such small samples of attitudes and opinions as began to be fitfully recorded a few
decades ago, but even today the available data are meager

enough, and there are practically no data available on attitude distributions or opinions beyond a few decades ago, against which comparisons might be made. At any event, the recent sample of students indicated that between a quarter and a half of such a sample still accepted the premises of astrology, palmistry, and phrenology. Mysterious powers are ascribed to "mental" processes by almost one half. Over three-quarters of such a sample thinks that man's perceptive processes are limited to the traditional "five senses," while over ninety percent believe that the power of "concentration" can be developed by playing chess or checkers, and that deep breathing exercises are healthful and should be systematically practiced.

Outside of academic and educational circles, matters are still in a sorry state. As recently as the year 1928 devils were still being driven out of people by Christian priests in the state of Iowa.[16] As recently as 1951 in Minnesota two women were flogged to death in whipping rituals practiced by a deviant cult which specializes in driving out devils presumably in possession of the bodies of cult members. Beliefs in witchcraft still prompt an occasional murder in the "Hex" counties of Pennsylvania. There is a continuing demand for dog fat as a charm against tuberculosis in some parts of New York City.

Social crises such as the depression during the nineteen-thirties produced convincing evidence of the profound psychological kinship of "primitive" and the more "modern" religions. By 1931 prayer marathons from dusk to dawn seeking for relief from the depression were reported by the United Press. In Boston the mayor took part in a ceremonial in which "General D. Pression" in a black coffin was tossed into the harbor from the stern of a ferryboat. The chauffeur of the car in which the mayor rode at the head of the procession, lost his job that very same day and complained in a letter to the mayor that they had "buried the wrong guy." On December 21, 1932, the United Press filed the following dispatch from St. Joe, Arkansas:

"In a huge subterranean cavern citizens will revive a custom of celebrating Christmas together in an effort to bring back better times, just as years ago the custom banished Civil War hatreds.

A Christmas tree will be planted in a cave ten miles from here. About its candle-lit branches the people of Cave Creek Valley will clasp hands while a minister reads the story of the nativity.

This custom was observed in 1874 to abolish war hatreds among residents who supported the North and the South.

A few years ago a cedar tree planted in the cave in 1874 was cut down. Citizens of the valley say their fortunes suffered from that time, so the custom is being revived."

Here we have cleanly and clearly illustrated the major behavior processes involved in all magic, ritual, and religion. There is the ascription of causality to the unusual antecedent; there is the assumption that the activity or ceremonials observed during the time that a previous crisis was resolved had produced that resolution; and there is the reversion to these same habits when a persistent and otherwise apparently insoluble crisis appears, even if the events are separated by over fifty-five years in time. But the "elders" recalled them with the vividness and conviction of primary memories, like the prayers and articles of faith indoctrinated with the very first verbal habits.

By 1933 the New York Times reported the following:

"The depression could be solved in twenty-four hours by a "good prayer meeting in Wall Street" at which the bankers and corporation heads would confess their sins, the Rev. Dr. Norman Vincent Peale, pastor of the Marble Collegiate Reformed Church, Fifth Avenue and Twenty-ninth Street, declared yesterday morning in his sermon there.

"It is not necessary to call the business leaders to Washington to tell Congress how to end the depression," he said. "Let the bankers and speculators and great corporation heads who are guilty get down not before the Senate but before God and confess their sins, and the air will be cleared."

Apart from a powerful faith in the supernatural's capacity to intervene effectively in mundane social affairs, we also have here a clear-cut illustration of the very human weakness for confusing moral judgment with causal explanation. But this episode is cited primarily to indicate the extent to which the lay mind reverts to animistic habits of thought and scapegoating when confronted with situations in which it is as helpless as is the savage in the crises in which he resorts to similar devices. Whether such sentiments as were here expressed represented genuine and earnest convictions on the part of the pastor is completely immaterial. What is significant is that they were uttered by one of our greatest contemporary experts in the art of effectively taking the measure of the public mind. It should thoroughly chasten us if we have even the smallest remaining traces of any smug feelings of superiority to the German citizens who succumbed to a systematic attack by such blandishments under far more desperate and trying conditions than confronted us here in 1933.

By November 1934 the New York Herald Tribune published the following letter under the heading: "A Day of National Prayer":

"The Presbyterian Church has designated next Sunday, November 25, as a day of national prayer to God to get us out of the terrible mess that we are in. All other denominations are invited to join the Presbyterian Church in this great and sensible act. This is the right way to get out of our troubles—let God help us out of them. He is the only One that can do it."

Lest anyone assumed that it was the circumstance of an unprecedented business depression that touched off such animistic revivals, let it be noted that about mid-1954 when a mild business recession had produced an increase of some 24% in cashed-in insurance policies over a corresponding period of the year before, and when the prices in the mail-order catalogues were some two or three percent below previous listings, similar reversions to a ritualism appeared. The letter of a business advisory service appearing at this time, recounted the evidences of gloom and asked:

"What can business do about it? Well, down in Fulton, Ky., local business men have started praying that things will improve. They hold a half-hour devotional every Monday morning before work."

These illustrations are chosen not with any special animus against the sects involved nor against businessmen. They are but a few of the many that come to hand every day of the

general area of the functions the current mentality assigns to
the domain of spiritual forces or agencies. They are cited only
to illustrate the varied levels of complexity of phenomena at
which significant sections of the populace begin to think in
animistic terms. And, if any religion is to survive in the face
of secular competition it must be ready to provide techniques
in the traditional manner and spirit for any new frustrations, or
sources of apprehension or insecurity that an evolving culture
cannot help but create. The hazards of the highway, complicated with a significant admixture of high speeds and inhibition
removing and reaction-time slowing alcohol, cannot help but
sell a lot of insurance. But it also gives rise to anxieties that
no amount of paid-up insurance can allay. Thus it came about
that the New York Times could report on February 8, 1931, the
start of the custom of the ritual blessing of automobiles in its
city. If I have been correctly informed, this has become standard practice with some worshippers. In the days before the
menace of objects that might be dislodged under impact had
been well publicized, medals believed to have special pro-
tective powers for the traveller were sometimes attached to the
windshields of autos. Thus it was that the New Yorker Magazine, with its taste for the ironies and whimsies of life could
shortly report that the only bodily injury suffered by the pas-
sengers in such a car that was involved in an accident resulted
from the medal which broke loose because of the impact of
the collision and struck a passenger in the eye. Yet who knows?
They might all have been killed but for the saving grace of the
medal! At any event, by the year 1939 the pastor of Trinity
Church, New York, was providing his parishioners with an
especially prepared "Motorist's Prayer," according to the New
York Times.

Even in a country such as this that provides secular education for the great majority of its children, we see pilgrims
flocking to tombs and shrines in long processions. The occasional case in which long-standing habits of invalidism are
broken under conditions of great excitement and suggestion
provide the fuel that keeps all but the most statistically minded
at least in a state of doubt but what perhaps at times faith can

achieve the impossible. But the run of the mill of the faithful accept their miracles without question, and see miraculous results where there is no reason for expecting anything more complex than the normal homeostatic mechanisms and well-proven secular remedies. Nor does the average individual limit his credulity in the miraculous to official sectarian beliefs. A real-estate broker recently reported that any room or suite numbered 711 would rent for ten to twenty percent more than equivalent space on the same floor.[17] Similarly, whenever the 13th of a month falls on a Friday there is regularly reported almost everywhere in the United States a decided drop in the number of marriage licenses issued and the number of marriages performed on that day; in the New York City area this drop usually runs to around fifty percent of the normal quota for an ordinary day.

Lest one become intolerant of, or disturbed by, such whimsical peccadilloes, consider some of the aberrant cults. There are the Penitentes in New Mexico who flog each other's backs raw and bloody with thorny cactus bushes. In the daily press there are occasional references to the activity of snake cults. The United Press sent out the following dispatch from Huntsville, Alabama, July 17, 1954:

"Mrs. Wayne Gore, who believed that faith would make her immune to the serpent's bite, let a rattlesnake sink its fangs into her at a snake cult service and died two hours later, it was disclosed yesterday.

The 50-year-old zealot refused to let a doctor be called when she collapsed a few minutes after being bitten four times in her home. A large crowd watched the rite."

This cult, like many another deviant group, seems to take as its chief point of departure some particular passage in the Christian Scriptures, in this case probably the statement in regard to faith making one whole. Such is the price we pay for dispensing with authoritative interpreters of our Holy Writ!

But the logic of events in a world dominated increasingly by a scientific technology is slowly leaving its effects on popular beliefs. The survey of popular beliefs previously referred to showed that while some 95% accepted a "belief in God" only 73% were at all confident about some sort of an after-life. Hell was mentioned spontaneously by only 13%, but when pressed specifically, 52% thought the post-mortem life was divided into hell and heaven. In the face of a generally increasing popularity of organized religion in the last decade there has been also an unquestioned decline in beliefs in hells, devils, and the essential sinfulness of man. "Life" Magazine, in the issue of May 15, 1950, submitted to its readers the following comment on the modern creed:

"F. A. Voigt, a respected British essayist, has undertaken to sum up and deplore the religious beliefs common to Christendom in the past 10 years. His "articles of the contemporary creed" appear in a British Catholic publication called *The Month*, and they are worth pondering.
They include:
"Religion without God; Christianity without Christ; Christ without Antichrist; Heaven without Hell; works without faith; a God of Love but not of Wrath; a Church that can bless but cannot curse.
"We believe that God, almighty and incarnate, is but a benevolent Spirit; that Satan does not exist; that Christ was the author of an ethical code, but not the Godhead crucified. We profess to believe that He existed, for agnosticism is no longer the fashion.
"We believe that Gospels must conform with our time and not our time with the Gospels.
"We believe that man is by nature good and can, by his own efforts, attain perfection, although what 'perfection' is we do not know and hardly even care—."
This adds up to a harsh accusation. Many will think it goes to the root of the "Christian" world's troubles."

It would seem that the good essayist had done a pretty accurate job of factual reporting. There can be no doubt about the general trend in what is popularly accepted of the traditional doctrines. Apparently others have been alarmed, well before our British essayist took his pen in hand. Some time during 1936, the New York Times published a small but significant item under the heading:

Drive to Inspire Ministers Planned.
"Meetings in 25 Cities Set for Next Fall to 'Revitalize' Faith of Clergymen.
To "revitalize" faith in the Christian Gospel among ministers, twenty educators and religious leaders have been appointed to conduct meetings in twenty-five cities next Fall under the auspices of the National Preaching Mission."

That is a rear-guard action at best. Another way of meeting tendencies toward the abandonment of beliefs that might begin to look a bit incredible is to move to the offensive. When a tendency arose to question the authority of the Bishop of Rome some eighty-five years ago, Rome answered the challenge with the doctrine of papal infallibility. Recently the same pressures that produced the state of affairs lamented above by the Briton and which have resulted in much soft-pedaling, in Protestant circles, of Biblical content that puts a strain on the credulity of today's reader, has been met by the Catholic church by making a dogma out of the belief in the bodily assumption into Heaven of the Virgin Mary. It may well be that in the battle for the spirit the best defensive strategy is the attack!

It has frequently been noted that with wars and social crises there is a quickening of interest in the supernatural generally. After World War I there was, particularly in countries that had suffered heavy losses in men killed in action, a great revival of interest in attempts at communicating with the dead. Under fire from both the orthodox churches and skeptical scientists, such "spiritism" has had but feeble signs of revival in the recent post-war period, with the possible exception of West Germany where the business throve for a time. But the hard core of faithful "Spiritualists" remains, some of whom are organized into groups or "churches" and whose beliefs have acquired a characteristic immunity to contrary evidence. Such

people are surrounded by millions who take post-mortem survival of the individual for granted, and for whom the mere
addition of the possibility of effective communication with departed "spirits" represents no great obstacle. The death of a
near and dear one can easily provide the keen desire that makes
the belief completely acceptable. A new worker of minor miracles, some "medium" with just the proper approach nicely
attuned to the times, might well swell the rolls of the believers.
Professional performing magicians such as the man known as
Duninger could acquire a flock of faithful believers overnight,
merely by "admitting" to having supernatural or extra-sensory
aids in their performances. A sizeable fraction of the population is ready to insist that his performances are "impossible"
without the aid of supernatural agencies. The professional
magician, John Mulholland[18] reports that professional magicians again and again are credited by their audiences with
having supernatural powers, even in the face of their stout and
repeated denials. Apparently nothing will break down beliefs
once established. The famous Fox sisters, who as very young
and prankish girls started the vogue of spirit rappings one All
Fools' day about a century ago, repeatedly confessed their
trickery. Such confession did not prevent them from again
drawing large audiences and private clients when again the
low state of their fortunes prompted them to fall back upon
their old means of support. Currently, we have seen a professor of plant physiology and a professor of philosophy still
continue to seek for sources of "psychic" powers in spirit mediums admittedly caught in attempted deceit or in relaying
"spirit messages" from non-existent and purely fictitious characters such as the niece invented by G. Stanley Hall to test the
famous "medium," Mrs. Piper. All too many people have the
most childishly naive confidence in their ability to detect deceit
in the performances of experts in deceiving under conditions
determined by the experts in such deceit. Saddest of all is the
grim fact that evidence of deceit in part of the performance
does not seem to discredit the rest of it in their eyes. People
do have the most amazing confidence in "what they can see
with their own eyes," blissfully unaware that the trickster's skill

lies precisely in keeping them from seeing the things that would give the show away. A prior belief in the reality of such super-natural phenomena can be counted upon to provide rationalizations and interpretations that will permit the believer to hang on to his old beliefs. When a spirit "medium" reveals relatively obscure facts about a client's life almost anything is believed except that the medium has had investigators hired to dig up the facts that are then dramatically revealed. Until the investigator is revealed many will prefer to postulate mysterious psychic powers as the source of information.

There is a happy optimism in church circles in the current post-war inflationary period. Church building and church membership are at an all time high. An important factor in this growth is the rising standard of living which has made it possible for many more families to achieve lives of quiet small-town and suburban respectability. Church membership has traditionally gone with the status of the solid or aspiring citizen, and many more families now have such prospects. The actual figures on church membership, however, are probably not up to the standards of truth-telling so staunchly advocated officially by the churches. In "Up From Methodism," Herbert Asbury relates how he tried for years, but in vain, to have his name removed from the rolls of that church. He came to the conclusion that not even death could remove a name from such lists once it got on one. Similar experiences can be duplicated by practically any family that has taken up residence elsewhere than at the place where once they were church members. An army colonel recently related to me that he found, much to his surprise, that he was still on the membership roll of a church he had not entered in ten years. He had written, years past, informing that body that he no longer could consider himself a member. No doubt it is nostalgic pangs that keep most such names on the old rolls. The spirit is still there, even if the flesh is absent.

Even more important in keeping the churches filled is the happy fact of their gradual transition and evolution in creed and in function. To keep a church filled these days practically demands that the pastor make no specific demands on precisely the beliefs each communicant professes. Furthermore, he must somehow provide in many cases a day nursery, a youth forum, organized sports, and a basement young-people's meeting and mating ground, as well as expert counseling and psychotherapy. The creeds, services, and sermons, must be nicely attuned to the exact degree of secular enlightenment of the congregation, or at least the more vocal and influential members thereof, particularly in such bodies in which the local group has the power to hire and fire the parson at will. And if that is not trying enough, there are even more disturbing products of the machine age come to complicate the lives and disturb the sleep of these faithful servants in the Lord's vineyards. As was already mentioned, in June 1955 a Scarsdale, N. Y., pastor made one-minute inspirational prayers available to telephone callers by way of tape recordings. Shortly the calls were so numerous that the telephone company had to add duplicate outlets to handle the traffic. By September a similar arrangement was made in Cleveland, Ohio, where quickly ten installations were needed to prevent a complete traffic jam from paralyzing the entire exchange which served the church. Counting "busy" signals as calls, telephone officials estimated that a hundred thousand calls might well have been placed there in one two-day period! Certainly that is technology in the service of religion! One is reminded of the ingenious psychiatrist who solved the problem of getting an insomniac to sleep. He found that hypnosis did the trick. The next stage was to do that by telephone. Then he had a phonograph recording made of his routine in inducing the hypnotic sleep, which proved to be quite effective. Then too, Christian "Science" practitioners have "treated" their clients by telephone for many years now. There is no reason why the tape-recorded prayer should not remain in reasonable demand for some time. Such developments merely point up the fact that if a religion is to have a mass following it must provide real and concrete services. It must have applicability in the workaday world of at least some of its communicants.

Above all, the current revival of religion is but part of the general wave of conservatism that has its roots and structure in the fundamental economic events in the current world scene, and is far from a simple process. The United States is without doubt its focal point.

Probably far more directly than we suspect are our fundamental outlook and evaluation structure a product of the economics of the current scene. In some aspects of the process, there is no better illustration of the failure of history to repeat itself than the contrast between the two post-war periods of the two world wars in the United States, in spite of the many similarities that these two periods provide. To begin with, there never was any real period of post-war prosperity after the first world war. The era of silk shirts for the workers—which somehow symbolized the wasteful and luxurious living standard the worker was presumed to have reached if he worked in a shipyard instead of being in uniform—ended almost with the Armistice celebrations. And, while corporate profits rose beautifully and output per worker soared, the wage increase was at best a ten percent rise in purchasing power for those that were employed. And the rolls of the unemployed kept mounting. During all this pre-depression period the American was treated to the spectacle of a slow discrediting of many of the then current sacred cows. To begin with, the myth of the moral crusade that the war was supposed to have been was progressively discredited by the coming to light of such items as those revealed by the Russian diplomatic archives, by the economic realists here at home who kept reminding us of the part played by the loans of the House of Morgan to the Allies in developing local pressure to enter the war, as well as the fundamental roots of the rivalries in economic competition that were probably the most important single factor making for war in the first place. Then the hated Bolsheviks whose early demise was confidently predicted by all right-thinking opinion makers and leaders in the world, perversely refused to lie down and die, and instead began to excite the world with talk of planned industrial expansion. What with the publicity attendant upon the legal fireworks in regard to evolution theory in the state of Tennessee, orthodoxy of all sorts had come upon difficult days.

And it was high time that the mythology that cloaked our economic, religious, and political institutions was given a thorough "debunking," as it was called in those days. The scandals of the Harding administration added effective water to the mill of the critics. On top of the discredited respectabilities came the depression. College student opinion sampled during the period 1929-1932 showed a three-fold increase in the percentage of opinion favoring a collectivistic economic order in each of the three schools sampled.[19] And, with that went similar changes in political and religious orthodoxy. It is significant that with the inauguration of the New Deal measures in 1933 and 1934 there was a complete arrest of the leftward trend in these attitudes, even if the rate of economic recovery was slow and irregular up to the outbreak of the second world war.

In this second war, nature showed a perverse zeal to imitate art. Where in the first war we had to cut German atrocities practically out of whole cloth and make martyrs out of spies that were executed when caught, all according to accepted practice in "civilized" wars, this time a paranoid paper-hanger provided us with millions of bona fide atrocities. Our entry into this second war was tarnished by no such shady manipulations as in 1917. There is some dispute over the messages President Roosevelt sent, but our ambassador holds that the mischief was done by deliberate mistranslation in the Japanese governmental machinery somewhere, by individuals who wanted war. At any event, we were "in," and the war was fought with an effective planned efficiency to a victorious conclusion.

Here the western, the non-Communist powers had permitted another disastrous war to start, and the war's end left no doubt as to who was the victor: Russia, who promptly established communistic states wherever her troops took over, in pursuing the German armies westward.

Meantime, the capitalistic societies in the west, not by any means healthily dynamic since the first war, were now in a state of economic paralysis that suggested to many a citizen the advisability of trying something radically different. There was a genuine crisis confronting the "West," as the traditionally "free enterprise" areas are now designated. To meet the threat that the long disgruntled European voter would turn to economic and political dictatorship required the launching of something of a crusade. Such crusades demand that the full fury of all available moral wrath be mobilized against a clearly definable devil. Russian communism, as long directed by the paranoid Stalin, could easily qualify as a devil for practically everyone in the West. The ardent advocate of political democracy, the libertarian, those apprehensive of state powers in general, those to whom private enterprise has turned its pleasanter face, and, above all the authoritarian theologian, together see the end of all that they live for and by with the advent of the spectre of communism.

Political forces are always more easily mobilized against than for something, and the New Conservatism is such an alliance. It is of such a united front backed up by all the elements made apprehensive by the social empiricism of the New Deal period, that the current "return to religion" is a part. It is an alliance held together by the bond of a common fear. Under the impact of this emotion the economic conservative who saw doom in the picayune New Deal spending, votes billions to shore up tottering social systems abroad, meanwhile venting his wrath against government "waste" by cutting a few paltry millions off social services at home.

Such is the dialectical character of social causation that the prosperity wrought at home by loans and spending abroad has the effect of making the voter even more conservative, even more inclined to forget the lessons learned during the late depression, and even more ready to eschew radical or critical opinion. This is no doubt contributed to by the active prosecution of the dissident groups that had provided the spearheads for unionization drives during the depression—whenever such activities happened to be compatible with the shifting directions of the "Moscow line," and to be called off when Moscow foreign policy called for a different turn. But with a decade of prosperity, and an increasing ratio of voters who have no significant recollections of depression years, the conservative alliance is riding high. And organized religion is part of the wave of conservative respectability.

The significant thing about the current religious revival is that it has nothing whatever to do with faith, belief, theology, or dogma. In the Protestant domain there is even a considerable move in the direction of soft-pedalling of traditional doctrinal differences, of avoiding areas of dispute or conflict, of combining forces and exchanging memberships when convenient. Such religious return as exists is largely an increasing support of religious organizations and institutions. Religious content is minimized. The Catholic church of course keeps a tight rein on doctrine and belief but bends every effort to cash in on the favorable and pro-religious atmosphere created by the anti-Communist drive and seeks to circumvent the traditionally hostile attitudes toward it, and if possible win such concessions as it can from the state in support of its parochial educational system. It began with pressure to have transportation supplied, and having won this concession in some areas is now gunning for aid in school construction.

But by and large, areas once lost to science can not be recovered by the priesthood. Where are the areas in which we could conceivably witness a revival of authority for faith? The old faiths lost their battles against the rising scientific method and could hardly be expected to recover ground long lost. With currently arising problems religion would have to compete on the basis of its capacity to deliver the goods, and to do so against competition from the scientific methodology. Are there any remaining areas in which it might effectively compete? Compelled to make a guess, one would probably do well to point to the general area of psychotherapy, that is, to that part of it that still seeks to attain its ends by the methods that can be broadly characterized as techniques of habit-making and breaking. Here is a vein well worth working, while yet it can be, before the entire area of abnormal behavior deviations is taken over by the biochemist and endocrinologist. Until a major fraction of the populace has been educated to the point of having a deterministic attitude toward habit processes, religious symbols and concepts might well provide as effective verbal "shock therapy" as the spicy dialogue of the psychoanalyst. Certainly the next decade will see an enormous increase in attempts in this direction by the Protestant clergy. Organized religion can get along well without an elaborate dogma, but it must have some live and practical function; if worst comes to worst it must at least provide a setting in which to compare milady's new bonnet against those of her social rivals. It did, during the years when clothing involved a larger fraction of the budget than it does today, and might perhaps again.

In part, the increase in church attendance is a cyclical phenomenon much after the manner of cycles of interest in phonograph records, amateur musical renditions, or charades. It is not just a function of establishing group membership or of a rush into respectability. Church membership and attendance declined when rival interests in golf, motoring, movies, radio or other entertainment began to claim larger shares of the available time. During that period, home piano playing, and musical efforts generally suffered a decline, as probably did card playing, stereoscopic viewing and many other once popular activities. But with the passage of time, a new generation, one perhaps not alienated from churches by having had to attend while too young and suffering boredom in consequence, or for which the other activities have become commonplace, can find an interest in the modern church which in the meantime had added the attractions of shorter sermons, card parties, club rooms, young people's activities, and perhaps even good music. It is similar improvements that have sparked a revival of interest in record playing, to wit, the possibilities of really high fidelity reproduction. Then too, exposure to a wide variety of musical selections on the radio has developed individual tastes, the desire to hear particular tunes when just in the mood for them. The motion picture theatres that were emptied by the television sets were filled again with the advent of technological improvements and really good pictures. Enough effort has gone into the churches so that on technological grounds alone they should be drawing near capacity houses. But it is not "the old time religion" that is provided; it is a streamlined modern version. It is more nearly attuned to the customers for whom it is making the pitch: customers who, what with a five-day working week gotten them by the trade unions, now have somewhat more time available for the religion they all along felt should be supported.

CHAPTER XIII

ETHICS AND RELIGION

Assiduously cultivated in many circles is the thesis that religion and ethics are, if not identical, then certainly two aspects of some higher unity, perhaps even a higher mystery. The priestly caste in the western world considers it not immodest to claim authoritative dominion in the field of morality and ethics. Ethical factors are frequently held to distinguish magic from religion and certainly the layman is by and large incapable of marking a distinction between correctness in religious ritual and morality. It would be both interesting and instructive to trace the origin and evolution of this theory of the identity of the ethical and the religious. It is a safe guess that the priestly caste has simply preempted jurisdiction and certainly has not been too effectively challenged in its authority. But the linkage seems to be an unquestioned axiom even among the early anthropologists. Marett[1] has the following to offer:

"Mana is selected by me for special emphasis merely because it comes nearer than any other available term to the bare designation of that positive emotional value which is the raw material of religion, and needs only to be moralized—to be identified with goodness—to become its essence."

Characteristically, if a modern scientist or philosopher "confesses" a religion or finds a place and need for it, it is a religion as a source and buttress of morality that emerges from their writings as is clearly apparent in Whitehead, Eddington, and many others. In fact, the commonest conviction one encounters today in the literature of ethics is that all "values" must stem from transcendental sources, be they moral or aesthetic. Karl Stern,[2] puts it this way: "Values, good and bad, or beautiful and ugly—are not the object of science." A few pages on and this is encountered: "Values are transcendental. They lie in an area which accumulative knowledge cannot reach." Apparently fully aware that there is a determinism in the acquisition of aesthetic tastes, that such things are cultural acquisitions, he none the less adds: "We might even find factors which would account for these differences in taste. Yet the question of intrinsic value—what makes one thing more beautiful than another —remains untouched." When "values" in the concrete, the particular, do turn up as deterministic products this author saves the day for himself by falling back upon a Platonic universal! This pure essence is still not accounted for, this abstraction has a pure existence apart from any particulars! It is preeminently respectable these days to assert that ethical codes can not be extracted or derived by scientific method. With this thesis goes the firm belief that values have a transcendental, a spiritual, a theological, in short a religious source. It is the currently accepted myth. It is this presumed identity of the ethical with the religious that has caused such puzzlement and worry in philosophers from Plato to the present when myths ascribe immoral acts to the gods. Here were these old Greek gods, on occasion displaying very human immoralities which just should not be if religion and morality are identical or almost so. The fate of that Old Testament Sad Sack who inadvertently touched the ark of the covenant has worried many a "right thinker" who assumed an identity of the religious and the good, and what was worse, mistakenly assumed that the right and the good were such for all time.

But there has been no lack of serious thinkers to doubt this identity of religion and ethics. Honorable mention here must go to Kant[3] who asserted: "Morality in no way needs religion for its support—but by means of pure practical reason is sufficient to itself." That alone would explain the general lack of enthusiasm for him in theological circles! Long ago, John Stuart Mill saw that morality does not follow from religion or grow out of it; religions rather tend to be or provide justifications for patterns of morality already established. Henry L. Mencken[4] denied the significance of the role of ethics in religion. In his words, "Religion—is primarily a theory of causes and only incidentally a scheme of conduct."

It seems probable that where particular religions spread geographically into areas formerly occupied by quite different cultures an increasing emphasis upon behavior deviations can be expected in the various aspects of religious activity. In such culture contacts there is indeed a winnowing out of the relatively more plausible and widely significant from those idiosyncratic to a particular culture. The "universalistic" characteristics frequently claimed for the Judeo-Christian morality, insofar as there is substance to that claim, is no doubt such a product. At any rate, it is apparent that in primitive societies, that is, relatively isolated and long stable cultures, there seems to be but little concern with morality; their behavior patterns are well integrated and the individuals are subjected to but few cross-pressures making for behavior deviations. Certainly there is but little use made of supernaturals as agencies for the enforcement of cultural norms. Chantepie[5] quotes Felix Dahn[6] on the Vikings to the effect that there were skeptics among them, and that many were godless, and that on the whole the influence that the belief of the Vikings in their gods exerted on their conduct and mental attitude cannot have been great. In speaking of morality among the Teutons Chantepie,[7] says: "This morality is not hallowed by religion; it would be a very difficult task indeed to collect from the heroic saga examples of pagan teutonic piety. But the material that represents the moral side is all the richer." It would seem then that while there is no denying that there is a great concern with morality in some contemporary religions that must not be assumed to be a universal state of affairs.

Paul Deussen[8] develops a thesis that religion derives from a fusion of mythology and morality. The "higher" the religion the less of the former and more of the latter. Such a theory would seem to imply that as religion is refined to its pure essence it loses one of the essential elements of the initial fusion that produces it! When such a dilemma has been reached in logical processes it is a sure sign that we are having word trouble, and that it is high time that we establish objective referents for our nouns!

The sociological facts behind Deussen's thesis are that in contemporary western culture where scientific research and method have trimmed function after function and area after area away from what was traditionally the field and function of the priesthood there is a decided tendency to react to the traditional mythology of western religion with a tongue-in-cheek attitude and at the same time not to dispute too actively the dominance of the priesthood in a certain abstract or "Sunday" morality. Science, historical scholarship, and archaeology have reduced the official mythology to a group of somewhat imaginative tales, largely borrowed from older cultures, among which we are occasionally surprised to find one whose content bears considerable relation to some recently established historical fact. The "Sunday" morality continues to exist side by side with the practical adjustments we learn to make with our fellows in the workaday world and with which it offers a minimum of interference, largely because, the facts of the psychology of habit being what they are, we acquire habits specific to the particular situations in which we practice them. Verbal abstractions couched in an archaic tongue do not generalize too readily to the situations of everyday life which one learns to meet on their own terms in the specific situations offered. I recall a lusty proletarian who reported having several adulteries to his credit before he knew what the seventh commandment referred to. It seems he had acquired his vocabulary or learned that commandment during the period when there was a great to-do over the passage of pure food and drug acts with their strictures on adulterations and adulterants! Such traditional morality tends to remain a mixture of concern over purely ritualistic observances having absolutely no significance in the workaday world and abstract platitudes in regard to conduct, completely out of tune with the realities faced by an individual in the sharp practices of the business world. Or, having learned a commandment against killing, he is then assigned the task of killing as many citizens of a neighboring state as possible, and is honored in so doing. Were the religious leadership seriously to take sides in the disputes in the marketplace accordingly as it interpreted the events in the light of its moral principles or theological commandments it would quickly lose its comfortable role as generally approved social ornament. It would become but one of a group of contending disputants, and vulnerable in case it had backed the wrong horse. By and large, the priesthood has played its cards well. It has managed and influenced the general culture so as to create for itself the role of official moral guardian and to link this in the popular mind with religion. This linkage is so strong that even in areas where there is no established religion the average individual hesitates to announce himself as lacking a religion since, in the popular mind, that is tantamount to admitting to a lack of morality. To have salvaged this much prestige and power in rear-guard actions after a succession of defeats and the consequent surrender of extensive areas is no small achievement.

There is a common psychological dilemma that confronts all beliefs and value systems that must be instilled and perpetuated in the face of pressures and conflicts. To get them accepted they must be taught under emotional pressures that have the almost unfailing result of producing behavior rigidities which do not succumb to the conditions which normally produce habit adjustments, even under circumstances in which it is highly advantageous to the individual to change. This is the basis of the peculiarly rigid character of sectarian beliefs acquired under conditions of conflict or competition with other value systems. It is notorious that individuals raised in a culture in which there are no competing religious systems are comparatively easy victims of the propagandists of competitive beliefs in comparison with people who have for similar periods of time "held true to the faith" in an area where there has all along been live competition and exposure to the blandishments of the competitors. Such firm adherence to the faith means at the same time the loss of the flexible and adaptive character of human behavior. It reduces the shifty, opportunistic character of human behavior so well suited to the trial and error solution of concrete problems as they are encountered, and even more interferes with the realistic anticipation of approaching dilemmas or problems. Yet, if uniformity and predictability of behavior can be produced by no other means, the price of an impressive rigidity is perhaps not too excessive, for any kind of organized social relations demands of human behavior that it be predictable. To put it another way, it is this predictability of the behavior of particular individuals that constitutes any kind of social organization. It is highly desirable that a pattern of social behavior should be efficient, but before it can be efficient it must be predictable. Organized effort becomes possible when people begin to behave predictably toward each other; when they cease to do so the result is anarchy. What sometimes appears as a zeal for conformity for conformity's sake has this sound basis in the practical facts of human behavior. The premium tends to be upon conformity since only thus is the individual deviant kept in line. To conform is to be approved, to be good, to be moral. No morality has any other basis or any other foundation.

It offends many good people to be told that their morality is but an accident of geography, or a monument to the personality quirks of some highly ascendant individual who impressed his idiosyncrasies upon the group about him. Such a cavalier verdict should be supplemented by pointing out that such a morality could not have been too preposterous or too handicapping else any group practicing it should have long been extinct. This implies a sort of natural selection hypothesis in regard to morals. It seems, in fact, that there has been, and is, such a process in operation where human stocks tend to survive, not on the basis of specific biological virtues or shortcomings, but rather on the basis of the excellence of their social organization, their "morals," if you will. For only in the more modern, more complex societies do we find distinctions between law and morality, or mark off any special aspects of social behavior as involving "morals" as distinct from other socially significant activity.

Questions of "morals" then are always questions of conformity to the behavior norms of a particular group. There is no other criterion of the "moral." Moral values or moral judgments do not begin as an objective, functional analysis of concrete or general problems to be solved followed by an evaluation of the diverse possibilities of their solution. They begin as an unquestioned acceptance of the values and customs of some particular culture. These values and customs are frequently ascribed to the commands of a supernatural agency. They may well be thought to be an inherent aspect of the fibre and core of the cosmos, or, as with Kant, be used to "prove" the existence of a god who presumably laid down these moral laws and gave each of us a conscience that somehow knew just what these laws are.

An intellectual fare that includes even a meagre ration of anthropology will quickly point up the inadequacy of such notions. But some philosophers still claim that there are universally recognized "goods." There are, if you but make them in the form of generalizations that are broad enough. Thus, it might be held, that man everywhere seeks happiness. That might well be true enough as far as it goes. But unless that knowledge tells us whether his formula for happiness includes the eating of his fellow men, or the use of them for lion-bait, that could hardly be thought of as significant information. There probably is great zeal for "justice" everywhere, but there is no better definition of justice than the traditional expectations of a particular culture.

If there are any limitations whatever, any universals at all in the field of morality, they are but the bounds and limits set by the conditions of human survival. It is a safe bet that any of the various moralities the face of the globe has seen are more or less workable norms of behavior, given the circumstances and conditions in which they appeared. It would be a reckless person indeed who would venture to defend the thesis that any given morality was the best possible morality for that particular time or place; too many different moralities have existed, and still do, under what seem to be largely similar circumstances and conditions. But just so long as any culture with a particular set of morals exists, we are compelled to grant its workability. Nor can the criterion of survival be pushed too far since it might result in a ruthless, conquering,

and exterminating horde becoming the "moral" one and setting
the standard on the basis of such eloquent evidence of the favor
of the gods.

The term "ethics" is a monument to the fact that serious
thinkers recognized the limitations of the various moralities and
were striving to attain to a knowledge of conduct more accurately attuned to the true nature and needs of man. Thus
it is at once apparent that the historical speculations on the
subject of ethics could be no more intelligent than the then
current knowledge of man, his true characteristics, needs, and
potentialities. Nor could they transcend the limitations in their
knowledge of the world in which man must of necessity function. But from Socrates on, the attempts to challenge local
moralities and point out their limitations have had a hard row
to hoe, and quite understandably. Any local morality had the
advantage of a demonstrated workability; and any innovation,
however small, would constitute a disruption of the nicely
integrated pattern. Even a desirable modification that could
be introduced without serious disturbance to the balance of
the pattern would none the less tend to destroy its aura of
timeless sanctity and in effect encourage trends toward heterodoxy. The development of a scientific ethics had to await the
formulation of a far more accurate knowledge of both man
and his world, a knowledge so impressive that it could even
compel acceptance in the area of that emotionally charged
subject, the rules of human conduct.

It is opportune at this point to puncture and deflate the
contention of theologians in the western world that the ethics
of conduct has from the beginning been the province of religion; that it has been the priestly caste's special function to
cultivate and nurture this fragile flower. Nothing could be
further from the truth. It is the current and local moralities
that the priesthood has been avidly defending all these years.
Or, when attached to an expanding or conquering culture,
they have simply established their own moralities as absolutes,
drawing the line at nothing in their zeal to demand and get
conformity to their own rules and patterns. All the priesthood
has ever done is to attempt to universalize its own moralities.

What else, might one well ask, could it indeed do? To provide a basis for ethics sounder than the apparently workable pattern it represented, would require a priesthood long devoted to a quest for empirical knowledge. It would have demanded of a priesthood that it doubt every untested assumption, every article of faith, every sacred revelation, everything that could not be demonstrated. Such a priesthood would of necessity be one of doubters, of challengers, of super-skeptics, of empiricists. But particularly in the western world it has been the misfortune of the priesthood to be cast in a quite contrary role, that of the suppressor of precisely the kind of inquiry and skepticism that is absolutely essential if ever the kind of knowledge is to be collected and organized that has any prospects whatever of giving mankind a foundation upon which a sound ethics of conduct might eventually be constructed. This is the really critical, the key insight into the problem of the relation of religion to ethics.

It is not the purpose of this inquiry to cast any aspersions whatever upon the historical role of the priesthood or on any of the practices that by any stretch of terminology or the imagination might be called "religious." But it must be insisted upon in the interests of historical objectivity that even an innovating priestly leader could at best correct but a few of the more preposterous errors of the pattern from which he was deviating. It should be obvious that a not insignificant series of changes have from time to time been introduced into current practices by dissident practitioners of the priestly arts. Certainly, if there has been such a thing as "progress" in the evolution of the priestly doctrines and arts, it has come about through the innovations of dissident and revolutionary leaders in previous techniques, practices, or routines. Many of these innovations are today conceded a considerable significance; by all Christians, for example, in the case of the innovations and changes in Judaism initiated some two thousand years ago in the course of its adaptation to western European cultures. They remain a regrettable heresy to all Jews, much as the 16th century deviations in Christianity are still apostasies and heresies to those faithful to the older dispensation. Apparently, no matter how authoritatively or convincingly the gods may have spoken at one time in history, their messages seem to dim with the years and to require a new orchestration to keep them in a more acceptable harmony with current themes. But such changes can in no way be equated with a transition from mere morality to ethics. Any scientific improvement over the historical trial-and-error of even the most brilliant or successful culture would have to draw on a rich and varied diversity of historical experience in a great variety of cultures in addition to an exact knowledge of the environmental forces with which man must come to terms. Most important of all, such improvement would have to wait upon a truly scientific knowledge of the nature of man.

Where at one time the members of any one culture probably knew but little of the ways of their immediate neighbors, and that little of an unfavorable sort due to misunderstanding, conflict, and hostility engendered by economic or biological competition, today there are objective accounts of at least a respectable fraction of the possible ways of life as illustrated by contemporary anthropological diversity. There is less and less excuse for the shocked incredulity which was formerly the standard reaction to even trifling deviations in the familiar pattern of life and morals. It is true that these accounts are often barely extracted from the wreckage wrought by contact with the now dominant western culture, but the convincing diversity is there for all to see. The physical problems and limitations of the material world in which man has to live are now coming to be understood in fairly exact and quantitative terms. The ethics of conduct must take full account of such important factors. Finally, the scientific method has invaded the domain of human nature itself, where the impact of its advent is probably even more dramatically significant than it has been in the other two areas.

If there was a reluctance on the part of moralists to accept the scientific account of the external world, nothing short of a violent resistance has greeted the invasion of the scientific point of view into the domain of human nature. The western moralistic view of man was made up of some amazing contradictions. On the one hand there was the human soul which was asserted to be of a peculiar god-like quality. But its sovereignty over the activities of the body was always in a dubious battle with "the flesh" or "original sin" which are assumed to be of a peculiar depravity amenable only to a very special kind of ritual cleansing. This illustrates a very common moralistic fallacy, the confusion of moral judgment with understanding or explanation. Once a moral judgment is made nothing more need be said or done. Such is the intellectual atmosphere where moral judgments are predominant. And there can be no question whatever of the role that religion, that is, the priesthood, has played: it has tended to preserve, often in complete disregard of all other considerations, the traditional moralities. Far from having taken an empirical position, a willingness to test the workability of other possible patterns, the priesthood has tended to throw its weight with the established past, since it is with that established past that their special authority and competence is identified. As no doubt with the rest of us, they tend somehow to see virtue as parallel to their own vested interests. That early American dissenter, Roger Williams, put it this way:

"The truth is that herein all the priests in the world, Mahumetan, Popish, Pagan and Protestant, are the greatest peacebreakers in the world, as (fearing their own cause) never rest stirring up Princes and people against any (whether Gods of Devills instruments) that shall oppose their own religion and conscience, that is in plaine English, their profits, honours, and bellies."[9]

Considering the time in which he made this judgment, we can perhaps forgive him the intensity of his invective.

But the knowledge necessary to a sound ethics has been accumulating apace. It is now obvious to all but the most benighted bigots that no one culture ever has had or now has a corner on virtue; that some people managed to live a life about as good as ours under different gods as well as under different skies; that whatever gods may be, they have permitted, or have been unable to prevent the worship of each other by millions over the millennia. With the years we have slowly substituted a sound knowledge of nutrition with its details of calories, minerals, and vitamins for the irrationalities of totemic and food taboos. We need no longer plague the gods with prayers to prevent pestilence. The food we eat is no longer a ritual matter, it is but a problem in economics, individual preference, and physiology. We combat plagues by putting a certain percentage of us to work at the task of finding out precisely what practical measures to take rather than maintaining a large retinue of experts who, when catastrophe strikes, can only tell us that we have been remiss in the performance of some bootless rite. Amusingly enough, the proper steps which we now discover should be taken, become in turn "moral" or ethical! We condemn strongly, and in moral terms, the individuals who are negligent in having themselves vaccinated or immunized, who breed without regard to the economics of reproduction, or who carelessly pass on their diseases to others, or who raise children without enlightening themselves with the latest facts in scientific child-care. And we save our deepest scorn for those who allow the ritual rules of their older morality to stand between them and the practice of a sound "ethics," namely the practices dictated by the best knowledge now currently available.

There is no doubt but that we are developing a sound "ethics" of conduct in the area of the physiological, where objective criteria of normal physiology and of sound health are readily available. But how are we faring in the domain of the "purely psychological," the area of human desires, needs, motives, and values? Certainly a fine beginning has been made in understanding the relations existing between the physiological or "lower" organic animal needs and higher ethical values. The general outlines of what constitutes psychological well-being are now quite familiar, as well as the general character of the conditions conducive to it. No longer need we exalt "the spirit" and bemoan or regret "the flesh." "Values" are no longer things from the realm of pure spirit, but something very much in the domain of things psychological where they can be anticipated, predicted and controlled.

Evaluational attitudes are not wholly fortuitous and idiosyncratic. They have, up to a certain point, organic determinants in the tissues of the organism. At the most fundamental level we have the deficiency drives which must be met if the individual is to survive. Here are the oxygen need, the temperature norms that must be maintained, the complex nutritional and fluid needs to be met. Their common denominator is simply that if these needs are not met the organism shortly ceases to be. These needs have an understandable priority over those not of a deficiency character. It is to be noted that when a deficit of any considerable extent exists in any of these areas, any "higher" motives simply do not exist for such an individual. Similarly, with an increase in deficiency needs goes an increasing disregard for the conditions involving tissue integrity or other threats to what are well classified as "security" needs. Sex drives illustrate an interesting border-line between those involving definite tissue conditions or hormonal factors and those produced by habit mechanisms. Sex drives have indeed an organic, hormonal basis, but they are in no sense deficiency drives. Yet under their impetus, reactions to security drives are considerably varied and the relative strength of other deficiency drives much modified. But what is of practical significance for the problems of ethics is just that the higher ethical values are not a substitute for the "lower," more primitive urges, but instead are best acquired under conditions of adequate satisfactions of all the needs "lower" in the hierarchy, of those closer to, and in the nature of deficiency drives. The socially "higher" needs are evaluated more highly by those whose needs, both "high" and "low" are regularly and adequately satisfied. Typically then, the pursuit of "higher" values is more effectively executed by those in whom the more fundamental needs have been adequately met. A sound, practical ethics can not be expected to be produced or developed in individuals who are starved or frustrated on the more primitive levels of satisfaction. The individualities and idiosyncrasies of which people are capable cannot be expected to emerge until the more primitive levels of satisfaction have been realized. At the lower levels of needs we are pretty much alike. We differ *significantly* in our activities *after* the more primitive needs are met, when the individuals' activities are increasingly a function of the factors and processes in which they differ greatly from one another. These differences can emerge only when the prepotent physiological needs and lower level drives have been satisfied.

Even a casual examination of the general classes of conduct that meet with social approval practically everywhere will reveal rather significant facts about approved conduct. While it will be universally conceded that the "lower," the deficiency drives must be satisfied, social approval is meted out to the capacity to defer, reduce, or postpone such satisfactions in the interest of "higher" needs, such as love (whether sexual, familial, or general fraternal concern for his fellow man) or the esteem of his fellows, or the pursuit of highly individualized or idiosyncratic values popularly characterized as "self-expressive," and which, in the long run, are the sources of such values as can be shared by all mankind.

We can now glimpse the outlines of sound criteria of ethics, far indeed from the blind addiction to venerable rules out of the past that has characterized all mere moralities. Such ethics will be little concerned with ritual details, but will have a clear grasp of the practical ends to be attained. It will tolerate a fluidity of means, and respect individual idiosyncrasies wherever and whenever possible. Instead of registering a great concern lest there is here and there a ritual violation it will take pride in its capacity to tolerate, to adjust to, and if possible make use of human deviations, both in structure and behavior. It will have learned the profound lesson that anything really new anywhere must of necessity seems absurd, preposterous, and even sinful. It will approach such deviations with a live curiosity, with tolerance and charity, and seek to channel them into constructive activities. Or failing that, into innocuous outlets; or, as a last resort, repress with regret. It will have learned that "to each according to his needs, from each according to his means" is not a paternalism gone wild but rather the most intelligent form of constructive social policy. It will be axiomatic that an individual not functioning at his highest possible level is a loss, not only to himself but to all the rest of us.

A good society will be one in which relatively small fractions of the total energy will be spent on the more primitive values or needs. Drudgery has values only in the eyes of those who do not have to perform it. For those for whom its performance brings rewards in the form of need satisfaction it rates at best a grudging tolerance. The lower levels of needs are relatively easily satisfied. It is the satisfaction of the higher needs of man that makes large demands and for which efficiency must be introduced into basic need satisfaction that there be plenty of time and energy left over for expenditure on the higher.[10] Concern with higher needs can arise only where a margin in basic need satisfaction makes it possible. A fairly objective criterion of the ethical values involved in any situation or alternative is to be found in the kind of satisfactions as well as the amounts promised by the alternatives. Here one might well make errors or miscalculations, but profit could be had from experience. If there is to be improvement in anything there must be opportunity to profit by experience. An ethics that makes no provision for such growth and experience is axiomatically and hopelessly invalid. We have no measure of value but that derived from our own functions. In so far as we can have preferences as to the activities to engage in, we have provided ourselves with objective value criteria. In a changing world, such criteria, subject to day to day revision, will probably prove more valid guides to conduct than even the best and most venerable guesses out of the past. It must never be forgotten that, apart from the practical merit of any system of conduct or values, its quantitative efficiency in providing both lower and higher level satisfactions or "values" to its members, an established order of any sort can offer as justification for its continued existence in competition with a new or revised pattern only such losses in efficiency as admittedly follow on the heels of the ending of any set of predictable relations between individuals. And there are definite limits to such losses.

It is thus clearly apparent that the current religions have much housecleaning and soul-searching on their hands before they can lay claim even to being on terms of civil communication with a genuine ethics. It is safe to assert that at best but few of the more forward-looking and less ritually bound fractions are making any contribution whatever to a sound contemporary social ethics or show a promise for growth that might make them significant forces in the future. Other than these, the linkage of religion with ethics is the tenuous and dubious coincidence of some few and perhaps relatively unimportant items in which the particular morality of which it is the self-appointed guardian happen to have concrete content and instrumental value in a scientific formula of sound conduct. To date, organized religions have shown little capacity for anything other than contributing their blessings to the major political, economic, and military agencies dominant in their culture. Any claim to ethical leadership will have to be validated with a record of far more effective and constructive counsel and responsibility than has thus far been forthcoming. An ethics whose values are tied to conformity and obedience is childish, and richly deserves the replacement it will certainly get at the hands of a more dynamic social philosophy.

Such a social philosophy will have to make a frank and frontal assault upon the hoary mythology that pretends that a great gulf separates the empirical-scientific from the value-judgmental. It will have to recognize and assert brazenly that religion is human behavior, no more, no less. It must recognize that the merit of any ethics or any religion cannot exceed its functional relevance to human needs, desires, or well being. And no ethics and no religion can contain any wisdom that can transcend man's own knowledge about the immediate and future consequences of his own behavior. Every religion and every ethical system must recognize that it might well be made obsolete by any extension of human knowledge in almost any area.

The contributions of any ethics or of any religion to human well-being are fundamentally of two sorts, the first of which are the advantages resulting from the predictability and stability provided by any enforced rules. These advantages are very real and are completely independent of any advantages or disadvantages, merits or demerits, the system may have as compared with other possible systems of formalized conduct.

An inefficient predictability can easily outweigh what may well be relatively more efficient but less predictable. This advantage, of necessity accrues to any established system, whether it involve polygamy or widow-burning, vegetarianism or cannibalism. Some of these practices might well constitute an inefficient use of human energies; but unpredictable cannibalism or widow-burning, even if of rare occurrence would disturb the efficient functioning of a group far more than its regular and continuous practice. But any established system makes this gain, has this advantage; and the fact of its establishment will mean that, with rare exceptions, it will seem good, true, and beautiful to those who are accustomed to it. To question its merits will elicit but a crop of socially acceptable fictions and rationalizations which justify it. The advantages shared by any and every system will be presumed to be unique to the familiar system. Where an empirical basis is lacking, transcendental or supernatural sanctions for it will be claimed.

In addition to the efficiency that is the product of predictability, every way of life must make some sort of showing in effectiveness vis-à-vis its competitors, since the efficiency resulting from predictability accrues to any pattern however inefficient basically. Furthermore, the individual is far more likely to become aware of deviations in conduct from the expected than he is of even an obvious inefficiency in the basic pattern, particularly if, as so often happens, any considerable concern develops for conformity as an end in itself, when mere conformity is an unquestioned virtue, and any deviation ipso facto an evil, regardless of its possible contributions to a basic social efficiency. It should be emphasized here that in the calculus of social efficiency it is immaterial from what source advantages accrue, be it from such effective interpersonal relations as are commonly thought of as ethics or morals, or from mechanical advantages hit upon in the manipulation of the material word. Nor are these two sources independent of each other; they are, in fact, in a continuous interaction, each subject to changes due to events in the other. No system of rules for effective human relations can remain meaningful where there have been profound changes in the area of the mechanical-technological. Where such changes have taken place, no system of morals can hope to escape serious overhauling or revision. Any moral code is of necessity nothing other than emotionally crystallized habits based upon the problems that confronted man in the past. There is even no guarantee that they were at any time the best of all possible patterns; it would actually be a safe bet that they never were. There is a sound motive behind Bernard Shaw's self-confessed tendency to attack any and every institution over ten years old. In a rapidly changing world the odds begin to rise that it needs revision in that time. Any culture that finds itself in a crisis is thereby confessing that it has been remiss in its self-criticism and empiricism. It has omitted from its structure the most important single item: an effective machinery for revising it. The problem of ethics is not something limited to a small segment of a culture; it is rather a question of the fundamental efficiency of the entire pattern.

The priesthoods and their apologists are still reiterating the old claim of religion to "eternal truths," though there is increasing reluctance to a specific listing of them. For example, "Religion claims to give knowledge, and knowledge of eternal truth; by its capacity to justify this claim it will stand or fall."[11] Insofar as any specific truths are ventured, they will today be found increasingly limited to the area of the ethics of conduct, and indeed to rather narrow limits in that field. The time when the western priesthood dared to speak authoritatively in areas of cosmology, geography, biology, and pathology is happily in the past. For an impressive survey of the priestly role in these areas the reader is strongly advised to make a pilgrimage through the pages of Andrew D. White's monumental "History of the Warfare Between Science and Theology in Christendom."[12] The methods and principles of the theologicans are still the same; they have merely abandoned certain fields as no longer profitable for exploitation and have concentrated their efforts in the psychological and sociological areas where they are still claiming "eternal truths." The moral authority claimed by organized religion proves upon examination to be nothing better than traditional beliefs in regard to things psychological and sociological, derived out of a distant past. Their sole claim to validity today derives from the extent of their social acceptability, not from any empirical validation. To preserve that social acceptability organized religion bends its every effort to keep "controversial" topics out of public educational institutions and to provide as much parochial education as possible for as many of the "faithful" as possible. Their most recent victory has been that of prying their god into the school-children's oath of allegiance in obvious violation of the federal constitution.

The "eternal truths" of religion, if one can judge by the causes recurrently and persistently championed by the priesthood, prove upon examination to be venerable items out of ancient codes of conduct, which, far from remaining practical or significant today are frequently bad in every possible sense. Take, for example, the almost hundred percent opposition of the priesthood to all forms of population control, particularly contraception and abortion. The social opposition to such measures has been far from universal in the past. Both methods of population control have been common in areas of limited land surface and food supply. But where the conditions of survival involved much numerical competition with rival groups, and where infant death rates were high, it has been frequently considered anti-social for anyone not to do his utmost to maintain and increase the group numerically. In some groups this pressure went so far as to demand mating as early as it is biologically possible and to leave no unmated females about that might be kept breeding, even if it meant polygamy or other familial adjustments. Such "morals" were no doubt excellent where survival rates are low. A sufficient premium on viable offspring has made it not only moral but economically advantageous for a young woman to be able to bring to a marriage as many children as possible, begotten by no one cares whom, just so they are there. But it is ethical imbecility or indeed madness to preserve such morals into a day where infant deaths have practically disappeared, where the survival rate is high, where population presses upon a food supply, where crowding makes a good life extremely difficult, or where population pressures in one area can become contributory to military hostilities between cultures, or even where a conflict between cultures might be waged in hospital delivery rooms. No culture can disown the consequences of its behavior, no matter how "moral" it may hold itself to be.

Christian apologists have long boasted that it was Christianity that "discovered" the individual, made each individual soul equally precious. That claim can be best validated if the equality and preciousness is limited to evaluations and events post mortem. In the here and now however, the weight of the organized religions has invariably attempted to force the individual into the limitations of the past. It is doubtful that the theological mind is capable of even imagining a functional code of conduct based upon sound and objective rather than ritual criteria of the significant rights of and respect for individuals. Such rights, and such respect will of necessity begin by demanding that each individual have an effective right, first of all, to a sound heredity; that individuals should not be incubated where a good probability of serious heritable defects exists. Next, even a minimum of respect for the individual should assure him the right to be incubated under propitious gestational conditions, and any pregnancy should be terminated when significant evidence appears that a handicapped individual is likely to result, as is the case during certain kinds of virus infections during pregnancy. Such willingness is the acid test of a true respect for individuality. Similarly, minimal spacings should be assured between pregnancies since a disregard of this factor probably results in an individual handicapped by poorer than average vitality and a ten point handicap in intelligence quotient. To continue with the list of the specific demands of respect for individuality, every individual should be guaranteed that those assuming the burden of his gestation, parturition, nursing, nutrition, care, and education really desire that individual and make plans and proper provision for him. There is not the slightest excuse for one single individual being born without this prerequisite being fully met. Modern science and skill can guarantee it. What objections can possibly be raised against even an abortion when with proper equipment and properly trained operators the mortality risk can easily be reduced below its present negligible level of something like one tenth of the hazards involved in the normal delivery of a full-term infant.[13] That today's American woman is really acting on such sensible considerations rather than conforming completely to the official hypocrisies is eloquently attested to by the fact that while in 1938 there were roughly 800,000 live births in the U.S.A. there were an estimated 780,000 abortions performed that year, which is something very close to a 1-1 ratio.[14] And let it be remembered that the great bulk of these abortions are performed upon respectably married women, as a procedure agreed upon with their husbands. Furthermore, these couples with but rare exceptions already have one or more children, and for good and sufficient reasons, usually economic or physiological, are determined enough not to have more children that they will flout both law and current morality to that end. What is even worse, they are all too frequently driven to patronizing untrained, ill-equipped, and unscrupulous operators of "abortion-mills," the quality of whose services bears much the same relation to what modern medicine and surgery can provide as the "bath-tub gin" of prohibition days bears to the vintage wines of Bordeaux and Burgundy. Deaths resulting from abortions can be laid to nothing other than the current hypocritical laws in our land that boasts its rugged individualism. But desperate women somehow manage to get their abortions when needed. With but rare exceptions, the illegitimate children that are born today come from stock of such poor quality that they represent at best no asset to the land, and at worst, which is not at all infrequently, they are a biological and social liability. We can well dispense with a morality that insists that certain poor, unfortunate children be born with the stigma of illegitimacy, not to mention the sadistic vengeance we insist on inflicting upon their mothers. On some perhaps not too distant tomorrow, such a morality will appear barbarous indeed!

The New York Times of October 30, 1955 carried a Tokyo dispatch dealing with that county's grappling with its problem of overpopulation. Pointing up the need local authorities felt for better methods of birth control and their wider application was their estimate that there were about as many abortions annually as live births: one and a half million. Effective birth-control techniques, easily available, certainly are superior to abortions; but let those who would prefer the additional million and a half children to be born annually in that crowded land speak up and be counted!

Then there is that little matter of what we have a right to expect the social world should provide for the individual. First of all, let it be understood, I shall limit my list of expectations only to the things we now know how to provide as far as the technical skills involved go. We may not have a social machinery for its universal provision, but we well know what should be done and what can be done. Every normal parent will of course want all these things for his children, and would no doubt forego many things to provide them. To begin with then, our individual should be properly tested and measured, frequently enough on standardized tests till there no longer is any reasonable doubt as to the level of abilities at which he can be made to function. This information is vitally important to parents and educators even before the child is aware of the process, so that the parent can be properly and intelligently guided in the expectations he should make of this individual. The optimal level for each individual is one complex and difficult enough for him so that it offers a challenge, but it must be well within the range of his capacities and abilities so that honest and guided efforts will bring a modicum of success and reward. These things can be quite accurately measured and determined. Would you think it desirable that your children should have it? Shouldn't every child be entitled to it? All we need is some twenty times more psychologists and testers than we now have to do the work—and to pay them of course for doing it. It is just possible that we might have to divert some high-pressure salesmen into a different occupation, or learn to take pride in something other than the fact that we have twenty competing fuel oil delivery trucks making the rounds of the same street.[15] Then there are the dimensions of personality other than sheer intelligence that need to be tested and watched as they evolve in our individual that we protest we respect so very much. Here we can first of all use some king-size research programs, something comparable, let us say, budgetwise, to the annual cigarette and automobile advertising campaigns. But much already useful is ready at hand. It need but be applied to produce very much worth-while results in preventing the formation of twisted personalities that are far costlier in the long run when they become criminals or frustrated personalities perhaps following paranoid political leaders. We need the moral courage to demand and get a school system in which either a child has interest in the curriculum aroused in him or else is permitted to work; yes, has a job provided for him that is well within his capacities, regardless of his age.

Do we want "moral" individuals, striving for what are by common consent called "higher" satisfactions and seeking to satisfy "higher" needs? Then we know the answer: we must see to it that we provide them with efficient and effective means of satisfying their "lower" needs. No one can strive for higher satisfactions until the lower needs are under control, until there is provision for satisfying them with some time and energy left over. Do we laugh at the tastes of the Nouveau riche? It takes time to acquire the kinds of tastes that "good taste" approves!

Then there are the troubled people, those not on good terms even with themselves, the potential suicides, the drug addicts. Do we respect the individual? Then we must stop treating such cases as crime problems with our stupid laws. Can anything be more ridiculous than a law forbidding a man to attempt suicide? Were we willing to respect a man's "right" to commit suicide we could no doubt prevent nine-tenths of all suicides and all the incidental deaths caused by suicides in asphyxiating themselves with gas or jumping from high buildings. A whole host of problems confronts us in trying to improve the adjustment levels of matings in marriage, but that is no reason for not applying what is already known. Impossible? Look what a little intelligent legislation has done in the way of cradle-to-grave security! Has it made people lazy? What has finally been demonstrated here in America is that the number of people working is a function solely of the number of jobs available. All other factors are statistically insignificant. The individual must have a chance to work and earn.

Professions of concern or respect for the individual all too easily remain empty lip-allegiance. They are not to be taken as anything but hypocrisy unless they embody a genuine program of action. Before we can accept at face value any claim to a concern for the individual let us see it validated with a program of intelligent steps having an empirical basis. Such a program will not deal with moral absolutes and certainties. It will instead, attempt tentatively to try a given program with a view to evaluating its effectiveness. It will not be hamstrung by a blind allegiance to the formulae of the past. "Eternal Truths" are a delusion and a snare. An institution that consumes the fraction of social energy devoted to religion had better find more significant functions than those of resolving the apprehensions it has itself aroused in its communicants, and become again a constructive social force. To be that it has to burn with a holy zeal. It has to be aroused to demand and get action. It can no longer afford to be respectable. It will have to descend to the market place and demonstrate its potency as a social force. It will have to arm itself with the best knowledge science can provide. And far from giving it a belated and grudging recognition for its achievements it must make itself the prophet of science, making it meaningful even to those who are incapable of grasping it in detail. It will have to prove that it is earning its keep. There is no evidence that it now does so.

Professor John Dewey somewhere expressed his misgivings about the value of contemporary religion as follows:[16]

"It seems to me that the chief danger to religion lies in the fact that it has become so respectable. It has become largely a sanction of what socially exists—a kind of gloss upon institutions and conventions. Primitive Christianity was devastating in its claims. It was a religion of renunciation and denunciation of the "world"; it demanded a change of heart that entailed a revolutionary change in human relationships. Since the Western world is now alleged to be Christianized, a world of outworn institutions is accepted and blessed. A religion that began as a demand for a revolutionary change and that has become a sanction to established economic, political, and international institutions should perhaps lead its sincere devotees to reflect upon the sayings of the one worshipped as its founder: "Woe unto you when all men shall speak well of you," and "Blessed are ye when men shall revile you and persecute you."

Yes, Christianity had its constructive phases when it was a dynamic social movement, when it was in effect at war with the established and the respectable. That phase of its history is definitely over, and the same can be said with equal confidence of the rest of the world's religions. There is but a limited future to be predicted for an institution whose activities are increasingly limited to providing mechanisms of renunciation, reconciliation, and vicarious satisfactions generally, although this has long been a function of religious machinery. As Guthrie and Edwards[17] put it:

"Religion has traditionally offered a number of devices for the relief of distress, not the least of which is the central faith itself which, like wartime patriotism, may serve to give meaning to a life which the individual is incapable of working out for himself."

With such passive functions the contemporary religions have offered no effective competition to fascism where it became a social movement, and in some areas they have even become adjuncts to communistic states.

Can one indeed find evidence of any respectability, statistically, that religion as it is today is playing a useful or constructive role? If there is any it has eluded me. Every survey ever undertaken of the composition of the criminal population reveals a percentage of the avowedly religious higher than a random sample of the population will show. The percentage of avowed infidels and pagans, on the other hand, appears to be but a small percentage of its chance quota. The higher secular education that on every survey ever made decreases the religiosity of its partakers seems to be an almost fool-proof vaccination against catching prison stripes. One survey in New York State found only four college graduates among the 22,000 prisoners surveyed! On the face of it, there is one item that seems to support the cause of religion, and that is the matter of divorce incidence. People married in a church have a lower divorce rate than those "spliced" before a justice of the peace. But the difference is so small that the apparent superiority of church weddings disappears into the larger factor of the general economic and social stability of people who have their "roots" in a community, of which church membership is a concomitant rather than a cause.

A very recent and extensive research seeking only clues and indications as to the role of religion in the socialization of the individual came up with the folowing conclusion: "Little or no relationship was found between the presence or absence, intensity, or kind of expression of religious faith, and conduct or moral standard. Some of those who were most skeptical, or who denied all need of faith or concern with religious problems, were unimpeachable in behavior, kind and helpful to others, and of high integrity."[18]

Dr. George R. Mursall of the Ohio Department of Welfare found that reformatory inmates had received fully as much religious training as had the average child of matched age and status not in trouble with the law.

The many attempts to find evidence that religion or its practice have desirable consequences in crime prevention have without exception ended in failure. P. M. Smith[19] was forced to conclude that there seems to be no convincing evidence that conventional religion, of itself, has proved an effective antidote to crime. The sociologist, Negley K. Teeters, similarly found no evidence that church goers have less criminal tendency. A recent elaborate report on juvenile delinquency in the public press specifically reported finding no relationship between a lack of religious training and a boy's misconduct.

But how about the desirable effects of church membership and attendance wholly apart from its relation to crime? One significant piece of research[21] examined the effects of church affiliation upon friendship choices. Of six denominations studied, not one showed any reliable effect upon the number of friendship choices received by an individual. But *students without church affiliation* received statistically significantly more friendship choices than those having church affiliation! One might well wonder if there is a sound basis for the apprehensions frequently expressed by parents that church affiliation is necessary to provide an adequate friendship circle for their children. The apprehensions probably disguise a fear that friendships might perhaps be formed outside the sectarian bounds. Sectarian prejudice has been again and again shown to go hand in hand with orthodoxy and church membership. One particularly significant study[22] found race prejudice far higher among students who reported that religion was a marked or moderate factor in their upbringing than in those reporting it as a slight or non-existent factor. Happily churches also contain some individuals that are low in prejudice but on the face of it, the evidence must give the professional apologists for orthodoxy some uneasy hours.

The researches into the matter of honesty among children and its relation to religious beliefs and practice all came up with similar negative results. Some differences could be detected in the way the different social classes behaved in particular situations. And the intelligence level of the child too, showed some tendency to influence the kind of crime a child might commit, or its "honesty" behavior in a given situation. But religious differences failed to show, whether of the different religions or the amount and intensity of the indoctrination of each. In a pioneering and monumental experimental work on deceit in school children, Hugh Hartshorne and Mark A. May[23] after finding small differences, sometimes in favor of Sunday School attendance and as often against it, summed up their findings as follows:

"Yet so far as the facts go, we may say that neither the length of time that children are associated with Sunday school nor the regularity of their attendance seems to be at all associated with their tendency to deceive either at school or on work taken home."

One might well wonder what the basis is for the smug assumptions so commonly made that ethical and aesthetic values are contingent upon animistic agencies, the supernatural, or upon a firm belief in their existence. Here is a typical example: "I have seen many atheists in rapture over a Bach fugue or a Haydn quartet; they little realized that they would have to burn all the great musical scores in a bonfire if they really lived what they preached."[24] Just what is being assumed here anyhow? That the emotional reactions conditioned to some unusual auditory cues are something beyond the ordinary physiology and neurology of human behavior? Is it also true of, let us say, the reactions to boogie-woogie? To be-bop? Does he imply that a disbelief in animistic agencies is in any way related to a refusal or incapacity to acquire a taste for particular kinds of musical sounds, or that aesthetic experiences or enjoyment is something "out of this world" and proof of the existence of one god? Or two? Or a dozen? Or could this be an illustration of what textbooks in elementary logic call a non sequitor?

The notion of an objective or absolute ethics dies hard. The process by which the average individual acquires a modicum of socialization in his behavior habits, the respect for persons other than his own, and the distinction between mine and thine, is such that they seem to have importance not only in his little social world but also to the entire universe. The moral horizon of a social world seems readily to stretch out to infinity. The social world seems to live by a purposive moral order, particularly if such teleological notions are taught in church and Sunday School and echoed by parents and prestiged persons generally. Such ideas, once acquired, are practically immune to evidence and argument to the contrary. And even after such ideas have been given up on the intellectual or verbal level, they remain as conditioned visceral reflexes, even more resistant to extinction processes. To such an individual the scientific picture of a "mechanical" world will never seem right, and such disapproved ideas will be credited with producing all manner of evils, thereby well illustrating the general principle of emotional and ethical congruence or compatibility in perceived cause-effect relations. That is, in naive perceptions of causality, ethically or emotionally approved causes are practically always assigned to approved effects, and vice versa. Thus Stace:[25]

"Is it too far-fetched to suggest that the older more harmonious music reflected the idea of a world made harmonious by its obedience to a divine plan, while current music by its jarring discords suggests the uselessness of all things and all life?"

And again, on the following page we find:

"Much of the darkness, perplexity, and loss of sanity in the modern world, perhaps even the vast increase in the number of neurotic individuals and nervous breakdowns in our time, can be traced back ultimately to that loss of faith in the existence of any purpose or plan in the world-process which has been one of the results of the work of the mainly devout and pious men who were the founders of modern science."

Stace concedes that a few murderous world wars probably had something to do with a loss of confidence in old value-systems, but the above suggestions of the causal processes involved really bear closer examination. If music provides a subtle reflection on the Weltanschauung of the cultures that produces it, what, might one well ask, was the social and spiritual state that produced Oriental and Asiatic musical structures? Or, apart from the contributions of Portuguese traders and hymn-singing missionaries, just what kind of world-ideas are reflected by Hawaiian music? When it is remembered that one culture's funereal tempo is another's cue for gaiety and merriment it could seem that a relatively fortuitous learning process was a more likely determiner of musical structures. It has long been known that the learning process can change the perception of what once was "discords" to pleasant musical experience, even if the sounds differ markedly from conventional harmonies. And, if the lovers of the modern "discords" are impressed with the "uselessness of all things and all life" it is yet apparent that such impressions do not subtract from their keen enjoyment of that life!

But the suggestion in regard to the sources of the "loss of sanity" in the modern world must be given more serious consideration. It is of course true that the overall incidence of all forms of mental abnormality, with the exception of paresis, is now higher than it was in times past. Yet nothing could be more dangerous than a quick jumping to conclusions as to the significance of that fact. It also happens to be true[26] that in the native African the incidence of mental illness of all sorts is only one-tenth that of the white and negro population in western Europe and the U. S.A.! But in the United States, for the period 1930-1940, negroes had a higher rate of first admissions to mental hospitals than the whites. Are we to conclude that the savage life is more "normal" to man and more conducive to mental health? Hardly. The raw incidence of mental abnormality in a race of culture is completely meaningless except in terms of a comparison on the basis of the percentage of each population found in the various age classes. The older the average age of a population the higher the incidence of mental abnormalities. Where a high death-rate keeps down the average age level, few cases of mental abnormality will be found, not only because of the lower average age of the group but also because high death-rates tend to eliminate early the individuals of marginal vigor, more prone to all illnesses, including the "mental." Yes indeed, the higher incidence of mental pathology in our culture is positively a function of our "materialism," the materialism that has reduced death rates and lifted our average life expectancy to somewhere in the neighborhood of seventy years! The older one gets to be, the greater the probability that at some time or other one will be hospitalized for behavior disorders of a serious sort. Manic-depresive insanity, with a typical age of onset in the late forties, is relatively rare where the life-expectancy is somewhere between twenty-five and thirty years, as in India. Post-revolutionary Russia, having just come through a period of years with famine, hardships, and very high death-rates, had a marked decline in the incidence of manic-depressive insanity. As the average age of its population again rose, so did the incidence of that disorder.

The conception of ethics as somehow absolute is a twin sister of the doctrine of a moral or purposive universe. The two tend to stand or fall together in the good graces of man. There is by now, hardly a better publicized fact than that the moral beliefs and practices of the various cultures and peoples differ widely. The naive still react to deviations from their own familiar practices as to moral evils. The entire movement toward a "relativism" in ethics was but an assertion that differences in moral standards from those with which one happened to be familiar were not, ipso-facto, proof of the inferiority of the unfamiliar. This is, after all, the great psychological hurdle that practically everyone has to overcome. But nowhere, has it ever been assumed to my knowledge, that there could not possibly be one set of morals or ethics that could be an improvement over any other. The accusations commonly leveled at moral relativists that they held to such nonsense are completely unwarranted. What is commonly held by these "relativists" and what is unquestionably true, is just that whatever the practices of a culture, they are held to be "moral" in that setting and by that people. It could even be asserted with considerable confidence that, insofar as a given culture was surviving, its practices had at least an overall balance on the survival side. The moral "absolutists" are fond of head-hunting as their horrible example of an obvious "evil" that is not relative. Of course it is an "evil." It is obvious that it would be far better to solve the problem of the humans-to-available-game ratio by means less wasteful of human protoplasm, such as birth control, or even abortions. But the obviousness of it as an evil stems more from its rather dramatic character than from the gross quantity of the evil which is represents. After all, there is little enough to choose between the head-hunting which keeps down the number of people to be supported by the game produced in a given area, and the periodic wholesale slaughter engaged in by "civilized" peoples in their battles for the control of equally vital economic resources, and for which slaughters the blessings of our religions have never failed to be forthcoming. One might well wonder why the "absolutists" wander so far from home for their examples. The head-hunters practice their quaint art precisely for the same reasons that we arm to the teeth and on occasion fight each other, namely because our neighbors do. It is their way of surviving, and who is to say that surviving by such devices is worse than being exterminated?

When your moral relativists asserts that whatever behavior standards obtain anywhere are there considered "moral" he is not asserting that there is nothing to choose between the various moral systems. He is merely bidding us not to take our own standards as absolute. He is inviting us to develop objective and if possible quantitative criteria for a sounder ethics, an ethics that forswears absolutes, that recognizes no power superior to human wisdom in devising patterns of conduct, but yet recognizes with humility the limitations to human powers in determining too far in advance what will be effective and desirable behavior standards in the future. "One step enough for me," as the good old hymn has it. It is precisely in this area that the organized and institutionalized religions have been our greatest sinners. They have made absolutes and certainties in ethics out of the behavior norms and rules of conduct that were observed, not without considerable remissness and coercion, by some tribes emerging out of the neolithic age.

A quite irrational awe surrounds the entire area of the rules of conduct of man to man. A pretense is made that but for some awesome supernatural sanctions that prevented it, man would be so busy flying at the throat of his fellow man that only mutual extinction could posibly result. The whole point of view is most probably a myth assiduously cultivated by the self-appointed authorities and spokesmen for some of the major systems of supernaturalism, the balance of whose wisdom in its entirety has long been laughed out of court or at best been converted into quaint poetry or parable. But by some peculiar quirk of human behavior, the metaphysics, psychology, and ethics which these same systems taught are solemnly held to be "divinely inspired" or of superhuman or supernatural penetration and validity. Thus do we overrate the traditions peculiar to our own particular cultural lineage. Even a cursory glance at history should disabuse us of such childish notions. The great bulk of mankind has somehow managed to exist, create, dream, and inspire, and to do it without what to us seem our absolutely indispensable, and divinely inspired rules of behavior. And, should we look to see wherein our superiority, vis-à-vis these other people lies, we would find it precisely in the areas in which we had most successfully fought to a show-down these same "divinely inspired" rules; where we have most effectively freed ourselves from the dead hand of the past. Our superiority over the teeming, starving, Asiatic millions was bought at the price of violating the "divinely inspired" ethics of the past, at least as it was interpreted "authoritatively" by the traditional experts in those matters.

In thousands of cultures people live, and have long lived, interesting and happy lives under rules evolved under their own peculiar histories. What evidence have we of the superiority of any one pattern of the ethics of conduct over any other? Nothing beyond the criteria of survival. And we do not even know if the survival of a given culture with its ethics is a survival in spite of its ethics or because of it. We assume monogamy to be of course superior to polygamy. But the Children of Israel whose god we have borrowed and whose ethics have contributed much to our own, waxed great and strong under a polygamy. Should some particular biological type of man come to be at a premium in some global competition, monogamy would be as fatal a handicap as it would be today in our barnyards. In such an event, we could find excellent scriptural justification for our polygamous reversions, were we driven to them. We cannot know too far in advance what has functional utility. The monogamous family was a "must" where food was scarce and where, as with man, reproduction involved the year-round support and maintenance of very slowly maturing and helpless infants. To that end man had to lose his seasonal rut and acquire one that was perpetual. In an era of plenty with a system of high differentia in individual acquisitions and rewards, the surviving monogamous traditions limit polygamy to the successive type.

When certain similarities are discerned, as frequently there can be in the ethical rules of behavior in the diverse cultures, this should be no cause for awe and wonder. After all, the nature of the human organism does set some limits, does enforce certain minimal uniformities in the rules or regulations under which he can function effectively. But once it is assumed that ethics are the product of some divine inspiration, such common elements perceived in other ethical systems are written down as the product of some "imperfect" vision of the true faith, rather than as evidence of the operation of convergent factors in the historical process.

Ethical rules, which are quite commonly today presumed to have some contranatural source, come to be surrounded by an aura of the sacrosanct. They simply cannot be questioned. The popular attitude, assiduously cultivated and encouraged by the priesthood, has it that while progress might even be inevitable elsewhere, it is by definition impossible in the area of the correct and proper in human behavior. Why, indeed, is it thus? Is the development of effective rules of interpersonal behavior a matter of such transcendent complexity and metaphysical subtlety that man has forever to be content with what he achieved some three or four thousand years ago? Merely to raise that question should dispose of it. But it obviously does not for the great majority of "believers" in Christendom and out. Here is a source that has proved to be, to put it generously, something short of infallible in matters of simple history, geography, astronomy, cosmology, pathology, and dietetics, to mention but a few areas. Yet in the face of all the evidence of all too human limitations, the ethics taken from that same source is still held to be infallible, to contain such transcendent wisdom that even to question it is treated as an invasion of the domain of the gods. Probably some time in the twenty-first century man will attack the task of the construction of a scientific ethics. It will be high time that we begin to question the wisdom of preserving standards of sexual ethics, prescribed and interpreted by a priesthood leading biologically perverted and psychologically frustrated lives. We learned long ago that it was wholly undesirable to have too high a concentration of frustrated spinsters among those in charge of the education of the young. Emotionally healthly, if perhaps a bit overworked married women have long been known to provide teachers superior to a crop of either frigid or frustrated celibates. It will probably be centuries before we evolve a sound functional ethics of sex, trimmed with an aesthetics that is finally freed from the unfortunate attitudes that were the product of the dubious battle against the combined evils of overpopulation and venereal disease. Such ethics can hardly be expected to be evolved where

the entire subject is blanketed by attitudes dominated by surviving notions of shame, taboo, and sin. A celibate priesthood
is a living monument to the dominance and persistence of these
attitudes. It is not just fortuitous chance that the nucleus of the
organized resistance to the evolution of a functional ethics of
sex is to be found in the organizations of celibates. A world
facing a population problem can no longer take its moral
guidance in this area from such a poisoned source. Happily it
is no longer waiting for the consent of the self-appointed experts
in the Eternal Verities before making sound, sensible, and
aesthetically acceptable adjustments to contemporary reality.
The following Reuters dispatch to the New York Times, date-
lined Rome, November 20, 1953 and published December 13,
speaks eloquently of the entire process:

> "Terruggia is a cluster of stone houses on a north Italian
> hilltop, resembling thousands of similar villages in this
> rugged land.
> But something revolutionary has happened in Terruggia.
> The Terruggians, stanch Roman Catholics in every other
> respect according to their priest, decided early this year
> to have no more children.
> They say the reason for their decision is economic.
> Half of the men in this village of 940 souls are land-
> owners who grow and sell grapes; of the other half, most
> hold moderately well paid positions in factories at nearby
> Casale. Only a few are laborers.
> When the war ended, they enjoyed a boom in wine and
> farm produce prices and they were able to buy smart clothes
> and ride into town on feast days by car or motorcycle.
> Outside, their houses looked like those of any other
> north Italian village, but inside were installed all the con-
> veniences of town life.
> 'We reaped the benefits of long years of hard work, a
> great deal of sweat, and small returns,' one told the village
> priest. 'Now we are organizing our lives so that we may
> have small families and pleasant homes, instead of large
> broods and pigsties.'"

The youngest baby in Terruggia is 10-month-old Sergio Pessina. It was in June that the village priest began to get anxious about his flock, remembering that only in March the Bishop of Casale had exhorted them all to have large families, "which are the blessing of God."

'It is no use at all having fine clothes if you have no children' he said.

Few of the women who heard him had more than one child.

So the village priest, Don Giuseppe, whose benign, bespectacled face hides the firmness of his convictions, began to ask around. His adult parishioners told him their decision.

Birth statistics over the last sixty years show up the seriousness of the step that Terruggia men and women have taken.

In 1895, a record year, forty-three babies were born. The average until the first post-war years was thirty-two, but in 1944 only thirteen were born. There were twenty-six in 1947, at the height of Terruggia's boom, then seventeen in 1948, twenty in 1950 and suddenly, in 1951, the number dropped to eight, rose again to eleven in 1952, and will be nil this year.

But if this seems defiance on the part of Terruggia's men and women, Don Giuseppe never complains of their attendance to other religious duties.

Even though half of them voted Communist and Socialist in the last general election, they all go to church on Sundays. The priest says that crime is unknown in the village.

Don Giuseppe proclaims these facts with pride. But suddenly he throws up his hands:

'If only it weren't for this matter of the children. What can have got into my people?'

And some Italians say the devil has ridden into Terruggia on a scarlet motorcycle, carrying a television set under one arm and a vacuum cleaner under the other."

Here we have the keen eye of the journalist sensing history on the move, and transcribing it for posterity in the only terms in which history can be recorded, namely, in terms of the concrete changes in the human behavior that is history. Here we see the motivation that gives rise to the vigilance that is necessary, as Anatole France put it, to defeat nature's plans. And make no mistake about it, all civilization is a victory over nature, a decided improvement over nature. Whatever "nature" does, it is but a challenge to man to improve upon it, or at least to find out exactly what it is that nature "does."

Given half a chance, practically all humans will strive and strive hard to "get out of the pigsty." One might well be very suspicious of the motives of any institution that would instead seek to keep them there, that would prefer large number of people in dire poverty to relatively fewer, but "out of the pigsties." Today, any institution seeking to validate its claim to ethical leadership would have to lead the way in such moves, rather than grant them belated and grudging acceptance when a failure to do so would almost surely result in a progressive isolation of such an institution from the people it presumes to lead.

On some fine day it will be more generally realized that the wisdom needed to get a few geographical or astronomical facts straight is of a simple order indeed when compared to the broad knowledge about both man and his environment that is essential if man is to launch confidently a series of projects involving his own destiny. Yet all too many of us adhere blindly to some rules-of-thumb that have come down to us out of the past when scientific methodology was not yet even dreamed about. Too long such rules have been palmed off on us as having supernatural sources. The development of intelligent rules of social conduct, nicely adjusted to the objective facts of man's state, presents a real challenge to our scientific knowledge and our emotional objectivity. And, although errors are unavoidable, we can console ourselves that some fine day the break with the barbarian past when our criteria of good conduct were accepted blindly from tradition, is inevitable.

Such negations of the old are simple and obvious enough. They will but clear away the accumulated rubbish of the ages and allow the serious work to begin. First of all, a generation must be raised that is aware of the nature of the problem that confronts man; a generation that has been taught that it has no heavenly crutch to lean upon in this area and that man has a man-sized job ahead of him. Then a genuine respect for individuality must be taught as the sine qua non of an efficient society. Most difficult of all will be the problem of reconciling a multitude to a frank program of trial-and-error in which programs of social action are launched as devices for moving toward particular objectives. Where, for example, we learn to attack the problem of alcohol as a problem in effecting a reduction in its consumption rather than launching a crusade that attempts the impossible. Or, even more complex, initiating an approach to the problem of balancing the aspirations aroused in people with what is a reasonable probability for realization. No easy formulae or solutions; just problems to solve where there are no perfect solutions but where at worst we can channel aspirations and interests where there is work to be done. The ritualists have dominated the field of ethics far too long. It is high time the problem is turned over to objective students of human behavior.

It is fashionable in some circles to hold that a proper reverence for personality is impossible without a belief in a god and the immortal soul that each personality must have. The Reverend Harry Emerson Fosdick could wax eloquent on this theme. Such doctrine is reminiscent of the arguments that formerly were offered as objections to scientific astronomy, geology, and even biology as they appeared to challenge the mythology of Judaism. Without a deity brooding over them, the heavens were presumed surely to lose their glory, the earth its grandeur, and all life its poetry. With personality but a fortuitous product of a material universe, and having no destiny beyond its mundane span, how could anyone take it seriously, let alone make it an object of reverence and perhaps even of material struggles and sacrifices in this vale of toil and sin?

The answer to such nonsense is of course that we have no necessary or innate ideas or conceptions about the future. Living things were good, lusty, capable entities long before they were capable of worrying about what was to become of them post-mortem. A good part of the human race still does not concern itself much over such problematical matters about which it has no information. Of the balance of us that do concern ourselves about the post-mortem functions of our personalities a good part bemoans the survival in an existence that is presumed to be inescapably cursed by desires and urges that are by definition evil. All such notions, be they of a desirable state of affairs or of round after round of burdensome trial from which there is but a slim chance of escape into oblivion, are but little tricks man has learned to play upon himself with self-provided verbal cues. They have no other reality, no other existence. We can ourselves decide if we shall bring up our children to plague themselves with concerns about which we can give them no information whatever. We can make their lives a life-sized hell right here by getting them to worry about ritual violations that have obscene consequences. Or, we can choose to get them interested, even excited, about the possibilities that confront them in the world that leaves no reasonable doubt as to its reality and validity.

A plague on those scorners of the mundane, on the belittlers who bemoan it as at best a hurdle or a proving ground on the road to the wish-fulfillment phantasy of some unimaginative and probably frustrated slave. Such visions are the product of defeated and stunted personalities who failed to see the possibilities offered them by the world they scorned. What could any other realm of reality offer as a long-term guarantee against boredom that is superior to the possibilities inherent in the chemistry of carbon? Or to the challenging combinations of protons, electrons, neutrons, positrons or what have you in the atom? Or, better yet, the endless complexities and possibilities that is each personality, right here under our eyes and hands. There are things to be learned about these super-constellations of chemical systems whose behavior is so challenging. There is ready at hand the strongest of all possible motives for discovery in this area, for it is about ourselves. And, were we not so long misled by the promise of poppy-dreams by the mystics we could have so enriched our lives that the lot of today's most fortunate individuals were by comparison that of a galley slave. The energy spent in placating the powers presumed to be potent post-mortem, properly applied, could give us command over some of the knottiest problems that plague us today and do it in short order. No need to worry about running out of problems either; each "solution" but opens the view to many more.

Where is the evidence that without a belief in personal immortality things generally, and ethics in particular, would go to pot? The primitive societies in which such a belief is absent show no evidence of social or individual moral deterioration. To this day, in Mohammedan cultures, it is solemnly taught and believed that women have no souls. Are their women of notoriously degenerate moral fibre because of that belief? Do they make bad wives, mothers, cooks or housekeepers as a result? Was the Council of Macon meeting in 585 A.D. finally moved to concede women a soul because without that assurance females were lagging seriously behind males in moral development, purity, piety, and chastity? If so, the historians have been singularly silent about this shameful episode in our history that would be chargeable to the lack of the saving grace of a true faith and a correct doctrine in regard to personal immortality. Let's face it frankly; our behavior in this or any other situation is largely a function of the real world we here encounter; the role played by a few verbal sing-songs referring to situations with which by definition we can have no contact can be very easily overestimated. Such beliefs seldom have a role other than that of rationalizations for acts and habits acquired on far more solid grounds or determinants. The apprehensions felt in regard to the dire consequents of the loss of such an item of belief are but the familiar reaction to any threat to ideas and faiths long held to be unquestioned and axiomatic. With an emotional or economic vested interest in such beliefs, any threat to them can come close to striking terror in all but the most insightful of individuals.

This concern for the loss of the individual personality were it not preserved or resurrected beyond death has no sensible or reasoned basis. Just which of the many personalities each of us was at some time between the cradle and the grave, is it that

is to survive? Even Heraclitus knew some two and a half millennia ago that one could not talk to the same personality twice!
So if I survive death, is it the exhibitionistic child, the bumptious adolescent, the domesticated husband, the enthusiastic
heretic, or the doddering arteriosclerotic that, given any reasonable luck, I am yet to become that will survive? It cannot
be all, nor even any two of them. On that count, even biology
is frustrating because no one can leave an exact duplicate of
himself behind, even as far as the chromosomal content goes,
not to mention the myriad fortuitous environmental factors that
have gone to produce a relatively unique individual; and would
have, even had the chromosomal limitations not existed. But
the egotist who insists that something of him must survive, that
he must somehow cheat complete oblivion by however small a
margin has a world full of opportunity open to him. He can
leave his marks and imprints here behind him. He has but to
choose his field of endeavor. Should his egotistical urges take
a biological turn he might slip into the wilds of Idaho and
there acquire five or more wives and twenty or so children, as
the public press recently reported of one lusty male in those
parts. Or he could start a campaign to preserve the Bottle-
necked Whozzis from extermination. Or crusade for a stop-light
at the corner of South and Main streets, thereby preventing the
untimely death of the child that ultimately became Orwell's
Big Brother or the biochemist who hit upon a device for
measuring the level of activity of the anterior lobe of the pituitary gland, or devised a way to screen out the twenty-four
chromosomed sperms, thereby initiating a period of imbalance
in the sexes which did more for the status of women than was
achieved by all the ardent crusaders for the seventeenth amendment! In truth, no one can spend any time whatever upon this
earth without leaving it permanently changed in some dimension. Even the child that dies in early infancy leaves behind it a
pair of parents who are now quite different from what they
might have been but for this circumstance. The individual personality does count, frequently too heavily; there is no such
thing as completely annihilating any personality, and all it was
and achieved, if perhaps unwittingly. *That* is the genuine im-

mortality each of us possesses in his very material nature. It has genuine, objective, and historical possibilities that can be demonstrated here in the flesh and the sticks and the stones of the material world. It offers us concrete and specific programs of constructive action. Who are these schizoid individuals that dwell apart in a phantasy world and yet busily recruit addicts for their spiritual hasheesh when a world of concrete action beckons at every turn?

It would be silly to pretend that the existence of gods, devils, heavens, hells, or immortality tortured or blissful, could be disproved. Such concepts are, by definition, placed beyond the realm of secular evidence or proof. The probability of the truth rather than the falsity of propositions at random is, however, slim indeed. So slim, in fact, that any action upon the assumption of the truth of any one of them would have to be rated as reckless gambling. The prospects of the truth of a particular combination of elements are of necessity even slimmer, if that is possible. Speculations in regard to the possibilities of truth in even the wildest guesses would remain relatively innocuous did they not come to absorb a palpable fraction of human effort and energy that could always be better expended on finite endeavors. The possibilities in regard to a post-mortem existence have never been properly exploited by a really live imagination. And, admittedly, it would be impossible to disprove the truth of anything that the liveliest imagination might invent. Note the evident satisfaction derived by the believers in some particular kind of personal survival, from their challenges to the non-believer that he cannot *disprove* their fond beliefs! It is often argued against the genuineness of contemporary "spirit messages" delivered via practicing "mediums" that the messages are so obviously lacking in wisdom or insight even as judged by earthly standards. Yet what reason is there for suspecting that with death a personality should suddenly acquire capacities it lacked during its normal lifetime? If personalities do survive death it must be assumed that either they are impotent or lack the required ingenuity to get any form of authentic communication back to those that outlived them, or, that they are so transformed at death as to lose even the smallest traces of earthly sentiments toward even those whom they had diapered some two to four thousand times, and fed some twenty thousand meals, in the case of parents preceding their children in death.

If, as is frequently asserted, there is a unity to things spiritual, then the survivors of this material earth must be thrown in together with similar refugees from other planets in other solar systems. Since the tempo of evolution of living forms on the various planets obviously cannot have been synchronized, do they then have a problem of the relation between early and late arrivals? Do some of the later comers arrive with superior "spiritual technology," the equivalent of muskets over bows and arrows; and do they justify their spiritual sovereignty over the "backward" spirits with the rationalization of more effective utilization of spiritual possibilities and potentialities? Come, come, you believers; you cannot disprove such possibilities either!

Perhaps sentimental attachment to old friends, relatives, and neighbors is no part of the make-up of the post-mortem personality, but most portrayals of heavenly bliss have featured it. Are there then family reunions, get-togethers of the old Bridge or Skat or Pinochle players, class reunions and alumni associations, not only of school classes but of trade unions, political parties, war veterans, Kiwanis clubs, chapters of the Loyal Order of Moose, perhaps even a World Alumni Association for those personalities from this particular planet as against the dubious characters arriving from goodness knows what messy places on the as yet unguessed planets no doubt circling at least some of the multitudinous suns in the equally numerous galaxies of the physical universe? Once we begin to asume spiritual doubles it would be the crudest of provincialisms that would not at once recognize as equally valid the claims of other regions of the cosmos. But just the same, we'll have an especially warm spot for those souls that arrive from our old stamping grounds. "Did the Democrats win that next election?" "What happened to the horsepower race in auto engines?" "Did the Dodgers ever win another Series?" "Did that displaced phase-angle method of measuring a BMR pan out?" Perhaps with the passage of time the questions might take somewhat different turns. "Did the Maine coastline continue to sink?" "Are the glaciers still retreating on Mt. Rainier?" "What progress are they making in a more adequate balance between capital goods and consumer goods expenditures?" "Have they ever again tossed the really big firecrackers at each other in anger?" One wonders indeed what of high comedy and tragedy the spirit world might offer that could rival the attractions so scorned right here. The Heavenly choirs eternally chanting His praises sounds on the face of it even worse than the naming of factories, towns, and streets everywhere after a paranoid dictator. We'll have none of it!

CHAPTER XIV

SUMMARY

Patient inquiry fails to reveal any universal theme, belief, motive, or logic to the behaviors called variously magic or religion, together or separately. Nor is there to be discovered any belief or behavior that has anything even remotely approaching universality. The variety of things done, and variously called magic or religion is legion. Nor is there even remotely any general agreement that any particular things or situations can be distinguished as secular or sacred. Attitudes deemed appropriate to the sacred, for example, may well be elicited in situations that in another culture are thought to be wholly secular.

The dichotomy of the "spiritual" as opposed to the "material" which forms the theoretical basis and foundation of much of western religion, specifically providing the contemporary priesthood with an area in which to claim authoritative knowledge, to wit: the domain of "the spirit" or "spiritual values," or "the eternal," is not the product of contemporary scientific insights. It is not made necessary as a simplifying hypothesis to cover important facts of experience. Instead, it is a concept that has had a very complex and interesting history in its development. Briefly summed up, the course of its development in Western culture is something about as follows:

1. Practically all primitive cultures develop terms and concepts for what is conceived to be an active causal agent accounting for the activities of living things, personalities, or many of the more striking or dramatic phenomena of nature. Such agencies are presumed to be of a rarefied, diffuse, or gas-

eous nature, but are presumed of course to be material; they must be palpable to the senses at least at some times or under some conditions. They may be identified with shadows, reflections, or images, or with the breath. They are usually credited with volitional powers. As in the Vedas, mind is an evolved form of matter, and opposed to spirit.

2. A concept of "spirit" arose in several culture areas. This concept was presumed to account for the more abnormal activities of humans for the most part, such as the manifestations of mania, epileptic seizures, hallucinations, the effects of drugs and intoxications of all sorts including the fatigue induced by physical excesses such as extreme thirsts, fastings, dancing till completely exhausted, or self-torture. The normal activities of what we refer to today as the "higher mental processes" were definitely excluded from this concept. But it was these abnormal experiences that were presumed to participate in, or make contact with, a higher spiritual reality which gave the product of such visions or hallucinations a convincing authority over the evidences or information derived from the more commonplace, prosaic senses, and the more normal psychological states.

Professor McDougall's "refinement of the conception of God"[1] was a process then, by which pathological states generally were ascribed to non-material processes or agencies which were widely personified, particularly in the cases where the drugs inducing hallucinations or dramatic conscious experiences were deified and denied the material bases or nature that were taken for granted in ordinary experience states or mental processes. Instead of deifying some material object, as in the case of the soma plant, there was a shift of attention to the conscious states induced by consuming this potent plant, and the conscious drug experience became the theological entity, the "spiritual" reality. Abnormal conscious states, particularly the hallucinatory, not induced by drugs but perhaps by fasting and exposure, were elsewhere similarly apotheosized and dematerialized. A similar dematerialization of the more normal processes of the individual soul or mind then took place, increasing the kinship of human soul and god, and making plausible the "revelations" of gods, speaking through a human "soul" or spirit. Most religious innovators claimed their authority on the basis of such revelations, and the multitudes at large still show a penchant for such inspired or mystical wisdom.

3. In the more sophisticated circles there is now developing an increasing skepticism amounting almost to outright rejection of all pathological states as dependable sources of fact or information. But the belief in the existence of the "spiritual realm" which was a product of having accepted these pathological experiences as unquestioned evidence, has survived, and is questioned by but few. The history of the origins of this animistic belief is not even guessed at by all but a rare few idly curious individuals who have been motivated to take a look behind the impressive facade of the currently unquestioned fictions. Nor is the validity of some of the past products of such dubious psychological states questioned if they form the bases of the institutionally organized and socially respected belief systems current in the individual believer's culture. In general, any new products of such suspicious psychological states are rejected unless they limit themselves to a confirmation of the already established and accepted social fictions or beliefs. Most current religions, and even most systems of metaphysics are representative of this state of belief structure. Here the activities of all living things, and particularly the higher mental process of man are now offered in evidence and testimony of "things spiritual," of forces or agents that "transcend the material" and are now rushed into the breaches made by an encroaching determinism. The normal phenomena of mental activity, which were presumed to be material by the ancients who constructed the concept of the spiritual or the sacred out of the abnormal or pathological experience, or phenomena, must now provide the evidence for that transcendent type of reality once presumed to have no material basis. When the experience of the sacred resulted from drugs, as from the soma with the Hindus, that drug was itself presumed to be the essence of spirit or the sacred, and not a material phenomenon such as the activities of a mere mortal mind. The Hebrews at one time made a similar distinction. With some Greeks too, spirit was discernible only in extreme ecstasy, or mania, or

madness. The Latin word sacer means sacred, but also crazy or demented. The Greek word has a similar duality of meaning. The German word *selig* (sacred, holy) has similar roots with the English word silly.[2]

Where it is "living things" that are presumed to be the locus of current manifestations of such spiritual forces, the believers are currently made uncomfortable by the researches that crystallize, dissolve, recrystallize, and break down the chemical compounds that are these viruses and even synthesize them again to restore the original capacities of "living" things which the component parts definitely could not manifest.[3] Hence the recourse to semantic "solutions" such as denying the status or quality of "LIFE" to such viruses. Yet since these viruses infect man and proliferate in his system with consequences seemingly identical to the layman with those caused by the somewhat larger organizations, the bacteria, any "solution" that denies "life" to the viruses will not carry too much weight or conviction with the average man. Viruses will probably remain in his general semantic catch-all of "bugs."

4. Over the past half-century the frontiers of the scientific inquiry into the nature of living things and particularly the processes involved in the higher mental processes in man have been pushed steadily forward. First, the forced movements or tropisms of plants and animals were shown not to be a purposive but rather a deterministic process, completely understandable in chemical, gravitational, or electrical terms; or perhaps in terms of the permeability of membranes, surface tensions, solution concentrations etc. Then the behavior of the higher animals too was seen not to demand the operation of animistic agents. A few diehards still hold out on man himself. Here, they insist, an animistic agency or process of some kind must be operating that "transcends" the limitations and capacities of the purely "material." Practically without exception, such animists are completely innocent of any knowledge of what has been going on in the modern studies in the associative and higher thought processes. Their very most modern item of information in this area usually consists of having read some popularized account of Professor Watson's conditioning little

Albert to fear a white rabbit. Most often they still speak of "the five senses" as limiting the deterministic possibilities in human behavior. If they have heard of kinesthesis they give no indication of having grasped the significance of these omnipresent receptors in providing a deterministic dynamics for behavior. It can now be confidently asserted that science has come full-circle, back to the single universe of primitive peoples. All the phenomena of his experience are embraced by common scientific asumptions and methodology. Souls, spirits, ghosts, shades, devils and gods are but nightmares out of his unscientific, if perhaps imaginative, past. In making that tragic circuit, from primitive monism to scientific monism man has learned that the way of faith is a sterile, blind, and tragic alley. It is to skepticism and empiricism that man owes everything in which, in the light of longer history, he can take pride. The skepticism evolved but slowly out of a past dominated by what can only be called the magico-religious point of view or perhaps way of life. Just what is the essence of the magico-religious?

If there is such a thing as commonality or universality to the magico-religious it is this: in situations or circumstances important or vital to man, and in which he yet lacks effective means of control, and where overt trial-and-error procedures are either abandoned or have never been applied, he frequently acquires habitual ways of behaving that are obviously not attempts to get at the material nature of the problem nor to solve it on those grounds. In fact, as seen from the contemporary scientific point of view, such activities could of themselves never solve the problem, nor even lead to knowledge of how it eventually might be solved. The amount of confidence the practitioners have in these activities varies widely, and seems to be a personality variable. On the basis of over a decade of research into personality structure by the methods of factor analysis, my colleague, Professor Thomas N. Jenkins, who is interested in such personality variables, describes it as a tendency to accept solutions of problems or difficulties by *postulate*. The desired solution is verbalized or "postulated" and the verbalization is then accepted as more or less real by the personality. It is one of the common forms of neurotic adjustment. The normal personality applies such "solutions" only in limited and usually socially approved areas. Literally minded objectivists find no use whatever for them. They may have a high frustration tolerance or prefer to face problems for what they are and to concern themselves with practical solutions. At the other extreme, a delusionary system completely displaces objective reality. In between are to be found a variety of systems of logic-tight ideas, with their necessary supporting rationalizations.

But effective or not, magico-religious activities are yet persisted in; they are the more or less permanent way in which these people meet such situations. Such behavior is fixed as habits, not by its causal efficacy which of course it does not have, but rather by virtue of the fact that it is persisted in until either:

(a) the situation resolves itself favorably, or

(b) the practitioner persists in the activities, even in the face of failure or catastrophe, until his emotional reactions to the failure have eventually exhausted themselves, as they must in the end anyhow.

In both these cases, the psychology of the learning process is such that the activities engaged in when the situation changed for whatever reason, will recur with the appearance of another or a similar situation or crisis, since in both cases these were the responses practiced in the crisis situation. It is entirely unnecessary that such ritualistic activities have anything to do with resolving or ending such crises: it is only necessary that they be persisted in until the situation changes. The term "situation" here includes the emotions or attitudes of the suppliant. With a recurrence of a crisis, the activities practiced during similar emotional disturbances will recur; and belief follows on the heels of practice or action. That is why it is perfectly possible for one set of rituals or practices to displace another without the new having any mechanical advantage over the old. Circumstances need but conspire to have the new activities in action when crises are resolved, or failure, loss, or defeat have been emotionally accepted. Magico-religious behavior is causally effective only on the behavior of its practitioners or devotees.

The advantages that practical or "scientific" devices and techniques have in getting acceptance is just that very often the crises are resolved, directly the correct things are done. Where any considerable time elapses between the time even the most "scientific" thing is done and the results appear, the odds increase that credit for the success of "cure" will go instead to something that happened to have been going on precisely when an improvement was noted. Frequently surgery or medication produces no, or but few, immediate benefits. A holy shrine visited after secular therapy frequently gets the credit for the "cure," since the visit might well coincide with some impressive changes in the patient's subjective feeling state.

Precisely what sort of activities are engaged in, or become the habitual mode of meeting crises is a highly fortuitous matter. The effects produced are much the same no matter what is done. Even a casual pursuit of the literature of religion and magic quickly leaves but one question to answer, namely: is there indeed anything that the human organism might conceivably do that is not the standard procedure somewhere? The answer is that the ordinarily assumed "limits" of the possible are given a very good work-out and an even better stretching! Yet here, as elsewhere, factors operate to set limits, to favor responses or behavior of one kind as against another so that while yet great variability obtains there are none-the-less factors making for similarities in such ritualistic behavior. Among such limiting factors are the following:

(a) Any habits previously acquired in whatever situation might be called out as relatively complete patterns by some minor similarity in any frustrating or critical situation. Habits appropriate to a child vis-à-vis a parent might appear in an adult placed in a hopelessly distressing situation. In general, patterns of behavior found effective elsewhere in a culture have good prospects for appearing as rituals in crisis situations. If entreaty, for example, is socially effective in a culture, then its rituals are likely to embody it.

(b) There are obvious advantages that favor minimal or symbolic activities since they can be persisted in for long periods at minimal energy expenditure and with a minimum of interference with ongoing practical efforts. Note how postures, verbal formulae, and minor gestures recur in practically all systems of magical or religious practices. Verbalizing requests or desires is widespread indeed and retains a high repute even in areas where scientific methods and principles are otherwise respected.

(c) Other things equal, probability will favor activities that symbolize, caricature, or duplicate some part or aspect of the problem or its desired outcome as illustrated by the prevalence of water sprinkling in rain making ceremonials; or, even better, the making of golden "emerods" and mice to stop the bubonic plague.[4]

(d) The odds favor activities engaged-in in deadly earnest since they are more likely to be long continued, and hence have better prospects of being engaged-in when a crisis is resolved for whatever causes.

(e) The odds also favor activities of a highly exciting or orgiastic sort since such activities better fill time, distract more effectively, and hence more effectively shorten time psychologically, thus seemingly terminating crises more quickly. Pageantry, sacrifice, orgies, tableaux, chants, and dances are almost universal, at least at some times or under some circumstances.

(f) The odds also favor a certain amount of mystery and secrecy in such procedures, particularly when they are the province of a specialist. Hence we have magical cantrips, secret verbal formulae, unmentionable names of gods, rites and chants in archaic or mysterious languages, etc.

Lastly, it must not be forgotten that usage and tradition can make anything seem possible and reasonable; and, once established in habit and expectation, any interference with, or modification of the familiar can be expected to be greeted as an unquestioned evil and to arouse intense emotion.

Where the individual resolves conflicts or problems "by postulate" as Professor Jenkins puts it, a threat to such a postulate becomes a threat to the structural integrity of the personality. This is the psychological factor in the individual "believer" that has made it easy for a priesthood to enlist its followers in sanguinary wars of extermination against rival or competing systems. An unbeliever constitutes a threat just by his very existence, since he threatens the belief-structure of the postulate.

We are now in a position more intelligently to ask as well as answer such questions as: "Is man naturally religious?", "Has man a religious instinct?", "Does man have to believe in something?", etc. As a matter of fact, these questions are actually but very seldom asked; the answers to them are, instead, frequently asserted without substantiating evidence in simple declarative sentences such as: "Man is naturally religious," "Religion is instinctive to man," or as it was emphatically put to me recently by the garbage collector, "Ya gotta believe in sumptin."

If we restate the first question in some such manner as this: will man continue to fixate as habits whatever activities he happened to have been engaged in when crises are resolved, problems solved, or when emotions of fear, frustration, or depression have finally spent themselves, the answer is a positive "yes." For these same learning processes also turn up inventions, discoveries, and solutions of problems, as well as fixate non-causal, ritualistic, or ceremonial activities. But how about the activities that make no material contribution to the solution of such problems as man encounters? Will he continue to retain such habits or activities? Since many such activities have direct repercussions or effects back upon his own behavior, (as do all beliefs, faiths, verbalized or unverbalized hunches, theories, and hypotheses, frequently keeping him actively trying, or patiently waiting for favorable outcomes of his problems), the answer again must be that such habits already current in a culture are rather likely to survive until they become altogether too incompatible with the balance of the cultural acquisitions. For example: the making of golden mice and bubos to control bubonic plague has been replaced by large scale rodent extermination programs. However, new ritualisms will probably keep turning up as man encounters new problem situations for which he has no more effective secular means of control.

Now any given culture can maximize the role and importance of such ritualism, or it can bend every effort toward minimizing it. It can, as in old Tibet, put about one-fourth of its effective man-power to spinning prayer-wheels or telling off beads in keeping track of ritual sequences. Or, it might begin a process of luring the priests back to the secular economic life with imported Chinese girls making up the shortage of local women resulting from infanticide on local female babies, and sweetening the deal with offers of state loans to tide them over in the period of adjustment to the material world, as was reported from Tibet on page 22, column 1, of the New York Times on October 2, 1955. The writer is always saddened at any news of the passing of any of the quaint folk-ways anywhere on the earth. He would like nothing better than to keep Dobuans pursuing their paranoid existence, Trobrianders allowing their adolescents unlimited license, Fiji Islanders continuing to regale themselves with their cannibal feasts, and Tibetans pushing on toward a theoretical goal of having 100% of their manpower applied to beads and to prayer-wheels. To this end he would gladly volunteer to do guard duty anywhere on earth, for a reasonable period of service, to keep Yankee traders, religious missionaries, and Communist agents out of these historical museums for the indefinite future. We will need them around in the flesh for some time to confound the breed of human that is forever telling us that this, that, or the other minor social variant, or political or economic innovation couldn't possibly be made to work, usually because it is held to be "against human nature."

So it should be obvious that there is no particular human situation or contingency in which man must *of necessity* have recourse to ritualistic, non-interventive, or stereotyped behavior, whose sole claim to our loyalty grows out of its having been our traditional way of meeting such situations. In any culture once touched by the magic wand of science such activities are abandoned in wholesale batches. We rejoice when it is the futile ritualism of cultures other than our own that is thus made technologically obsolete. But everywhere, the priesthood that has come to live by, for, and on such activities, quite under-

standably takes a dismal view indeed of such losses suffered
by the traditional and the venerable. Man's inborn equipment
makes it probable that in some situations he will fixate ritualistic
activities as more or less permanent habits. But there is no compulsion or necessity stronger than the rigidities of habits once
acquired that demands that such activities be institutionalized
or retained in perpetuity in all situations or even in any situation. Certainly there have always been individuals who have
summarily rejected the local tribal irrationalities or have bowed
to them under silent protest. As for the "necessity of believing
something," it has long been apparent that even where the
pressures to conform to belief in local fictions is strong, an
increasing percentage of well educated people find that statistical probabilities provide far superior objects of faith, in that
they prove far less disconcerting and destructive to the core
of the personality when more or better data demand their revision. Those who insist that a faith in an anthropomorphic god
is essential to a stable personality are willfully overlooking the
fact that millions of humans have lived the good life believing
nothing of the kind, and are continuing to do so.

One glance at any of the current anthropomorphic deities
is sufficient to demonstrate to all but those hopelessly indoctrinated during their helpless infancy, that these gods were
created by man when he was not too well informed. Therefore,
on current standards, they are not very moral. If the god or
gods presumed to be running the affairs of this earth are all-
knowing and all-powerful, then their ethical standards must
remain forever an enigma to human reasoning processes. On
the obvious face of things, they might be powerful and knowing but devoid of moral content. They might be knowing, and
moral, but then they would have to be far short of all-powerful.
It is increasingly difficult in these days to conceive morality
separated from wisdom.

And just how wise have the various man-concocted gods and
their vicars and prophets been? Is there any evidence whatever
that any wisdom directly or indirectly credited to the gods has
in any way transcended the capacities of mortal minds? The
simple truth of the matter is that nowhere is there any such

evidence. All known systems of supernaturalism have been derived by way of some minor modifications of previously existing systems with here and there some evidence of a more violent reaction against some specific aspects of the older cults, as for example the vigorous reaction of Moses against the unbelievable proliferation of gods and idols of the Egyptians. Certainly there have here and there been innovators and leaders in this field much as there have been ingenious specialists in all other endeavors. But where is the historical evidence that the individuals who claimed to be gods or to speak for them have demeaned themselves any more morally or intelligently than has the secular leadership of less presumptuous mortals? If there is any such evidence it has effectively evaded my prying eyes. The performance of the American clergy as hatemongers in the first world war is all too typical.[5]

Have religious institutions been any more humane in the process of consolidating their power than has secular machinery similarly occupied? The taste for slaughter exhibited by the sons of the Prophet was more than matched by that of the Christians who liquidated heathen and heretic with the ruthlessness, thoroughness, and zeal shown by Chicago prohibition-time beer-barons "rubbing out" their rivals, or by Hitler in liquidating Jews, or Stalin liquidating Trotzkyites, or rival politicians in the banana republics in liquidating each other. Let us face it; we are all ready to be savage in some cause. The more dogmatically and absolutely "right" we feel ourselves, the more savage we are likely to be. That is why many of us prefer the company of people who have forsworn certainties and instead limit themselves to mere probabilities, which guarantees that the possibility of being wrong is never absent from them. Most dangerous of all are the moral certainties we feel when a belief or a program of action is shared 100% by a crowd which produces and maintains such attitudes by the usual devices of crowd behavior. It is so safe and so very easy to agree with the crowd. Probably the most valuable type of moral courage that man is capable of is that called for in standing up against solid majorities, in holding unpopular opinions. It is so very easy to be "convinced" by a logic that everybody echoes.

Organized religions have been particularly intolerant of such deviates and hold-outs. It is an interesting paradox in the psychology of belief that the poorer the evidence for a belief and the stronger the evidence against it, the greater the emotional heat, zeal, and intolerance with which such a faith must be held. The better the evidence for a theory or belief and the weaker the evidence against it, the easier such a belief can be held without excessive heat and intolerance. This is the great handicap suffered by the scientific point of view vis-à-vis any and all dogma. The more a dogma feels itself under attack the more vigorous the offensives it launches. The scientific point of view by its very nature tends to dissipate any emotional heat since it involves no conflicts that generate it. Hence the frequent attacks by theologicans on "Godless Scientists." The scientists with neither conscious nor unconscious misgivings in regard to the probabilities underlying their opinions are seldom moved to reply in kind. This has social disadvantages since an unthinking ignorant rabble tends to fall in behind a noisy attack.

It is difficult to imagine motivation persistent enough to maintain the heat necessary to pursue to the bitter end the famous Hundred Years' War, or even the Thirty Years' War, without some such source in the conscious and unconscious doubts of the participants. And let it be remembered that these were wars of religious bigotry. For no other motive has man maintained such organized hostilities for so long. And the savageries of the inquisition were not again matched until a paranoid P.F.C.[6] took over the leadership of a bankrupt industrial capitalism, some four hundred years later.

In Europe's dynastic wars religions were, like the bishops on the chess board, just one of the various kinds of the kings' defenders. The same god was invoked and was presumably active on both sides of all the wars in Christendom. The only possible theological hypotheses that could be made to fit European history are either the assumption of a single, cynical and sadistic god, or several gods, rivaling each other in power, cruelty, and cynicism. One wonders at the paranoid compulsion that drives some personalities to project their emotional and security needs into their perceptions of the universe. Otherwise there should be far less resistance to seeing the world as it actually is in relation to man, namely ethically neutral. Man undoubtedly is, as the Genesis myth has it, a product of the dust of the earth. He remains closely related to that earth: its products nourish him, its air keeps his oxidative processes going, and his equilibrial senses and his muscles are nicely matched to local gravitational relationships. Here is to be found such "evidence" as there is of man's special importance to the universe, of man somehow being "in tune" with it. But it is evidence only if it is first set on its head so that it is read as if the universe were planned to fit man, rather than seeing man as the more or less fortuitous product of that universe.

The Northern theologians who were convinced during the Civil War that their God was on the side of the anti-slavery forces were matched by those in the South who were equally eloquent and scripturally armed in favor of slavery. If there was a southern church that spoke up against the callous savagery of Andersonville it has left no record of its protests. Organized religion has always managed to provide prayers and thanks for victories in bloody wars. That is what long ago motivated Robert Burns to write:

"You heretics, are these your pranks—
To murder men and give God thanks—"

In more recent history, including two world wars, is there any evidence that organized religion anywhere did anything but bless the battlers on both sides? Did any church anywhere loudly blow the alarm when Franco applied arms and terror to a democratic state? Alas! No. But there is strong evidence that one church did mobilize all its influence to pressure legislation through the American congress forbidding the sale of arms to that democratically elected government during its ordeal by fire. It is to Franklin Delano Roosevelt's undying credit that he twice publicly admitted the error of that part of American policy. Vigorous and timely action then might well have headed off the second world war.

Is there any evidence that religion has provided a superior brand of wisdom for the guidance of secular affairs, or in the burning social issues of the day? With the population of the earth growing by geometric leaps from unchecked fertility but with epidemics and diseases well under control, what religious leaders spoke up for the necessity of planned parenthood? Not one! But many did hound Margaret Sanger to prison for her constructive work in that direction. Today, with birth control not yet freed from hypocrisy, ("Sold only for the prevention of disease".') yet almost universally practiced against all the threats of hell-fire that the theologians were able to call down upon it, it has become a prerequisite for orderly social existence, everywhere. Even the hopelessly miserable Orient is turning to it, happily without serious opposition from their priesthoods.

Meanwhile, over here it is again the forces of institution-alized religion that are in the van of the fight to keep parent-hood from becoming completely voluntary. This time they are bending every effort to prevent the repeal of anti-abortion laws. What is more, they are the ardent spirits behind the needling of law enforcement officers to see to it that all practitioners are prosecuted, lest the laws against it succumb to their violation as did the prohibition amendment. When laws fail to conform to the actual practices of a people they are bad laws indeed. With about as many "illegal" operations being performed in the land as there are live births, we are obviously dealing again with another "prohibition" law. But in this case we are not dealing with a drive to satisfy a more or less pathological form of drug addiction. We are dealing with a matter of high ethical motivation. Only the ignorant, the careless, and the completely uninhibited can lightly launch another individual into this "vale of toil and sin." The commitments involved must give pause to even the dullest wit that can yet make crude calculations in regard to the future. For the educable young, the cost of an adequate education alone is a matter of some ten to twenty thousand dollars per child. To withhold even one such sum from the clutches of the landlord, the super-market, the tax-collector, and the installment seller is well beyond the capacity of the average wage earner. Is there then any wonder why highly moral people wish to, and do in the case of a failure of contraceptives, reduce their biological commitments by illegal means if necessary? They consider it far more immoral to have children for whom they cannot provide that which they know in their hearts that a child should have if it is to have an even break in this world.

But are our experts in the transcendental and the supernatural, our self-appointed authorities in the eternal verities leading the fight to bring our legal structures into line with the practices dictated by our awakened moral sensitivities? Indeed not. They assure us instead that no morality even exists other than that developed by some barbarous tribes about twenty-five hundred years ago, when they were fighting in a dubious battle for survival under a particular set of conditions.

So in this matter, moral leadership in the world goes by default to the Scandinavian countries, and even to Russia, now staggering back toward sanity after over two decades of paranoid leadership under Stalin. Meantime, over here, student attitudes at three widely scattered colleges, and as long ago as 1929, have consistently shown majorities of from 55 to 61 percent favoring the legalizing of abortions.[7]

Lest it be assumed that it is only in matters pertaining to sex and reproduction that the church has been reluctant to abandon obsolete moralities and face the social realities of a rapidly changing world, where are the theologians or priests who spoke up for old age pensions, unemployment insurance, state support for otherwise destitute families, mothers' pensions, and workmen's compensation laws, all now solidly accepted social provisions? There were a miserly few at best; and they were "beaten to the draw" several decades by the godless Socialists at that!

There is no better test of morality than the social wisdom of the tenets of that morality, and time has a way of putting it to the proof. Have our priests provided us with guidance that can pass such a test? Sad to relate, most significant social ameliorations have come against the best efforts of the priesthood to prevent them. There is of late even some evidence that at least some fraction of the clergy is becoming acutely aware of this sad state of the institution. One hears loud cheers for the Catholic Church for its admittedly belated but none the less welcome stand against the imbecilities of the southern caste system, and for the welcome ending of Jim Crow in the conclaves of the Protestant pastors in that same unfortunate American area. Under communist needling, the tide has turned. The churches are keeping step, not leading, the van. But where is there ever any evidence of any wisdom emanating from the clergy of whatever stripe that suggests that they are privy to any source of information or guidance that has any advantages whatever over that which man can himself dig out with scientific methods, or even can offer it what could remotely be considered competition of any sort? Where indeed? Their pretense to inspired wisdom in the field of ethics will not stand critical examination.

Instead, there is all too much evidence that a concern with the supernatural inevitably distracts and deflects human energies from the tasks of solving very real and immediate problems that confront man in the here and now. No matter what contributions they make make in the future, the priesthoods of whatever stripe can never live down, nor make amends for, their disgraceful role in retarding the development of modern science during the past millennium in Christendom. But what is even worse, they seem to have learned nothing from that defeat and are now closing ranks, better to fight the same sort of a battle in the area of the social sciences and ethics. Their insistence in this area, that the means for ameliorating man's estate lies in some transcendent "beyond" goes far to justify the worst charges that supernaturalism is, in its social functions and consequences, a dangerous opiate. And, what is perhaps even worse, it discourages objective attempts at intelligent social trial-and-error, planning, and even research, and undermines man's faith in his own resources. It is again a dangerous force, apparently aiming to duplicate in the area of man's social and ethical knowledge what it so effectively did in the development of the physical sciences; namely, fought the progress of secular knowledge until the priesthood was forced to admit grudgingly and ungracefully, and item by item, that its domain was the "spiritual" and not the "material" world. But science has caught up again with these medicine men. It challenges loudly the duality of the spiritual and the material and asserts again that this is indeed a Universe in which we are functioning, and that thus far no key to its mysteries other than that of scientific method, is anything more than the wish-fulfillment phantasy of emotionally infantile individuals. Professor John Dewey had no illusions in regard to the role played by supernaturalism when he wrote:

"What is the inevitable effect of holding that anything remotely approaching a basic and serious amelioration of the human estate must be based upon means and methods that lie outside the natural and social world, while human capacities are so low that reliance upon them only makes things worse? Science cannot help; industry and commerce cannot help; political and jural arrangements cannot help; ordinary affections, sympathies and friendship cannot help. Place these natural resources under the terrible handicap put upon them by every mode of anti-naturalism, and what is the outcome? Not that these things have not accomplished anything in fact, but that their operation has always been weakened and hampered in just the degree in which supernaturalism has prevailed."[8]

It is a strange phenomenon, this insistence that man is somehow incapable of bringing his powers to bear on the problem of a sensible code of conduct for himself. Right, Wrong, Good, True, and Beautiful presumably are Absolutes that transcend man and his capacities. But, might one ask, if man is incapable of learning a better, more effective pattern of behavior for a particular situation, where is he to look for a more infallible guide? The supply of self-appointed authorities in such matters is generous indeed. A high dignitary of an organized system of supernaturalism just recently was quoted in the press as asserting that the power hierarchy of which he constituted a cog was appointed by supernatural agencies as final arbiter in matters of faith and morals, *including political* behavior, namely voting. That is no new pretense; but old or new, it is just about the most audacious claim that ever was based upon a pun,[9] the humor of which was, I fear, lost on the countless victims of the inquisitions designed to discourage any suspicion that the pun was anything other than deadly earnest. Let me hasten to add that I fully agree with this dignitary that everything man does, and believes, not only his moral ideas but his political behavior as well as the lowliest, most prosaic act of his practical, economic life, has moral consequences. It is ridiculous to pretend that the acts having moral consequences or implications are limited to a few narrow areas. I merely question the soundness of his morals. When the church hierarchy began modestly to limits its claims of infallible authority to matters of faith and morals, that was a retreat from its historical position that all mundane sovereignty was exercised with and by permission of supernatural forces whose authoritative spokesmen this priesthood pretended to be. Time was when the hierarchy could make a king stand barefooted in the snow till he admitted precisely who was boss. And it has continued to exercise such powers wherever possible and until abrogated by the authority of force. Like any other vested interest, it claims everything in sight and then perhaps generously disavows claim to some of what it has been perhaps compelled to surrender and sees no hope whatever of recovering. Such power drives are quite comprehensible in human society and are certainly nothing unique or particularly reprehensible. Even history will judge them not so much on the basis of the rationalizations they managed to invent for their actions, nor even on the extent to which they violated the traditional expectations of the citizenry over whom they exercised sovereignty, but rather on the basis of the kind of life they made possible for the people of the culture pattern they established. Few indeed are the individuals who bemoan, here in the United States, the ruthless displacement of the aboriginal peoples and culture that once "owned" this continent. We do not even question the long run superiority in every dimension of the now dominant culture, and perhaps grin a bit at the mention of the bounty once paid for the scalps of the "varmints." We consider that the results more than justify the means by which they were achieved.

Power struggles are nothing new in history. We can learn to identify the various parties to the controversies, and see which of them is more nearly aligned with our own interests: economic, intellectual, moral, or aesthetic. Having identified the contending parties we can take their respective claims with the proverbial grain of salt. When one such party makes the claim that there cannot possibly ever be any objective or factual bases upon which to erect or modify an ethical structure, that instead we are forever dependent upon their particular interpretations of rules derived long ago from supernatural sources, even the most gullible might well begin to suspect that such a position just cannot muster any evidence whatever of the more conventional sort to carry conviction. If one is to assume that our particular gods designed our particular code of conduct, who then gave the heathen *their* ways? Were they designed to provide amusement and smug self-satisfaction for the devout here in this world and stimulating wails of agony from their brimstone griddles in the next? Time was when precisely such motives and beliefs in the faithful were deliberately cultivated. They are still good coin in some of the lower and more frustrated strata of the faithful. In both Islam and Christendom the naive believers have over long periods been taught that it was their duty to slaughter the unbeliever, or whoever refused to accept their particular version of divine guidance. They have not had a change of heart; they have just been shorn of the powers for mischief.

The effective organization and conduct of human affairs calls for intelligence, not blind faith. It demands the application of scientific method to the human equation both in its individual and its social dimensions. It calls, first of all, for objective insight into those blind, emotionally reenforced and persistent behavior tendencies that we call—when others exhibit them—rigidity and stubbornness; but when we demonstrate them they are monuments to the power of the "true faith." Faith, whose authority was unquestioned, did not prevent the bloodiest of warfare, no more when states were practically theocracies than when their priesthoods were reconciled to a role in which they but sanctified the decisions of a military or entrepreneurial state. There is no evidence that a decline in faith preceded the downfall of the various cultures that once waxed strong; nor did a brand new faith stay the downfall of the Roman Empire.

Apparently many complex cultures had developed a priesthood, authoritative in ritual and dogma, but not all did. The

Chinese civilization did not, and it is still with us, at the moment making the transition to an industrial society and still lacking a priesthood, in spite of millions spent by Christian missionaries of varying stripe. It has been estimated that, even counting "rice Christians," i.e. those people who attached themselves to the mission machinery because it meant a means of livelihood in that overpopulated land, the cost per convert calculated from the expenditures of the boards of missions was around ten thousand dollars! Nor did the Greece of the Golden Age have a priesthood with a dogma, and that tiny city-state, having about as many free citizens as Walla Walla, Washington, created a culture that can truly be said never to have died. Any constructive social research into the question of the precise conditions giving rise to significant human creativity must seriously consider the possibility that this creativity in the absence of a class with a vested interest in a dogma was not just pure chance. Generalization from a few cases is dangerous, but right-thinking people today almost unanimously identify the monstrosities perpetrated by the paranoid Stalin, with the abandonment of private ownership of capital goods, overlooking completely the evidence of pathology in that leader. It should be added that they do not identify the operation of Hitler's gas ovens with the profit economy he was desperately trying to preserve, nor do they ascribe the savagery that produced Pearl Harbor to the type of economy the Japanese ruling class was trying to maintain. Mark well these instances of emotional and moral congruence in the perceiving of cause-effect relations! They remind one of the "causes" of the fall of Rome so glibly assigned in popular oratory. At any event, any claims of the indispensability of the priesthoods with their dogmas to civilization rests upon foundations that will not bear examination.

The problems that confront us call for science and more science. On some, I hope not too distant day, we will see to it that our political leaders can pass tests of emotional stability at least as drastic as those which reject men for selective service in the ranks, not to speak of those necessary for commissioned officers. A few psychopaths still slip by, or become that way while in service, but not many. The chief obstacle to any such programs is a public intelligently appreciative of the probability principle as a basis for decision and action. A public taught to revere blind faith is in a very poor position to acquire an intelligent respect for probability. We have a supreme court for legal decisions; what is to prevent us from coming to accept the verdict of a board of experts on the fitness of a politician to hold office? Does the Supreme Court destroy political democracy? The problem is but one of some research into the specific problems involved, and a public intelligently "sold" on the conception of qualified experts with specifically limited functions. Those rooted in the past will swell the chorus of "You can't this, and you can't that," but surely all of us were sometime told that "Can't never did anything."

Intelligent political leadership will some day toss out suggestions to be kicked around, something after the manner in which some of the later New Deal measures first were suggested. Programs can be suggested as possibilities, not as infallible cure-alls, or revelations. Along with this should come an inventory of persons and institutions and vested interests likely to oppose such innovations and the obvious reasons for such probable opposition. There is sadly lacking a technique of sound statesmanship, but it can be developed. The problem again is with a public that demands the categorical absolutes so long indoctrinated by institutionalized religions.

Moral absolutism is the greatest enemy of scientific objectivity. Divest any system of values of its supernatural sanctions and it stands revealed as the archaic habit systems of a long dead past. It is difficult enough to make sound and objective evaluations of rival or alternative behavior patterns without complicating the problem with the rigidities of behavior that of necessity follow upon any assumption that the last and final word on any matter was said long ago. Intelligent social action is difficult, if not impossible, in any area in which popular attitudes remain at the level of moral absolutes. The reason that organized religions have been almost completely impotent in providing intelligent and effective moral leadership is simply that they have had none to give. Intelligent social leadership must begin with what is actually present on the human scene today, not with a moral judgment emphatically made thousands of years ago of something now presumed to have been identical with, or to have the same relevance to, the events of the present. Such beginning must be followed by the application to that current scene of the very latest and best scientific fact-finding devices. Practical goals then must be set, based upon relevant fact rather than upon two thousand year old absolutes. Organized religions cannot provide this type of leadership because the priesthood is by definition and training expert in archaic traditions, and cast in an institutional role where it can do absolutely nothing but defend and support that tradition. It is this orientation toward the past that has made organized religion the natural ally of all reactionary social forces. It rarely overcomes this handicap. Its moral myopia, evident when it takes a stand on social issues, is likely to result in the support of causes such as the ill-fated prohibition amendment. During the days of business stagnation there was a bit of moral carping at business enterprise from some of the religious leaders, but with inflationary prosperity they vie with one another in their denunciaticns of Godless Communism. Far from any evidence of far-sighted and consistent leadership, the clergy has shown nothing other than the all too human tendency to fill their sails with whatever winds of public opinion may blow, and always with their vested interest firmly at the helm.

With a subject having ramifications as wide as has religion, only a limited treatment of but a few of the various aspects of the subject can be attempted in the confines of a single volume. What has been attempted here has been but a brief outline of the many theories presuming to account for religion, with or without magic, together with the principal shortcomings and limitations of some of the more common ones. This has been followed by a critical analysis of the chief metaphysical assumptions upon which most religions rest, together with the evidence from contemporary science for abandoning them. The actual beliefs and behavior commonly identified as religious are then treated as problems in the psychology of habit which easily accounts for any and all the phenomena of the magico-religious. The nature of the priestly caste and its role in the institutionalization of their special interests is given far less space than it richly deserves. The priesthood deserves a large volume all to itself. The manifestations of the magico-religious habits of thought and action in the modern world are briefly reviewed, as well as the linkage of the magico-religious with the ethics of conduct.

The author is motivated by no special animus against any particular faith or creed. If illustrations are drawn from some specific religion it is only because one must of necessity draw upon the familiar. Certainly there has been no intention to make invidious comparisons of one creed against another nor to evalute any of them, except on specific items under examination. But it is insisted that religions are historically a trial-and-error product exactly like every other element in our culture, and, as such are proper subjects for objective analysis and study. It is high time they are one and all stripped of their pretenses of having some special, transcendental character. They are but behavior; human, all too human!

I INTRODUCTORY

1. Thus: E. H. Page, "The Psychology of Religion After 50 Years," Canadian Journal of Psychology, 1951, 60-67—"neither theology nor psychological theory, as at present understood, seems likely to gain deeply from the attempt to apply the empirical operations of psychology to the phenomena of religion."

2. E. Washburn Hopkins "Origin and Evolution of Religion," Yale University Press, 1923, pp. 3-5.

3. Alfred M. Lee, "The Press and Public Relations of Religious Bodies," Annals of the American Academy of Political and Social Science, Philadelphia, March 1948, pp. 120-131.

4. See an excellent discussion of this point in Ellis Freeman, "Social Psychology," Henry Holt, N. Y., 1936, Chapters XIV and XV.

5. Treatise on the Gods, N. Y., A. A. Knopf, 1930.

6. N. Y. Modern Library (Random House), p. 84.

7. Varieties of Religious Experience, Longmans, 1925, p. 31.

8. Floyd Allport, "Institutional Behavior," Chapel Hill, N. C., U. of N. C. Press, 1933, p. 423 and 427-428.

9. Religion in the Making, Macmillan, 1926, p. 119.

10. op. cit., p. 158.

11. op. cit., p. 37.

12. op. cit., p. 16. Later, (p. 27) he holds: "But religion is still a thoroughly social phenomenon."

13. "Sociology of Religion," University of Chicago Press, 1944, p. 383.

14. Structure of Social Action, Glencoe, Ill., The Free Press, p. 424.

15. N. Y., The Macmillan Co., 1950, p. 22.

16. Marett, R. R., "The Threshold of Religion."

17. The Individual & his Religion, N. Y., The Macmillan Co., p. 52.

18. See Paul Radin, "Primitive Man as Philosopher," N. Y., D. Appleton & Co., 1927, p. 375.

19. Kluckhohn, Clyde, and D. Leighton, "The Navaho," Cambridge, Mass., The Harvard University Press, 1946, p. 122.

20. T. H. Gaster in Ferm, V. (ed.) "Forgotten Religions," p. 117. N. Y. Philosophical Library, 1950.

21. For this information I am indebted to Professor Richard Lessing of the University of California.

II SOME POPULAR EXPLANATIONS OF BEHAVIOR AND RELIGION

* Philosophy of Religion, N. Y. Macmillan and Co., 1914, p. 4.
1. Howells, William, "The Heathens," Doubleday, 1948, pp. 18-19, 87.
2. T. Veblen, "Theory of the Leisure Class," chapter on devout observances.
3. "Primitive Religion, Its Nature & Origin," N. Y., Viking Press, 1937, p. 282.
4. John Cyril Flower, London, Kegan Paul, Trench, Trubner and Co. Ltd. 1927.
5. From "Collected Poems," N. Y., Dodd Mead, 1924.

III SEX AND RELIGION

1. From: A Treasury of Humorous Verse by Samuel Hoffenstein, N. Y. Liveright.
2. Life Among the Lamas of Choni, National Geographic, Vol. 54, Nov., 1928, pp. 569-619.
3. New York Times, October 21, 1956. Page 22 of the magazine section.
4. "Look" Magazine, Nov. 29, 1955, p. 28 estimates the U. S. Jews at 3.5% of the population, having 10% of the total personal income and 20% of the 9,000 millionaires!
5. Life Magazine, August 20, 1956. pp. 95-104.
6. The Egyptian Bull-god Apis was believed to have been born of a virgin cow!
7. Sidney Hartland, "Primitive Paternity," Vol. I, pp. 63-64, quoted by Chapman Cohen, in "Religion and Sex," London, T. N. Foulis, 1919. p. 108.
8. See Chapman Cohen, op. cit. p. 165 ff.
9. James H. Leuba in "The Psychology of Religious Mysticism," N. Y., Harcourt-Brace, 1926, cites a mass of impressive evidence for its linkage.

IV MIND AND RELIGION—ANIMISM

1. E. Washburn Hopkins, "Origin & Evolution of Religion," p. 350.

2. Varieties of Religious Experience, p. 12.

3. E. W. Hopkins, "Origin and Evolution of Religion," p. 27 ff, says the plant produced an intoxicant, and was held, both in Iran and India, to be identical with the moon which it resembled in color and in "swelling." Later, in India, the priests only were permitted to partake of it.

4. Friederich Paulsen, "Einleitung in der Philosophie," Berlin, Wilhelm Hertz, 1901, 7th Ed., p. 384 and 387.

5. Wm. McDougall, Body and Mind, p. 29. Tertullian's views were accepted until the 5th century A.D.

6. Body and Mind, Methuen, London, 8th Edition, 1938, p. 30.

7. Body and Mind, Preface p. xiii

8. "Experimental Study of the Motor Theory of Consciousness," Jour. of Comp. Psych., Vol. 24, No. 2, Oct., 1937, p. 307.

8a. W. Rowan, "The Riddle of Migration," Chap. IV. Baltimore, Williams and Wilkins, 1931.

9. Physiological Foundations of Behavior, N. Y., Henry Holt & Co., 1924, p. 1.

10. See Wolfgang Kohler, "The Mentality of Apes," N. Y., Harcourt-Brace, 1927.

11. Already by 1937 Professor Razran's excellent bibliography contained 1111 titles. (Psch. Bulletin, Vol. 34, no. 4, April 1937.)

12. J. Lang and J. M. D. Olmstead, "Conditioned Reflexes and Pathways in the Spinal Cord." Amer. J. Physiol., 1923, 65, 603-611.

13. See Ivan D. London, Psychology in the USSR, American Journal of Psych., July 1951, Vol. 64, No. 3, pp. 422-428.

14. Charles Shagass, "Conditioning of the Human Occipital Alpha Rhythm to a Voluntary Stimulus." Journal of Ex. Psych., 1942, 31, No. 5, Nov., 1942, 367-369.

15. Anthropologists have reported the same phenomenon when people for the first time are shown black and white photographs.

16. Lewis Gellerman, "Form Discrimination in Chimpanzees and Two Year Old Children," J. Genet. Psychol., 1933, 42, 3-50.

17. General Psychology, Appleton, N. Y., p. 159.

18. L. B. Hoisington, Program of the 34th Annual Meeting of the American Psychological Association, Dec. 1925, p. 10.

19. Gregory H. S. Razran, "Conditioned Responses." Archives of Psychology, No. 191, N. Y., Oct., 1935. Also his excellent classified bibliography

on "Conditioned Responses," Psychological Bulletin, Vol. 34, No. 4, April, 1937. Also, "The Nature of the Extinctive Process," Psychological Review, Vol. 46, No. 3, May, 1939. Also "Salivating, and Thinking in Different Languages," The Journal of Psychology, 1, pp. 145-151. Also "The Conditioned Evocation of Attitudes (Cognitive Conditioning)," Journal of Experimental Psychology, Vol. 48, No. 4, 1954, pp. 278-282. Also, "Conditioning and Perception," Psychological Review, Vol. 62, No. 2, 1955, pp. 83-95.

20. Ivan D. London. Psychology in the USSR. Am. Jour. Psych., July 1951, Vol. 64, No. 3, pp. 422-428.

21. Bernard Riess, "Genetic Changes in Semantic Conditioning." Jour. of Exper. Psych. V. 36, No. 2, April 1946, pp. 143-152.

22 "Images as Conditioned Sensations," Jour. of Exper. Psych., V. 26, No. 3, March 1940, pp. 345-351. Also, see Leuba and Dunlap "Conditioning Imagery," Same Jour. Vol. 41, No. 5, May, 1951, pp. 352-355.

23. loc. cit. pp. 349-350.

24. Reported in conversation by a former student of James.

25. Louis W. Max. "An Experimental Study of the Motor Theory of Consciousness": I. Critique of Earlier Studies." Jour. of Gen. Psych., 1934, 11, pp. 112-125.

26. Knight Dunlap, Johns Hopkins Cir., 1914, No. 3.

27. Margaret Washburn, "Movement and Mental Imagery." Boston: Houghton Mifflin, 1916.

28. Agnes Thorson, "The relation of tongue movements to internal speech." Jour. Exper. Psychol., 1925, 8, 1-32.

29. op. cit.

30. L. E. Jacobson. "The Electrophysiology of Mental Activities." Am. Jour. of Psych., 1932, vol. 44, pp. 677-694.

31. An Experimental study of the motor theory of consciousness: I. Critique of earlier studies, Jour. of Gen. Psych., 1934, 11, 112-125; II. Method and apparatus, Jour. of Gen. Psych., 1935, 13, 159-175; IV. Action current responses in the deaf during awakening, kinaesthetic imagery and abstract thinking, Jour. of Comp. Psych., Vol. 24, No. 2. Oct., 1937.

32. (IV, p. 335 ff)

33. op. cit. p. 327.

34. IV. p. 334.

35. See Knight Dunlap, "The short-circuiting of conscious responses." Jour. Philos. 1927, 24, 263-267.

36. William James, "Essays in Radical Empiricism," N. Y., Longmans, Green & Co., 1912, p. 2.

37. "Origin and Evolution of Religion," (Yale University Press, 1923) p. 354.

38. p. 355.

39. W. T. Stace, "Religion and the Modern Mind," (Lippincott, 1952) p. 248.

40. C. V. Hudgins, "Conditioning and the Voluntary Control of the Pupillary Light Reflex," Jour. of Gen. Psych., 1933, 8:3-43.

41. W. S. Hunter, "The Delayed Reaction in Animals and Children," Animal Behavior Monographs, 1913, No. 1.

42. Wm. James, "Does Consciousness Exist," in "Essays in Radical Empiricism," p. 2.

V MAGIC AND RELIGION

1. Boston, Ginn & Co., 1902.
2. "History of Magic and Experimental Science," (Macmillan Co., N. Y., 1923). By permission of Columbia University Press, copyright holder.
3. op. cit., p. 337.
4. As quoted in Thorndike, whom all readers interested in this historical phase of the subject should consult.
5. Thorndike, op. cit., V. II, p. 666.
6. op. cit., pp. 976 ff.   ....
7. Parenthetical additions mine. Anyone not familiar with this monumental work of Thorndike's is emphatically advised to savor the rich fare of historical material he has made available and for which this writer is much indebted.
8. op. cit. p. 978.
9. See, for example, Charlevois, "Histoire de la France Nouvelle."
10. James H. Leuba, in Ferm, V. "Religion in Transition," p. 184.
11. Eli Burris, "Taboo, Magic & Spirits," (N. Y. Macmillan and Co., 1931).
12. Bronislaw Malinowski, "Magic, Science & Religion," (The Free Press, Glencoe, Ill.), p. 20.
13. Hutton Webster, "Magic," (Stanford Univ. Press), p. 114. Quoted from 47th Annual Report, Bureau of American Ethnology, p. 494.
14. E. W. Hopkins, "Origin and Evolution of Religion," p. 78.
15. "The Religion of the Teutons," p. 385.
16. Parenthetical additions mine.
17. William J. Goode, "Religion Among the Primitives," (The Free Press, Glencoe, III., 1951) p. 59 ff.
18. Norman Maier, "Frustration and Conflict," (McGraw-Hill, 1949).
19. Nock, quoted by T. Parsons, "Structure of Social Action," p. 425.
20. op. cit. p. 52 ff.
21. See A. D. White, "History of the Warfare of Science with Theology in Christendom," (Appleton, N. Y., 1896).
22. James G. Frazer, "The Golden Bough"
23. Paul Radin, The Winnebago Tribe, 37th Annual Report of the Bureau of American Ethnology, Washington (Quoted by Lowie, "Primitive Religion," p. 137).
24. E. W. Hopkins, "Origin and Evolution of Religion," p. 4.
25. B. Malinowski, "Magic, Science and Religion," p. 28.

26. op. cit., pp. 20-21.
27. Wm. Goode, "Religion among the primitives," (The Free Press, Glencoe, Ill.), p. 55.
28. Life Magazine, April 11, 1955, p. 147.
29. Charles S. Braden, "These Also Believe" (N. Y. Macmillan, 1950).
30. K. Diven, "Certain Determinants in the Conditioning of Anxiety Reactions." (Journal of Psychology, 1937, 3; pp. 291-308).
31. Samuel Mercer, in "Forgotten Religions," (ed. by V. Ferm, N. Y. Philosophical Library, 1950), p. 41.
32. This writer unfortunately gives us no further clue as to precisely what constitutes "scientific prayer"!
33. George Hedley, "The Superstitions of the Irreligious," (N. Y. Macmillan, 1951).

VI   THE THEORY OF RELIGION IN EVOLUTION

1. See A. Lang, "Magic & Religion," (1901), and "The Making of Religion," (1909, N. Y., Longmans, Green and Co.)
2. Note, for example, the ratio of "Hail Marys" to "Our Fathers" in the Catholic rosary.
3. R. R. Marett, "The Threshold of Religion," (London, Methuen & Co., Ltd., 1914), p. 14, ff.
4. Bronislaw Malinowski, "Magic, Science, & Religion," p. 28.
5 loc. cit.
6. Life Magazine, April 25, 1955, p. 157.
7. i.e., Tacoma, Wash., Dec., 1929—Public prayer for rain; or "Victory" prayers by all contending nations, 1914-18 and 1940-45.
8. See Floyd H. Allport, Harper's Magazine, Feb., 1930.
9. See Paul Hutchinson, "Have We a New Religion," Life Magazine, April 11, 1955, p. 147.
10. See Vergilius Ferm, ed., "Forgotten Religions," (N. Y. Philosophical Library, 1950) p. 148.
11. E. Washburn Hopkins, "Origin and Evolution of Religion," (Yale Univ. Press, 1923), p. 323.
12. See E. Washburn Hopkins, "Origin and Evolution of Religion," (Yale Univ. Press, 1923) p. 89.
13. loc. cit.
14. Curt J. Ducasse, "A Philosophical Scrutiny of Religion," (N. Y., Ronald Press, 1953), pp. 3, 349-350.
15. op. cit. p. 350.
16. A. Bronson Feldman, "Freudian Theology," Part 2. Psychoanalysis, 1953, 1 (4) 37-53, as summarized by L. E. Abt in Psychological Abstracts, Vol. 28:2515.
17. (Boston, Little, Brown & Co., 1926).

VII LEARNING AND RELIGION

1. See for example: the entire book of Leviticus.
2. Norman Maier, "Frustration." (N. Y., McGraw-Hill, 1949) p. 35.
3. Burrhus F. Skinner "Superstition in the Pigeon." Jour. of Exp. Psych., 1948, 38) pp. 168-172.
4. See Edwin R. Guthrie, "The Psychology of Learning," (N. Y., Harper and Brothers, 1952), p. 268.
5. Virginia W. Voeks, "Postremity, Recency, and Frequency," Jour. of Exp. Psych., (1948, 38), pp. 495-510.
6. op. cit.
7. Edwin R. Guthrie, "Psychology of Learning," Rev. Edition, p. 265 (N. Y. Harper Brothers, 1952).
8. William H. Prescott, "History of the Conquest of Mexico," Chap. III, reports that as many as 70,000 prisoners were sacrificed at one time when the social crisis of the Spanish invasion was met with the orgy device.
9. G. V. Hamilton, "Objective Psychopathology," (St. Louis, The C. V. Mosby Co., 1925), pp. 251 ff.
10. Norman Maier, "Frustration," (McGraw-Hill, 1949) p. 30.
11. The nine-day Navaho healing ceremony well illustrates the application of the general "orgy" principle.
12. Raymond B. Cattell, "Psychology and the Religious Quest," (N. Y. Nelson & Sons, 1938), p. 37.
13. "History of Magic & Experimental Science," (N. Y. Macmillan & Co., 1923) p. 337.

VIII BELIEF AND FAITH

1. W. O. Jenkins & J. C. Stanley, "Partial Reinforcement: A Review and Critique." (Psychological Bulletin, Vol. 47 No. 3) pp. 193-234.
2. op. cit., p. 231.
3. As reported by Walter Duranty in the New York Times, according to Current History Magazine, April, 1930, p. 38.
4. Wm. James, "The Will to Believe and Other Essays," (Longmans, N. Y., 1896, p. 29).
5. E. Washburn Hopkins, "Origin & Evolution of Religion," (Yale Univ. Press), p. 70.
6. loc. cit.
7. Hopkins, op. cit., p. 321.
8. Hopkins, op. cit., p. 87.
9. George Hedley, "The Superstitions of the Irreligious," (Macmillan, 1951), p. 39.
10. op. cit., p. 27.
11. Thomas H. Howells, "A Study of Religious Orthodoxy," Uni. of Iowa Publications, 1929.
12. "The Measurement of Social and Political Attitudes and the Related Personality Factors," Jour. of Abn. & Soc. Psych., Vol. XXV, No. 2, July-Sept. 1930, pp. 149-189.
13. "Religious Beliefs of American Scientists," (Harper's Magazine, 1934), V. 169, pp. 291-300.
14. Anne Roe, "A psychological study of physical scientists," Gen. Psych. Monogr., 1951, 43, pp. 121-231.
15. p. 189.
16. p. 231.
17. See the chapter on Contemporary Magico-Religious Manifestations.
18. Dr. Warren Weaver, Look Magazine, Apr. 5, 1955, p. 29.
19. Britanicus, in G. B. Shaw's "Caesar and Cleopatra."
20. W. T. Stace, "Time and Eternity," (Princeton Uni. Press, 1952) p. 4.
21. "Religion Among the Primitives" (Free Press, Glencoe, Ill., 1951) p. 220.
22. "Religion in Transition," p. 146. Allen & Unwin Ltd., London 1937. Edited by V. Ferm.
23. "Origin and Evolution of Religion," (New Haven, Yale University Press, 1923) p. 73.

24. Victor Robinson, M.D., "The Story of Medicine" (Ft. Pierce Beach, Florida, Froben Press, 1943), p. 25.

25. Episode provided by Dr. H. Russell Meyers, Professor of Neural Surgery, Iowa State College of Medicine.

26. Jean Piaget, "Language and Thought of the Child" (N. Y., Harcourt-Brace).

27. "The Need to Believe," (N. Y., International Universities Press, 1954) p. 155.

28. Vol. LVIII, No. 4, p. 387, Oct. 1930.

29. H. J. Eysenck & D. B. Prell, "The inheritance of neuroticism: an experimental study." (Jour. of Ment. Sci., 1951) pp. 441-465.

30. W. T. Stace, "Religion and the Modern Mind," (N. Y. Lippincott, 1952) p. 220.

31. Quoted from V. Robinson, M.D., "The Story of Medicine," Ft. Pierce Beach, Fla., 1943. The Froben Press, p. 51.

32. "The Third Revolution," (Harcourt, Brace, 1954).

33. R. J. Williams, et. al. "Individual metabolic patterns, alcoholism, genetotrophic diseases." Proc. Nat. Acad. Sci., Wash., D.C., 1949, V. 35, p. 265.

34. Look Magazine, April 5, 1955.

35. "The Will to Believe," p. 10.

36. William James, "The Will to Believe," (N. Y., Longmans, Green & Co., 1917) p. 14.

37. "Essays in Radical Empiricism. Does Consciousness Exist?" p. 2.

38. "The Will to Believe," p. 28.

39. op. cit., p. 14.

40. The author has elsewhere examined incest taboos as a learning problem; Jour. of Abn. & Soc. Psych., Vol. 23, No. 2, July-Sept., 1928, pp. 232-240.

41. Sigmund Freud, "The Future of an Illusion," (N. Y., Horace Liveright and the Institute for Psychoanalysis, 1928), p. 74.

42. Henry Alden Bunker, "Psychoanalysis and the Study of Religion," in G. Roheim, "Psychoanalysis and the Social Sciences."

43. "The Mystery of Religion," (N. Y., Harper & Bros., 1924).

44. "The Psychology of Hymns," Jour. Abn. & Soc. Psych., Jan., 1926.

45. Abraham Kardiner (Columbia Univ. Press, 1947), p. 426.

46. Oman, "The Brahmans, Theists, and Muslims of India," p. 173. Quoted by E. W. Hopkins, "Origin and Evolution of Religion," (Yale University Press, 1923) p. 28.

IX THE RELIGIOUS EXPERIENCE—MYSTICISM

1. Letters (Boston, Atlantic Monthly Press, 1920) Vol. II, p. 127.
2. "Does Consciousness Exist" in Essays in Radical Empiricism (N. Y. Longmans, Green & Co. 1912) p. 2.
3. Thomas V. Moore "The Driving Forces of Human Nature." (Grune and Stratton, N. Y. 1948) p. 417.
4. ("Wissen, Glauben und Ahndung," Göttingen, Vandenhoeck & Ruprecht, 1905) p. 176.
5. Quoted in Rudolph Otto, 13th German edition of "Das Heilige" Chapter 18.
6. One might well wonder how a writer comes to adopt a word like Ahndung for his especial purpose, particularly when that word has long had a perfectly good usage (resentment, revenge, or requital), and when the term as he uses it has an obvious similarity to "Ahnung" (foreboding, hunch, presentment.)
7. Rudolph Otto "The Idea of the Holy," (Oxford Press, 1928) p. 10. Otto claims that his usage of the concept "Numinose" follows that of Zinzenderf, which in turn claims identity with Melanchthon's "Sensus Dei."
8. Joachim Wach, "Sociology of Religion" (University of Chicago Press, 1944) p. 16.
9. (op. cit. p. 234).
10. Wright, H. W., "The Religious Response," (N. Y., Harper & Bros. 1929) p. 18.
11. Wm. James "Varieties of Religious Experience" (Longmans, Green & Co. 1929) p. 379.
12. Henri Bergson, "Two Sources of Morality and Religion" (N. Y. Doubleday-Anchor) pp. 220-221.
13. Wm. James "Varieties of Religious Experience" (Longmans, N. Y.) p. 379.
14. See James Leuba, "The Psychology of Religious Mysticism" (N. Y. Harcourt-Brace 1926) p. 240 ff.
15. op. cit., Chs. V. & VIII.
16. W. T. Stace, "Time and Eternity," (Princeton University Press, 1952) p. 17.
17. "The Psychology of Religious Mysticism," (N. Y., Harcourt, Brace and Company, Inc. 1926).
18. "Varieties of Religious Experience," p. 413.
19. A. A. Al-Taftazani, "Psychology of Mysticism," Egyptian Jour. of

Psych., 1949-50 (2), pp. 291-295, (as briefed in The Psychological Abstracts), V. 26, 5357 & 5358.

20. "The Individual and his Religion." (Macmillan, 1950) p. 62.

21. W. T. Stace, "Religion and the Modern Mind," (N. Y., Lippincott, 1952) p. 278.

22. op. cit., p. 245.

23. Louis W. Max, "Experimental Study of the Motor Theory of Consciousness," Jour. of Comp. Psychology, V. 24, No. 2, p. 307.

24. F. M. Davenport, "Primitive Traits in Religious Revivals," (Macmillan, 1906).

25. "Religion in Transition," (ed. Vergilius Ferm, N. Y., The Macmillan Co., 1937) p. 221. Also Catherine C. Cleveland "The Great Revival" (Uni. of Chicago Press, 1916).

26. Morton Prince, "The Unconscious," (N. Y., The Macmillan Co.)

27. op. cit., p. 226.

28. Solomon Diamond, "A Study of the Influence of Political Radicalism on Personality Development," Archives of Psychology No. 203, June, 1936.

29. "Religion in the Soviet Union," Current History, Vol. 32, No. 1, April, 1930, p. 27.

30. Same article, p. 31.

31. Gordon W. Allport, James M. Gillespie, and Jacqueline Young, "The Religion of the Post-War College Student," Jour. of Psych., 1948, 25, pp. 3-33.

32. "Psychology and the Religious Quest," (N. Y., Nelson & Son, 1938) p. 37.

33. J. B. Carter, "Religious Life of Ancient Rome," (Boston, Houghton, Mifflin, 1911).

34. George B. Vetter & Martin Green, "Personality and Group Factors in the Making of Atheists," The Jour. of Abn. & Soc. Psych., Vol. XXVII, No. 2, p. 186.

X PRIESTHOOD—THE WORLD'S OLDEST PROFESSION

1. (London, Macmillan and Company, Limited, 1920).
2. (N. Y. Viking Press, 1937 p. 107).
3. (Erwin Rohde, "Psyche," N. Y. Harcourt Brace 1925 p. 29 ff.).
4. (Hopkins, E. W. "Origin and Evolution of Religion" p. 207).
5. Pope Pius XI once expressed regrets at the church having "lost" the allegiance of the proletariat during the 19th century.
6. (Myth, Ritual & Religion, London, Longmans, Green and Co., 1887, Vol. 1 p. 121).
6a. Hopkins, E. W., Origin and Evolution of Religion, p. 2.
7. Upton Sinclair, "The Profits of Religion" (Published by the author, Pasadena, California 1918).
8. A recent report has it that in the American middle west there is a trend toward the full-time "Priest" or professional by whatever name he is known, among the Quaker congregations.
9. The "Witnesses" now have full time promoters.
10. It was about this time that the New Yorker Magazine published a cartoon reflecting the current paradox in regard to science and religion. Two men in clerical garb were depicted looking out of a tall Gothic window against which rain was beating vigorously. One cleric is saying to the other: "I wonder, is it theirs or ours?"
11. It should be noted here there is currently a great increase in the frequency of malpractice suits. This probably indicates a general decline of the tendency to stand in awe of any special skills, including the priestly.
12. Boisen, A. T. "The Minister as Counselor," (J. Pastoral Care, 1948, 2, 13-22).
13. "It may be asserted as a principle of human organization that when new types of social organization are required, respectable, well-thought-of, and conservative people are unable to take part in them." Arnold, Thurman W. "The Folklore of Capitalism" (Yale University Press, 1937, p. 3).

XI SOCIAL MOVEMENTS AND RELIGION

1. For a functional analysis of the structure of the Roman Catholic Church, see Daniel Katz and Richard Schanck, "Social Psychology" (New York, John Wiley & Sons, 1938).
2. Joachim Wach, "Sociology of Religion" (University of Chicago Press) 1944 p. 307.
3. Robert V. Hine, "California's Utopian Colonies," (San Marino, California, The Huntington Library).

XII CONTEMPORARY MAGICO-RELIGIOUS MANIFESTATIONS

1. New York Times, Sunday, September 18, 1955, page 11.
2. William McDougall, "Body & Mind" p. viii.
3. Curt J. Ducasse, "A Philosophical Scrutiny of Religion," (Ronald Press New York, 1953) p. 393.
4. J. B. Rhine, "New Frontiers of the Mind," New York: Farrar and Rinehart, 1937 p. 249.
5. Harold O. Gulliksen, "Extra-Sensory Perception: What is it?" The Am. Jour. of Sociology, Vol. XLIII, No. 4, Jan., 1938, pp. 623-631.
6. pp. 629-630.
7. New Frontiers of the Mind, p. 30.
8. op. cit., p. 630.
9. "New Frontiers of the Mind," p. 110, 234, & 270; Extra-sensory Perception, p. 133.
10. R. A. Fisher, "Statistical Methods for Research Workers."
11. "Beware Familiar Spirits," pp. 221-227.
12. See: Kendon Smith, & Harry J. Canon, "A methodological refinement in the study of ESP and negative findings." Science, 1954, 120, pp. 148-149.
13. "A Philosophical Scrutiny of Religion," (The Ronald Press, N. Y., 1953) p. 403.
14. "Conditioning Imagery," Jour. of Exp. Psych., Vol. 41, No. 5, May, 1951, pp. 352-355.
15. F. L. Marcuse and M. E. Bitterman, "A Classroom Demonstration of 'Psychical Phenomena'." Jour. of Abn. and Soc. Psych., 1944, vol. 39, pp. 238-243.
16. See, "Begone Satan" by the Rev. Karl Vogel, (publ. by Rev. Celestine Kapsner, O.S.B., St. John's Abbey, Collegeville, Minn., 1935).
17. The popularity of such a number no doubt stems from the fact that the numbers 7 and 11 are winning numbers in gambling with dice.
18. See his "Beware Familiar Spirits!", (N. Y., Charles Scribner's Sons, 1938) p. 307.
19. Unpublished data collected by the author.

XIII   ETHICS AND RELIGION

1. Robert R. Marett, "Threshold of Religion," (London, Methuen & Co., Ltd. 1914, p. xxxl (introduction).

2. "The Third Revolution," (N. Y. Harcourt, Brace, 1954, p. 75).

3. Werke, Berlin Edition, V. I, p. 3.

4. "Treatise on the Gods" (N.Y. A.A. Knopf, 1930, preface, p. viii).

5. Chantepie de la Saussaye, "Religion of the Teutons," (Boston, Ginn & Co. 1902, p. 408).

6. "Skepticismus und Goetterleugnung in nordgermanischen Heidenthum."

7. (op. cit. p. 406).

8. "Allgemeine Geschichte der Philosophie," (Vol. 1, 2nd Ed. 1906, pp. 77 ff.).

9. "Bloudy Tenet of the Lord Made Yet More Bloudy by Mr. Cotton's Efforts to wash it Clean." 1645.

10. For a most stimulating discussion of the psychological bases of need and value differences, see A. H. Maslow, "Higher" and "Lower" Needs, Jour. of Psych., 1948, 25, pp. 433-436.

11. W. G. DeBurgh, "From Morality to Religion," (London, MacDonald & Evans, 1938) p. 294.

12. N. Y. D. Appleton & Co., 1896.

13. During the first period of legal abortions in Russia, at one report 55,000 operations had been performed without a single fatality.

14. J. L. Gillin, & J. P. Gillin, "Cultural Sociology," (N. Y. Macmillan, 1948). Quoted in Peter R. Hofstaetter, "Einfuehrung in die Socialpsychologie," Humboldt Verlag, Stuttgart Wien, 1954, p. 346.

15. The American Petroleum Institute recently boasted this number for a city of eighty thousand (In an advertisement).

16. I wish someone would locate this quotation for me! I'd like very much to be able to ask the copyright holder for permission to quote.

17. "Psychology," (Harper & Bros., 1950), p. 199.

18. C. W. Heath, "What People Are." (Harvard University Press, 1945) p. 42.

19. "Organized religion and criminal behavior," (Sociology and Social Research, 1949), V. 33, p. 363.

21. Merl E. Bonney, "A study of friendship choices—," Jour. of Soc. Psych., 1949, 29, 153-166.

22. Gordon W. Allport & B. M. Kramer, "Some roots of prejudice," Jour. of Psych., 1946, 22, p. 25.

23. "Studies in Deceit," (N. Y., The Macmillan Co., 1930) pp. 357 & 360.

24. Karl Stern, "The Third Revolution" (N. Y. Harcourt Brace, 1954) p. 76.

25. W. T. Stace, "Religion and the Modern Mind," (J. B. Lippincott, 1952) p. 101.

26. J. C. Carothers, "The African Mind in Health and Disease," World Health Organization Monograph, Series 1953 No. 17.

XIV SUMMARY

1. Already quoted in this volume, p. 81.

2. Peter R. Hofstaetter, "Einfuehrung in die Sozialpsychologie" (Humboldt-Verlag, Stuttgart-Wien, 1954) p. 285.

3. See for example the dramatic work reported by H. Fraenkel-Conrat and Robley C. Williams, in the Proceedings of the National Academy of Sciences, Vol. 41, No. 10, pp. 690-698, Oct., 1955. Recently hybrid viruses have been produced by these methods.

4. I Samuel: 6:5
   This little scriptural episode very strongly suggests that the Philistine priests and diviners already then had a hunch in regard to the relation existing between rodents and the bubonic plague. "Emerods" were swellings, "bubos." In I Samuel 5:9 "emerods in their secret parts."

5. For a highly readable account of the shortcomings of the clergy, see Harry Elmer Barnes, "The Twilight of Christianity" (N. Y., The Vanguard Press, 1929).

6. The English language press, through an error in translation, has given Adolf Hitler a promotion that the German army denied him. His top rank was "Gefreiter," i.e., Private first class. He was *not* "Obergefreiter," Corporal!

7. Unpublished researches by the author.

8. "Anti-Naturalism in Extremis," Partisan Review, X, Jan.-Feb., 1943, p. 33. Also quoted in V. T. Thayer, "Religion in Public Education" (N. Y., Viking Press, 1947), p. 122-123. An excellent volume.

9. Matthew 16:18. In Latin, Peter = Petrus = rock. The Catholic doctrine of the "priority of Peter."

INDEX